The Realities of International Criminal Justice

The Realities of International Criminal Justice

Edited by

Dawn L. Rothe, James Meernik and Þórdís Ingadóttir

MARTINUS NIJHOFF PUBLISHERS

LEIDEN · BOSTON

2013

Originally published as Volume 13, No. 1 (2013) pp. 7–318 in Brill's journal *International Criminal Law Review.*

Library of Congress Cataloging-in-Publication Data

The realities of international criminal justice / edited by Dawn L. Rothe, James Meernik, and Thordis Ingadottir.
pages cm
Includes index.
ISBN 978-90-04-25110-6 (hardback : alk. paper) -- ISBN 978-90-04-25111-3 (e-book) 1. Criminal justice, Administration of. 2. International criminal law. I. Rothe, Dawn, 1961- II. Meernik, James David. III. Ingadottir, Thordis.
K5001.R43 2013
345--dc23

2013015532

ISBN 978-90-04-25110-6 (hardback)
ISBN 978-90-04-25111-3 (e-book)

This book is printed on acid-free paper.

MIX
Paper from responsible sources
FSC® C109576

Printed by Printforce, the Netherlands

Contents

Acknowledgements

We want to extend our gratitude and appreciation to Michael Bohlander, as without his initiative, this project would not have happened. It was through his first efforts, contacts, and planning that we were able to finish this book. For that, we are eternally thankful to him. We also wish to thank all of the contributors for their role in making this project a reality. As always, we are also grateful to our many colleagues, friends and family who continue to support us and our work.

Introduction
The Realities of International Criminal Justice

Dawn L. Rothe

The international criminal justice system (ICJ), as with domestic mechanisms of social control, inherently poses various challenges and prospects for states, the international political community, perpetrators, and victims. Given the vast amount of research that recognizes the primary and secondary consequences of states' responses to crime and violence at national levels, criminologists, socio-legal and criminal law scholars have, in general, neglected examining these same concerns at the international level. Consequentially many questions remain in terms of the role, impact, challenges and prospects of ICJ– both normative and practical.

Nonetheless, often what is touted, is the ideal or overvalued interpretations of the impact of the international criminal justice system, from the ad hoc courts (e.g., International Tribunals for Rwanda and the former Yugoslavia), hybrid courts (e.g., Special Court for Sierra Leone) to the International Criminal Court (ICC). This has especially been the case when proponents of ICJ speak to its ability to end impunity and serve as a deterrent. Many actors within the field of international criminal justice have heralded the deterrent power of the ICJ system and its ability to remove impunity for violations of international criminal law. However, the empirical evidence is mixed at best as to the realities behind the assumed deterrent power to date.

Advocates of the 'international criminal justice system' have noted the advances to the treatment of victims from many domestic criminal justice systems. This claim has particularly been made by backers of the International Criminal Court (ICC) in relation to the improvements of victims' rights of the International Criminal Tribunal for former Yugoslavia (ICTY) and International Criminal Tribunal for Rwanda (ICTR). Scholars have also pointed to the dangers of an ICJ system that is active during ongoing conflicts, and/or conflict resolution periods. The concern here has been on the impact of peace processes and negotiations. Additional concerns include the issue of enforcement, state-compliance, and selectivity of situations, cases, and subsequent charges. Other areas of interest include issues related to legitimacy, due process, sentencing, and the impact of ICJ on domestic fronts, from the legal to the social.

The chapters in this special issue take a coherent, analytical and critical look at the development and impact of the major instruments of international criminal justice since the 1990s with the advent of the ICTY and the ICTR. The issue begins with a chapter by Alette Smeulers, Barbora Hola, and Tom van den Berg that provides an excellent overview of the realities of the modern international criminal justice system over the course of the past 65 years. The authors note that the ICJ system consisted of 9 international criminal courts and tribunals of which 6 are still operational. In all, there have been 172 concluded cases with 745 suspects indicted, 356 were actually tried with 281 convictions, and 34 suspects are currently on trial with 22 at large. The remaining chapters are devoted to examining the ad hoc and hybrid tribunals, followed by issues related to the International Criminal Court.

For example, Stephan Parmentier and Elmar Weitekamp provide new insight into the subsequent notions of justice at the domestic level nearly twenty years after the creation of the International Criminal Tribunal for the former Yugoslavia. They note that while the international political community has put a major emphasis on and push towards the criminal prosecution and conviction of the persons mostly responsible for the war crimes committed in the region, there remains an absence of discussions and reflections of the population's perceptions of whether or not justice has been served. In an effort to fill this general lack of focus, Parmentier and Weitekamp conduct a population based survey that provides significant insight into the perceptions of the Serbia people regarding impunity of and accountability for the war crimes committed, prosecutions, and other forms of transitional justice in the Country. Delineated down to two main issues-the quest for justice and the search for truth through the eyes of the population-Parmentier and Weitekamp conclude by showing that a large majority of the respondents believed it was of utmost importance that the 'truth' about what happened during the war be established and that this is most favored when done through the courts and truth commissions: an official validation of 'truth'. Additionally, they found that the issue of accountability was most noted in the context of prosecutions at the ICTY and the national level and linked to the more senior political and military leaders with less emphasis and concern on 'direct' perpetrators who were seen as carrying out orders.

Kenneth Rodman focuses on the Special Court for Sierra Leone, the conviction of the former Liberian President, Charles Taylor and prosecution of other perpetrators. Rodman pays particular attention to the role and interventionist strategies of Western governments and international and regional institutions. The analysis shows that the prospects for prosecutions, post-conflict, are most likely determined by the political strategies the international political community employ to end the violence. Rodman continues by suggesting that international criminal justice also presumes interventionist forms of politics. Rodman explicitly states that the discourse surrounding international criminal justice is overly optimistic as to its role in resolving on-going conflicts. Rather, attention needs to be paid to international criminal law's dependence on politics in conflicts and post-conflict responses and prosecutions.

The hybrid tribunals, the Special Court for Sierra Leone, the Extraordinary Chambers in the Courts of Cambodia and the Special Tribunal for Lebanon are then discussed in Georgia Tortoras' chapter. The chapter begins with an overview of how countries' opposition to the ad hoc tribunals (ICTY and ICTR) framework shaped the decision making processes and subsequent policies for the final financial and administrative arrangements of the three hybrid Courts or Special Tribunals. Tortora then examines the uncharacteristic financial and administrative features of each of these institutions. It is argued that their funding mechanism and oversight structure resulted in greater confidence among donor states about their cost-effectiveness and offered states greater means to intervene in instances of mismanagement. This is due in part, to the Courts' need to rely on voluntary funding and the role of the steering/management committees that generated a 'vested interest' in the success of the Tribunals.

Cedric Ryngaert's chapter focuses on the International Criminal Tribunal for Rwanda and the dichotomy between states' duties to cooperate with the ICTR and the reality of state noncooperation. An in-depth analysis of two central factors associated with cooperation, namely the arrest of fugitives by countries and the referral of cases to national jurisdictions. Ryngaert finds that while Rwanda has used cooperation, it has done so as a bargaining tool to gain desired concessions from the Tribunal. Likewise, while states have a statutory obligation to cooperate with the ICTR in terms of arrests, providing documentation, to relocate acquitted individuals and those that have completed their sentence, and a moral duty to accept cases of referral from the ICTR, and to relocate acquitted individuals and those that have completed their sentence, it has been the case that states have not always complied with their obligations to the ICTR.

The following chapters examine the impact, challenges, and prospects of the International Criminal Court. Rosa Aloisi begins this section with an analysis of the political independence of the Court. Specifically, Aloisi examines the impact of the political relationship between the United Nations Security Council's power to refer or defer situations to the Court, and the ICC's ability to carry out 'justice'. It is argued that clashing political and judicial interests have hindered the implementation of international justice. Aloisi suggests that when matters of referrals to the Court should or do occur, power and political discourses surrounding the discussions of and subsequent decision-making is impacted in spite of the realities of a claim for international justice.

A similar theme of contradiction is highlighted by James Meernik's chapter on the International Criminal Court and its power to issue arrest warrants but not the political power to carry out enforcement of those warrants. Rather, the ICC must rely on states to comply with their obligations to carry out the arrest warrants.

Given that states' leaders, international political actors, and suspected war criminals all have divergent and at times contending interests that guide their actions, political disputes arise, negating state compliance and support. Specifically, Meernik argues that while the principal interest of the International Criminal Court is supposed to be justice, those indicted by the ICC have interests of maintaining or attaining power. Consequentially, given the limitations of the ICC in terms of enforcement, Meernik contends that the Court's ability to gain custody of suspects is, and will be, largely determined if a shift occurs in the international political community and state actors ideology that places justice over peace.

On a related, yet different perspective, Dawn L. Rothe and Victoria Collins suggest that the International Criminal Court's presence in conflict and post-conflict situations poses other challenges and secondary unintended costs that have not only hampered the goal to end impunity and a deterrent effect, but also secondary unintentional consequences of additional violence. They begin by examining the Court's ability to effectively act as a catalyst to end impunity by first discussing the core ideology behind retributive justice; deterrence. Here Rothe and Collins suggest that the assumed belief in deterrence that undergirds the ICJ system and ICC is further hampered by practical, structural and procedural issues including jurisdictional limitations, and the backlash of its involvement in, and issuance of arrest warrants during highly contentious conflicts. This chapter offers some insight into these issues and the obstacles they present to the success of the International Criminal Court in ending impunity and future cases of such criminality. Rothe and Collins then draw on two case examples, Uganda and Columbia, to draw out the challenges posed by the Court in ongoing conflicts and post-conflict situations.

The following chapter by James Meernik provides an excellent analysis of 5161 survey respondents' perceptions (from seven countries) of ICC intervention in Sudan to understand how views and support for the Court are determined, linking this to issues of legitimacy. His findings suggest that support for the ICC's case against President Al Bashir was contingent upon individuals' religion and ethnicity and the dominant narrative of these groups regarding who was responsible for the crimes under investigation, the perceived bias of the Court and/or the West. Individuals who identified as Muslims and individuals from Arab states were most likely to oppose the ICC case against Al Bashir whereas individuals from Sub-Saharan African states were more likely to support the ICC. Based on his findings, Meernik concludes with suggesting that winning the support of publics and thereby deriving legitimacy from positive impressions will be difficult for the International Criminal Court.

The chapter by Isabella Bueno and Andrea Diaz Rozas delves into the situation of Columbia and the ICC within the broader debate of approaches to past mass crimes: between retributive and restorative justice. They suggest this debate becomes more complex when the ICC begins to exert influence in states' responses to mass crimes. Bueno and Diaz Rozas offer a detailed analysis of the complexities including the quagmire between complying with the Court and implement national traditional responses and legislation that can be in contradiction to the Westernized push of a retributive system.

Along the same theme, Steven Roach draws on the case of Northern Uganda and its local procedure of *mato oput* as practiced by the Acholi tribe in connection with the ICC. Roach provides a detailed understanding of the central features of local justice in the region and its relationship to the state in general and the ICC's victims' unit and trust fund. Noting that while there has been some complementarity between *mato oput* and the Court, there remains some obstacles to developing a more effective relationship between the local practices and the victims' resources of the ICC.

Jonathan O'Donohue examines another pragmatic area of ICJ that is often ignored, the financial side of the ICC. In particular, he analyzes the financial investment of the Court in terms of its efficiency, control over its operations and finances, and its value by achieving impact. He begins by identifying an emerging set of negative attitudes towards the overall cost of ICJ followed by a detailed discussion of the ICC's financial situation and expenditure practices. O'Donohue then suggests that the principle factors that 'ought' to be the focus of the ICC's budget are currently not being met. As a result of this, he proposes several policy proposals that would allow the Court to be more fiscally efficient: one of which O'Donohue suggests is to enhance the complementarity principle of the Court.

The final chapter in this special issue examines the issue of genocide. Mark Findlay suggests that prosecution of genocide can be pursued through the international courts in terms of criminal liability as well as under the states' rights/responsibility legal paradigms. Findley suggests that while being procedurally problematic is in keeping with the human rights direction of international criminal justice. Further, this would allow judges to consider the more realistic complexities involved in genocide, enhancing courts' ability to address and respond to the multiplicity of victims' interests.

This special issue raises many of the challenges and prospects of international criminal justice from procedural to substantive issues. Indeed, the goals of an ICJ system present their own trials and tribulations. This is not necessarily different than state local criminal justice systems, yet the complexities of cases, the politics of the international arena do pose additional challenges to the goals of ending impunity and enhancing the rule of law.

Sixty-Five Years of International Criminal Justice: The Facts and Figures

Alette Smeulers,[a] Barbora Hola[b] and Tom van den Berg[b,*]
[a]Department of Criminal Law, Tilburg University, Tilburg, the Netherlands
[b]Department of Criminal Law and Criminology, VU University, Amsterdam, the Netherlands

---

Abstract

The international criminal justice system comprises nine international criminal courts and tribunals; six are still operational and three have closed down. On average, they operated for almost nine years apiece and concluded 172 cases in which over 250 judges and 23 chief prosecutors were involved. All in all 745 suspects were indicted, 356 were actually tried and, of these, some 281 defendants were convicted. Currently 34 suspects are on trial and 22 are still at large. The 'average' convicted perpetrator is male, aged 40 and a member of a military or paramilitary organisation from Europe, Asia or Africa who is acting on behalf of his government. These are just some of the facts and figures which we present in this article: an overview of the empirical reality of the international criminal justice system which has currently been functioning for just over 65 years.

Keywords

International criminal courts and tribunals; international crimes; judges; prosecutors; perpetrators

1. Introduction

The judgment delivered by the International Military Tribunal (IMT) in October 1946, marked the birth of an international criminal justice system, a system which is now just over 65 years old.[1] In this article, we focus on the empirical reality of the international criminal justice system and present the facts and figures from these last 65 years.[2] We end with the convictions of Thomas Lubanga on 14 March 2012, the first person ever to be convicted by the International Criminal Court (ICC) in The Hague, and Charles Taylor, who appeared before the Special Court for Sierra

---

*) The authors wish to thank Joris van Wijk and Tijs Kooijmans for their help in translating the relevant parts of the case law of the Special Panels of Dili.

1) The Treaty of Versailles, which was concluded after the First World War, provided for the prosecution of Kaiser Wilhelm II but he fled to The Netherlands and was granted asylum.

2) The data were processed up to May 2012.

Leone (SCSL) on 26 April 2012 and was the first former head of state ever to be convicted by an international criminal tribunal.

As well as presenting an overview of the empirical reality of the international criminal justice system, we fill in a gap in the literature. Scholarly articles have usually focused on legal and doctrinal issues and, thus far, a comprehensive overview of the empirical data of the international criminal justice system has been lacking in academic literature. Not only is there an absence of empirical research into international criminal justice but the few empirical studies that have been completed have usually focused on just one aspect of the tribunals' functioning and covered only one tribunal at a time. In contrast, we describe many aspects of the functioning of the international criminal courts and tribunals, including their establishment, court composition, procedural aspects and sentencing practice. We also focus on the main subjects of the international criminal justice system: the defendants.

The article is descriptive and does not strive to provide explanations but to establish a starting point for further research. We have gathered information predominantly from the statutes, official documents and reports released by the courts and tribunals, the official websites of these tribunals and courts, from case law and the work of other scholars. In some cases we have used additional sources on the internet to corroborate our findings.

In the next section, we briefly introduce the various international and internationalized criminal courts and tribunals that have been established and discuss when and how they were set up. In the third section, the focus is placed on the background of the prosecutors and judges involved and, in the fourth section, the figures on the functioning of the tribunals, such as case composition, length of proceedings and sentencing are outlined. The fifth section shifts the focus to the defendants who have been tried by international criminal courts and tribunals. Who are they? What are their ages, sex and rank? Are they civilians or members of the military? In the sixth section, we briefly refer to the trials conducted by domestic courts and the suspects who were tried for international crimes in these courts who should have been tried.

2. International Courts and Tribunals: Types and Establishment

There are a total of nine international criminal courts and tribunals. The International Military Tribunal (IMT) and International Military Tribunal for the Far East (IMTFE) were established by the Allies after the end of the Second World War. The IMT was established by a treaty[3] and the IMTFE by a special

[3] Charter of the International Military Tribunal of 8 August 1945.

proclamation of the Supreme Commander of Japan, General McArthur.[4] The International Criminal Tribunal for former Yugoslavia (ICTY) and the International Criminal Tribunal for Rwanda (ICTR) were established in the early nineties by United Nations Security Council Resolutions.[5] The International Criminal Court (ICC) was set up by a statute which states can become a party to. Agreement on the statute was reached on 17 July 1998 in Rome[6] and, on 1 July 2002, after the sixtieth state had ratified the statute,[7] the ICC became operational. The Special Court for Sierra Leone (SCSL),[8] the Extraordinary Chambers in the Courts of Cambodia (ECCC)[9] and the Special Tribunal for Lebanon (STL)[10] were all established after an agreement between the governments of the country and the United Nations (UN). The internationalized court in East Timor, which is generally referred to as the Special Panels of Dili (SPD), was created as part of the transitional UN administration of UNTAET.[11] As well as these international and internationalized courts, there are also national courts which prosecute international crimes; there are also a few national courts with an international dimension such as the courts in Kosovo and the War Crimes Chamber in Bosnia. These courts, however, will not be included in our analysis as there is too much data to be discussed here.

Of the nine international criminal court and tribunals which are discussed in greater detail, five can be considered international courts (IMT, IMTFE, ICTY, ICTR and ICC), and the other four (SCSL, ECCC, STL, SPD) internationalized, mixed or hybrid courts. International courts have international judges only, while the internationalized, mixed and hybrid courts usually have a mixture of national and international judges (for more detail, see Section 3.2). The ICC is the only permanent court, all other courts are temporary. The IMT, IMTFE and the SPD have all closed down, while the ICTY and ICTR are working on their closing strategies. The SCSL has finalized all its cases with the exception of the Charles Taylor appeal. The ECCC is fully operational: it has concluded one case and a second case, which involves three high-profile perpetrators, is currently on-going. The STL is about to

4) Charter of the International Military Tribunal of the Far East of 19 January 1946.

5) SC Resolution 827 of 15 May 1993 and SC Resolution 955 of 8 November 1994.

6) UN Doc A/CONF. 183/9.

7) On 11 April 2002 at a special UN ceremony ten countries deposited their instrument of ratification simultaneously, reaching the threshold of the sixty ratifications needed for the Statute of Rome to enter into force. As of July 2012, 121 states are party to the statute.

8) Statute of the Special Court for Sierra Leone of 16 January 2002.

9) Agreement between the United Nations and the Royal Government of Cambodia concerning the Prosecution under Cambodian Law of crimes committed during the period of the Democratic Kampuchea (Extraordinary Chambers in the Courts of Cambodia) of 6 June 2003.

10) SC Resolution 1757 of 30 May 2007.

11) UNTAET, which stands for United Nations Transitional Administration in East Timor, was established by UN SC Resolution 1272: the resolution referred to the need to investigate the crimes committed after the referendum. In UNTAET Regulation 2000/11 the idea of a hybrid court was launched for the first time.

start its first trial. The ICC has finished one case and is currently investigating sixteen cases in seven different situations.

All the courts and tribunals have limited temporal and territorial jurisdiction. Four tribunals were established after an armed conflict. The IMT and IMTFE were established after the Second World War and had jurisdiction for the crimes committed during this war, only prosecuting perpetrators who belonged to the Axis. The ICTY and SCSL were established after a civil war and prosecuted perpetrators from more than one party within the conflict. Three courts and tribunals deal with one-sided violence; the ICTR, for example, deals with the genocide committed by Hutu extremists in 1994,[12] the ECCC with the crimes committed by the Khmer Rouge regime during their reign in power (1975-1979) and the SPD with the violence committed by the militias and the Indonesian army in 1999 after the ballot for independence. The STL deals with the fatal attack on Prime Minister Hariri, it thus has a temporal jurisdiction which is very limited and only prosecutes crimes related to the attack on 14 February 2005. The ICC has the broadest mandate as it can potentially prosecute all international crimes committed from 1 July 2002, the date of its establishment. It has to be noted, however, if the state in which the crimes were committed has not ratified the statute or the state from which the perpetrator originates has not ratified it then a Security Council Resolution based on Chapter VII of the UN Charter is required to start proceedings.[13] With the exception of the STL, all tribunals have jurisdiction over war crimes and crimes against humanity. The ICTY, ICTR, ICC, SPD and ECCC also have jurisdiction over genocide.[14] The IMT and IMTFE, in their time, had jurisdiction over crimes against peace, which is similar to the current crime of aggression which the ICC will have jurisdiction over.

The mixed and hybrid courts also have jurisdiction over non-international crimes according to domestic criminal codes: the SCSL has jurisdiction over crimes committed under Sierra Leonean law such as offences relating to the abuse of girls or the wanton destruction of property; the ECCC has jurisdiction over the crimes of homicide, torture and religious persecution according to Cambodian law and the SPD have jurisdiction over murder, sexual offences and torture. All courts and tribunals have jurisdiction over natural persons and there are no

[12] The genocide was committed during a period of civil war in which the Rwandan Patriotic Front (RPF) committed crimes too. The ICTR however only prosecuted crimes committed by the Hutus as part of the genocidal campaign. Carla del Ponte, Chief Prosecutor of the ICTR tried to also prosecute members of the RPF but was prevented from doing so. *See* Carla Del Ponte, *Madame Prosecutor: Confrontations with Humanity's Worst Criminals and the Culture of Impunity*, (Other Press, 2009).

[13] *See* Art. 12 jo. 13 of the ICC Statute.

[14] The IMT and IMTFE did not have jurisdiction over genocide. The concept was not internationally accepted at the time. Lemkin had coined the term in 1944 but it wasn't until 1948 and thus after the IMT finished its work that it was legally established in the Genocide Convention.

systems of immunity (or amnesty) that can be used to protect heads of states and other governmental officials from prosecution.

The Hague is often referred to as the legal capital of the world because the ICTY, the Appeals Chamber of the ICTR, the ICC and the STL all have their seat there. The IMT was also seated in Europe, namely in Nuremberg. Two of these European based courts (IMT and ICTY) dealt with crimes committed in Europe (although the crimes of Nazi Germany stretched beyond the boundaries of Europe). The STL deals with crimes committed in the Middle East, while the ICC can potentially deal with crimes committed anywhere in the world but so far has mainly dealt with crimes committed in Africa. The three courts seated in Asia (IMTFE, ECCC and SPD) deal with crimes committed in Asia, while the two courts seated in Africa (SCSL and ICTR) deal with crimes committed in African countries.[15]

3. Prosecutors and Judges

One of the distinguishing features of international and internationalized criminal courts and tribunals is the involvement of international prosecutors and judges.[16] In the section below we focus on these prosecutors and judges and their characteristics.

3.1. *Prosecutors*

In total there were 23 chief prosecutors involved in the nine international and internationalized criminal courts and tribunals, seven of whom are currently still in office (for more detailed figures, see Table 1). Most tribunals have one chief prosecutor at a time with the exception of IMT which had four chief prosecutors and the ECCC which has two chief prosecutors. Initially the function of chief prosecutor at the ICTY and ICTR were combined but these functions were separated in 2003. The SPD and the ECCC also have investigative judges.

Males are overrepresented amongst the prosecutors: 18 out of 23 (78 per cent) prosecutors were male whereas there were just five females (22 per cent). The average age of a prosecutor is 50 years old. The youngest prosecutor was 33 (Longuinhos Monteiro at the SPD) and the oldest 66 (Da Silva at the SCSL). Most

---

15) The trial of Charles Taylor by the SCSL was conducted in The Hague at the premises of the ICC for security reasons.

16) For a discussion of this phenomenon and its implication for judicial policy-making, *see* Jared Wessel, 'Judicial Policy-Making at the International Criminal Court: An Institutional Guide to Analyzing International Adjudication', 44 *Columbia Journal of Transnational Law* (2005-2006) 377-452; and Sebastian Jodoin, 'Understanding the Behaviour of International Courts: An Examination of Decision-making in the ad hoc International Criminal Tribunals', 6 *Journal of International Law and International Relations* 1 (2010) 1-34.

Table 1. Prosecutors

	IMT	IMTFE	ICTY	ICTR	ICC	SCSL	SPD	ECCC	STL	Total[1]
Number	4	1	4	4	2	4	2	3	2	23
Simultaneously	4	1	1	1	1	1	1	2	1	1.4
Male	4	1	2	2	1	3	2	2	2	18
Female	0	0	2	2	1	1	0	1	0	5
Age[2]	45	58	51	53	51	58	41	41	54	50
Time in office (yrs)	1	2	4	3	9	2	2.5	4.5	5	3[3]

[1] The figures in this column do not all add up but this is because in counting the total numbers we took into account that three of the four chief prosecutors at the ICTY combined this position with their role of chief prosecutor at the ICTR.
[2] We could not trace all data on year of birth. For four prosecutors the year of birth was missing – on the basis of the information provided when they received their MA we have estimated their year of birth.
[3] The figure was calculated by taking all prosecutors (those who left office and those still in office) into account. The outcome does not change if we only take those who left office into account.

prosecutors have a background as a prosecutor, judge or attorney-general and have stayed in office to date for an average of three years – differences in time in office can be related to the length of time that the tribunal was operational. The longest operating prosecutors were Ocampo (ICC) and Jallow (ICTR) who both have nine years service, closely followed by Del Ponte (ICTY) who was in office for eight years. The prosecutors are predominantly from western countries, namely six from Europe, five from the United States and three from Canada; three came from Africa, one from Latin America and one from Asia.

3.2. *Judges*[17]

In total there were over 250 judges involved in the international criminal trials including alternate judges, reserve judges and *ad litem* judges.[18] Of them

[17)] The data on the judges of all the international courts are fairly complete with the exception of the SPD. We were able to gather all the information we required about the judges of the IMT, IMTFE, ICTY, ICTR and ICC. Of the judges of the SCSL, ECCC and STL we could not find enough data about their ages or years of birth to include in our analysis as these tribunals do not provide this information on their website and we could not retrieve the information in any other manner. The data on the judges of the SPD is incomplete as there are no lists of all the judges. By looking through the judgments and the notifications of the Special Representative of the Secretary General of East Timor we estimated that there were about twenty-eight judges involved of whom fifteen were international judges and thirteen national judges. We could not however discern any further information with sufficient certainty (apart from the overall count) so these judges have therefore been excluded from the analysis.
[18)] The IMT had four substitutes who participated fully in the deliberations. A number of courts used alternate or reserve judges, while the ICTY and ICTR appointed so-called *ad litem* judges who are usually assigned to just one case.

24 judges have served as presidents of the international criminal courts and tribunals; most judges served at the ICTY and fewest at the IMT (for further details, see Table 2). The early war courts (IMT and IMTFE) as well as the two international criminal ad hoc tribunals (ICTY and ICTR) and the ICC have international judges only. The so-called hybrid courts have both national and international judges. In all of the mixed and hybrid courts, with the exception of the ECCC, international judges have a majority.[19] Of the total of 256 judges, 222 (87 per cent) were international judges and 34 (13 per cent) were national judges.

Initially judging war criminals was an entirely male concern and all 19 judges at the IMT and IMTFE were male. Since then 61 female judges have been appointed, making up roughly one out of four judges (27 per cent). The first female international judges were Gabrielle Kirk McDonald and Elizabeth Odio-Benito appointed on 17 November 1993 as judges of the ICTY. Most female judges were appointed to the ICTY (22) but the ICC has the highest average of female judges (47 per cent). This can probably be explained by the fact that according to the Rome Statute (Art. 36(8) ICC Statute) there should be a fair representation of female and male judges. Five women have served as presidents of different tribunals.

The average age of the judges at the time of their appointment is 62 years old[20] and the average leaving age is 67. On average the judges at the IMTFE were the youngest, appointed at 55 years old and the ICTY judges at 63 years old were the oldest. The youngest judge ever to be appointed was Bert Röling, the Dutch judge of the IMTFE, appointed at 40 years old. The oldest serving judges were David Pedro of Argentina and Arpad Prangler of Hungary who were both 82 years and served at the ICTY. Judges at the international criminal courts have usually been of a rather advanced age. This fact might be explained by the requirement that international judges be persons of high moral standing with extensive professional experience in the international or domestic arenas (Cf. Art 36(3) ICC, Art 13 ICTY).

The average time judges served in office is four point eight years. On average judges at the SCSL served the longest terms while the judges at the IMT served for less than a year which was the time span of the only trial held at the IMT (for more detailed information, see Table 2). Twenty judges served more than

---

19) At the ECCC this was one of the major points of discussion. The UN wanted a majority of international judges but Cambodia wanted a majority of national judges. This was one of the most important reasons behind why the negotiations took so long but finally the UN gave in. *See* Tom Fawthrop and Helen Jarvis, *Getting Away with Genocide? Elusive Justice and the Khmer Rouge Tribunal* (Pluto Press: London, 2004). The group of experts who had been appointed by the Secretary General of the UN had advised that the majority of judges should be international but the Cambodian government decided otherwise. *See* Report of the Group of Experts for Cambodia, established pursuant to the General Assembly Resolution 52/135, 1999 – Report: A/53/850.

20) The figures are based on the IMT, IMTFE, ICTY, ICTR, ICC data where only few numbers were missing. Since there is a lot of missing data on judges' ages the SCSL, ECCC, STL, and SPD we have not included them in the analysis.

Table 2. Judges

	IMT	IMTFE	ICTY	ICTR	ICC	SCSL	SPD	ECCC	STL	Total
Number	8	12	81	37	34	18	28	26	12	256
International	8	12	81	37	34	14	15	13	8	222 (87%)
National	0	0	0	0	0	4	13	13	4	34 (13%)
Male	8	12	59	27	18	13	MD	20	10	167 (73%)
Female	0	0	22	10	16	5	MD	6	2	61 (27%)
Youngest	43	40	47	46	50	MD	MD	MD	MD	40
Oldest	66	65	82	77	81	MD	MD	MD	MD	82
Av. age	58	55	63	61	62	MD	MD	MD	MD	62
Av. term	1	1.8	4.8	6.2	4.7	6.8	MD	5.1	2.7	4.8
Longest term	1	1.8	14	17	9	10	MD	5.1	2.7	17
Presidents	1	1	6	6	2	6	MD	1	2	25
Male pres.	1	1	5	4	2	4	MD	1	2	20 (80%)
Female pres.	0	0	1	2	0	2	MD	0	0	5 (20%)

Key: MD = Missing Data

ten years (nine at the ICTY, five at the ICTR and six at the SCSL) 17 of whom are still in office. The longest serving judge is William Sekule of Tanzania who was appointed in 1995 at the ICTR and is currently still in office (thus serving for more than seventeen years). Patrick Robinson from Jamaica is the longest serving judge at the ICTY – he was appointed in 1998 and is still in office.

If we take the home country of the judges into account most judges come from Europe – 86 out of the 228 judges (38 per cent). Africa and Asia also have a large share of international judges (between 21-22 per cent). The smallest percentage of judges comes from Australia (see Table 3 for exact figures). If we look at the table we can see that international criminal justice has become more cosmopolitan during the years. While the IMT was a pure western tribunal the other courts strive for a fair geographical balance, although European judges were still dominant at the ICTY. The ICTR had many European and African judges. The two first African judges to be appointed were Georges Abi-Saab from Egypt and Alphonse Karibi Whyte from Nigeria who were both appointed in 1993 at the ICTY. The first Latin American judge was Elizabeth Odio Benito from Costa Rica appointed in 1993 at the ICTY.

In general judges come from three different backgrounds: first of all academia – renowned scholars who have specialized in international law or international criminal law; secondly judges who have been diplomats who represented their countries or worked for them in international organizations and thirdly judges who come from national criminal law courts who have many years of experience on the bench.[21]

---

[21] Cesare P.R. Romano, 'The judges and prosecutors of internationalized criminal courts and tribunals', in Cesare P. Romano, André Nollkaemper and Jann K. Kleffner (eds.), *Internationalized*

Table 3. Judges, Geographical Spreading

	IMT	IMTFE	ICTY	ICTR	ICC	SCSL	ECCC	STL	Total
Europe	6	4	36	14	14	3	5	4	86 (38%)
US & Canada	2	3	6	0	1	2	1	0	15 (7%)
Latin America	0	0	10	1	7	0	0	1	19 (8%)
Africa	0	0	11	14	7	11	3	1	47 (21%)
Asia	0	3	15	6	5	2	15	4	50 (22%)
Aust. & NZ	0	2	3	2	0	0	2	2	11 (5%)

4. International Criminal Courts and Tribunals: Functioning

In this section we have gathered information on the functioning of the international criminal courts and tribunals.

4.1. *Start-up and Trials*

With the exception of the ICTY all the ad-hoc courts started operating after their respective conflict ended and most courts and tribunals started functioning within one or two years of the conflict ending (see for further details, Table 4). The STL began operating three and a half years after the attack on Hariri while the ECCC started operating 27 years after the fall of the Khmer Rouge regime. The reason for this exceptionally long delay was that Vietnam had invaded Cambodia and remained in power while the international community continued to recognize the Khmer Rouge government in exile as the legitimate regime.[22] It lasted until the mid-nineties until the international community finally stopped supporting the Khmer Rouge. The negotiations between the government of Cambodia and the UN on an agreement for the tribunal started soon thereafter but lasted a very long time.

With the exception of the STL and the ICC, all the tribunals managed to issue their first indictments within 18 months of operation. It took the courts from between one to ten years before the first judgment was delivered. Within one year of their establishment, the SPD and the IMT decided their first case whilst it took the IMTFE and the ICTR more than two and a half years, the ICTY three years and the SCSL and ECCC over four and a half years. The ICC had the longest starting period; after becoming operational it was almost ten years before it managed to

Criminal Courts – Sierra Leone, East Timor, Kosovo and Cambodia (Oxford University Press, Oxford, 2004), p. 249.

[22] *See* extensively on this issue Fawthrop and Jarvis, *supra* note 19.

Table 4. Operational Times of Courts

	IMT	IMTFE	ICTY	ICTR
Crimes	1939-1945	1939-1945	1991-1999	1994
Court operational	18-10-1945	29-4-1946	17-11-1993	27-11-1995
1st indictment	20-10-1945	29-4-1946	4-11-1994	22-11-1995
1st trial started	20-11-1945	3-05-1946	7-5-1996	9-1-1997
1st Judgment	1-10-1946	12-11-1948	29-11-1996	2-9-1998
Time Lapse	11.5 m	2 y 6.5 m	3 y	2 y 10 m
Years operational	1 y	2.5 y	19 y	17 y
	ICC	SCSL	SPD	ECCC
Crimes	2002-	1996	1999	1975-1979
Court operational	1-7-2002	1-7-2002	6-6-2000	18-01-2006
1st indictment	8-7-2005	7-3-2003	15-11-2000	19-9-2007
1st trial started	26-1-2009	3-6-2004	18-1-2001	30-3-2009
1st Judgment	14-3-2012	20-6-2007	25-1-2001	26-7-2010
Time Lapse	10 y	4 y 11 m	6.5 m	4.5 y
Years operational	10 y	10 y	5 y	6.5 y

Key: y = years, m = months.

convict its first accused (Lubanga). The explanation for these differences may stem from the fact that the rules and procedures at the earlier tribunals (IMT and IMTFE) were less burdensome than those of the later courts and tribunals (ICTY, ICTR and ICC) and some tribunals were able to start off with relatively straightforward cases (SPD, ICTY) whereas others were not (ICC). To try international criminal cases is, by definition, a difficult task because so many people and organizations are involved and the countries in which the crimes were committed are often war-torn. Much depends on the availability of evidence and the willingness of the respective states to cooperate with the tribunals.

All in all 172 cases were tried involving 356 suspects and 17 cases are still ongoing (see for further details, Table 5). Most of the cases were tried by the SPD which tried 60 cases involving 88 suspects, closely followed by the ICTY and ICTR which conducted 54 and 50 cases respectively. On average, a case in front of an international criminal court or tribunal involves one point nine suspects. The largest cases by far were conducted at the IMT and IMTFE where one trial was held of the accused conjointly (22 and 28 respectively).

4.2. *Length of Proceedings*

The time lapse between the indictment and the start of trial was very brief at the IMTFE; the indictments were read out on 29 April 1946 and the trials started just

Table 5. Cases

	IMT	IMTFE	ICTY	ICTR	ICC	SCSL	SDL	ECCC	Total
Suspects	22	28	118	74	11	10	88	5	356
Cases concluded	1	1	54	50	1	4	60	1	172
On-going[1]	0	0	9[2]	1	6[3]	1	0	1	17
Average	22	28	1.9	1.5	2	2	1.5	2.5	1.9

[1] Only on-going trial cases are included.
[2] One in the pre-trial phase and eight on-going cases.
[3] Two cases are actually on-going, three cases involving six suspects in total are scheduled to begin in 2013 and one case is still in its pre-trial phase.

four days later. For the other courts, the average time lapse between issuing an indictment and the start of the trial was two years. It was shortest at the SPD (one year) and longest at the ICTY (three point six years) and ICTR (four point five years). This might be due to the lack of enforcement powers and political support at the beginning (securing cooperation) of the functioning of these tribunals. Internationalized courts may have more domestic support and engagement as their respective countries feel more ownership of the on-going proceedings.

On average the time length between the indictment (I) and the trial judgment (TJ) at the international criminal courts and tribunals is four point nine years (for further details, see Table 6). The average length of the trial is two point nine years (time lapse between start of the trial and judgment). The shortest trial was conducted at the SPD and lasted seven days whereas the longest trial was conducted at the ICTR and lasted ten years.[23] On average the fastest working tribunal is the SPD with an average length of trial close to four months, followed by IMT, ECCC and ICTY who all, on average, conclude the trial proceedings within two years. It took the IMTFE and ECCC two and a half years. It is remarkable that the IMT and IMTFE were amongst the fastest tribunals as they tried all defendants (22 and 28) in just one case.

The longest trials on average are conducted at the ICTR and the SCSL which take over three years for a trial, as the ICC did in its first trial. These differences could be explained by the type of cases tried. The SPD usually focused on single incidents, the cases were not very complicated and the defendants often plead guilty. At the ICTR there were many high-ranking figures and the cases covered genocidal campaign, often organized by these defendants, including multiple incidents of killings and mistreatment of victims. Similarly, the trials at the SCSL

[23] This was the so-called Butare case against Pauline Nyiramasuhuko and five others. *Prosecutor v. Nyiramasuhuko et al*, ICTR-98-42-T. The trial commenced on 12 June 2001 and the judgment was rendered on 24 June 2011.

Table 6. Length of Proceedings (I-ST-TJ)

Proceedings	IMT	IMTFE	ICTY	ICTR	ICC	SCSL	SDL	ECCC	Av.
Length of first full proceedings (I-TJ)	11 m	2.5 y	2.3 y	2.6 y	6.1 y	4.3 y	2 m	2 y	1.7 y
Shortest full proceedings (I-TJ)	11 m	2.5 y	7 m	4 m	6.1 y	3.6 y	2 m	2 y	2 m
Longest full proceedings (I-TJ)	11 m	2.5 y	12 y	15 y	6.1 y	9.2 y	4.3 y	2 y	15 y
Av. length of full proceedings (I-TJ)	11 m	2.5 y	5.6 y	7.6 y	6.1 y	5.3 y	1.5 y	2 y	4.9 y
Av. time lapse before start trial (I-ST)	1 m	4 d	3.6 y	4.5 y	2.3y	1.7 y	1.1 y	2.4 y	2 y
Shortest trial (ST-TJ)	10 m	2.5 y	6 m	2 m	3.2 y	2.3 y	7 d	1.3 y	7 d
Longest trial (ST-TJ)	10 m	2.5 y	3.9 y	10 y	3.2 y	4.9 y	2.1 y	1.3 y	10 y
Average length of trial (ST-TJ)	10 m	2.5 y	1.9 y	3.9 y	3.2 y	3.6 y	4 m	1.3 y	2.9 y
Guilty pleas	0	0	21 /118	9/74	0	0	27 /88	0	57/356
Percentage of guilty pleas	0	0	18%	12%	0	0	31%	0	16%

Key: I = indictment, ST = start trial, TJ = trial judgment, y = years, m = months, d = days.

had a multiplicity of high-ranking defendants and deal with multiple crimes. Evidentiary issues of linking these defendants to the crimes committed consumed a lot of trial time. The fact that there were both international and domestic judges with different backgrounds and experiences on the bench might have played a role at both the ECCC and SCSL. Of influence on the length of the trials is also the practice of pleading guilty which generally shorten the proceedings,[24] whereas no one pleaded guilty at the IMT, IMTFE, SCSL, ECCC and ICC, 27 defendants (31 per cent) pleaded guilty before the SPD, 21 defendants (18 per cent) pleaded guilty at the ICTY and nine defendants (12 per cent) pleaded guilty in front of the ICTR.

24) It has been argued that, at the ICTY in particular, the practice of plea agreements was implemented because of concerns about time constraints and lengthy proceedings before the Tribunal. *Cf.* Nancy A. Combs, *Guilty Pleas in International Criminal Law, Constructing a Restorative Justice Approach* (Stanford University Press, 2007).

Table 7. Indictees

	IMT	IMTFE	ICTY	ICTR	ICC	SCSL	SPD	ECCC	STL	Total
People indicted	24	28	161	90	28	13	392	5	4	745
Withdrawn due to death	1	0	10	1	2	2	0	0	0	16
Others withdrawn	1	0	20	2	4	0	304	0	0	331
Referrals	0	0	13	7	0	0	0	0	0	20
Still at large	0	0	0	6	11	1	0	0	4	22

4.3. *Indictments and Convictions*

In total, 745 people were indicted by the international criminal courts and tribunals; most of these by the SPD and the fewest by the ECCC and STL (for further details, see Table 7). Almost half of all the indictments, namely 347 were withdrawn before they went to trial; 16 withdrawals were due to the death of the suspects: 13 indictees died before their arrest and three others after their arrest but before the trial started. The ICTY and ICTR referred 20 cases to national jurisdiction and withdrew those cases for that very reason. By far the most indictments were withdrawn by the SPD (304) because the accused could not be found and the tribunal was about to close down. The other 27 cases were withdrawn for reasons other than those already mentioned above, such as judicial economy, lack of evidence or because the accused was not fit enough to stand trial. At the ICC, four cases were terminated because the pre-trial chamber did not confirm the charges. A total of 22 indictees are still at large (although some of them may have already died), most of them were indicted by the ICC. The ICTY and ECCC are the only two tribunals which are still functioning and no longer have anyone at large.[25]

Out of the 745 people indicted, only 356 (47 per cent) actually went on trial. Of these, 281 were convicted and 29 acquitted, the indictments of 12 defendants were withdrawn during the trial (ten of them because the person on trial had died) and proceedings against 34 individuals are still on-going, such as cases against some prominent defendants, e.g. the one against Gbagbo, former president of Ivory Coast at the ICC, and Karadzic and Mladic at the ICTY (for further details, see Table 8). The overall conviction rate (i.e. the percentage of those convicted after a trial has been started against them) is 87 per cent, while nine per cent ended in an acquittal and four per cent were withdrawn. All the courts have a conviction rate

[25] Last year on 26 May 2011 and 20 July 2011, respectively, Ratko Mladic and Goran Hadzic were the two last fugitives of the ICTY to be arrested.

Table 8. Suspects Tried and Outcome of Trial

	IMT	IMTFE	ICTY	ICTR	ICC	SCSL	SPD	ECCC	Total
Suspects tried	22	28	118	74	11	10	88	5	356
Trial still ongoing	0	0	18	2	10	0	0	4	34
Suspects died (suicide)	0	2	6 (1)	1	0	1	0	0	10 (1)
Withdrawals	0	1	0	0	0	0	1	0	2
Acquitted	3	0	13	10	0	0	3	0	29
Convicted	19	25	81	61	1	9	84	1	281
Convictions rate	86%	89%	81%	85%	100%	90%	95%	100%	87%
Acquittals rate	14%	0%	13%	14%	0%	0%	3%	0%	9%
Withdrawal rate	0%	11%	6%	1%	0%	10%	2%	0%	4%

of above 80 per cent. The ICC and the ECCC stand out with a 100 per cent conviction rate so far, but this is due to the fact that they have only concluded one case each and in both cases (*Lubanga* and *Duch*) the respective courts found the defendant guilty. The SPD has a conviction rate of 95 per cent and the SCSL has a conviction rate of 90 per cent due to the fact that one person died during the trial and consequently could not be convicted. So far, four courts have had no acquittals. This is not surprising for the ICC and ECCC which have only concluded one case but is telling in the case of the IMTFE and the SCSL. The IMT, ICTY and ICTR all have an acquittal rate of 13-14 per cent.

In comparison to ordinary criminal courts, the conviction rates at the international tribunals are rather high and this provides reason for some, Schabas for one,[26] to doubt the fairness of the procedure. An explanation for the high conviction rate, however, is possibly that the international criminal justice system is very selective and has successfully picked those individuals against whom enough evidence was available. If, on the other hand, we look at the number of people who were in some way involved, in comparison to the number of people tried, the conviction rate is very low, much lower than in relation to ordinary crimes.[27]

26) *See* William A. Schabas, 'Independence an impartiality of the international judiciary: some lessons learned and some ignored', in E. Hughes, William A. Schabas & R. Thakur (eds.), *Atrocities and International Accountability*, (United Nations University Press, Tokyo, 2007), pp. 182-207.

27) Mullins estimated that 'fewer than one percent of the perpetrators of international crimes have been brought to justice', Christopher W. Mullins, 'Conflict victimization and post-conflict justice 1945-2008', in M. Cherif Bassiouni (ed.), *The Pursuit of International Criminal Justice: a World Study on Conflicts, Victimization, and Post-Conflict Justice*, (Intersentia, Antwerp, 2010), pp. 67-108.

The international criminal courts and tribunals usually have jurisdiction over the three core international crimes: genocide, crimes against humanity and war crimes (for exceptions, see above Section 2). The majority of all the convicted perpetrators at the international courts were convicted for crimes against humanity (71 per cent) and a large number were convicted for war crimes (41.3 per cent).[28] Fifty-nine (21 per cent) individuals were found guilty of genocide, most of them at the ICTR. Genocide as a criminal concept was not fully developed when the prosecutions at the IMT began, so the Holocaust was qualified as a crime against humanity rather than genocide. In East Timor the first 12 cases were qualified as murder cases rather than crimes against humanity.[29] At the IMT and IMTFE most perpetrators were prosecuted for crimes against peace (aggression) which is an offence which has not been prosecuted since.

4.4. *Sentencing*

Of the 356 suspects tried, 281 were convicted and received a prison sentence. Of the 281 convicted perpetrators, 19 (7 per cent) were sentenced to death, 45 (16 per cent) received a life sentence while the vast majority (77 per cent) received a determinate sentence. The shortest determinate sentence[30] was handed down by the SPD and was 11 months and the longest, at 52 years, was handed down by the SCSL. The average determinate sentence was 15.3 years. If we compare the different courts and tribunals (for more details, see Table 9) the sentencing practice seems rather varied and sentences at different courts are quite divergent. The differences among individual courts, however, can be explained by sentencing options, case compositions and prosecutorial strategy.

An important difference between the IMT and IMTFE, on the one hand, and the rest of the courts, on the other, is that these courts were the only ones that could sentence suspects to the death penalty. The IMT sentenced 12 out of 19 convicted perpetrators to death (which is 63 per cent of the perpetrators convicted by the IMT) while the IMTFE sentenced seven (28 per cent) convicted perpetrators to death. Seventeen people were actually executed: ten at Nuremberg on 16 October

[28] At the IMTFE, no distinction was made in the indictment between war crimes and crimes against humanity and both were grouped under Group III counts 53-55. The literature seem to agree, however, that the crimes grouped under these counts should be considered war crimes rather than crimes against humanity and are usually referred to as the former, *see* Yuma Totani, *The Tokyo War Crimes Trial: The Pursuit of Justice in the Wake of World War II* (Harvard University, Harvard, 2009), p. 103. These crimes have also been considered as such in our data.

[29] According to Suzannah Linton, 'East Timor Special Panels', in Antonio Cassese (ed.), *The Oxford Companion to International Criminal Justice* (Oxford University Press, Oxford, 2009), p. 307 this was 'because there were no resources on which to develop crimes against humanity cases'.

[30] Shorter sentences have been given by the courts for misconduct during the process itself, such as contempt of court and giving false testimony, but these have been excluded here.

Table 9. Sentences

	IMT	IMTFE	ICTY	ICTR	ICC	SCSL	SPD	ECCC	Total
Convicted	19	25	81	61	1	9	84	1	281
Death Sentences	12	7	N/A	N/A	N/A	N/A	N/A	N/A	19
Life imprisonment (still in appeal)	3(0)	16(0)	4(3)	21 (7)	0	N/A	N/A	1	45 (10)
Prison term not life (still in appeal)	4	2	77(14)	40(8)	1	9(1)	84 (0)	0	217 (23)
Minimum sentence	10	7	2	6	14	15	11 m	Life	11 m
Maximum determinate sentence	20	20	40	45	14	52	33.3	N/A	52
Maximum sentence	Death	Death	Life	Life	14	52	33.3	Life	Death
Average determinate sentence length	16.25	15.7	15.9	22.6	14	38.6	8.8	N/A	15.3

Key: N/A = Not Applicable, m = month.

1946, and seven in Tokyo on 23 December 1948. Goering committed suicide the day before he was to be executed and Bormann was never arrested, but convicted in absentia.[31] No other international criminal court or tribunal since has had the option of handing down a death penalty. Because of the development of international human rights standards, the death penalty had been abolished by the majority of states and was, therefore, also excluded as a penalty for international criminal courts and tribunals.

The maximum possible sentence that could be handed out at the post-cold war international tribunals was therefore life imprisonment (art. 24 ICTY and 23 ICTR).[32] A life sentence was given to 45 out of 281 (16 per cent) sentenced perpetrators, ten of which are still under appeal at the ICTY and ICTR.[33] Most

---

31) It is now assumed that Bormann had already committed suicide before the trial started. He was officially declared dead in 1954. Later, in 1973, his body was exhumed and identified.

32) This, by the way, created a strange situation in Rwanda where the most senior perpetrators could receive life imprisonment but less important perpetrators who were prosecuted at the local courts in Rwanda could face the death penalty. According to Schabas, twenty-two individuals were executed in Rwanda in April 1998. However, in 2007, under international pressure, Rwanda abolished the death penalty. William A. Schabas, 'Post Genocide Justice in Rwanda', in Philip Clark and Zachary D. Kaufman (eds.). *After Genocide. Transitional Justice, Post-Conflict Reconstruction and Reconciliation in Rwanda and Beyond*, (Hurst Publishers Ltd: London, 2008).

33) Interestingly, a total number of eight life sentences were converted to determinate sentences on appeal. Stakic saw his life sentence converted by the ICTY, while seven defendants saw their life sentences overturned at the ICTR. These sentences were converted to determinate sentences ranging from fifteen tot forty-five years. In three other cases, one at the ICTY and two at the ICTR, determinate sentences were converted to life sentences on appeal. These

sentences of life imprisonment were handed down at the ICTR. It has sentenced 34 per cent of all the convicted individuals (21 suspects) to life in prison. This high percentage of life sentences can be explained by the fact that 52 out of 61 sentenced perpetrators were convicted for genocide, generally considered to be the most heinous of all crimes, and many high-ranking perpetrators stood trial at the ICTR and were all convicted of multiple killings. At the ICTY so far, only four perpetrators have been sentenced to life while three of them are still awaiting the outcome of their appeals.

The IMTFE handed down 16 sentences of life imprisonment but all the perpetrators who were convicted were paroled after serving less than ten years.[34] The last was Kenryo Sato who was paroled in Japan in 1956.[35] At the IMT, three people (Hess, Funck and Raeder) were sentenced to life; Hess committed suicide in prison in 1987, the other two were released due to ill health in the mid and late 1950s. Duch, the only person convicted so far at the ECCC, also received a life sentence. Initially a 35 year sentence had been imposed but this was changed into life imprisonment after a successful appeal by the prosecutor. Duch, was the first of four indictees to be sentenced and was a middle-ranking perpetrator, whereas the other three are all high-ranking state officials and organizers. Even though little can be concluded after just one conviction, this could possibly indicate that the ECCC may ultimately sentence all suspects to life imprisonment (since high-ranking officials are usually punished more severely). Notably, however, some tribunals, such as the SCSL, lack jurisdiction for the imposition of life sentences.

The great majority of convicted perpetrators, some 217 (77 per cent), received determinate sentences; the longest being the 52 year sentence handed down by the SCSL to Isay Sesay of the AFRC/RUF (Armed Forces Revolutionary Council/ Revolutionary United Front of Sierra Leone). Sesay was the highest-ranking officer after Sankoh and Bockarie, the two leaders of the RUF who died. Alex Brima, the leader of the AFRC, and Charles Taylor, the former president of Liberia, both received a 50 year sentence at the SCSL. The longest determinate sentence handed down at the ICTR was 45 years and at the ICTY 40 years. Three perpetrators at the SPD were sentenced to 33 years and four months; they were all convicted in the

---

involved Galic, whose twenty-year sentence was converted to a life sentence at the ICTY and Gacumbitsi and Seromba, whose thirty-year and fifteen-year sentences respectively were converted into life sentences by the ICTR.

34) *See* R. John Pritchard, 'International Military Tribunal for Far East and the Allied National War Crimes Trials in Asia', in M. Cherif Bassiouni (ed.), *International Criminal Law*, (Transnational Publishers: Ardsley, 1999), p. 142.

35) The fact that of all convicted perpetrators, Kenryo Sato was the last to be paroled is remarkable as he is generally considered to be the person least responsible. http://www.enotes.com/tokyo-trial-reference/tokyo-trial.

same trial which dealt with the militia group called Team Alfa. All the sentences were, however, reduced to 25 years by a presidential decree.

The highest average determinate sentences of 38 years were handed down at the SCSL and the ICTR has an average determinate sentence of 22.6 years, while the average sentences at the IMT, IMTFE and ICTY are all about 15 to 16 years. The reasons for this variance may be related to the fact that the SCSL could not hand down any life sentences and thus relied on long determinate sentences for those most culpable. The ICTR prosecuted predominantly high-ranking individuals for committing genocidal killings. As this type of crime can be considered one of the most serious, it may not be surprising that as well as the high number of life sentences handed down, many ICTR suspects received long prison sentences. At the IMT and IMTFE, the determinate sentences are relatively low but this can be explained by the fact that the majority were sentenced to death or life imprisonment with only six receiving a determinate sentence. The lowest average sentences are handed down by the SPD, a court which convicted mainly low-ranking perpetrators for usually one single incident. In some cases, the crimes were not even qualified as international crimes but as ordinary crimes. The perpetrators facing this court received an average sentence of just under nine years. The ICC has recently handed out a sentence of fourteen years to Thomas Lubanga for his participation in the war crime of conscripting and enlisting child soldiers.

4.5. *Appeals*

Overall, on 175 occasions, the outcome of a case was appealed (either by a defendant or prosecutor or both). The IMT and IMTFE did not allow appeals. If we take this into account, then 66 per cent of all the cases which could be appealed were appealed (for further details see Table 10). All the judgments handed down by the SCSL were appealed. At the ECCC and ICC the only cases finished on trial so far (*Duch* and *Lubanga*) were appealed. Over 80 per cent of the outcomes were appealed at the ICTY and ICTR, whereas by far the lowest appeal rates are at the

Table 10. Appeals and Sentences after Appeal

	ICTY	ICTR	ICC	SCSL	SPD	ECCC	Total
Concluded trials	94	71	1	9	88	1	264
Appeals (pending)	75 (17)	58 (17)	1(1)	9(1)	31	1	175 (36)
Percentage	80%	82%	100%	100%	35%	100%	66%
Lower after appeal	22	13	0	0	15	0	50 (36%)
Higher after appeal	5	3	0	3	6	1	18 (13%)
No change on app.	31	25	0	5	10	0	71 (51%)

SPD, with only 35 per cent of the cases being appealed. In total 36 appeals are still pending, 17 each at the ICTR and ICTY, and one each at the SCSL and ICC. In 50 cases (36 per cent), the sentence was lowered by the Appeals Chamber and in 18 cases the Appeals Chamber actually increased the trial sentence (12.9 per cent). This practice is controversial because of human rights standards and many judges at the ICTY and ICTR filed dissenting opinions in this respect (referring to the 'prohibition of reformation *in peius*' which means a person should not be placed in a worse position as a result of filing an appeal).

4.6. *Closing Down*

The IMT, IMTFE and SPD have closed down while all the other courts are still operational. To date, the courts operating the longest are the ICTY and ICTR which have been operating for 19 and 17 years respectively, but both are now working on their closing strategies. The ICC and SCSL have been operational for more than ten years, while the IMT and IMTFE have been operating for one and two and a half years respectively. On average, the international criminal courts and tribunals were operational for eight point eight years. The ICC is the only permanent court.

5. Profile of Convicted Perpetrators

The nine international criminal courts and tribunals convicted all together 281 individuals. Most people, some 84, were convicted by the SPD; this is 30 per cent of all convicted perpetrators. The ICTY convicted 81 (29 per cent) and the ICTR 61 (22 per cent). The IMTFE convicted 25 people (9 per cent) and the IMT 19 (7 per cent), while SCSL convicted nine people (3 per cent) and the ICC and ECCC one person each (less than 1 per cent). In this section we look at the extent to which we can find any general characteristics about the kinds of individuals who are convicted by the international criminal justice system and the differences between the typical profile of the perpetrators convicted by each tribunal, as prosecutors can exercise quite a large amount of discretion in choosing defendants, depending on the type of conflict, the cases investigated and the available evidence.

5.1. *Rank*

We distinguished four ranks: high, middle, low and those without any authority at all. Top political or military authorities who make decisions at policy level were considered to be high-ranking. Middle-ranking individuals were those at the intermediate level of power and authority who implemented and executed policies determined by the top level authorities such as regional political leaders, higher ranking military commanders, heads of executive units within the state bureaucratic apparatus. The low-ranking perpetrators are those with very limited authority over others, such as camp commanders, shift leaders, local army commanders and local politicians. Foot soldiers, very low level bureaucrats and civilians were ranked as having no authority at all. If we combine all the figures (see Table 11) and look at the percentages of convicted perpetrators, then all four different ranks are more or less equally represented. The various tribunals however show remarkable and revealing differences.

The Nuremberg and Tokyo tribunals strove to prosecute only those with the greatest responsibility in the main international trial, trying the minor perpetrators in the follow-up trials without this being explicitly stated in the statute (see Section 6). With the possible exception of Julius Streicher, who owned the influential and racist newspaper *Der Stürmer*, all the others convicted at the IMT and IMTFE held high positions within the state hierarchy or were high-ranking military leaders who could be considered as the highest level organizers of international crimes committed during WWII. The ICC has only convicted one person to date, namely Thomas Lubanga who was the leader of the rebel movement UPC and considered to be an influential rebel leader in the Congo. Although he did not have a position within the state, he can nevertheless be considered high-ranking as he carried a large amount of authority and was a key member of his rebel group. These three tribunals almost exclusively convicted high-ranking perpetrators.

The United Nations Security Council (UNSC) initially did not specify who the ICTY and ICTR were to prosecute. Art. 1 ICTY and Art. 1 ICTR refer in general terms to those responsible for serious violations and thus leave it to the discretion of the

Table 11. Rank of Convicted Perpetrator

	IMT	IMTFE	ICTY	ICTR	ICC	SCSL	SPD	ECCC	Total
Convicted	19	25	81	61	1	9	84	1	281
(Percentage)	(7%)	(9%)	(29%)	(22%)	(0.4%)	(3%)	(30%)	(0.4%)	
High rank	18	25	9	17	1	8	0	0	78
(Percentage)	(94.7%)	(100%)	(11.1%)	(27.8%)	(100%)	(88.9%)	(0%)	(0%)	(28%)
Middle rank	1	0	23	31	0	1	1	1	58
(Percentage)	(5.3%)	(0%)	(28.4%)	(50.8%)	(0%)	(11.1%)	(1%)	(100%)	(21%)
Low Rank	0	0	37	11	0	0	29	0	77
(Percentage)	(0%)	(0%)	(45.7%)	(18%)	(0%)	(0%)	(35%)	(0%)	(27%)
No authority	0	0	12	2	0	0	54	0	68
(Percentage	(0%)	(0%)	(14.8%)	(3.3%)	(0%)	(0%)	(64%)	(0%)	(24%)
Military	9	16	67	14	1	9	83	1	200
(Percentage)	(47%)	(64%)	(83%)	(23%)	(100%)	(100%)	(99%)	(100%)	(71%)
Civilians	10	9	14	47	0	0	1	0	81
(Percentage)	(53%)	(36%)	(17%)	(77%)	(0%)	(0%)	(1%)	(0%)	(29%)

prosecutor to decide which perpetrators he or she would focus on. From the start, the aim was to focus on those most responsible, but circumstances could make the work very difficult. This was especially the case for Goldstone, the first prosecutor of the ICTY, who with very little support had to construct the entire institution while the war in Yugoslavia was still on-going.[36] Goldstone consequently decided to make a start with low-ranking perpetrators who could easily be apprehended such as Tadic and Erdemovic and then subsequently build up cases against the high-ranking perpetrators. In 2002 the ICTY prosecutor made it clear that he would focus his efforts exclusively on high-ranking perpetrators and in 2003 and 2004 the tribunals were given clear instructions by the UNSC to focus on those most responsible.[37] So far the ICTY has convicted nine high-ranking perpetrators, 23 middle-ranking perpetrators, 37 low-ranking perpetrators and 12 perpetrators who had no authority at all. Thus over 60 per cent of the people convicted at the ICTY had little to no authority.

The ICTY was the first international criminal tribunal to indict a sitting head of state when it indicted Slobodan Milosevic on 24 May 1999. Milosevic lost the elections, was arrested and transferred to the tribunal on 29 June 2001. His trial began on 12 February 2002, the first time that a former head of state had been put in the dock. His trial was a long and difficult one, as Milosevic demonstrated little respect for the court and used the court as an arena for promoting his political views. His trial ultimately did not lead to a conviction as Milosevic died in his cell on 11 March 2006. A number of important and high-ranking suspects such as Mladic and Karadzic are currently still on trial. That no one is at large anymore is a huge achievement of the ICTY, this is, however, in some part because of the number of cases (13) that have been referred to national jurisdictions.

Figures at the ICTR show a rather different picture: of the 61 perpetrators who have been convicted 17 (27 per cent) could be qualified as high-ranking, 31 (51 per cent) as middle-ranking, 11 as low-ranking (18 per cent) and two (3 per cent) as having no authority at all. Most high-ranking perpetrators have indeed been tried and it is not a surprise that such a large percentage of middle-ranking perpetrators were prosecuted as, in reality, this group is much bigger in comparison to the limited number of the top state and military officials. Low-ranking perpetrators were only prosecuted in exceptional cases.

---

36) *See* Frederiek de Vlaming, *De aanklager – Het Joegoslavië-Tribunaal en de Selectie van Verdachten*, (Boom Juridische uitgevers, 2010).

37) *See* SC Resolutions 1534 (2004) of 26 March 2004 and UN SC Res 1503 (2003) on 28 august 2003 but *see also* statement of the president of the SC in S/PRST/2002/678. This was initiated after President Claude Jorda wrote a letter to the Secretary General in relation to this issue. See S/2002/678 (http://daccess-dds-ny.un.org/doc/UNDOC/GEN/N02/434/47/IMG/N0243447.pdf?OpenElement) and also to UN SC Res 1329(2000) November 2000.

The SCSL was the first court at an international level which had a statute specifically referring to those 'who bear the greatest responsibility' (art. 1).[38] It indicted 13 suspects and convicted nine perpetrators, all of whom can be considered high-ranking leaders (with the possible exception of one individual, Kanu). The most well-known defendant was Charles Taylor, former head of state of Liberia and the first former head of state to be convicted as a war criminal for aiding and abetting war crimes. In the same way as the SCSL, the ECCC strove to focus on senior leaders and those most responsible (art. 1 Agreement); of its five indictees, four were, indeed, amongst the most senior leaders. So far Kaing Guek Eav, better known as Duch, has been the only person convicted by the ECCC. He was the director of the infamous Tuol Sleng (S-21) prison which was, in fact, a torture and extermination centre. Duch's main job entailed the supervision and running of this prison at which probably as many as 12,000 people were tortured and executed including (allegedly) many Khmer Rouge cadre members.[39] Apparently only 14 prisoners survived. Duch cannot be qualified as a one of the highest ranking leaders as he did not have any political or decision making power. Duch was, however, head of the most important prison for political prisoners and so, nevertheless, held a crucial position in the state administration.

The SPD tried predominantly low-ranking perpetrators who were the hands-on perpetrators, the ones who used force and violence killing the pro-independence supporters: 99 per cent of those convicted can be qualified as either low-ranking or without any authority at all. They were virtually all East Timorese militia members acting on the orders of the Indonesian army.[40] Many of the highest-ranking leaders were Indonesian military leaders such as General Wiranto whom Indonesia refused to extradite to East Timor for trial. The SPD was consequently forced to withdraw all these indictments and, in the end, only prosecuted perpetrators who had very little to no authority.[41] However, if we ignore the figures of the SPD which

---

38) There was some discussion as to the difference between greatest responsibility and most responsible but the clear aim of the UN was to have those in leadership positions to be prosecuted. *See* Report of the Secretary General on the establishment of a Special Court for Sierra Leone. *See* also Renate Winter, 'The Special Court for Sierra Leone', in Roberto Bellelli (ed.), *International Criminal Justice: Law and Practice from the Rome Statute to its Review* (Ashgate, 2010), p. 106.

39) For more on the role of S-21, *see* Ben Kiernan, *The Pol Pot Regime – Race, Power and Genocide in Cambodia under the Khmer Rouge, 1975-1979* (Yale University Press, New Haven, 1996); David Chandler, *Voices from S-21 – Terror and History in Pol Pot's Secret Prison* (University of California Press, Berkeley 1999); Alex L. Hinton, *Why did they Kill? Cambodia in the Shadow of Genocide*, (University of California Press, Berkeley, 2005) and on Duch's role *see* Nic Dunlop, *The Lost Executioner: the Story of Comrade Duch and the Khmer Rouge*, (Bloomsbury, London, 2009).

40) *See* Sylvia de Bertodano, 'East Timor: Trials and Tribulations', in Romano et al., *supra* note 21, p. 94 who notes that: 'overwhelming evidence [existed] from other sources that the violence was instigated and controlled by the Indonesian military.'

41) *Ibid*, p. 81.

prosecuted mainly low-ranking perpetrators and was the court which received the most criticism, then 40 per cent of all those convicted were high-ranking, 29 per cent were middle-ranking, 24 per cent low-ranking and only 7 per cent were civilians or foot soldiers who had no authority at all.

Most convicted perpetrators (71 per cent) were members of the military while just over one quarter were civilians (29 per cent). In comparison to the other tribunals, most civilians were prosecuted by the ICTR, the IMT and the IMTFE. This comes as no surprise as the crimes were instigated by the state and many of the convicted perpetrators were politicians who were drafting and implementing state policies.

5.2. *For or against their Government*

Almost all the convicted perpetrators acted on behalf of their governments. The crimes prosecuted by the IMT and the IMTFE were committed on behalf of the government as were the genocides committed in Rwanda and Cambodia. In East Timor, the crimes were committed by the militias under the orders of the Indonesian military (TNI) who at the time were still in power in East Timor.[42] The crimes committed in former Yugoslavia were committed during a civil war by various groups and militias. Due to the existence of difficult power relations during the conflict, and the fact that many groups and *de facto* governments were involved, categorizing crimes in the former Yugoslavia along these lines is a highly complicated matter. In Sierra Leone members of the three main parties within the conflict were convicted: the Civil Defence Forces (CDF) which represented the government and the RUF and the AFRC which were both rebel groups which successfully committed a coup on 25 May 1997 but were overthrown in February 1998 by the Economic Community of West African States (ECOMOG). Two of the convicted perpetrators were from CDF, while six others were from RUF and AFRC. Interestingly enough, the perpetrators of the CDF were initially given fairly low sentences of six and eight years as they were, according to the judges, fighting for a just cause (to defend the democratically elected government). In appeal these arguments were quashed and the suspects received much higher sentences, namely 15 and 20 years. The ninth perpetrator convicted was Charles Taylor, President of Liberia who supported the RUF.

The ICTY and SCSL were the only two courts to prosecute perpetrators from two different opposing sides. The IMT and IMTFE only prosecuted crimes committed by the Axis power and none of those committed by the Allies. There is no

[42] East Timor had declared its independence in 1975 when the Portuguese left but they were invaded by Indonesia soon after. The violence erupted after the ballot in 1999 when the East Timorese population voted for independence rather than autonomy. East Timor finally became independent in 2002.

doubt that Nazi Germany and Japan were aggressors and that they committed much more serious crimes, but some acts of war such as the bombings of the German cities of Hamburg and Dresden and the atomic bombs dropped on Hiroshima and Nagasaki, arguably, may also have deserved investigation. Carla Del Ponte, prosecutor of the ICTY and ICTR attempted to prosecute Tutsis from the Rwandese Patriotic Front (RPF) as well but was prevented from doing so. The Rwanda government was very much opposed to this initiative threatening to withdraw all cooperation with the ICTR.[43] It must be noted that the prosecution of international crimes is, to a certain extent, a political decision. There are often so many people involved that prosecuting all the perpetrators is simply impossible and justice, as a consequence thereof, is by definition selective. A prosecutorial strategy is often determined by pragmatic considerations (such as at the beginning of the ICTY) and is arguably influenced by political factors as well (such as the failed attempt to prosecute RPF crimes at the ICTR which is described above).

5.3. *Sex*

The most outstanding characteristic of the convicted perpetrators is that more than 99 per cent of them are male (for further details, see Table 12). To date only two women have been convicted by international criminal courts and tribunals. The first was Biljana Plavsic, a leading Bosnian Serb political figure who, as part of a plea agreement, was sentenced to eleven years for persecution by the ICTY and Pauline Nyiramasuhuko, a Rwandan politician, who was recently given a life sentence for incitement to genocide by the ICTR thus becoming the first ever woman

Table 12. Convicted Perpetrators' Sex and Age

	IMT	IMTFE	ICTY	ICTR	ICC	SCSL	SPD	ECCC	Total
Male	19	25	80	60	1	9	84	1	279
(percentage)	(100%)	(100%)	(99%)	(98%)	(100%)	(100%)	(100%)	(100%)	(99%)
Female	0	0	1	1	0	0	0	0	2
(percentage)	(0%)	(0%)	(1%)	(2%)	(0%)	(0%)	(0%)	(0%)	(1%)
Youngest (crimes)	32	46	19	24	41	25	14	32	14
Youngest (TJ)	39	53	25	36	51	35	17	67	17
Oldest (crimes)	66	74	61	70	41	48	51	32	74
Oldest (TJ)	73	81	72	78	51	64	55	67	81
Av. Age (crimes)	48	57	39	43	41	36	32	32	40
Av. age (TJ)	55	64	49	55	48	48	37	66	49

Key: TJ = Trial Judgement.

[43] *See* Del Ponte, *supra* note 12.

in history to be convicted by an international tribunal for genocide. At the ECCC a third woman, Ieng Thirith, a Cambodian politician under the Khmer Rouge regime and the wife of Ieng Sary, one of the other defendants, and sister-in-law of Pol Pot, was until recently one of the defendants in an on-going trial. However, she successfully plead for her release on the grounds of being mentally unfit to stand trial and was consequently freed on 13 September 2012.

The predominance of males is not remarkable as women are under-represented in governments and within the militarized organizations such as the army, police and secret services in particular and these are the main organizations which are responsible for these crimes. Women have played a role in international crime but it has been a less prominent one compared to men. When they have been involved – as for instance in the Rwandan case[44] – many of them were hands-on perpetrators, accomplices or accessories rather than leaders.

5.4. *Age*

The average age of the convicted perpetrators was just under 40 years old (39.84) at the time of the crimes (for further details, see Table 12). The youngest perpetrators are those convicted at the SPD who, on average, are 32 years old, closely followed by the SCSL where the perpetrators have an average age of 36. The average age of the perpetrators at ICTY and ICTR is around 40 years, whereas the perpetrators convicted at the IMT had an average age of 48 at the time of their crimes. With an average age of 57 at the time their crimes were committed, the perpetrators convicted at the IMTFE are by far the oldest perpetrators. The oldest person convicted by an international criminal court or tribunal is Hiranuma Kiichiro who was 74 when he committed the crimes and 81 when he was sentenced. Kiichiro was prime minister of Japan in 1939, a minister from 1940 to 1941 but then withdrew from government. Nevertheless, he was sentenced to life by the IMTFE but paroled in 1952; he died shortly after his release. The second oldest to be tried was Elizaphan Ntakirutimana who was convicted by the ICTR and was 70 years old at the time of the crimes. He was the first of the clergy to be convicted for genocide. Ntakirutimana was sentenced to ten years imprisonment for his participation in genocide while judges emphasized his advanced age and state of health as important mitigating factors. Ntakirutimana was released after he served his sentence and died shortly thereafter.

The youngest person ever convicted was 14 years old at the time of the crimes and aged 17 when he was in the dock. He was convicted for murder and

---

44) *See* African Rights, *Rwanda: Not so Innocent; when Women Become Killers*, (African Rights, London, 1995).

sentenced to one year imprisonment by the SPD. His name and date of birth were deleted from the files in order to protect his identity.[45] So far he is the only minor convicted by an internationalized criminal court or tribunal. The dilemma of prosecuting minors was discussed most prominently at the SCSL; many child soldiers were involved in the conflict as members of the infamous 'small boys units' which committed atrocious crimes. The SCSL had jurisdiction over persons of 15 years of age and above (Art. 7 SCSL) and could thus prosecute suspects between 15 and 18. The Secretary General and the Security Council of the UN clearly stated that it would be better if the Truth and Reconciliation Commission (that was also established in Sierra Leone after the conflict) could deal with juveniles.[46] The prosecutor David Crane noted furthermore that he would not prosecute minors: 'although the children of Sierra Leone may be amongst those who have committed the worst crimes, they are to be regarded first and foremost as victims and not as the ones who bear the greatest responsibility'.[47] Two convicted perpetrators, however, alleged that they had been abducted and their careers thus possibly started as child soldiers.[48] Art. 26 ICC Statute excludes persons who were under 18 years of age when their crimes were committed from the jurisdiction of the ICC. Amongst the indictees at the ICC is Dominic Ongwen who was abducted as a ten year old child but advanced to the rank of brigade commander and who is now indicted for war crimes, crimes against humanity and specifically the recruitment of child soldiers. Although Ongwen, without doubt, has committed atrocious crimes one may wonder whether he is not simultaneously a victim and a perpetrator.[49]

5.5. *Geographical Background*

Amongst the perpetrators who have been convicted, there are no Americans, Australians or anyone from Latin America. All the convicted perpetrators came from Asia, Africa and Europe. This is not surprising as the crimes prosecuted by

---

[45] *The Prosecutor* v. *X*, Case No. 04/2002, 2 December 2002. *See* also Linton, *supra* note 29, p. 307.

[46] Letter from the President of the Security Council addressed to the Secretary-General (31 January 2001) UN Doc S/2001/95. *See* also William A. Schabas, 'Internationalized courts and their relationship with alternative accountability mechanisms: the case of Sierra Leone', in: Romano et al., *supra* note 21, p. 163.

[47] *See* report UN SG S/2000/915 of 4 October 2000. *See* also Luc Côté, 'Special Court for Sierra Leone', in Cassese, *supra* note 29, p. 516.

[48] *See*, for instance, the defence of Issay and Kallon who state that they joined the forced because they were forcefully abducted. *See* also Schabas, *supra* note 46, p. 140 who notes: 'the older military leaders of both the RUF and the pro-government militias had begun their careers as child soldiers.'

[49] For general information on this topic, *see* E. Baines, 'Complex Political Prisoners: Reflections on Dominic Ongwen', 47 *Journal of Modern African Studies* 2 (2009) p. 163; and Mark A. Drumbl, *Reimagining Child Soldiers in International Law and Policy* (Oxford University Press, Oxford, 2012), p. 90.

international criminal courts and tribunals were all committed in Europe, Asia and Africa. The largest proportion of convicted perpetrators is from Asia which has 110 out of 281 (39 per cent). Most of these are East Timorese (82) and Japanese (25) as well as two Indonesians and one Cambodian. The second largest group is from Europe with 101 perpetrators (36 per cent), most of them German and Yugoslavian, while 70 convicted perpetrators (25 per cent) come from Africa, most of them from Rwanda and Sierra Leone. So far crimes committed by Americans, Australians or within Latin America have not been investigated by international criminal courts and tribunals. The ICC has however started preliminary investigations in Columbia and Honduras.

5.6. *Education, Marital State, Children and Criminal Records*

We have also tried to gather information on the level of education, marital state, children and criminal records of the convicted perpetrators but many data are missing as judgments do not systematically record personal details of the defendants. We have, therefore, provided an overview based on the existing data; this may not necessarily be representative of the whole population of defendants ever tried by the international criminal justice system.

First of all, it becomes clear that perpetrators from all levels of education have been convicted for committing international crimes. Of the 124 convicted perpetrators whose educational backgrounds we could trace 53 (43 per cent) have studied at university (many of them law) while 54 (44 per cent) had professional training.[50] This often entailed getting a degree after having successfully completed a military academy. The official data on the level of education of the perpetrators convicted at the SPD are missing but it is stated in a number of cases that many suspects were 'illiterate farmers'.[51]

The data seem to show that the high-ranking perpetrators, in particular, had a rather high level of education whereas the low-ranking perpetrators had little or no education. A lot of the educational data on the perpetrators at the ICTY are missing but, of the 42 perpetrators whose education we could trace, 17 went to university and 19 had professional training, whereas only six had primary or secondary school. At the ICTR we were able to trace the educational level of 34 perpetrators: 17 went to university and 15 had professional training. We also tried to trace information on the convicted perpetrators marital state and whether they had children. Although data was missing on a 119 (42 per cent) of the

---

50) Professional training means specialized education aimed at acquiring specific skills/knowledge after finishing secondary level education *e.g.* military academy, police training, training for auto-mechanic, electrician etc.

51) De Bertodano, *supra* note 40, p. 81.

perpetrators, 154 of the 162 perpetrators (95 per cent) were married and 150 individuals (95 per cent) did have children. Very few perpetrators seem to have had a criminal record prior to their involvement in international crimes. We found only nine cases in which the convicted perpetrator already had a criminal record and some of these were related to political crimes such as a failed coup attempt.

6. Others Prosecuted and Those Who Were not Prosecuted

Focusing solely on people convicted by international criminal courts and tribunals, however, does not tell the entire story of the atrocities committed within each conflict. A number of perpetrators are tried by national courts, dealt with by the Truth and Reconciliation Commission or not brought to justice at all. In the Subsection 6.1 we discuss the people prosecuted in relation to the abovementioned conflicts and in Subsection 6.2 we examine the suspects and perpetrators who should have been prosecuted in relation to these conflicts but were not.

6.1. *Other Prosecutions*

As well as the trial of the main war criminals in Nuremberg, 12 trials were conducted by the Allies under the authority of the Control Council Law No. 10, amongst which were the prominent *Einsatzgruppen* case and the case against the Nazi doctors. A total number of 185 alleged perpetrators were indicted, of whom a 142 were convicted and 35 acquitted, while eight cases were withdrawn (three indictees committed suicide, one died, one case was withdrawn because it was considered a mistrial and three cases were terminated because of the ill health of the suspect).[52] Twenty-five convicted perpetrators were sentenced to the death penalty and 20 to life imprisonment. The maximum determinate sentence was 25 year and the shortest one and a half years. Many more people were prosecuted in countries occupied by the Nazis during the Second World War besides these national military tribunals. The UNWCCC documented 89 war crimes trials,[53] some of which attracted a lot of worldwide media attention such as the trial of Eichmann in Jerusalem in 1961, Klaus Barbie, nicknamed the Butcher of Lyon tried in France in 1987 and John Demjanjuk in Germany in 2011.[54] In Japan too

---

52) *See* Kevin J. Heller, *The Nuremberg Military Tribunals and the Origins of International Criminal Law* (Oxford University Press, Oxford, 2011).

53) Kai Ambos, *Der Allgemeine Teil des Völkerstrafrechts – Ansätze einer Dogmatisierung* (Duncker & Humblot, Berlin, 2002), p. 140.

54) For trials against crimes committed during the Holocaust, *see* Stephan Landsman, *Crimes of the Holocaust – the Law confronts Hard Cases*, (University of Philadelphia Press, Philadelphia, 2005).

there were many domestic trials[55] as well as those held at the IMTFE. Chen notes that:

> Of the 5,700 accused of Class B and Class C crimes, 984 were condemned to death (some were later pardoned), 475 were given life imprisonment sentences, 2,944 were given finite imprisonment sentences, 1,018 were acquitted and 279 were not brought to trial or not sentenced. Between 1945 and 1951, over 2,200 trials were held outside of Japan against 5,600 Japanese nationals and Japanese collaborators accused of various crimes. More than 4,400 were convicted and about 1,000 were sentenced to death.[56]

Most of those prosecuted by other courts were the middle and low-ranking perpetrators which may explain the difference in sentencing. Sometimes, however, high-ranking perpetrators were prosecuted such as General Yamashita, who was tried by an American military tribunal in the Philippines, found guilty on 7 December 1945 and sentenced to death. He was executed on 23 February 1946.

The ICTY and ICTR have referred a number of cases to national courts and will continue to do this as part of their completion strategy. The Bosnian War Crimes section, for example, has prosecuted 74 accused[57] and many others have stood trial at the courts in Kosovo and the Serbia war crimes tribunal. In the overcrowded prisons of Rwanda, at one point, almost a 120.000 suspects were awaiting trial. More than 10.000 have been tried for genocide by national criminal courts in Rwanda and a number of the convicted perpetrators received the death penalty and were executed.[58] The death penalty was officially abolished in 2007 but no executions had been carried out since 1998. Doubts were raised as to whether these trials were fair. In order to solve the problem of overcrowded prisons the Rwandan government set up the *Gacaca* system which began operating in March 2005 and wound down in June 2012. The total number of cases tried was over 1.958.634. Of those indicted, some 84 per cent were found guilty while 277.066 (14 per cent) were acquitted.[59] The people who committed international crimes during the war in Sierra Leone were given amnesty and, apart from the ones who were prosecuted by the SCSL, no other people were prosecuted. In Cambodia there was just one trial held against Pol Pot and Ieng Sary who were both convicted in

---

55) Robert Cryer, Hakan Friman, Darryl Robinson and Elizabeth Wilmshurst, *An Introduction to International Criminal Law and Procedure* (Cambridge University Press, Cambridge, 2010), p. 120 and Neil Boister, 'The Tokyo Trial', in William A. Schabas & Nadia Bernaz, (eds.), *Routledge Handbook of International Criminal Law* (Routledge, London, 2011), p. 21.

56) *See* the info on the website: http://ww2db.com/battle_spec.php?battle_id = 221. Class A suspects were the most important ones while Class B and Class C suspects were the less important.

57) Fidelma Donlan, 'Hybrid courts', in Schabas & Bernaz, *supra* note 55, p. 99.

58) *See* website: http://www.un.org/en/preventgenocide/rwanda/about/bgjustice.shtml

59) Summary of the Report Presented at the closing of Gacaca Courts Activities, National Service of Gacaca Courts, Kigali, Republic of Rwanda, June 2012, pp. 34-35.

absentia for genocide in 1979 so many years before the ECCC started operating.[60] Sary was pardoned in 1996 when he defected from the Khmer Rouge and now has to stand trial before the ECCC which did not acknowledge either the first trial or his pardon. Apart from the mentioned trial and the suspects tried by the ECCC no one was prosecuted.

Indonesia promised the UN that it would prosecute the Indonesians responsible for the violence in East Timor[61] and a body of inquiry, the Indonesian National Commission of Human Rights (KPPHAM) was established which issued a report into the human rights violations in East Timor. After the publication of the report, the Human Rights Court was established which had the authority to inquire into cases of gross human rights violations perpetrated by Indonesians in East Timor. In March 2002 an ad hoc panel in Jakarta indicted 18 military and police officers, militia members and civilian officials.[62] Of this 18, some 12 were acquitted and six were found guilty receiving sentences from three to ten years. This panel also convicted the former East Governor of East Timor, sentencing him to three years and the commander of Aitarak militia who received a ten year sentence of imprisonment. Both were ethnic East Timorese.[63]

6.2. *Who Were not Prosecuted but Should Have Been?*

One of the obvious and inevitable questions which arise when discussing the people who were prosecuted, tried and convicted is: who, given their status and involvement in international crimes was not prosecuted but should have stood trial in front of an international court? At the IMT in Nuremberg the most prominent absentees were Hitler, Goebbels and Himmler; all Nazi leaders of the highest-rank who committed suicide at the end of the war and thus prevented the Allies from apprehending them. At the IMTFE Emperor Hirohito was the most prominent absentee in the dock simply because he was not indicted. This was remarkable as the Australians had called him 'the war criminal number one'.[64] Cryer noted that 'his immunity was necessary for Japan's post-war stability'.[65] Other members of the Emperor's family were also absolved from prosecution. Amongst

[60] Judgment of the people's revolutionary court of Phnom Penh of 19 august 1979. *See* also Subhash Kashyap, 'The Framework of the Prosecutions in Cambodia', in Kai Ambos and Mohammed C. Othman (eds.), *New Approaches in International Criminal Justice: Kosovo, East Timor, Sierra Leone and Cambodia*, (Max Planck Institute, Freiburg i. Br. 2003) p, 189; and Craig Etcheson, 'The politics of genocide justice in Cambodia', in Romano et al., *supra* note 21, p. 214.
[61] *See* De Bertodano, *supra* note 40, p. 79 and 94.
[62] *Ibid*, p. 84.
[63] Mohammed Othman, 'The frame work of prosecution and the court system in East Timor', in: Ambos and Othman, *supra* note 60, p.106.
[64] Boister, *supra* note 55, p. 18.
[65] Ibid, p. 22 and *see also* Cryer et al. 2010, *supra* note 55, p. 119..

them was Prince Asaka who played an important role in the Rape of Nanking, which occurred in 1937 in China when 300.000 Chinese civilians were brutally tortured, raped and murdered.[66] Many others who had originally been arrested and described as the most important, so-called Class A suspects were never prosecuted. Among these was Nobusuke Kishi who became prime minister of Japan in 1957.[67] Individuals who did bacteriological research and supported bio warfare, leaders of industrial conglomerates and the ones responsible for the 'comfort women' system escaped the attention of the IMTFE.[68]

As already noted from the original list of the ICTY, no one is at large anymore and, with the exception of the ten people who died before their arrest or before they could be convicted, one can assume that the individuals most responsible for the crimes have all been tried. Amongst those who died before they could be arrested was Arkan, the infamous leader of the Arkan Tigers, who was murdered in Belgrade in January 2000.[69] Six suspects died in prison after their transfer to the Tribunal.[70] Amongst them one of the key figures in the conflict - Slobodan Milosevic, former president of Serbia and the Federal Republic of Yugoslavia, who was found dead in his cell on 11 March 2006, four years after his trial had begun. All the other important figures appear to have been tried or are still on trial. The ICTR was less successful in that regard and six indictees are still at large, amongst them some of the ring leaders, according to Cryer.[71] One of the major failures of the ICTR, as already mentioned, was that it did not prosecute the offences committed by the RPF.[72]

The Lome Peace Agreement, which was signed by the various warring parties in Sierra Leone, provided a full amnesty for combatants on all sides and envisaged the setting up of a Truth and Reconciliation Commission (TRC); legislation to do this was adopted on 22 February 2000.[73] Although the SCSL did not find itself bound by the amnesty, it could however only try individuals who carried the most responsibility. The SCSL had a list of 13 indictees but three of these suspects died two before their arrest and one during the trial proceedings. Koroma, who became

66) *See* Iris Chang, *The Rape of Nanking*, (Penguin Books, London, 1997).

67) Boister, *supra* note 55, p. 22.

68) *Ibid*, p. 22.

69) For more information on Arkan, *see* Christopher S. Stewart, *Hunting the Tiger – the Fast Life and Violent Death of the Balkans most Dangerous Man*, (Thomas Dunne Books: New York 2007).

70) For their names, *see*: http://www.icty.org/action/cases/4.

71) Cryer et al., *supra* note 55, p. 140.

72) *See* book by Del Ponte, *supra* note 12.

73) *See* Truth and Reconciliation Act 2000 s 6(1). *See* also William A. Schabas, 'A synergistic relationship: the Sierra Leone Truth and Reconciliation Commission and the Special Court for Sierra Leone', in: W.A. Schabas and S. Darcy (eds.), *Truth Commissions and Courts: the Tension between Criminal Justice and the Search for Truth*, (Kluwer Academic Publishers, The Hague, 2004), p. 3; and Schabas, *supra* note 46, p. 157.

head of state for a short period of time after the successful coup of the AFRC, is still at large although he may also have died.[74] President Kabbah was not indicted while the leaders of the pro-government CDF forces were.

A number of prominent figures of the genocide in Cambodia escaped justice as did all middle and low-ranking cadres. Pol Pot died in 1998 and so could not be prosecuted. Son Sen and his wife Yan Yat, both high-ranking Khmer Rouge leaders, were murdered by Pol Pot and Ke Pauk, who was also a member of the inner circle of leadership, died in 2002. Ta Mok, one of the senior leaders of the Khmer Rouge, was apprehended but died in prison in 2006.[75] In this respect we should note that two ECCC co-investigating international judges resigned because they felt obstructed in their search to find the truth. They wanted to indict and prosecute more people but were prevented from doing so.[76]

East Timor tried mainly low-ranking perpetrators. High-ranking militia members and commanders of the Indonesian military were indicted but could not be apprehended as Indonesia would not cooperate with the Tribunal.[77] General Wiranto, for instance, was one of those high-ranking officers who was indicted but never apprehended. His indictment led to a political uproar and even president Gusmao 'expressed regret' in relation to the indictment and stressed the important of good relations with Indonesia.[78] Indonesia refused to hand over any of the Indonesian suspects but promised to prosecute them instead. As already noted above, Indonesia indeed prosecuted a few suspects but, as De Bertodano remarks: 'it is generally felt that those tried represented the 'second division; and not the top command'.[79] Wiranto one of the senior leaders responsible for the crimes committed in East Timor, for instance, was not indicted by the Indonesian courts and later even became a prominent figure in Indonesian politics. The commanders who were indicted were charged mainly with criminal negligence.[80] Othman states that the outcome of the trials was disappointing: the court acquitted the former chief of police and five senior military and police officers, a former Dili Military commander and three senior leaders. The court could not establish a structural link but 'this finding is at odds with the indictments for the special panels'.[81] The SPD only had jurisdiction for crimes committed in 1999 after it was

---

74) If he is captured he has to be tried by a national court, *see* Winter, *supra* note 38, p. 118.

75) Etcheson, *supra* note 60, p. 204.

76) *BBC News*, 19 March 2012: http://www.bbc.co.uk/news/world-asia-17432484.

77) De Bertodano, *supra* note 40, p. 81.

78) *Ibid*, pp. 84-85.

79) *Ibid*, p. 93. Wiranto was accused of being one of the main perpetrators of the violence, according to an Indonesian Human rights Commission report which was published in January 2000.

80) *See* report of International Crisis Group: Indonesia: implications of the Timor Trials 8 May 2002; and De Bertodano, *supra* note 40, p. 93.

81) Othman, *supra* note 63, pp. 105-107.

announced that a ballot would decide whether East Timor would become completely independent or only receive autonomy within Indonesia. The violence and repression of the previous twenty-five years under the reign of Indonesia, which was much worse and cost 200,000 people their lives, was not prosecuted.[82]

7. Summary and Conclusion

This article has presented an overview of the empirical reality of the international criminal justice system which is represented by nine international criminal courts and tribunals which, on average, have operated for almost nine years. Together, these courts have concluded 172 cases in which over 250 judges and 23 chief prosecutors were involved. Overall 745 people were indicted and 356 actually tried. This number is less than half of the people indicted but is mainly due to the fact that the SPD had to withdraw 304 indictments because Indonesia refused to hand over the suspects. If we exclude SPD from our calculations, then 353 suspects were indicted, of whom 268 were actually tried, which is 76 per cent. Of all those indicted 16 died, 27 cases were withdrawn for other reasons in addition to 20 cases which were referred to national jurisdictions. There are currently 34 defendants on trial while 22 are still at large, half of these indicted by the ICC.

In total, 281 defendants were convicted, 29 were acquitted and 12 cases were withdrawn after the trial had started. The overall conviction rate of international criminal courts and tribunals is 87 per cent, with only 9 per cent of the defendants were acquitted. The average time-lapse between an indictment and the trial judgement was four point nine years while the trials lasted on average two point nine years. This is long but can be explained by the complexity of the cases and that, despite the horrendous nature of the crimes, the human rights of the defendants still had to be taken into account. A total number of 19 convicted perpetrators were sentenced to death, 45 to life imprisonment and 217 received a determinate prison sentence ranging from 11 months to 52 years. The average determinate prison sentence was 15.3 years and 66 per cent of the cases were appealed.

The convicted perpetrators are almost all male (99 per cent) and mostly members of a military or paramilitary organisation (71 per cent). The vast majority acted on behalf of their government and they were, on average, 40 years old. The age span varies from 14 to 74. All levels of education (from illiterate to academic) were represented amongst the perpetrators and almost all the perpetrators of

---

82) The CAVR, a truth and reconciliation commission, dealt with this period and produced a report. Beth S. Lyons, 'Getting Untrapped, Struggling for Truths: the Commission for Reception, Truth and Reconciliation (CAVR) in East Timor', in Romano et al., *supra* note 21, p. 100.

whom we could find data seemed to be married and have children. Most perpetrators came from Asia, Africa and Europe, which is not surprising as the crimes prosecuted by the international criminal courts and tribunals were committed in these three continents. Perpetrators from all four different ranks (high – middle – low – no authority at all) were prosecuted and, if we take all courts into consideration, the convicted perpetrators are fairly evenly distributed over the four ranks. If, however, we ignore the figures of the SPD, which prosecuted mainly low-ranking perpetrators and is in general the court which was very much criticized, then 40 per cent of all those convicted were high-ranking, 29 per cent were middle-ranking, 24 per cent low-ranking and only 7 per cent were foot soldiers with no authority at all.

The case law produced by the nine international criminal courts and tribunals forms an extremely rich body of law which can guide national states as well as the ICC in their future prosecutions of international crimes. It is expected that no international criminal courts and tribunals or mixed or hybrid courts will be established in the future and that national states will prosecute international crimes themselves. The ICC can only be, and should only be, the court of last resort. The best response to international crimes is, arguably, prosecution by the national states; the international community should intervene only if these national states are unwilling or unable to prosecute. Furthermore, the establishment of the ICC has led many national states to incorporate legislation related to international crimes into their national system and some states have indeed prosecuted perpetrators of international crimes. The ICC is taking an active stance; it has 16 cases involving seven situations which are currently under investigation and is conducting preliminary examinations in an additional seven cases.

If we look at all these data, it cannot be denied that only an extremely small percentage of all the people involved in international crimes are prosecuted. On the other hand, although many perpetrators go free, others are prosecuted, convicted and punished, amongst them heads of state and high-ranking leaders. In so doing, the international criminal courts and tribunals have sent a clear message to the world. Although the chances of getting caught are still slim, perpetrators of international crimes can no longer rely on impunity. Heads of state who order or commit international crimes should be warned. Among the 28 people indicted by the ICC, there are four (former) heads of state. Although the deterrent effect which is created by international criminal prosecutions on middle and low-ranking perpetrators might be limited, high-ranking perpetrators definitely have more reason to worry than they had 65 years ago. Furthermore, as these high-ranking perpetrators pull all the strings, the deterrent effect of these prosecutions and indictments might be larger than anticipated. The Human Security Report, for instance, suggests that these prosecutions have helped to prevent international crimes; this is also found by Kim and Sikkink who conducted empirical research and concluded that human rights prosecutions definitely have a deterrent effect.[83] From our data we cannot tell whether this is true, nor can we conclude whether the international criminal justice system has been a success or failure so far. We have simply provided an overview of what has been achieved so far – which may be much more than most people could have anticipated some 65 years ago.

---

83) Human Security Report 2009/2010, 77; Hunjoon Kim and Kathryn Sikkink, 'Explaining the Deterrence Effect of Human Rights Prosecutions for Transitional Countries', 54 *International Studies Quarterly* (2010) 939-963.

Punishing Perpetrators or Seeking Truth for Victims: Serbian Opinions on Dealing with War Crimes

Stephan Parmentier[a,1] and Elmar Weitekamp[b]
[a]Professor of Criminology and Human Rights, Leuven Institute of Criminology, University of Leuven, Leuven, Belgium;
Secretary General of the International Society for Criminology
[b]Professor of Victimology and Restorative Justice, Institute of Criminology, University of Tübingen, Tübingen, Germany

Abstract
The debate on how to deal with the past in Serbia is still ongoing almost twenty years after the end of the armed conflict in the former Yugoslavia. From the very start the international community has put major emphasis on the criminal prosecution and conviction of the persons mostly responsible for the war crimes in the region, both by establishing the ICTY and encouraging national prosecutions. In the discussions about 'dealing with the past' in Serbia little if any attention has been devoted to the views and expectations of the local population, although they provide an additional source of information about the strategies and the mechanisms for dealing with the crimes of the past and reconstructing the future. The objective of this chapter is to find out what people in Serbia think about the central debates around impunity and accountability for war crimes, and more specifically which importance they attach to criminal prosecutions and truth commissions in the country. For this purpose, it reports about the main findings of a quantitative survey conducted in Serbia in 2007, and concludes that the picture is not black and white but complex instead.

Keywords
war crimes; truth-seeking; truth commission; prosecutions; international criminal justice; Serbia; population-based research

By Way of Introduction

In the Serbian chapter of its latest (2011) annual report the Dutch non-governmental organisation Impunity Watch starts with the following passage:

[1] The authors gratefully acknowledge the financial support of the Research Fund of the University of Leuven for the four-year research project of which the Serbian survey was a part. They also wish to express their sincere thanks to Vesna Nikolic-Ristanovic (University of Belgrade) and Johan Goethals (University of Leuven) for their insightful comments on earlier versions of the empirical part of the survey, and to Marta Valiñas (OSCE, Sarajevo) for her great efforts in organising the data collection in Serbia and writing the preliminary report.

> The legacy of the Serbian state's pivotal role in the wars that took place on the territory of the former Yugoslavia in the 1990s, and the crimes that accompanied them, continues to affect the country. Even after the fall of its war-time leaders and criminal proceedings against many of them at the ICTY in The Hague, incomplete institutional reforms, unreformed security services and the existence of firmly entrenched groups with an interest in preventing accountability for those crimes have disrupted attempts to fully democratise Serbia and stabilise its political scene. Impunity for war crimes in Serbia is by no means over.[2]

Indeed, nearly two decades after the beginning of the disintegration of Yugoslavia and of the conflicts that ravaged the whole region but most intensely Croatia, Bosnia and Herzegovina, Serbia and Kosovo, each of the countries is still struggling to find suitable way(s) to address the atrocities of the past and their consequences and to rebuild trust among its citizens.

The debate on how to deal with the past in Serbia is an ongoing one. The international community has put major emphasis on the criminal prosecution and conviction of the persons mostly responsible for the war crimes in the region. Since 1993 the International Criminal Tribunal for ex-Yugoslavia has indicted 161 persons, of which 126 have been tried (September 2012) of international crimes in the territories of the region.[3] Also in the country itself new criminal justice mechanisms have been created, such as the War Crimes Chamber in the Belgrade District Court. Other transitional justice approaches, such as a truth commission or reparation programmes, continue to be discussed. The debate about dealing with the international crimes of the past thus remains of high relevance to the people, organisations and institutions of Serbia. In our view, international crimes as a relatively new concept differs from the older concept of state crimes in two ways:[4] on the one hand, state crimes constitute a wider category than international crimes, as they also involve behaviour that is not traditionally regarded as violent, such as instances of treason, espionage or corruption; on the other hand, state crimes are to be seen as narrower than international crimes, as the former are committed by institutions or persons entrusted with state powers, while the latter crimes can also be committed by non-state actors, such as guerrilla groups or private individuals.

All in all the Yugoslav and the Serbian cases are similar to other debates about 'dealing with the past' or 'transitional justice', as they are taking place between or among elites, political, economic, and from civil society, both in the country concerned and at the international level. Likewise the views and expectations of

---

2) Impunity Watch, *Annual Report 2011* (Impunity Watch, Utrecht, 2011) pp. 19-21.

3) See the website: www.icty.org.

4) David Friedrichs (ed.), *State Crime*, 2 vols (Ashgate/Dartmouth, Aldershot, 1998); David Kauzlarich, Christopher Mullins and Roger Matthews, 'A complicity continuum of state crime', 6 *Contemporary Justice Review* (2003) 241-254; Dawn Rothe and Christopher Mullins (eds.), *Crimes of State: Current Perspectives* (Rutgers University Press, Piscataway, NJ, 2010).

the local populations in any given country are not very well known, let alone taken into account. Although the last decade has witnessed a rapid development of empirical researches conducted in post-conflict situations and sometimes in ongoing conflicts, they still remain the exception that confirm the rule.[5] In our view, population-based research provides an additional source of information about the strategies and the mechanisms for dealing with the crimes of the past and for reconstructing the future, and also allows further debate to take place in the countries concerned and beyond.

The core question in this chapter is to find out what people in Serbia think about the central debate around impunity and accountability for war crimes, and more specifically which importance they attach to criminal prosecutions and truth commissions in the country. The chapter takes the following structure: we first highlight the design of the population-based research carried out by our research team in Serbia in 2007; then we focus on two main issues of the survey, namely the quest for justice and the search for truth as seen through the eyes of the population. The main objectives of our contribution are twofold: on the one hand, we wish to demonstrate the value of empirical research on post-conflict justice with local populations, and by doing so, contribute to a transitional justice approach "from below" as aptly formulated by McEvoy and McGregor;[6] and on the other hand, we intend to situate our findings in the context of the possible establishment of a truth and reconciliation commission in Serbia and the whole region of the former Yugoslavia.

1. Post-conflict Justice in Serbia "from Below"

What do people in Serbia think about the crimes committed during the war and about the strategies and mechanisms to deal with the horrors of the past? These were the two leading questions that led us to design and to conduct a quantitative survey with the Serbian population in 2007. The survey constituted part of the broader research project 'Mass victimisation and restorative justice. In search of the position of restorative justice in an integrated approach to mass victimisation

---

[5] See, *i.a.*: International Centre for Transitional Justice (ICTJ), *Iraqi Voices: Attitudes towards Transitional Justice and Social Reconstruction* (Human Rights Centre, University of Berkeley California / ICTJ, New York, 2004); International Centre for Transitional Justice (ICTJ), *Colombian Perceptions and Opinions on Justice, Truth, Reparations, and Reconciliation* (ICTJ, New York, 2006); International Centre for Transitional Justice (ICTJ), *When the War Ends: A Population Based Survey of Attitudes about Peace, Justice, and Social Reconstruction in Northern Uganda* (Human Rights Centre, University of Berkeley California / ICTJ, New York, 2007).

[6] Kieran McEvoy and Lorna McGregor, 'Transitional justice from below: An agenda for research, policy and praxis', in Kieran McEvoy and Lorna McGregor (eds.), *Transitional Justice from Below: Grassroots Activism and the Struggle for Change* (Hart Publishing, London, 2008) pp. 1-14.

in post-conflict situations. Case studies in Bosnia and Herzegovina and Serbia', carried out at the Leuven Institute of Criminology, University of Leuven, Belgium, between 2004 and 2008.[7] This project aimed at exploring what could be the role and the applicability of restorative justice principles in the process of dealing with post-conflict situations that include mass victimisation, taking Serbia and Bosnia and Herzegovina as the two case studies and thus carrying out very similar surveys in both countries. While the research focus was on restorative justice, it should be clear that the surveys themselves addressed many more issues in both post-conflict situations. We will limit ourselves here to a brief sketch of the four major steps, and refer to a previous publication for more details.[8]

1.1. *Objectives and Survey Design*

The aim of the survey was to inquire about the attitudes and opinions of individuals about the process of dealing with the past (or transitional justice) in Serbia,[9] with a particular focus on the 'possibilities' (or opportunities) and the potential of a restorative approach to such process. To analyse these attitudes and opinions we made use of the heuristic model developed by Parmentier, the so-called TARR model.[10] This model is composed of four building blocks that correspond to key issues in the process of dealing with the past by new regimes, namely: to search for truth about the past (T), to ensure accountability of the offenders (A), to provide some form of reparation for the victims (R), and to promote reconciliation between former enemies (R). This model arguably provides a useful framework to

---

7) The research team working on the above-mentioned research project was composed of Stephan Parmentier (promoter), Elmar Weitekamp (co-promoter) and Marta Valiñas (researcher). For the survey in Serbia the research team could benefit from the close cooperation with Vesna Nikolic-Ristanovic of the University of Belgrade and Chairperson of the Victimology Society of Serbia. The interpretation of the data remains the sole responsibility of the research team.

8) Stephan Parmentier, Marta Valiñas and Elmar Weitekamp, 'How to restore justice in Serbia? A closer look at peoples' opinions about postwar reconciliation', in Dawn Rothe and Christopher Mullins (eds.), *Crimes of State: Current Perspectives* (Rutgers University Press, Piscataway, NJ, 2010) pp. 262-274.

9) Attitude is *'a mental position with regard to a fact or state. Attitudes reflect a tendency to classify objects and events and to react to them with some consistency. Attitudes are not directly observable but rather are inferred from the objective, evaluative responses a person makes'*. An opinion is *'a person's ideas and thoughts towards something. It is an assessment, judgment or evaluation of something'*. These definitions were taken from the Encyclopaedia Britannica.

10) Stephan Parmentier, 'Global Justice in the Aftermath of Mass Violence. The Role of the International Criminal Court in Dealing with Political Crimes', 41 *International Annals of Criminology* (2003) 203-224; further developed in Stephan Parmentier and Elmar Weitekamp, 'Political Crimes and Serious Violations of Human Rights: Towards a Criminology of International Crimes', in Stephan Parmentier and Elmar Weitekamp (eds.), *Crime and Human Rights*, Series in Sociology of Crime, Law and Deviance, vol. 9 (Elsevier, Amsterdam / JAI Press, Oxford, 2007) pp 109-144.

analyse the various relations between two or more of its building blocks, it allows us to examine specific institutions and mechanisms of dealing with the past in relation to each of these issues, and finally it suggests that transitional justice approaches will result from the interplay between these four building blocks.[11] The survey was designed to include questions related to each of these four core issues.

The research method used in this study was a self-administered quantitative survey carried out through written questionnaires distributed all over Serbia. The methodology comprised four key steps:[12]

(a) creating an instrument of data gathering: the instrument used was a printed questionnaire with a total of 43 questions, some with mutually excluding answers, others with multiple possible answers, and in others respondents were asked to rank their level of agreement with given alternative answers to the formulated question; all of these questions were closed or semi-closed with one exception, namely one question on reconciliation; the questionnaire was developed by the members of the research team in the period between February and May 2006 on the basis of various sources; it was first used in a similar quantitative Bosnia in 2006, and later adapted to the specific situation of Serbia;[13]
(b) determining an adequate sampling method: given the difficulties to make use of reliable population census data in Serbia it was not possible to create an accurate national representative sample[14] and we opted instead for a 'quota sampling method';[15] this implied dividing the target population – the citizens and residents of Serbia– into subgroups or strata according to three criteria of particular interest to us, i.e. geographical distribution (throughout the country, with the exception of Kosovo), age (aiming at a large majority of persons between 26 and 64 years old, a small group between 18 and 25 years old and another small group over 65 years), and gender (equal groups of men and women), and determining the proportion of the sample in each category; in contrast to a similar survey in Bosnia, in Serbia, religion and/or ethnicity were not used as separate criteria for our quota sampling but we did ask respondents to indicate their religious/ethnic affiliation;

[11] Elmar Weitekamp, Stephan Parmentier, Kris Vanspauwen, Marta Valiñas and Roel Gerits, 'How to deal with mass victimization and gross human rights violations. A restorative justice approach,' in Uwe Ewald and Ksenja Turkovic (eds.), *Large Scale Victimisation as a Potential Source of Terrorist Activities. Importance of Regaining Security in Post-Conflict Societies* (IOS Press, Amsterdam, 2006) pp. 217-241.
[12] More information is available in the final report available upon request from the authors: Marta Valiñas, Stephan Parmentier and Elmar Weitekamp, *Survey 'Restoring Justice in Serbia'. Preliminary Report* (Faculty of Law, Leuven Institute of Criminology, Leuven, 2008).
[13] For more information on the methodology of the Bosnian survey, see: Stephan Parmentier, Marta Valiñas and Elmar Weitekamp, 'How to Repair the Harm after Violent Conflict in Bosnia? Results of a Population-Based Survey', 27/1 *Netherlands Quarterly of Human Rights* (2009) 27-44.
[14] When the characteristics of the population from which the sample is to be taken are not fully and accurately known, it is impossible to have a representative sample. For this reason, probability and random sampling methods may not be the most adequate.
[15] The difference between quota sampling (a non-probability method) and stratified random sampling (a probability method) is that in the former "*the sampling of individuals is not carried out randomly, since the final selection of people is left to the interviewer.*" Alan Bryman, *Social Research Methods* (Oxford University Press, Oxford, 2008) p. 102.

(c) collecting the data through the distribution of the questionnaire: the questionnaires were distributed in June 2007 in 16 different locations in Serbia by members of 19 Serbian NGOs who belong to the Association Joint Action for Truth and Reconciliation; each of these NGOs have diverse target groups, from refugees to victims of torture to war veterans, etc., and they were all given a similar number of questionnaires (around 50) and clear instructions on the criteria for the selection of the respondents; of the total number of 1.200 questionnaires distributed 922 were returned duly filled, which is a response rate of 85%, a high number typical of 'convenience sampling methods';[16]
(d) analysing the data gathered: a mask was created using SPSS software and all data were entered by a Serbian methodologist who also performed several levels of analysis, including univariate and bivariate analyses, correlations, and regression analysis.

All figures presented in the following paragraphs are the result of this four-step process of data gathering and data analysis.

1.2. *The Questionnaire*

Being aware of the impact that each person's experiences during the war have in their current opinions and attitudes towards issues of post-conflict justice we have tried to understand what had been the type and the extent of victimisation suffered by the respondents. The first part of the questionnaire therefore asked questions about forms of direct (e.g. physical injuries on the respondent) and indirect victimization (e.g. having lost family members). Moreover the respondents were asked about their perceived suffering in three categories, physical, material and psychological, and in two time periods, during and after the war. The responses allowed us to conclude that among our sample individuals have suffered mostly in emotional terms, both during and after the war, secondly they suffered material harm and thirdly that their suffering was of a physical nature. These results were completely in line with the results of the survey conducted in Bosnia in 2006.[17]

The second part of the questionnaire asked various questions under four different headings, i.e., seeking truth, establishing accountability, providing reparation and promoting reconciliation. In this contribution we limit ourselves to reporting some aspects on the issues of criminal prosecutions (under the heading of 'accountability') and truth commissions (under the heading of 'truth-seeking') in Serbia. Before looking into the most salient findings it is important to emphasise that all questions were asked to all the respondents in the survey and not only to those who might be legally or sociologically qualified as 'victims'. The reason is that in violent conflicts like the Yugoslav one it is virtually impossible to make such clear-cut distinctions between those who are only perpetrators and those who are only victims, since individuals can and sometimes do assume different

16) *Ibid.*, p. 100.
17) Parmentier et al., *supra* note 13, p. 34.

roles, even "reverse" roles, in different phases of a conflict.[18] For the purposes of this research we have preferred to ask to all respondents in Serbia for their opinions on post-conflict justice, thus going beyond a specific victim survey and extending into a broader population-based survey.

2. Main Research Findings

It is crystal clear that the debates about accountability for war crimes in Serbia have been strongly dominated, even monopolized, by strategies to bring the main perpetrators before a criminal tribunal or court, in the first place an international tribunal (ICTY) and in second instance a national court. While the international community, and individual states and other organizations, have consistently insisted on criminal prosecutions for the war crimes committed, virtually nobody has made any effort to check to which extent the population in Serbia supported this approach, or if specific viewpoints on criminal prosecutions could be identified. Even more, little if any research has been conducted about non-judicial scenarios to deal with war crimes, such as truth commissions or other mechanisms geared at knowing more about the past and addressing it in other ways than through criminal justice.

In the following paragraphs we sketch the most salient results of our empirical research work in Serbia in 2007. It will become clear that the picture is far more complex than what the dominant discourse tends to highlight, and that Serbs have very mixed opinions about prosecutions by national and international tribunals and also look beyond the retributive approach.

2.1. *Criminal Justice for War Criminals*

In the former Yugoslavia, the decision by the Security Council of the UN in 1993 to create the International Criminal Tribunal for the former Yugoslavia set the precedent of how the past human right violations were going to be dealt with at the international level and how it was suggested they should be dealt with at the national level: through criminal prosecutions. Since then, the prosecution of war crimes, genocide and crimes against humanity has been at the centre of international efforts in supporting the process of dealing with the past in the region. These prosecutions have also been put very little into question by human rights

18) On the concept of "role reversal", see: Paul Friday, J. Hartman, V. Lord and M. Exum, '*Batterers and the Battered: Role Reversals in Domestic Violence*', Paper presented at the annual meeting of the American Society of Criminology, Atlanta, Georgia, November 2007.

organisations, victim organisations and the international community. The creation of the War Crimes Chamber at the Belgrade District Court and of the War Crimes Prosecutor's Office in Belgrade have constituted additional steps towards accountability through criminal justice and have been generally regarded as important developments in the fight against impunity in the country.

There are, however, several questions surrounding prosecutions in the criminal courts that have been less often debated. For example, in a country in which such a large part of the population was actively involved in the war, which criteria determine who should be subject to criminal prosecution and who should not? In addition, what else could or should be considered as accountability measures, either in parallel with criminal prosecutions or as a replacement when prosecution does not take place?

Our survey aimed at exploring some of these questions. It tried to identify what the respondents thought about criminal prosecutions and other forms of accountability in order to get a better understanding of what 'accountability' meant to them in concrete terms. Also possible differences in opinion about how direct and non-direct perpetrators should be held accountable were explored.

First of all, respondents were asked who they thought should be held responsible for the things that happened during the wars in the former Yugoslavia, and given the possibility of choosing more than one of the options given. The aim was to understand whom accountability measures should be targeted at. As the figures below clearly indicate, political leaders were most often identified by respondents (accounting for 23.4% of all the responses). The international community came in second place, with 13.4% of the responses, followed by direct perpetrators (12.7%) and by NATO (11.5%). A hierarchical list of those seen to be most responsible would look like this:

1. Political leaders
2. International Community
3. Direct perpetrators
4. NATO
5. Military or Police leaders
6. The media
7. Religious leaders
8. The whole society
9. Members of other ethnic groups than your own.

It is interesting to note that very few respondents attributed responsibility for the war to 'members of other ethnic groups' (which accounted for only 4.3% of all responses). See Table 1.

The options chosen in this question within each ethnic group reveal some interesting observations: Albanian respondents, for example, were the only ones

Table 1. Who Do You Think Should Be Held Responsible for the Things that Happened during the Wars in Former Yugoslavia?

	Frequency	*Percent of responses*	*Percent of cases*
Direct perpetrators	380	12.7%	41.7%
Political leaders	702	23.4%	77.1%
Military or police leaders	329	11%	36.1%
Religious leaders	227	7.6%	24.9%
Members of other ethnic groups than your own	129	4.3%	14.2%
The whole society	158	5.3%	17.3%
The international community	402	13.4%	44.1%
NATO	346	11.5%	38%
The media	303	10.1%	33.3%
I do not know	26	.9	2.9%
Total	3002	100%	329.5%

not attributing any responsibility at all to the international community or to NATO; Bosniak respondents attributed them responsibility but at a lower level when compared to other respondents. Also, both Albanian and Bosniak respondents attributed more responsibility to members of other ethnic groups than other respondents did. Whereas for Bosniaks besides political leaders, also the military/police leaders and the media took a great share of responsibility, for Serb respondents following political leaders, it was the international community, NATO and direct perpetrators who hold more responsibility.

The main aim in this part of the survey was to understand what 'accountability' meant for the respondents, i.e., what measures of accountability should, in their view, be adopted or should take place. The question was split into two: one referring to the 'direct perpetrators' (person 'x' that directly inflicted harm upon the respondent) and another to 'non-direct perpetrators' ('the perpetrators' or 'those responsible' for the violence in more general and abstract terms). Respondents were first asked who could be considered as their 'direct perpetrators': in most cases the direct perpetrators belonged to official military or police forces (32.8% of all responses), as could be expected; but it was noteworthy to see that paramilitary groups and civilians together accounted for 35.2% of all responses, even more than the official forces, thus demonstrating the widespread involvement of individuals in these wars (going beyond the regular army forces), but also the militant and also individual nature of the conflicts. As has been reported several times, the Yugoslav war was not a classical war of armies but it in fact involved different groups, including underground and criminal groups as well as mere civilians who joined in the violence.

It was then asked what should happen to the persons responsible for the things that happened to the respondent *during* the war. Among the given options were included both processes and measures that would be implemented regardless of the will of the 'perpetrator' (or 'imposed obligations'), and also actions that would be more intrinsically linked to the perpetrator's will and attitude (or 'active responsibility'). A vast majority of the respondents gave priority to confession (84.8%), to the return of property and material goods (82.3%) and to apologies (75.3%). It is interesting to see that the options related to criminal prosecutions – although each gathering the support of over half of the respondents – scored lower in the overall set of priorities (see Table 2).

The accountability measures or actions favoured by respondents, from more to less, are as follows:

1. Confession by the perpetrator
2. Restitution of property and material goods
3. Apologies by the perpetrator
4. Monetary compensation (69.5%)
5. Community work (as replacement for restitution or compensation) (66.1%)
6. Prosecution in a criminal court in one of the countries of former (63.1%) Yugoslavia
7. Prosecution only of those with the highest responsibility (62.6%)
8. Prosecution in a criminal court outside the former Yugoslavia (57.8%).

Table 2. What Should Happen to the Persons Responsible for the Things that Happened *to You* during the Wars (i.e., the Persons Who Directly Committed the Things against You Described in Question 9)?

	I strongly disagree	I disagree	I agree	I strongly agree	I don't know
They should be prosecuted in a criminal court outside the former Yugoslavia	28.3%	5.4%	15.5%	42.3%	8.6%
They should be prosecuted in a criminal court in one of the countries of former Yugoslavia	18.3%	5%	25.5%	37.6%	13.7%
Only those with the highest responsibility for the violence (political and military leaders) should be prosecuted	14.8%	11.9%	16.5%	46.1%	10.6%
They should be obliged to pay money to their victims	9.2%	6.2%	16.3%	53.2%	15.1%

Missing values: option 1 14.7%, option 2 18.3%, option 3 21.3%, option 4 17.5%, option 5 15.7%, option 6 22.1%, option 7 16.2%, option 8 19%.

Acknowledgment and reparation thus figured as the main priorities for the respondents. Looking back at our hypothesis above, there was clearly a great importance given to acts or attitudes coming from the 'perpetrator' himself in comparison to externally imposed results. In material terms, the restitution of property is understandably a very important issue in Serbia as the country received a great number of refugees (from Croatia and BiH) and internally displaced people (from Kosovo) who left behind their houses and other material goods. Given the tangible character of such loss, it becomes easier to formulate claims of restitution but it is also closely linked to the more immediate need of individuals to rebuild their lives which naturally includes the need to secure housing and other property.

It is interesting to note that prosecutions in a court outside the former Yugoslavia was favoured by both Albanian and Bosniak respondents (for Albanians it was even the biggest priority), whereas for Serbs less than half of the respondents thought that prosecution should take place outside the former Yugoslavia, against 62.3% who thought it should take place within the former Yugoslavia. For both Serbs and Croats, confessions were the most important, followed by restitution of property. The latter came also as first priority (together with prosecution abroad) for Bosniak respondents.

In view of the dominant role that criminal prosecutions tend to assume in the public debate on how to deal with past violations in ex-Yugoslavia, it was crucial to understand what were the reasons given by respondents who thought that prosecutions should indeed take place. A vast majority of the respondents considered that prosecutions should take place 'so that it will not happen again' (90.5%); a very large number also believed that prosecutions should take place 'for justice to be done' (86.1%) and 'for the truth to be established in the court' (84.6%). When asked whether the reason behind prosecution was 'to take revenge' 65.7% said they disagreed/strongly disagreed and only 21.3% said they agreed/strongly agreed (see Table 3).

Thus the main function attributed by the respondents to prosecutions in a criminal court was that of prevention and/or deterrence – which are normally

Table 3. If You Think that They Should Be Prosecuted, what Are the Reasons for Your Answer?

	I strongly disagree	I disagree	I agree	I strongly agree	I don't know
To take revenge	55.9%	9.8%	6.9%	14.4%	13.1%
For justice to be done	4%	3.1%	17.6%	68.5%	6.8%
For the truth to be established in the court	4%	2.8%	15.7%	68.9%	8.6%
So that it will not happen again	4.6%	.3%	8.3%	82.2%	4.6%

translated into common language as 'for it not to happen again'. It reflects the widespread belief that prosecutions bear the potential of preventing future violations from taking place through the existence of a real threat of punishment. In other words, people seemed to believe that if there is a very real possibility of criminals to be tried and punished, and if some actually are, in the future other potential criminals will be discouraged from committing crimes because they can foresee a real possibility that they as well will be tried and punished. Irrespective of all arguments that can be found against deterrence as one of the consequences of criminal prosecutions, our survey suggests that such beliefs have penetrated Serbian minds as well as the public discourse. The fact that individuals primarily attributed to prosecutions a forward-looking function -to prevent the same violations from happening again in the future- might be related to the history of the region ravaged by previous conflicts and to people's wishes that history will not repeat itself.

The two other functions of criminal prosecutions regarded as important by the respondents were 'establishing the truth' and 'a sense of justice'. 'Justice' seemed to be more related to the reaffirmation of the fundamental values denied by the violations and the impunity that ensued. This could suggest that through prosecutions certain actions are clearly defined as 'wrong' and 'harmful', thus also leading to the acknowledgement and validations of the suffering of the victims (even if more indirectly). With revenge being refused by the majority of the respondents as a reason for prosecution, one can conclude that for the respondents the three important functions of trials were deterrence/prevention, doing justice and establishing the truth. The issue of truth will be analysed in the next section.

Our survey also tried to explore potential differences in the reactions of respondents in terms of accountability towards their 'direct perpetrators' and towards 'non-direct perpetrators'. The results, however, did not show any significant differences between these two categories, as only one or two percent differences were registered. Confession remained the option gathering more consensus (i.e., that a majority of respondents said they agreed or strongly agreed that it should happen) – 86.7% here, compared with 84.8% in the question about the direct perpetrators. The order of priorities remained roughly the same with only very slight changes, for example with community work coming in 4th place instead of 5th, and criminal prosecutions of only the highest responsible coming in 6th instead of 7th place.

2.2. *Truth-seeking for Victims*

Establishing the truth about the events of the past has become a central topic in the discussions on how to deal with the past in Serbia. Given that to a large extent the fuelling of the violence has been attributed to the manipulation of facts and public opinion and taking into consideration that one of the major obstacles to the process of dealing with the past today is the continued denial of war crimes, as well as multiple and contradictory versions of the truth, truth-seeking has been seen by many as absolutely crucial to set the foundations of a shared future for the citizens of Serbia and other countries of former Yugoslavia. The debate on truth-seeking has, however, been characterised by a significant degree of controversy. While the view that the past must be faced and the truth must be established has taken ground in the public as well as in the private discourse, the question remains how to establish the truth that does not continue to divide opinions. Our survey tried to understand first of all whether establishing the truth was important to the respondents, and then through which means and processes that this should happen. Particular attention was paid to the opinions on informal, small-scale initiatives of truth-sharing.

The importance of establishing the truth in more abstract terms or as part of the criminal justice process was asked in questions that are analysed below. For the moment, it is important to note that establishing the truth was seen by the respondents (almost 85%) as one of the main functions of prosecutions and that a great majority of the respondents said that it would make them feel better about what happened during the war if the truth about all facts and events of the war would be known (76%).

Furthermore, the respondents were asked in a separate question whether they thought that it is important for people to tell their experiences about the war. The majority of the respondents (63%) answered that both victims and perpetrators should be given a chance to tell their stories, while only 16% said only victims should be given a chance to tell their stories, and a small group (2%) said only the perpetrators should be given a chance to tell their stories. This makes up for 81% of the respondents who believed that it is important for people to tell their experiences about the war, against 6% who were of the opinion that it is not important. A small but still significant number of respondents did not know what to answer (14%). The obvious conclusion is that a majority of the respondents considered it important that people tell their experiences about the war and that among those, a majority thought that both victims and perpetrators should be given a chance to tell their experiences (see Table 4).

The respondents were also asked where they thought those stories should be told. A vast majority (74.6%) answered 'in the courts', immediately followed by 'psychologists' (73.2%), and thirdly in a 'Truth and Reconciliation Commission' (71.9%). In fourth place (chosen by 67.6% of the respondents) were public events (such as roundtables or workshops and in fifth were 'small groups in the community, in which members of other ethnic groups are present' (63.3%). Only 28% of the respondents thought the stories should be told in 'small groups in the

Table 4. Do You Think it Is Important for People to Tell About their Experiences about the War?

	Frequency	*Valid Percent*
Yes, but only the victims should be given a chance to tell their story	142	16%
Yes, but only the perpetrators should be given a chance to tell their story	15	2%
Yes, both victims and perpetrators should be given a chance to tell stories	560	63%
No, it is not important	57	6%
I do not know	121	14%

community, in which members of other ethnic groups are not present' and 26.5% said those stories should only be told to family and friends.[19] See Table 5.

These figures seem to corroborate the opinion expressed in the other question that the courts have an important role in establishing the truth, although they are placed almost at the same level of importance as psychologists and a TRC. It is at first surprising to see that psychologists appear as the second preferred place where such stories should be told – and if we look only at what respondents strongly agreed with, then psychologists even come in first place. This might be due to the increasing realisation of people that psychological trauma is a very real and very present consequence of the war, and that it tends to persist over time, but this issue should be further analysed. Excluding the case of psychologists – which probably figures very high because of the given reasons – there was a clear preference given to public truth-seeking *fora* such as the courts, truth commissions and public events. This may well have been related to the need of an official validation of the stories being told. Truth-telling seems not only associated with the need to 'tell' but with the need to 'be heard'. Following the same trend, small community groups where members of other ethnic groups are present are preferred over those where members of other ethnic groups are *not* present (63.3% against 28%, respectively).

Also interesting to note is that the highest percentage of respondents who did not know what to answer was registered in the option 'in small groups in the community in which members of other ethnic groups are *not* present' (23.5%), and secondly in the case of 'only family and friends' (19.9%). These two options were the ones in which a relative majority was more strongly against and also were

[19]) Here, as in other parts of the analysis, we grouped the respondents who answered 'agree' or 'strongly agree', and similarly those who answered 'disagree' or 'strongly disagree' to each of the alternatives presented.

Table 5. Where Do You Think that these Stories Should Be Told?

	I strongly disagree	I disagree	I agree	I strongly agree	I don't know
In the courts	8.5%	6.4%	28.7%	45.9%	10.4%
In public events (such as Round Tables or Workshops)	10.3%	6.3%	28.7%	38.9%	15.8%
In small groups in the community, in which members of other ethnic groups *are* present	10.8%	8%	25.5%	37.8%	17.9%
In small groups in the community, in which members of other ethnic groups *are not* present	29.5%	19.1%	14.5%	13.5%	23.5%
In a Truth and Reconciliation Commission	6.7%	4.7%	25.7%	46.2%	16.9%
To psychologists	5.7%	6.6%	24.2%	49%	14.6%
Only to family and friends	35.5%	18%	13%	13.5%	19.9%

(Missing Cases: Courts 10.5%, Public Events 13.8%, Small groups with other ethnic groups 17.5%, Small groups without other ethnic groups 19.7%, TRC 13.8%, Psychologists 16.1%, Family and friends 18.2%).

more respondents were undecided. This suggests that not many benefits were seen resulting from sharing stories in these very private and closed places.

Finally, it should be mentioned that both among Bosniak and Serb respondents, a majority thought that the best place where to tell these stories were the courts. Croats on the other hand favoured psychologists, a TRC or public events more than the courts. Also, comparatively speaking, Croat respondents (44.4%), together with Albanians (75%), were the ones who most supported small community groups which were ethnically homogeneous.

Another set of questions related to the establishment of a truth commission. The creation of a Yugoslav Truth Commission in 2001 by the then president, Kostunica, is said to have resulted mainly from international pressure than from a genuine national endeavour and consensus, and proved to be a failure in a strikingly short time. However, discussions on the creation of a truth commission in Bosnia and Herzegovina or at the regional level in the former Yugoslavia continued to be held at the time of conducting our survey, and in spite of the fate of the 2001 project. We therefore thought it was important to explore what were the views of the respondents on the importance and potential contribution of a truth commission.

First of all, respondents were asked whether they had heard about the Yugoslav Truth and Reconciliation Commission when it was created. A wide majority of the respondents (69.3%) said they had not heard about it, while 30.7% said they had.

Because the 2001 project of the Yugoslav TRC had not become a reality, the remaining questions on truth and reconciliation commissions were formulated in more abstract terms. First of all, we wanted to know whether the respondents knew what a Truth and Reconciliation Commission is: 72.2% said they did not know, while only 27.8% said they knew what it was. This also indicates that some people who had heard about the 2001 Yugoslav TRC did not know what it was about, which are indeed two distinct realities. In any case, the limited number of respondents who did not know what a TRC is and did not hear about the 2001 initiative proves that no serious and widespread discussion took place in the country on this issue and that for the same reason it is difficult to speak about popular support in Serbia for the idea of a truth commission or the lack thereof. This overwhelming evidence of the lack of knowledge of the population about the idea of a truth commission suggests that outreach efforts to raise awareness and knowledge about such initiative constitute a major challenge. At the same time it undermines the argument often repeated in the public discourse that the project failed because of lack of popular support, as such argument cannot be made without sufficient knowledge about the project in the first place.

The following questions were only asked to those who said they knew what a Truth and Reconciliation was. The respondents were asked whether they thought that a Serbian or a Regional TRC could be useful for them. As regards a Serbian TRC, a vast majority thought it could be useful (87.9%), out of whom 54.8% said they thought the TRC would not be useful for them personally, but that it could be for others, and 33.1% said the TRC could be useful. Only 9.2% said they thought the TRC would not be useful, and only 2.9% said they did not know the answer to this question (see Table 6).

As regards a regional TRC, even a larger majority (90.7%) thought it could be useful. Out of these, 49.8% did not consider the regional TRC useful for them personally, but that it could be for others, and 40.9% thought it could be useful. A very small percentage (5.1%) said it would not be useful and 4.2% said they did not know.

There was not a very significant ethnic variation in these answers among Serb, Bosniak and Croat respondents, except for the fact that Croat respondents thought that a TRC would be mostly useful for them personally while Serbs and Bosniaks considered the TRC useful but mainly for others than for themselves. Albanian respondents –as can be seen in other instances in the survey– tend to have more well-defined positions, i.e. normally choosing between the 'yes' and 'no' options. In this case, Albanians were in clear favour of a TRC (66.7% against 33.3% who said no). There was also a foreseeable large amount of Hungarian respondents who found the TRC useful but mainly for others (57.1%) and who did not know what to answer (28.6%).

As the idea of a national or regional TRC continued to be the object of public debate at the time of the survey, we found it important to explore what were the

Table 6. What Do You Think that such a Commission (Serbian or Regional) Should Be Responsible for Doing?

	I strongly disagree	I disagree	I agree	I strongly agree	I don't know
Establish the number and identity of victims	6.3%	3.6%	31.4%	52.5%	6.3%
Analyse what led to ethnic distrust and to the war	2.3%	3.7%	32.4%	56.5%	5.1%
Establish the moral responsibility of individuals in the course of the war	5.2%	5.7%	27.8%	51.9%	9.4%
Establish the moral responsibility of organisations and institutions in the course of the war	2.9%	3.8%	31%	56.2%	6.2%
Establish the role of actors outside Serbia in the war	9.3%	6.4%	28.4%	43.1%	12.7%
Establish the role of individuals who refused to take part in the violence and protected other individuals or groups	10.5%	8%	25%	47%	9.5%
Provide a forum for people to tell their experiences about the war	3.3%	4.3%	33%	51.2%	8.1%
Promote reconciliation in the former Yugoslavia	3.3%	1.9%	25.4%	63.6%	5.7%

Missing values: option a 6.7%, option b 9.6%, option c 11.3%, option d 12.1%, option e 14.6%, option f 16.3%, option g 12.6%, option h 12.6%.

respondents' views on such a commission's mandate. We opted to use the most recent proposal for a draft law on a TRC in the region at the time of this survey, in practice it was a draft law for the creation of a TRC in Bosnia and Herzegovina, which was made known to the public in an article in the Bosnian press.[20]

Given the controversy around this topic, it was quite surprising to see that a great majority of the respondents seemed to agree with what was being thought to be the elements of the mandate of a possible Serbian or Regional Truth Commission. The most important contribution that respondents associated with a TRC was the promotion of reconciliation (89%). Almost the same amount of respondents found it important for a TRC to 'analyse what led to ethnic distrust and the war' (88.9%) and to 'establish the moral responsibility of organisations

[20] See Nerma Jelacic and Nidzara Ahmetasevic, 'Experts query draft law on how the process would work, while victims complain they have not been consulted', in *Balkan Insight*, March 31st 2006.

and institutions in the course of the war' (87.2%). The TRC was also seen as an important 'forum for people to tell their experiences'. In fact this was the only alternative included in our survey that was not included in the mandate of the draft law mentioned above. The fact that 84.2% of the respondents thought this was an important contribution of a TRC corroborates the importance given throughout the survey to the issue of truth-telling, and is in line with the fact that TRCs were seen as the third most important place where people should tell their stories (see above).

On the basis of these percentages a hierarchical descending list,[21] showing what respondents saw as the most important tasks that a Truth and Reconciliation commission should be in charge of, can be drawn as follows:

a. promote reconciliation;
b. analyse what led to ethnic distrust and the war;
c. establish the moral responsibility of organisations and institutions in the course of the war;
d. provide a forum for people to tell their experiences;
e. establish the number and identity of victims;
f. establish the moral responsibility of individuals in the course of the war;
g. establish the role of individuals who refused to take part in the violence and protected other individuals;
h. establish the role of actors outside of Serbia in the war.

This list suggests that first reconciliation and then establishing the truth at a broader and national level (rather than the individual and even regional level) were seen as the most important functions of a TRC.

Since the time of our 2007 survey many developments have taken place in the region of ex-Yugoslavia, including the initiative led by NGOs to establish a Regional Truth Commission (RECOM) to examine war crimes and other gross violations of human rights committed on the territory of the former Yugoslavia between 1991-2001.[22] According to the Impunity Watch Annual Report quoted before, such commission "would not only help in bringing victims' voices forward but could also become an important tool to address war crimes denial in the region and to tackle revisionist tendencies within society as one of the most

[21] This list is drawn on the basis of the sum of the percentages of those who said they 'agreed' or 'strongly agreed' with the given option. This method was used since the distribution of answers for each option among the possible different ratings was not, in statistical terms, a 'normal distribution' and therefore it is not advisable to use the statistical means.

[22] Humanitarian Law Center (ed.), *Report about the Consultative Process on Instruments of Truth-Seeking about War Crimes and Other Serious Violations of Human Rights in Post Yugoslav Countries (May 2006-June 2009)* (Publikum, Belgrade, 2009).

important obstacles in dealing with impunity."[23] It would therefore be interesting to find out more today about people's perceptions on this new initiative.

By Way of Conclusion

Many reports continue to highlight that fundamental discussions are held in Serbia to discuss its role in the war and the strategies and mechanisms to deal with the war crimes. Not only the perpetuating debates about criminal prosecutions at the ICTY and national criminal courts, but also the ongoing discussions about setting up a truth commission in the region raise several interesting questions in the quest for accountability.

Our central objective was to find out the Serbian people's opinions about criminal prosecutions on the one hand, and the establishment of a truth commission on the other hand. As the survey sample was composed of a group of individuals targeted according to pre-established criteria that suited the research interests in this study, it cannot be considered 'representative' of the opinions of individuals that compose the population of Serbia as a whole. Nevertheless, it has generated many interesting results and also contributed to constructing a 'bottom-up' approach to transitional justice.

It was clear that a large majority of the respondents considered it important that 'the truth' about what happened during the war would be established and that people would tell their experiences about the war. This is not to say that none of the respondents wished that people would forget about what happened, or that telling their own experiences from the war would necessarily make them feel better. In fact, while there was great support for the truth to be known, opinions were more mixed when respondents were asked whether it would make them feel better if everyone would forget and move on, or if they could tell to others about their own experiences during the war. Such mixed opinions surface when questions are formulated in very personal terms, and naturally individuals deal with their own past, including their own suffering and trauma, in very different ways. However, there was clear support for establishing the truth and for those personal stories to be known. In the truth-seeking process, especially the courts and truth commissions were given an important role, which suggests that respondents valued an official validation or 'sanctioning' of the truth being told or established by evidence. Smaller-scale initiatives of truth-seeking or truth telling (such as public panels, roundtables, and community groups) were also regarded as positive by a considerable number of respondents. As to the specific issue of the creation of a truth commission in Serbia or a regional commission -controversies aside- it is

23) Impunity Watch, *supra* note 2, p. 20.

clear that there is much to be done in disseminating information among citizens on what such a commission consists of and what it would be translated into in these particular cases. Nevertheless, our survey clearly pointed to an 'informed' support for such a commission.

Finally, it is clear that the issue of accountability in Serbia and in the former Yugoslavia has been dominated by the role of prosecutions first at the international (ICTY) and then at the national level (ordinary courts and the War Crimes Chamber). These institutions have primarily tried to target the more senior political, and also military/police leaders against whom evidence was collected. In terms of the criminal justice system, the so-called 'direct perpetrators' posed the greatest challenge due to their overwhelming number and controversy (in spite of well-established principles by the ICTY) around the morality of convicting those acting under orders. Nevertheless, the direct perpetrators appeared in third place in the list of whom should be held responsible for what happened during the war. While the majority of these direct perpetrators belonged mostly to official military or police forces, a great number of such perpetrators were also civilians, which may complicate the process of evidence gathering through the criminal justice system.

Although these are just some findings, our survey suggests that almost twenty years after the beginning of the disintegration of Yugoslavia, many key issues in dealing with the past are still very present in the current debate on how to move forward. Therefore, this debate may benefit from putting in question certain assumptions on how accountability can be ensured and truth and justice achieved. The question of what approach to take in the process of dealing with the past – either a primarily retributive or restorative one – seems to be a very timely and necessary one in the current context of Serbia.

Justice is Interventionist: The Political Sources of the Judicial Reach of the Special Court for Sierra Leone

Kenneth A. Rodman
Colby College, Waterville, ME, USA

Abstract
The Special Court for Sierra Leone's conviction of former Liberian President Charles Taylor and its prosecution of perpetrators regardless of their political alignment have been hailed as milestones in the diffusion of international criminal justice norms. Yet what made these achievements possible were interventionist strategies by Western governments and international and regional institutions to defeat the rebellion in Sierra Leone and bring about regime change in Liberia. The broader lesson that should be drawn from this is that the prospects for prosecution in the aftermath of armed conflict are likely to be determined by the political strategies adopted by the international community to end the violence and that international criminal justice presumes an interventionist form of politics.

Keywords
international criminal justice; responsibility to protect (R2P); peace-enforcement; conflict resolution; peace versus justice debate

The Special Court for Sierra Leone's conviction of former Liberian President Charles Taylor on 26 April 2012 – the first of a head of state by an international tribunal since Nuremberg – and its prosecution of atrocity crimes committed not only by Taylor's allies in Sierra Leone, but forces aligned with the government as well – have been hailed as milestones in the diffusion of anti-impunity norms, demonstrating the reach of global justice regardless of a perpetrator's official position or whether he fought for the victors or the vanquished. Yet what made these achievements possible were interventionist strategies of Western governments and international and regional organizations to defeat the rebellion in Sierra Leone and bring about regime change in Liberia. In other words, it was not that the long arm of international criminal law had grown longer, but rather, that politics had lent to the law the platform from which it could extend its reach. And whether politics is willing or able provide this support in comparable contexts will be influenced by a myriad of factors in which criminal justice forms a small part – a factor that explains some of the limits of international accountability in the Sierra Leone case, as well as its absence at the end of the civil war in neighbouring Liberia. The broader conclusion that should be drawn from this experience is that the prospects for prosecution in the aftermath of armed conflict are likely to be shaped and constrained by the political strategies adopted by the international community to end the violence, and that international criminal justice presupposes an interventionist form of politics.

1. The Special Court for Sierra Leone and the Justice Narrative

The Special Court for Sierra Leone (SCSL) was established in 2002 to prosecute "persons who bear the greatest responsibility" for atrocity crimes committed on the territory of Sierra Leone after the Abidjan Peace Agreement on 30 November 1996. It was the first hybrid court negotiated between the UN and a member state in which trials were based in the country where the crimes occurred – in contrast to the distant justice of the International Criminal Tribunals for the former Yugoslavia (ICTY) and Rwanda (ICTR) – but with substantial international involvement to ensure fair trial standards and to guard against the politicized justice that national courts often mete out at the end of armed conflicts.[1] Under the SCSL statute, the trials were conducted under a mix of national and international law by a UN-appointed prosecutor and a government-nominated deputy, before a trial chamber of three judges (two international and one Sierra Leonean) and an appeals chamber of five judges (three international and two Sierra Leonean).[2] The court was located in Freetown, though the Taylor trial was moved to the facilities of the International Criminal Court (ICC) in The Hague for security reasons.[3]

The SCSL had its origins in a 12 June 2000, request by Sierra Leonean President Ahmed Tejan Kabbah to UN Secretary General Kofi Annan for assistance in prosecuting the leaders of the Revolutionary United Front (RUF), a rebel group notorious for using drug-addicted child soldiers to terrorize civilians in order to control the country's diamond resources. The RUF had been granted a blanket amnesty at the Lomé Peace Agreement on 7 July 1999, a provision that had triggered a disclaimer from the UN envoy to the negotiations that there would be no recognition of amnesties for international crimes.[4] The rebels returned to violence almost immediately after the agreement was signed, and in May 2000, took 500 UN peacekeepers as hostages. Given the assault on UN personnel, the Security Council responded positively to Kabbah's request with Resolution 1315(14 August 2000), which authorized the Secretary General to work with the government to set up an

---

1) Laura A. Dickinson, 'The Promise of Hybrid Courts', 97(2) *American Journal of International Law* (2003), pp. 305-308.
2) *Ibid.*, pp. 299-300.
3) Kingsley Moghalu, *Global Justice: The Politics of War Crimes Trials* (Palo Alto: Stanford University Press, 2008), p. 124.
4) David J. Francis, 'Torturous Path to Peace: The Lomé Accord and Postwar Peacebuilding in Sierra Leone', 31(3) *Security Dialogue* (2000), p. 366.

independent court. The negotiations were completed on 16 January 2002, and the agreement was ratified by the parliament and signed by the president by the end of March 2002.[5] In March 2003, David Crane, the Court's first prosecutor, obtained arrest warrants for 13 individuals, including Liberian President Charles Taylor and the leaders of the three main Sierra Leonean armed factions. The Court was able to gain custody of all but two of the indictees, of whom one disappeared and the other was killed in Liberia. Of those apprehended by the Court, two died in custody and the remaining nine defendants were convicted and sentenced to terms ranging from 15 to 52 years.[6]

The success of the SCSL in fulfilling its mandate has become part of the justice narrative put forward by those NGOs and international lawyers most supportive of prosecution. Not only did it reinforce the position that there can be no amnesties for international crimes; it also demonstrated, as Human Rights Watch noted, that "peace premised on a blanket amnesty may be a short-lived respite before the resumption of further armed conflict and its attendant crimes".[7] As a result of the breakdown of Lomé, one international criminal law scholar wrote that

> [t]he Government quickly mastered the situation, arresting many Revolutionary United Front supporters, in effect, shifting the fragile balance in the power-sharing that had been negotiated at Lomé. Then the Government of Sierra Leone 'reassessed' its position with respect to the amnesty.[8]

Another international lawyer observed that "[a]fter more conflict and more atrocities, the [amnesty] policy was reversed in favor of prosecution and punishment of those bearing the greatest responsibility for international crimes".[9]

This narrative suggests that prosecution is necessary for consolidating peace, and therefore, governments and mediators should make the right legal choice of accountability over amnesty. What the narrative misses is the dependence of the ability to make that choice on the relative power of the parties and the kinds of conflict resolution strategies that external actors are willing and able to undertake. In none of the three works cited above is there any mention of the British military intervention in Freetown following the breakdown of the peace agreement in May 2000, without which the Sierra Leonean government would not have

---

5) J. Peter Pham, 'A Viable Model for International Criminal Justice: The Special Court for Sierra Leone', 19(1) *New York International Law Review* (2006), pp. 78-89.

6) For an overview of the indictments and the trials, *see* Tim Kelsall, *Culture Under Cross-Examination: International Justice and the Special Court for Sierra Leone* (Cambridge, UK: Cambridge University Press, 2010), pp. 31-67.

7) Human Rights Watch, 'Selling Justice Short: Why Accountability Matters for Peace', July 2009, p. 4.

8) William A. Schabas, *The UN International Criminal Tribunals: The former Yugoslavia, Rwanda and Sierra Leone* (Cambridge, UK: Cambridge University Press, 2006), p. 35.

9) Darryl Robinson, 'Serving the Interests of Justice: Amnesties, Truth Commissions, and the International Criminal Court', 14 *European Journal of International Law* (2003), p. 396.

been able to master the situation and reverse its position on amnesty. Conversely, the amnesty negotiated at Lomé was not the cause of the breakdown of the peace agreement. Rather, it was a symptom of the weakness of the Sierra Leonean state and the unwillingness of external actors to defend it against a rebel group that was still supported by Liberia. In other words, prioritizing criminal accountability is not simply a legal choice; it requires compatible political strategies when directed against an entrenched regime or an active rebel movement, and this in turn, requires interventionist or coercive measures to defeat or marginalize perpetrators. As will be demonstrated in the next section, where such strategies were absent, impunity was an inevitable feature of efforts to end Sierra Leone's civil war.

2. Conflict Resolution and the Sources of Impunity in Sierra Leone's Civil War from 1991-1999

The SCSL's accountability mandate stands in sharp contrast to the policies used by the government and international mediators to address criminal violence from the outbreak of Sierra Leone's civil war in 1991 through Lomé in 1999. This was the direct result of international community's political approach to the conflict. One peacekeeping scholar referred to this as a strategy of "malign neglect", in which conflict resolution was left to the government and the major regional organization, the Economic Community of West African States (ECOWAS) and its ceasefire monitoring group (ECOMOG), with little in the way of international support.[10] As a result, the government alternated between two strategies for ending the war. First, it tried to defeat the rebellion by working with foreign forces (private security firms and ECOMOG) and local militias, all of whom were implicated in human rights abuses with no accountability except for a brief episode of victor's justice against the rebels. Second, it sought internationally-mediated negotiated settlements in which blanket amnesties were deemed necessary to persuade rebels who had not been defeated to lay down their arms. As long as these were the only approaches to ending the conflict, the prerequisites for international criminal justice were absent.

The civil war in Sierra Leone began in March 1991 when the RUF, led by Foday Sankoh, a former corporal who had been cashiered for participation in a failed 1971 coup, invaded Sierra Leone from neighbouring Liberia. The stated purpose of the rebellion was to liberate the people of Sierra Leone from the corrupt and repressive rule of President Joseph Momoh's All-People's Congress. In practice,

---

10) Adekeye Adebajo, *UN Peacekeeping in Africa: From the Suez Crisis to the Sudan Conflicts* (Boulder: Lynne Rienner, 2011), p. 161

however, the RUF had no discernible political agenda and its violence was directed against civilians, most notably through the forced recruitment of children as soldiers to terrorize people living in the diamond-producing areas in order to control those resources.[11] Sankoh's patron was the Liberian rebel leader Charles Taylor, whom he met while in military training in Libya, and who continued to support the RUF after Taylor was elected president of Liberia in 1997. Taylor's support was motivated both by the lucrative arms-for-diamonds relationship he established with the RUF and by revenge – "to make Sierra Leone taste the bitterness of war"– for its support for an ECOMOG intervention that prevented him from taking power in 1990.[12]

Neither the Momoh government nor the military junta that overthrew it in 1992 was able to defeat the rebels – in part, because a significant portion of the army was collaborating with the RUF in exchange for sharing in the spoils.[13] Given the unreliability of the armed forces, the government solicited the services of Executive Outcomes, a South African-based private security company, to lead the fight against the RUF. Executive Outcomes helped arm and train the Civil Defense Force (CDF), which consisted of traditional hunters, the best known of which were the *kamajors*, who had been loosely organized into self-defense militias to protect their communities from the rebels. Working under Deputy Defense Minister, Sam Hinga Norman, Executive Outcomes and the CDF conducted offensive operations that drove the RUF from Freetown and secured government control of the diamond-producing areas in the east of the country.[14] They also provided sufficient security for presidential elections in February 1996. The RUF tried to undermine the elections with some of the most brutal violence of the civil war – i.e., using child soldiers to hack off the limbs of civilians, both to terrorize them and physically prevent them from voting. The elections went ahead nonetheless, bringing into office a former UN official, Ahmed Tejan Kabbah.[15]

Kabbah initially sought a negotiated end to the war. On 30 November 1996, the parties signed the Abidjan Agreement in which the RUF agreed to a disarmament,

---

11) William Reno, *Warfare in Independent Africa* (Cambridge, UK: Cambridge University Press, 2011), pp. 182-184.

12) Arthur Abraham, 'Dancing with the Chameleon: Sierra Leone and the Elusive Quest for Peace', 19(2) *Journal of Contemporary African Studies* (2001) pp. 206-207.

13) Lansana Gberie, *A Dirty War in West Africa: The RUF and the Destruction of Sierra Leone* (Bloomington: University of Indiana Press, 2005), p. 82.

14) *See* Peter W. Singer, *Corporate Warriors: The Rise of Private Military Contractors* (Ithaca, NY: Cornell University Press, 2008), pp. 101-118; While most analyses note that Executive Outcomes had a considerably better record of civilian protection than other armed groups, there were serious alleged violations of international humanitarian law with regard to prisoners of war and civilian casualties. *See* David J. Francis, 'Mercenary Intervention in Sierra Leone: Providing National Security or International Exploitation?' 20(2) *Third World Quarterly* (1999), p. 332.

15) International Crisis Group, 'Sierra Leone: Time for a New Military and Political Strategy', Africa Report No. 28, 11 April 2001, pp. 8-9.

demobilization and reintegration (DDR) program and to transform itself into a political party in exchange for a blanket amnesty and the withdrawal of Executive Outcomes within five months. Executive Outcomes actually left only one month after Abidjan, before the initiation of the DDR process, and there was no UN or regional peacekeeping force that would replace it and ensure that the RUF would honour its commitments.[16] This turned out to be a critical mistake since the RUF stalled on disarmament and used the agreement to prepare for the continuation of the war, as became evident when Sankoh was arrested in Nigeria trying to purchase Ukrainian arms.[17] On 25 May 1997, Kabbah was ousted in a coup led by a group of junior army officers called the Armed Forces Revolutionary Council (AFRC), led by Major Johnny Paul Koroma, who had been imprisoned for an earlier coup attempt. The new junta then suspended the constitution and invited the RUF to join the government.[18]

Initially, ECOWAS and the UN imposed economic sanctions in order to coerce the junta to step down. In October 1997, Koroma signed an agreement at Conakry for Kabbah to return within sixth months in exchange for another blanket amnesty, but the junta reneged on its commitment.[19] As a result, a Nigerian-led ECOMOG force intervened, and working with the CDF, was able to push the RUF and AFRC out of Freetown in February 1998 and restore Kabbah to the presidency on 10 March 1998.[20] One consequence of this, as the International Crisis Group noted, was that ECOMOG "effectively became Sierra Leone's military".[21]

By stabilizing Freetown, ECOMOG enabled Kabbah to initiate prosecutions, not for war crimes and human rights abuses, but rather for treason in what amounted to an exercise in victor's justice. Over 2000 people were arrested for collaboration with the junta, many of whom were convicted and sentenced to death in trials that fell considerably short of international standards of due process. This included Sankoh, who was extradited from Nigeria on 25 July 1998. Since no one in Freetown was willing to defend him, the parliament passed a law stipulating that the absence of defense counsel would not invalidate the verdict. Sankoh was convicted and sentenced to death on 23 October 1998.[22]

Yet while ECOMOG secured Freetown, it could not defeat the rebels, who remained in control of much of the northern and eastern parts of the country, in

---

16) *Ibid.*, p. 11; *Also see* Singer, *supra* note 14, p. 114.

17) Eric G. Berman and Melissa Labonte, 'Sierra Leone', in William J. Durch, (ed)., *Twenty-First Century Peace Operations* (Washington, D.C.: US Institute of Peace and the Henry L. Stimson Center, 2006), p. 148.

18) Gberie, *supra* note 13, pp. 97-102.

19) Abraham, *supra* note 12, p. 216.

20) Adebajo, *supra* note 10, p. 149.

21) International Crisis Group, *supra* note 15, p. 7.

22) Abraham, *supra* note 12, pp. 217-218.

large measure due to continued support from Taylor.[23] Nor was it able to prevent the brutal January 1999 RUF-AFRC assault on Freetown – Operation No Living Thing – that involved some of the worst atrocities of the war.[24] The rebels were eventually dislodged by a three-week ECOMOG counter-offensive, which was fought with a "mercilessness that matched that of the rebels".[25] Yet while the RUF was repelled from Freetown, it still controlled much of the countryside. Moreover, the toll of the battle on ECOMOG, which took the lives of 700 soldiers, generated strong opposition to the deployment in Nigeria, which was undergoing a democratic transition and had been providing over 90 per cent of the troops.[26] As a result, Nigerian President Olesegun Obasanjo announced his intention to draw down the Nigerian presence and Kabbah was faced with the prospect of losing what amounted to his surrogate army.

Given their support for democratic consolidation within Nigeria, the US, UK and UN put pressure on Kabbah for a negotiated solution.[27] Sankoh, who was appealing his death sentence, was pardoned and allowed to lead the RUF delegation in peace talks in the Togolese capital of Lomé in May 1999. This resulted in the Lomé Peace Accords on 7 July 1999, which formally ended the conflict. While the agreement did call for the creation of a Truth and Reconciliation Commission, it also provided a blanket amnesty to all the parties and a power-sharing agreement in which the RUF was granted four cabinet positions. As part of the deal, Sankoh was appointed Vice President and the Director of the Strategic Mineral Resource Commission, giving him responsibility for the very same resources that were the object of his rebellion. In other words, the entrenchment of impunity went beyond Abidjan and Conakry by not only pardoning, but also rewarding criminal violence.[28] And as with previous agreements, it collapsed since the RUF had no intention of abiding by its word. Yet the amnesty was not the cause of this failure; it was rather the international community's unwillingness to replace the Nigerians with anything other than neutral peacekeepers and amnesty was a symptom of that political choice. It was only when external actors adopted an enforcement-based approach to peace-making that an accountability-based approach to peace-building became possible.

---

23) Berman and Labonte, *supra* note 17, p. 155.

24) Gberie, *supra* note 13, pp. 129-130.

25) 'Funmi Olonisakin, *Peacekeeping in Sierra Leone: The Story of UNAMSIL* (Boulder: Lynne Rienner, 2008), p. 33.

26) Julius Mutwol, *Peace Agreements and Civil Wars in Africa: Insurgent Motivations, State Responses, and Third-Party Peacemaking in Liberia, Rwanda, and Sierra Leone* (Amherst, New York: Cambria Press, 2009), p. 296.

27) International Crisis Group, *supra* note 15, p. 2.

28) *See* Olonisakin, *supra* note 25, pp. 35-38.

3. Explaining the Shift from Amnesty to Prosecution

The Lomé Agreement and its collapse represented watersheds in normative debates regarding amnesty as an instrument of conflict resolution. During the 1990s, the UN had facilitated a number of peace processes in which amnesties were a routine part of the bargain. Yet in mid-1999, it established a policy of opposing amnesties for international crimes given the Security Council's pioneering role in authorizing the ICTY and ICTR.[29] The blanket amnesty extended at Lomé was a direct challenge to that policy and triggered strong objections from international human rights organizations. While the UN was unwilling to oppose the agreement on those grounds, its envoy to the negotiations submitted a handwritten disclaimer withholding recognition of any amnesty for "genocide, crimes against humanity, war crimes and other serious violations of international humanitarian law".[30] This view was supported by international human rights organizations, both on legal principle and because they believed that peace without justice was unsustainable – a view that was seemingly vindicated by the RUF's subsequent return to violence.[31]

This attribution of Lomé's breakdown to the absence of criminal accountability confuses symptoms with causes. Amnesty was the inevitable consequence of international support for a negotiated solution at a time when the only force capable of containing the RUF was about to be withdrawn and its failure was due to the fact that the RUF was a total spoiler and the UN force that replaced ECOMOG had neither the capacity nor the credibility to deter the rebels from returning to violence. Prosecution – and the prospects for peace – only became possible when external actors, led by the UK, adopted a more enforcement-oriented approach toward the RUF and its Liberian sponsor. In other words, a prerequisite for the legal choice of demanding accountability is a political choice for enforcement over impartiality.

First, the reason why amnesty was an inevitable feature of Lomé was the impartial and non-coercive conflict resolution approach adopted by the international community, whose success depended on RUF consent. From a human rights perspective, this should have been unacceptable. David Scheffer, who was US Ambassador for War Crimes at the time, recalls a State Department colleague expressing her disbelief at the outcome at Lomé: "How in the world did the peace process allow Foday Sankoh to have such a prominent position?"[32] The answer is

---

29) Priscilla Hayner, 'Negotiating Peace in Sierra Leone: Confronting the Justice Challenge', (Geneva, Switzerland: Center for Humanitarian Dialogue and the International Center for Transitional Justice) December 2007, pp. 17-18.

30) Olonisakin, *supra* note 25, p. 40.

31) Human Rights Watch, *supra* note 7, pp. 57-61.

32) David Scheffer, *All the Missing Souls: A Personal History of War Crimes Tribunals* (Princeton, New Jersey: Princeton University Press, 2012), p. 310.

that while Sankoh had been in prison, he was also the leader of a rebel movement that had not been defeated and still occupied two-thirds of the country. Moreover, Sierra Leone was a failed state whose ability to contain the RUF was dependent on ECOMOG, which was about to leave.[33] As a result, the alternative to peace with amnesty was not peace with justice, but the continuation of the war without external support against a rebel group that was still being armed by Charles Taylor's Liberia.

The incompatibility between conflict resolution and legal accountability can also be seen in the initial character of the UN Assistance Mission in Sierra Leone (UNAMSIL), which replaced ECOMOG as part of the peace agreement. UNAMSIL was authorized by UN Security Council Resolution 1270 on 22 October 1999 – a force of 6000 that was increased to 11,000 because ECOMOG withdrew at a faster pace than had been anticipated.[34] UNAMSIL's mission was challenged by the RUF from the very start of its deployment in late 1999 as the rebels continued to use violence against civilians, resist disarmament, and obstruct access to the diamond-producing areas in the east.[35] Although UNAMSIL was authorized under Chapter VII, which allowed it to take enforcement actions against violations of its mandate, its operational policy was more in line with a Chapter VI mission in that it responded to RUF provocations through negotiation rather than confrontation. The premise underlying this policy was that both sides wanted peace and the role of the UN was to provide reassurance.[36] This approach misconstrued the character of the RUF and was the underlying source of its impunity since the rebels could challenge the agreement without consequences.

The catalyst for countering the RUF's impunity on the ground took place on 2 May 2000, when rebels seized 500 Kenyan and Zambian peacekeepers as hostages. This followed a decision by the commander of UNAMSIL to secure control of the diamond producing areas, which led to increased attacks on peacekeepers, culminating in the hostage crisis.[37] Not coincidentally, this escalation of rebel attacks on peacekeepers took place one week after the departure of the last ECOMOG forces from Sierra Leone – the only international force on the ground that had confronted the RUF militarily. While the UN and major powers placed pressure on Taylor to secure a negotiated release of the hostages, the crisis fundamentally changed the government's and the international community's approach

[33] John Hirsch, 'Sierra Leone', in David M. Malone, (ed.), *The UN Security Council: From the Cold War to the 21st Century* (Boulder, Co: Lynne Rienner, 2004), p. 526.
[34] *Ibid.*, p. 527.
[35] Mutwol, *supra* note 26, pp. 297-300.
[36] *See* the interviews with UN officials in Douglas Farah, 'Rebel Leader Exploited U.N. Weaknesses, Officials Say; Misplaced Trust, Slow Deployment Spurred Sankoh', *Washington Post*, 15 May 2000, p. A18.
[37] Hirsch, *supra* note 33, p. 528.

to the conflict. In Freetown, it led to a crackdown on the RUF. Sankoh was arrested on 17 May by army forces loyal to former AFRC chief Johnny Paul Koroma after he had fled following demonstrations outside his residence in which his bodyguards fired into the crowd, killing 19.[38] What made a tougher line possible, however, was not simply the determination of the government; more importantly, it was the change in the character of international intervention, which abandoned neutrality and sought to defeat the RUF.

The most decisive factor changing the power dynamics on the ground was the British intervention in Freetown following a plea from Kofi Annan for international assistance to prevent the hostage crisis from turning into another peacekeeping debacle comparable to UNAMIR in Rwanda or UNPROFOR in Srebrenica.[39] The initial deployment on 7 May – Operation Palliser – was designed to evacuate British and other Western nationals from Freetown, something that Western forces had done as well at the outset of the Rwandan genocide. Unlike the Rwandan case, however, the British stayed, providing forces to stabilize Freetown, secure Lungi airport from RUF control, and train the army and former militias into a military force capable of fighting the RUF and over whom it would have significant operational control.[40] It also maintained an "over-the-horizon" force with a visible demonstration of firepower to send a deterrent message to the RUF that "the British were prepared to unleash maximum damage should the rebels test their resolve".[41] The credibility of that resolve was further enhanced by military operations against rebels, such as the 17 May firefight with advancing RUF forces 12 miles outside of Freetown[42] and three months later, the Special Forces assault on the West Side Boys, an offshoot of the AFRC that had terrorized civilians and had taken a British patrol hostage.[43] These actions persuaded the rebels that "the war was unwinnable and that Freetown could not be taken".[44] According to the International Crisis Group, they also had a major impact on the confidence of the government in its security and in its determination to defeat the rebels and arrest its leaders.[45]

The hostage crisis also transformed the UN's approach to conflict resolution from one of strict neutrality to one of supporting the government and weakening the RUF. First, the Security Council imposed sanctions specifically targeting diamonds, which were the RUF's chief source of revenue and its link to its Liberian

---

38) Mutwol, *supra* note 26, pp. 311-312

39) International Crisis Group, *supra* note 15, p. 20.

40) Andrew M. Dorman, *Blair's Successful War: British Military Intervention in Sierra Leone* (Surrey, U.K.: Ashgate 2009), pp. 92-93, 117.

41) Olonisakin, *supra* note 25, p. 64.

42) Dorman, *supra* note 40, p. 94.

43) See Berman and Labonte, *supra* note 17, p. 162; Olonisakin, *supra* note 25, pp. 99-100.

44) David Keen, *Conflict and Collusion in Sierra Leone* (New York: Palgrave, 2005), p. 273.

45) International Crisis Group, 'Sierra Leone: Managing Uncertainty', Africa Report No. 35, 24 October 2001, pp. 1-2.

patron. Resolution 1306 (5 July 2000) established a certification program for Sierra Leone's diamond exports and called on member states not to purchase rough diamonds to staunch illicit exports.[46] After a UN panel of experts documented the extent of Taylor's ties with the RUF, the diamond boycott and other sanctions were extended to Liberia.[47] While the sanctions were less than airtight, one study concluded that "the growing difficulty of trading with Liberia appears to have significantly reduced rebel profits from the diamond trade".[48]

Second, the crisis catalyzed the transformation of UNAMSIL from a purely impartial and non-coercive mission into a more pro-active one that undertook some enforcement actions against the RUF. UNAMSIL's earlier problems coincided with the deliberations of a high-level UN panel on peacekeeping chaired by Lakhdar Brahimi. The Brahimi Report – released shortly after the hostage crisis – explicitly cited Sierra Leone acknowledging that "no failure did more to damage the standing and credibility of United Nations peacekeeping in the 1990s than its reluctance to distinguish victim from aggressor". As a result, peacekeepers should adopt a concept of impartiality not as "neutrality or equal treatment of the parties", but rather as impartiality toward the mandate. When that mandate is violated in ways that put civilians at risk, UN forces must have the authority and the resources to "confront the lingering forces of war and violence with the ability and determination to defeat them".[49]

The Security Council and Secretary General had these conclusions in mind when the size of UNAMSIL was increased to 17,500 – the largest UN peacekeeping operation at the time – which also included the 3000 US-trained Nigerian troops to provide the backbone of any peace-enforcement operations that might be necessary. In July 2000, UNAMSIL launched Operation Khukri, which rescued 200 hostages held by the RUF while inflicting heavy casualties on the rebels.[50] On 4 August, Security Council Resolution 1313 explicitly blamed the RUF for violations of Lomé and authorized UNAMSIL to "deter and when necessary decisively counter the threat of RUF attack by responding robustly to any hostile actions or threat of direct or imminent use of force".[51]

This shift to an enforcement-oriented mandate was not uncontroversial. India and Jordan withdrew their contingents because they objected both to the change in the mission and to Britain's unwillingness to put any of its forces under UNAMSIL command.[52] While those forces were replaced by troops from

---

46) Berman and Labonte, *supra* note 17, p. 181-182.
47) Olonisakin, *supra* note 25, p. 78.
48) Keen, *supra* note 44, p. 271.
49) United Nations, *Report of the Panel on United Nations Peace Operations*, A/55/305–S/2000/809, 21 August 2000, Executive Summary, pp. viii, ix.
50) Olonisakin, *supra* note 25, p. 93.
51) UN Security Council Resolution 1313, adopted 4 August 2000, paragraph 3(b).
52) Adebajo, *supra* note 10, p. 151.

Bangladesh, Kenya and Ukraine, there was often a reluctance to engage in actual enforcement missions or abandon negotiations, even in the face of continued RUF noncompliance. As a result, the most significant military actions were undertaken by the British-trained Sierra Leone Army (SLA) and the primary role of UNAMSIL was to consolidate territory liberated from the RUF.[53] This nonetheless represented a change in the mission from one of pure neutrality to assisting the government, which enabled it to pursue a two-track policy of deploying military pressure – or relying on it from the CDF and a reconstituted national army – and persuading the RUF to accept DDR and allow UNAMSIL to secure control of the diamond producing areas.

Another source of military pressure on the RUF came from Guinea, which was involved in a proxy conflict with Liberia in which it was backing anti-Taylor insurgents, probably with the support of the US and the UK.[54] A disastrous RUF incursion into Guinea prompted a fierce Guinean counter-offensive, using helicopter gunships to bombard RUF positions and supporting the *kamajors* and other militias fighting the RUF.[55] Since the RUF was now fighting against the Guineans, the SLA and the CDF with diminished assistance from Liberia, it became more receptive to UNAMSIL's DDR programs, if for no other reason than finding sanctuary from a fight it was losing. These pressures, in turn, contributed to the Abuja I and II cease-fire agreements in November 2000 and May 2001, in which the RUF and CDF agreed to a large-scale simultaneous disarmament that effectively ended the war. That demobilization was also a prerequisite for effective prosecutions, yet without a shift to a more interventionist approach to conflict resolution, they would likely not have materialized.

4. Enforcing Prosecution within Sierra Leone

In his opening statement in the CDF trial, David Crane declared that "politics must remain barred from these proceedings".[56] Indeed, many aspects of the SCSL's case selection exhibited an independence from politics in prosecuting the leaders of the three main armed factions regardless of their role in the peace process or their political alignment – an approach to prosecutorial independence advocated by many human rights organizations.[57] Yet what made this approach possible – and difficult to replicate in other post-conflict situations – was the interventionist

53) Dorman, *supra* note 40, pp. 97-101.

54) Keen, *supra* note 44, p. 268.

55) See *ibid.*, and International Crisis Group, *supra* note 45, p. 2.

56) The Special Court for Sierra Leone, *The Prosecutor of the Special Court* v. *Sam Hinga Norman, Moinina Fofana, Allieu Kondewa*, 3 June 2004, p. 12.

57) The advocacy of Human Rights Watch, Amnesty International and UN High Commissioner for Human Rights, Mary Robinson, for accountability on all sides of the civil war, is

approach to conflict resolution, which enabled foreigners to assume what amounted to supranational authority within a sovereign state.

First, the SCSL was able to assert its primacy over the peace process. In terms of legal principle, Article X of the SCSL statute asserted that amnesties for crimes against humanity or serious war crimes would not be a bar to prosecution, giving concrete meaning to the UN disclaimer at Lomé and the advocacy of human rights organizations. This was affirmed by the trial chamber in the RUF case, which supported the prosecution argument that there is a "crystallising international norm that a government cannot grant amnesty for serious violations of crimes under international law".[58]

The prosecutor also obtained arrest warrants not only for total spoilers like Sankoh, but also for perpetrators who took important steps in ending the conflict, such as Issa Sesay, who succeeded Sankoh as the leader of the RUF and played a cooperative role with UNAMSIL in ending the conflict, for which UN officials promised him immunity from prosecution, or Johnny Paul Koroma, who sided with the government during the May 2000 hostage crisis and whose forces captured Sankoh.[59] Both were indicted, and while Koroma escaped, Sesay was convicted and sentenced to 52 years in prison. To many advocates of international criminal justice, such an outcome should become the norm since the independence of courts from the political promises made by mediators will send the message to potential perpetrators that they cannot leverage their cooperation into immunity from prosecution.[60]

Second, the SCSL prosecuted those on both sides of the conflict by indicting the leaders of the CDF for violence against civilians perpetrated when it was fighting with ECOMOG against the AFRC and RUF from 1997-1999. This included the CDF's War Minister, Moinina Fofana, its High Priest, Allieu Kondewa, and Sam Hinga Norman, who was Deputy Defense Minister and National Coordinator for the CDF during the war. These indictments were controversial because the *kamajors* had fought on the side of the government and were seen by many as national heroes, particularly Norman, who stayed in the country after the 1997 coup to lead the fight against the junta.[61] Nonetheless, the *kamajors*, who came from the Mende tribe in the south of the country, viewed northern groups suspiciously as potential RUF/AFRC collaborators. As a result, those villages that did not fully cooperate

---

summarized in Peter Penfold, 'The Special Court for Sierra Leone – A Critical Analysis', in Lansana Gberie, (ed.), *Rescuing a Fragile State: Sierra Leone 2002-2008* (LCMSDS Press of Wilfred Laurier University, Waterloo, Ontario, 2009), p. 62.

58) *Cited in* Robert Cryer, *Prosecuting International Crimes: Selectivity and the International Criminal Law Regime* (Cambridge University Press, 2005), p. 109.

59) *See* International Crisis Group, "The Special Court for Sierra Leone: Promises and Pitfalls of a 'New Model', Africa Briefing No. 16, 4 August 2003, p. 5; and Keen, *supra* note 44, pp. 267-275.

60) *See* Human Rights Watch, The Meaning of the 'Interests of Justice' in Article 53 of the Rome Statute, Policy Paper, (June 2005), pp. 14-15.

61) International Crisis Group, *supra* note 59, p. 7.

with them were subjected to extrajudicial killings, rape, and looting.[62] And like their opponents, the CDF also relied extensively on child soldiers.[63] Desmond da Silva, Crane's successor as chief prosecutor, argued that the trial was necessary to demonstrate that such practices are never acceptable, even if "you are fighting on the side of the angels".[64]

While Norman died prior to the completion of his trial, Fofana and Kondewa were convicted. The two international judges agreed with the prosecution case that they bore command responsibility for CDF crimes because they knew or had reason to know of them and took no actions to stop them.[65] The Sierra Leonean judge dissented, defending their actions on necessity grounds – a view that had considerable public support.[66] Perhaps in deference to those sentiments, the trial chamber cited mitigating circumstances – i.e., that Fofana and Kondewa were fighting not to "destabilize the established constitutional order", but to "restore the democratically-elected government" – in sentencing them to six and eight years respectively rather than the Prosecutor's demand for 30 years.[67] The appeals chamber, with the Sierra Leonean judges dissenting, rejected the 'just ends' rationale for sentence mitigation and increased the sentence for Fofana and Kondewa to 15 and 20 years respectively.[68] Human Rights Watch, while acknowledging that CDF crimes were of "a smaller scale and a different nature", than those of the RUF, applauded this reversal, arguing that the trial chamber's decision "defies a well-settled principle in international humanitarian law that all parties are bound by and must be treated equally by international law" whether or not they are "on the 'right' side of the conflict".[69]

These achievements stand out from other post-conflict situations in which formal or *de facto* immunity was granted to the leaders of warring factions as part of peace agreements, as was the case for the leaders of the Khmer Rouge in the Paris Peace Agreements in 1991 or the peace settlement that ended the civil war in neighbouring Liberia.[70] In addition, the SCSL's ability to prosecute suspects aligned with the government differs from the Rwandan case, in which the ICTR

62) Kelsall, *supra* note 6, p. 29.
63) Pham, *supra* note 5, p. 73.
64) Thierry Cruvellier, "From the Taylor Trial to a Lasting Legacy: Putting the Special Court Model to the Test," International Center for Transitional Justice and Sierra Leone Monitoring Programme, 2009, p. 24.
65) Kelsall, *supra* note 6, pp. 63-64.
66) Cruvellier, *supra* note 64, p. 27.
67) *See ibid.*, p. 25; and Gill Wigglesworth, 'The End of Impunity? Lessons from Sierra Leone', 84(4) *International Affairs* (2008), p. 823.
68) Kelsall, *supra* note 6, p. 66.
69) Human Rights Watch, 'Political Considerations for Sentence Mitigation for Serious Violations of the Laws of War Before International Criminal Tribunals', Memorandum, March 2008, pp. 1, 5.
70) *See* Mats Berdal and Michael Leifer, 'Cambodia', in *United Nations Interventionism, 1991-2004* (Cambridge: Cambridge University Press, 2007), pp. 38-49, and David Harris, *Civil War and*

only prosecuted Hutus responsible for the genocide and not members of the Rwandan Patriotic Army, who are alleged to have killed over 20,000 Hutu civilians during the military campaign that ousted the genocidal regime,[71] or the Extraordinary Chambers in the Courts of Cambodia (ECCC), in which the Hun Sen government has been able to obstruct proceedings against former Khmer Rouge officials whose trial would be contrary to state interests.[72] While the SCSL has been subject to allegations of selectivity for not prosecuting Kabbah, who was Norman's superior,[73] its willingness to try both winners and losers has nonetheless been praised as an important precedent in countering victor's justice.[74]

Yet the ability of the SCSL to pursue exemplary prosecutions regardless of peace negotiations or political alignment was a function of political conditions absent in other cases. First, Sierra Leone was a failed state inordinately dependent on the international actors supportive of trials for security and economic reconstruction. Given this dependence, the government agreed to a statute for the court that minimized the potential for political interference. While it allowed the government to nominate a Sierra Leonean as deputy prosecutor, subject to UN approval, the power to apply for indictments was vested in the UN-appointed chief prosecutor. Moreover, the majority of international judges on the trial and appeals chambers insulated the judgments from national political considerations.[75] By contrast, the ECCC has a majority of Cambodian judges and Cambodian and international co-prosecutors and investigating magistrates of equal authority – rules that give the government more of an ability to obstruct politically inconvenient trials.[76] While Cambodia, like Sierra Leone, is dependent on foreign aid, much of that comes from China, which has backed the government position in resisting international pressures for broad accountability.[77]

Second, the strong international military presence on the ground minimized the risk that prosecution would destabilize the peace process. That was primarily because the UK and UN-supported enforcement missions effectively defeated the RUF, dismantling its command and control structures, and facilitated the disarmament of over 75,000 fighters from all the armed factions – outcomes that

Democracy in West Africa: Conflict Resolution, Elections and Justice in Sierra Leone and Liberia (London: I.B. Tauris, 2011), pp. 193-197.

71) *See* Victor Peskin, *International Justice in Rwanda and the Balkans: Virtual Trials and the Struggle for State Cooperation* (Cambridge University Press, 2008), pp. 207-231.

72) Open Society Justice Initiative, 'Political Interference at the Extraordinary Chambers in the Courts of Cambodia', July 2010.

73) Cruvellier, *supra* note 64, p. 25.

74) Human Rights Watch, *supra* note 69, p. 18.

75) Scheffer, *supra* note 32, p. 337.

76) Kelly Whitley, 'History of the Khmer Rouge Tribunal: Origins, Negotiations and Establishment', in John D. Ciorciari, (ed.), *The Khmer Rouge Tribunal* (Phnom Penh: Documentation Center of Cambodia, 2006), pp. 47-53.

77) On China's role, *see* Scheffer, *supra* note 32, pp. 382-383.

reduced the risk of violent reprisals against attempted prosecutions.[78] It was also due to a British program of security sector reform, which enabled British officers to exercise a significant degree of control over the SLA in reorganizing it to operate under civilian authority.[79] That meant that the SCSL could issue indictments for AFRC officers – including Koroma, who was still popular within the SLA[80] – with less risk of a military mutiny.

Yet nowhere did this foreign presence enable the SCSL to act as a supranational body than in Operation Justice – the plan devised by Crane to minimize the risk of violence while apprehending the first seven Sierra Leonean suspects, including Norman, who was at the time Minister of the Interior.[81] In pursuit of this goal, Crane convened a security group under the auspices of the British High Commission to Sierra Leone composed of the US ambassador, the inspector general of the Sierra Leonean police (who was a retired British policeman), the commander of UNAMSIL, and the British general in charge of training the SLA. Not a single Sierra Leonean was involved in the process, which was viewed as necessary to avoid political interference.[82] On 10 March 2003, UNAMSIL, with assistance from the US, the UK, and the SLA, apprehended all the suspects within one hour of each other and without incident. This included Norman, who was arrested in his office in the Interior Ministry, and who, in a normal sovereign state, would have control over the arresting units. Crane also made arrangements with the British Ministry of Defense for land and naval forces and with UNAMSIL for a rapid reaction team of Pakistani Special Forces to anticipate any potential violence.[83] The suspects were then transferred to Bonthe Island, 100 miles south of Freetown, where a detention facility – that in colonial days served as a transit centre for the Atlantic slave trade - had been built under the pretext of renovating prison for the national police.[84]

In a speech at Cardozo University Law School, Crane recounted this experience in the context of the slogan "African solutions to African problems". While acknowledging that this is the proper standard for Africa in the long-run, he noted that it was problematic in the near-term from an international justice

---

78) *See* International Crisis Group, *supra* note 59, p. 5.

79) *See* Peter Albrecht and Paul Jackson, 'Security System Transformation in Sierra Leone, 1997-2007', Global Facilitation Network for Security Sector Reform and International Alert, February 2009, pp. 51-64.

80) Jeremy Ginifer, 'The Challenge of the Security Sector and Security Sector Reform Processes in Democratic Transitions: The Case of Sierra Leone', 13(5) *Democratization* (December 2006), p. 796.

81) The details of the operation are laid out in David Crane, 'The Take Down: Case Studies Regarding 'Lawfare' in International Criminal Justice: The West African Experience', 43 *Case Western Reserve Journal of International Law* (2010), pp. 206-208.

82) *Ibid.*, p. 207.

83) *See ibid.*, p. 208, and Dorman, *supra* note 40, p. 123.

84) Gberie, *supra* note 13, p. 213.

perspective because it "could be used to avoid the international norms that the various nations in Africa have signed on to in order to avoid a just solution to impunity and criminal prosecution of one of their own."[85] While the government of Sierra Leone requested the SCSL and consented to its operation, had it been responsible for its own transitional justice mechanism, it would likely have involved victor's justice for the defeated (as with the 1998 treason trials), or immunity for those who fought with the government or played a cooperative role in the peace process. The reason why this kind of politics was barred from consideration was because outsiders played a disproportionate role in winning Sierra Leone's civil war for it, and therefore, assumed many of the prerogatives that would normally reside within a sovereign state.

5. The Prosecution of Charles Taylor and the Liberian Peace Process

The SCSL's most prominent trial was that of Charles Taylor, whose apprehension was more difficult than that of the Sierra Leonean suspects because he was in neighbouring Liberia where the court lacked the binding enforcement authority and capabilities it had in Sierra Leone. The strategy of prosecuting Taylor was ultimately successful because it comported with regional and international strategies to remove Taylor from power.

Initially, however, Crane's strategy was dissonant with conflict resolution because he unsealed the indictment just as the Liberian President arrived in Accra on 4 June 2003, for an ECOWAS-sponsored peace conference designed to end the Liberian civil war by persuading Taylor to step down. Crane believed that a dramatic move like this was necessary as long as Taylor resided in Liberia because he was outside the enforcement capabilities that had been brought to bear in Sierra Leone and because the SCSL lacked Chapter VII authority that would create a binding legal obligation for all member states to comply with its rulings. As a result, when the indictment was issued on 7 March 2003, Crane persuaded the judges to keep it under seal while he devised Operation Rope – a plan to publicize the indictment after Taylor left Liberia so as to maximize the legal, political and diplomatic pressure on third parties to arrest and extradite him.[86] That opportunity availed itself at Accra and Crane's message to Taylor's Ghanaian hosts was that they should surrender him for trial rather than negotiate with a war criminal.

The reaction to Crane's intervention on the part of diplomats was uniformly negative. The purpose of the Accra talks was to end the Liberian civil war at a time

[85] David Crane, 'White Man's Justice: Applying International Justice After Regional Third World Conflicts', 27(4) *Cardozo Law Review* (2006), p. 1687.
[86] Crane, *supra* note 81, p. 209.

when the two main rebel groups, Liberians United for the Restoration of Democracy (LURD) and the Movement for Democracy in Liberia (MODEL), were advancing on Monrovia. The mediators believed that the only way to avert a humanitarian catastrophe from a prolonged siege of the capital was by persuading Taylor to resign and accept sanctuary in a third country. Since the ECOWAS leaders who sponsored the talks were committed to a negotiated solution, they condemned the timing of the indictment – a view shared by UN and Western diplomats.[87] Ghana's President John Kufuor was particularly incensed since he had promised Taylor and the rebel leaders safe passage to attend. As a result, Kufour not only refused to execute the arrest warrant; he allowed Taylor to return to Monrovia on his private jet.[88]

Crane's decision was controversial because the Taylor indictment undercut international strategies of conflict resolution. Whereas the RUF prosecutions followed a commitment to defeat the rebels, Taylor was still in power and a successful diplomatic outcome required persuading him that it was in his interest to step down. While it is not clear whether there was a realistic prospect for securing his departure at that time – and retrospective interviews with participants in the negotiations indicate that they viewed such an outcome as unlikely[89]– the timing of Crane's intervention virtually guaranteed that an attempt to resolve the conflict in June would fail. As a result, fighting intensified after the breakdown of the Accra talks and "left over one thousand civilian dead, thousands more wounded, and hundreds of thousands starving as humanitarian organizations were unable to bring in supplies".[90]

Yet while this strategy was unsuccessful in gaining custody of Taylor, it did play a role in stigmatizing him, reducing his domestic and international legitimacy, and making it clear to the other stakeholders that he could not be part of any post-conflict political arrangement.[91] In fact, the Accra negotiations continued after Taylor's departure and produced a cease-fire on 17 July as well as plans for a transitional government that did not include Taylor.[92] Crane subsequently acknowledged that one of his goals was to "embarrass Taylor in front of his west African colleagues" and render him an unsuitable partner for the peace process because

87) Jess Bravin, 'A Prosecutor Vows No Deal with Thugs in Sierra Leone War', *Wall Street Journal*, July 28, 2003, p. A1.

88) Moghalu, *supra* note 3, pp. 109-110; International Crisis Group, *The Special Court for Sierra Leone*, 4 August 2003, p. 7.

89) Hayner, 'Negotiating Peace in Liberia: Preserving the Possibility for Justice', Geneva: Center for Humanitarian Dialogue and International Center for Transitional Justice, November 2007, p. 8.

90) J. Peter Pham, 'Politics and International Justice in a World of States', 4 *Human Rights and Human Welfare* (2004), p. 133.

91) Hayner, *supra* note 89, pp. 25-26.

92) J. Peter Pham, *Liberia: Portrait of a Failed State* (New York: Reed Press, 2004), p. 187.

any stable political settlement required the removal of Taylor from the political scene.[93]

The power of stigma associated with criminal indictments has often been touted by anti-impunity advocates as a means of reducing the influence and bringing about the eventual removal of criminal spoilers and the Taylor case has been cited in support of the ICC arrest warrant against Sudanese President Omar Hassan al-Bashir.[94] However, what made the stigmatizing impact of the Taylor indictment potent was that it comported with regional and international policies of coercive regime change (unlike the Bashir indictment, which did not change what amounted to a consent-based approach to resolving the Darfur conflict).[95] First, Taylor's destabilization of his neighbours generated opposition from almost all of ECOWAS and the two main rebel groups were supported by Guinea and Côte d'Ivoire.[96] Second, the UN Security Council maintained diamond sanctions and an arms embargo on Liberia even after it was no longer supporting the RUF, and added a timber boycott on 6 May 2003, contributing to the deterioration of its economy and further isolating it at a time when the government's neighbours were arming its enemies.[97] Finally, the US government was committed to the removal of Taylor because of his role in destabilizing the region, his political ties to Qaddafi's Libya and his purported economic ties to Al Qaeda. As a result, the Bush administration called on Taylor to step down and backed that up by sending three warships with 2300 marines off the coast of Liberia with the potential to intervene.[98]

In other words, while Crane's intervention in the peace process may not have succeeded as a judicial strategy eliciting compliance with the court's orders, it did augment the international community's political strategy of coercive diplomacy, a term used in the security studies literature to refer to the infliction of costs on a target, with the prospect of more to come, in order to persuade it to comply with the sender's demands.[99] From this perspective, criminalization aided the peace process by adding a political stigma to military and economic coercion to a point

---

93) Hayner, *supra* note 89, p. 8.

94) *See* Enough, 'The Merits of Justice', Strategy Paper No. 35, July 2008; and Human Rights Watch, *supra* note 7.

95) *See* Kenneth A. Rodman, 'Darfur and the Limits of Legal Deterrence', 30(3) *Human Rights Quarterly* (2008), pp. 546-549.

96) Charles T. Call, 'Liberia's War Recurrence: Grievance over Greed', 12(4) *Civil Wars* (2010), pp. 352-353.

97) Colin M. Waugh, *Charles Taylor and Liberia: Ambition and Atrocity in Africa's Lone Star State* (London: Zed Books, 2011), pp. 267-268.

98) International Crisis Group, "Liberia: Security Challenges," Africa Report No. 71, 3 November 2003, pp. 13-14.

99) For an analysis and critique of the use of international prosecution as an instrument coercive diplomacy with a focus on Libya, *see* Adam M. Smith, 'The Emergence of International Justice as Coercive Diplomacy: Challenges and Prospects', Human Rights Program, Harvard University, Research Working Paper 12-002, May 2012.

where Taylor and his allies realized that he had no choice other than to resign. As a result, Taylor agreed to step down on 11 August 2003, and accept asylum in Nigeria on the condition that he would not interfere in Liberian or west African politics.

The asylum deal was criticized by many human rights advocates as a violation of the duty to prosecute core international crimes that the UN had embraced in its rejection of the blanket amnesty at Lomé.[100] The reason why diplomats chose exile over prosecution lies in the difference between the conflict resolution strategy used in Sierra Leone – which aimed to defeat the RUF – and that employed at Accra, which required Taylor's cooperation to avoid a bloody endgame in Monrovia. For many of the African participants in the negotiations, this went beyond conflict resolution towards a need to elevate sovereignty norms over what was seen as an imperious supranational court that had interfered with their effort to find a regional solution to the problem. As a result, Taylor was escorted into exile in a show of head-of-state solidarity by the presidents of Nigeria, Ghana, South Africa and Mozambique.[101]

This clash between sovereignty and international justice norms would continue through Taylor's asylum in Nigeria. President Obasanjo initially resisted pressures to surrender Taylor from the court and international human rights groups as contrary to the agreement negotiated through ECOWAS, which ought to take precedence over a court without Chapter VII authority or a purported duty to prosecute international crimes. Obasanjo later amended that position, stating that he would surrender Taylor only if requested by a democratically elected Liberian government – that is, Nigeria would defer to a fellow African sovereign rather than a supranational court.[102] Yet when Ellen Johnson-Sirleaf was elected Liberia's first postwar president in October 2005, local politics weighed against such a request. That was because postwar Liberia was still a fragile state without effective security forces while many Taylor loyalists were still armed. Moreover, Johnson-Sirleaf needed the political support of some of Taylor's allies, who occupied influential positions in the Liberian parliament.[103] As a result, she told the BBC in January 2006 that arresting Taylor was "not a priority".[104]

---

100) *See* Amnesty International, "Nigeria: Impunity/ Legal Concern: Charles Ghankay Taylor', 12 August 2003, and Human Rights Watch, 'West Africa: Taylor Must Face Justice', 12 August 2003. For a more general critique of the incompatibility of exile with the new system of international justice, *see* Leila Nadya Sadat, 'Exile, Amnesty and International Law', 81 *Notre Dame Law Review* (March 2006), p. 959.

101) Abdul Tejan-Cole, 'A Big Man in a Small Cell: Charles Taylor and the Special Court for Sierra Leone', in Ellen L. Lutz and Caitlin Reiger (eds.), *Prosecuting Heads of State* (Cambridge, UK: Cambridge University Press, 2009), p. 215.

102) Moghalu, *supra* note 3, pp. 112-113.

103) Harris, *supra* note 70, p. 198.

104) Tejan-Cole, *supra* note 101, p. 217.

By March 2006, however, a number of factors worked to increase international pressure on both Liberia and Nigeria to alter their preferences. First, there were serious allegations that Taylor had violated the terms of his exile by interfering in the Liberian and regional politics. As a result, the UN Secretary General's Special Representative to Liberia called for his extradition and the Security Council authorized United Nations Mission in Liberia (UNMIL) to arrest Taylor should he set foot in the country.[105] Second, norm mobilization by international human rights organizations had resonance within Nigeria, and helped catalyze legal challenges to Taylor status. NGO lobbying also contributed to resolutions by the European Parliament and the U.S. Congress calling on Nigeria to surrender Taylor to the Special Court.[106]

Most important, however, was the decision by Western governments, particularly the United States, to exert pressure on behalf of bringing Taylor to justice. Johnson-Sirleaf was persuaded to reverse her position and ask for Taylor's extradition when US and EU development assistance was linked to compliance.[107] When Nigeria subsequently claimed that Taylor had escaped, the United States made clear there would be "consequences" for not arresting Taylor and threatened to cancel an upcoming summit between Presidents Bush and Obasanjo, scheduled to take place prior to the finalization of a restructuring of Nigeria's 30 billion USD debt.[108] Taylor was apprehended shortly thereafter and then transferred to Liberia, which then surrendered him to the SCSL in Freetown, after which he was transferred to The Hague, where he would be tried by the Special Court using the facilities of the ICC. Yet that road to The Hague required the US and the EU to act as 'surrogate enforcers',[109] using relationships of economic dependence to reverse the preferences of the Liberian and Nigerian governments.

6. Impunity Gaps

The SCSL was remarkably successful in fulfilling its mandate through exemplary prosecutions of the leaders of the main armed factions and the foreign head of state most responsible for criminal violence. As with any tribunal, however, there were 'impunity gaps', in which individuals with significant culpability escaped trial. For Sierra Leonean perpetrators, this was primarily a function of the political

---

105) Kimberly Lanegran, 'The Importance of Trying Charles Taylor', 6 *Journal of Human Rights* (2007), p. 169.

106) Tejan-Cole, *supra* note 101, p. 216.

107) *Ibid.*, p. 217.

108) *See ibid.*, p. 218, and Lydia Polgreen, 'Nigeria Finalizes Plan to Pay off $30 Billion Debt', *New York Times*, 21 April 2006.

109) This was a term developed by Victor Peskin to refer to third party pressure on states to comply with their legal obligations to international tribunals. See Peskin, *supra* note 71, pp. 9-13.

process that created the SCSL, which provided only those resources to try a relatively small number of high-level actors. It was also a function of the Prosecutor's decision to equate "bearing the greatest responsibility" with the leadership, rather than mid-level or regional commanders who used particularly brutal tactics, as had been advocated by some human rights organizations.[110] While these impunity gaps could have been closed by different donor preferences or prosecutorial choices, others are illustrative of how power realities and the political responses to them by states and intergovernmental organizations play a key role in determining who can and cannot be prosecuted.

First, there were no prosecutions of ECOMOG commanders or soldiers, who had been accused of serious human rights abuses and war crimes, particularly in repelling the RUF in the January 1999 battle for Freetown. These included summary execution, arbitrary detention, torture, sexual violence, looting, and firing cluster munitions in civilian areas.[111]

The SCSL statute effectively exempted foreign peacekeepers from its jurisdiction. Article 1(b) acknowledged UN Status of Mission Agreements in which the sending state has primary jurisdiction over any transgressions by its nationals in UN missions and extended that arrangement to peacekeeping forces authorized by regional organizations or which operated with the consent of the Sierra Leonean government. Article 1(c) did create the possibility of SCSL prosecutions if the sending state is unwilling or unable to prosecute, but only if authorized by the Security Council.[112] While ECOMOG did establish a Civil-Military Relations Committee to hear complaints and investigate allegations, there have been few sanctions, nor has the Security Council taken up the matter.[113]

To many human rights advocates, exempting international peacekeepers from the ambit of the international criminal law was viewed as selective prosecution that needs to be corrected to prevent the kinds of abuses that peacekeepers have committed in other contexts.[114] On the other hand, whatever ECOMOG's transgressions, they would likely fall outside the SCSL's mandate to prosecute those most responsible for atrocities committed during Sierra Leone's civil war.[115] Moreover, as US War Crimes Ambassador David Scheffer wrote, the allegations

---

110) Human Rights Watch, 'Bringing Justice: The Special Court for Sierra Leone – Accomplishments, Shortcomings and Needed Support', September 2004, p. 20.

111) Human Rights Watch, 'Getting Away with Murder, Mutilation, Rape: New Testimony from Sierra Leone', (July 1999), part V; *Also see* Olonisakin, *supra* note 25, p. 34.

112) Cryer, *supra* note 58, pp. 229-230.

113) See Marten Zwenenburg, 'Double Standards in Peacekeeping? Subcontracting Peacekeeping and International Humanitarian Law', 12(4) *Leiden Journal of International Law* (1999), p. 755.

114) For an overview of this issue and the advocacy surrounding it, *see* Melanie O'Brien, 'Protectors on Trial? Prosecuting Peacekeepers for War Crimes and Crimes Against Humanity in the International Criminal Court', 40 *International Journal of Law, Crime and Justice* (2012), pp. 223-241.

115) Cryer, *supra* note 58, p. 230.

against ECOMOG "had to be kept in perspective when compared to the magnitude and systematic nature of the atrocities committed by the rebels".[116]

Yet what Scheffer noted about ECOMOG could also be argued for the CDF – and was by the British High Commissioner for Sierra Leone.[117] The difference between the treatment of the two lies in politics and power relationships. CDF leaders could be prosecuted with minimal risk to the peace process since their militias had gone through the DDR process and international forces were deployed to contain any violent backlash. Prosecuting ECOMOG, by contrast, could be costly to peacekeeping in Sierra Leone and elsewhere. It would likely generate strong political opposition from Nigeria, which would be more resistant to cooperating with a supranational investigation of its own soldiers than it was in surrendering an unpopular foreign leader like Taylor. It could also have complicated participation in UNAMSIL – and perhaps peacekeeping more generally since states would be more reluctant to send their national forces on UN missions if soldiers and commanders were subject to international criminal scrutiny. These political realities were acknowledged by Scheffer, who concluded that "while logic pointed to inclusion [of jurisdiction over peacekeepers], political reality dictated exclusion".[118]

Second, no one in Liberia other than Taylor has been prosecuted for supporting atrocity crimes in Sierra Leone. Nor has Taylor been prosecuted for criminal violence in Liberia, where forces under his command – both as rebel leader and as president – used many of the same tactics for which the RUF was prosecuted. In fact, unlike Sierra Leone's transitional process, Liberia's involved neither national prosecutions nor an internationalized court comparable to the SCSL. As noted by Elise Keppler of Human Rights Watch on the day of Taylor's conviction: "Liberian victims of massacres, rape, and torture are every bit as deserving of justice as victims in Sierra Leone".[119]

The difference between Sierra Leonean and Liberian cases lies in the power dynamics of their respective civil wars and the political choices made by outsiders to address them. In the former case, prosecution was facilitated by UK, UN and regional interventions that defeated the RUF and exerted pressure on the warring factions to disarm. In the latter case, mediators at Accra sought a negotiated settlement between the government and the two rebel factions once Taylor was gone. They viewed this as necessary for the same reason they tried to secure Taylor's exile rather than his surrender to the court – namely, that the alternative was a bloody final battle for Monrovia. Moreover, no major power was willing to play a

116) Scheffer, *supra* note 32, p. 307.
117) Penfold, *supra* note 57, p. 61.
118) Scheffer, *supra* note 32, p. 335.
119) Human Rights Watch, 'Sierra Leone: Landmark Conviction of Liberian Ex-President', 26 April 2012.

role comparable to the British in Sierra Leone (or Australia in East Timor, which forced Indonesian-backed militias to withdraw and also led to the creation of a hybrid court), even though U.S. naval forces were poised off the coast of Liberia.[120] While the UN's Special Representative to the Secretary General called for the deployment of US ground troops – a position endorsed by the International Crisis Group – the Bush administration was unwilling to do so, in part because of its large-scale deployments in Iraq and Afghanistan, though perhaps because the conflict dynamics in Liberia – in which two armed factions were fighting the government – were different from those in Sierra Leone – where the goal was more simply to defeat a single spoiler.[121] An important consequence of that choice was that UNMIL had to contend with a less pacified environment with fewer enforcement capabilities than its counterpart in Sierra Leone.

As a result, the peace process had to make concessions to both the government and the rebels in terms of power-sharing and accountability in order to persuade them to end the war. The Comprehensive Peace Agreement (CPA) signed in Accra on 18 August 2003, created the National Transitional Government of Liberia to be followed by national elections by the end of 2005. In exchange, key government ministries were allocated to the leaders to the two main insurgent groups and the discredited former government. This was done without any vetting for past human rights abuses and allowed these officials to plunder the nation's resources to maintain their own patrimonial networks.[122] International mediators recognized the costs of this approach, but "were acutely aware that it was those with access to mortars and cannons who most needed to be appeased".[123]

That appeasement also extended to criminal accountability. The CPA neither required domestic war crimes prosecutions nor the creation of an internationalized mechanism like the SCSL. The mediators were successful in opposing the parties' preference for a blanket amnesty as contrary to international law and UN policy – a position that was supported by Liberian civil society organizations.[124] Instead, Accra called for a Truth and Reconciliation Commission (TRC) loosely modelled after its South African counterpart. While the TRC had the authority to recommend prosecutions, it was widely perceived by the rebels and the government as tantamount to amnesty.[125]

---

120) James Sloan, *The Militarisation of Peacekeeping in the Twenty-First Century* (Oxford: Hart Publishers, 2011), p. 220.
121) International Crisis Group, *supra* note 98, p. 13.
122) Call, *supra* note 96, p. 363; Hayner, *supra* note 89, pp. 15-16.
123) Jonny Steinberg, 'Liberia's Experiment with Transitional Justice', 109 *African Affairs* (2009), p. 137.
124) Hayner, *supra* note 89, p. 17.
125) Steinberg, *supra* note 123, p. 138.

One of the consequences of the CPA was that persons implicated in serious war crimes and human rights abuses were able to enter Liberian politics through the 2005 parliamentary elections. The most notorious was Prince Y. Johnson, a particularly brutal warlord and former Taylor ally, who was responsible for torturing and murdering former President Samuel Doe. Johnson had left Liberia after a falling out with Taylor, but returned after the peace agreement to win a seat in his home region in Nimba County.[126] Other members of the parliament included Taylor's former wife, his son-in-law – who became speaker of the lower house despite being subject to UN sanctions – and some of his most notorious allies. Other parliamentarians include officials from the Doe regime and rebel leaders from LURD and MODEL, all with dubious human rights records.[127] As one observer noted, "Commanders and generals who had been sworn enemies on the battlefield were now partners in the fiefdom of impunity".[128]

In theory, that partnership was challenged when the TRC released its final report in June 2009. It documented massive human rights violations committed by all parties and the absence of leadership efforts to control or mitigate them. As a result, it identified 98 individuals who should be subjected to criminal prosecution, including the leaders of all of the armed factions, many of whom were at the time in prominent positions in government, business, and academia. It also recommended a 30 year ban from politics for another 50 individuals because of their association with war criminals.[129] The TRC report was controversial, even to international human rights advocates who supported prosecution, because many of its conclusions were unsubstantiated. For example, it recommended the lustration of President Johnson-Sirleaf, who testified that she had briefly supported Taylor because of her opposition to the Samuel Doe dictatorship, but ended that support when she learned of his behaviour. The commission provided no evidence to contradict that claim in coming to its conclusion.[130] Whatever its flaws, however, the TRC report has strong resonance within Liberia and led many local civil society organizations to press for its implementation.[131]

Nonetheless, neither the government nor the international community has acted to demand criminal accountability even for a limited number of high-level perpetrators. In fact, Johnson-Sirleaf campaigned for re-election in 2011 promising not to implement the TRC recommendations (one of which would have barred

126) International Crisis Group, 'Liberia: How Sustainable is the Recovery?' Africa Report No. 177, 19 August 2011, p. 6.

127) *See* Peter Dennis, 'A Brief History of Liberia', International Center for Transitional Justice, May 2006, p. 6.

128) Aaron Weah, 'Hopes and Uncertainties: Liberia's Journey to End Impunity', *International Journal of Transitional Justice* (2012), p. 6.

129) Waugh, *supra* note 97, pp. 328-329.

130) International Crisis Group, *supra* note 126, pp. 19-21.

131) Waugh, *supra* note 97, pp. 329-330.

her from running). And a major factor in her victory in the presidential runoff was the endorsement of Prince Y. Johnson, who was at the top of the list of those the TRC recommended for prosecution, but who also came in third in the first round of voting.[132]

The source of this persistent impunity lies in political conditions in Liberia since the transition in 2003 and the means through which the international community has addressed them. Unlike the RUF – which could not win a single seat in Sierra Leone's first postwar election – many of Liberia's warlords have a regional power base in which they have political support and since they were not defeated or fully disarmed, they also have the ability to return to violence. Liberian police and judicial capacity, by contrast, is still very weak, and the government is dependent on UNMIL to maintain law and order against major disturbances.[133] While UNMIL was authorized under Chapter VII, it has defined its mandate as a reactive one, responding to violence against civilians or threats to the peace process.[134] If the UN were to establish some form of internationalized tribunal or refer the case to the International Criminal Court,[135] this would require UNMIL to play a pro-active role comparable to the international forces that implemented Operation Justice, but against a much wider range of perpetrators who have more of a capacity for violence than was the case in Sierra Leone. The improbability of such an intervention is a political reality that Johnson-Sirleaf understands and which dictates some level of accommodation with those identified as war criminals by the TRC. Barring a dramatic improvement in Liberia's security and justice sectors or a more robust international presence in Liberia – both of which seem unlikely in the foreseeable future – these are political realities that her successor will have to adjust to as well.

7. Conclusion

In *The Justice Cascade*, Kathryn Sikkink traces the increased strength and legitimacy of normative changes surrounding international criminal justice, much of which was evident in the history and practice of the SCSL. While Sikkink

132) *See* Clair MacDougall, 'Prince as Kingmaker: Can an Ex-Warlord Deliver Johnson-Sirleaf the Liberian Presidency', *Christian Science Monitor*, 15 October 2011, p. 1.

133) International Crisis Group, 'Liberia: Time for Much-Delayed Reconciliation and Reform', Africa Briefing No. 88, 12 June 2012, pp. 14-15.

134) Center for International Cooperation, *Annual Review of Global Peace Operations 2011* (Boulder: Lynne Rienner, 2012), pp. 40-43.

135) Chernor Jalloh and Alhagi Marong, 'Ending Impunity: The Case for War Crimes Trials in Liberia', 2 *African Journal of Legal Studies* (2005), pp. 72-75. While Liberia only ratified the Rome Statute after the war had ended in September 2004, placing the crimes of the civil war outside the reach of the prosecutor's *proprio motu* authority, a Security Council referral could extend the ICC's competence to when the Rome Statute entered into force on 1 July 2002.

acknowledges that power disparities explain the uneven application of the law, she does not view intervention as a means of narrowing them. In fact, in situations of mass atrocity or large-scale human rights abuses, she recommends that "foreign prosecutions and international tribunals can be cost-effective alternatives to military intervention".[136]

This language suggests that in situations of ongoing criminal violence, legal instruments are alternatives to political ones – a form of discourse that informs some of the scholarship on and much of the advocacy for international prosecution. For example, at the start of the debate that led to the Security Council's referral of the Darfur case to the ICC, Elise Keppler of Human Rights Watch characterized the UN's approach to the conflict as "woefully inadequate", but suggested that "investigation and prosecution by the International Criminal Court could hold the key ... [and] make a real difference".[137] Former ICC Chief Prosecutor Luis Moreno-Ocampo used similar reasoning in explaining his application for an arrest warrant for Sudanese President Omar Hassan al-Bashir:

> Persons indicted by the court should be arrested. They cannot be partners at the negotiating table. This is not about regime change, it is about the criminal responsibility of individuals. It is about stopping the crimes. No war, no invasions, but no inaction, no denial. Something between bombing and nothing.[138]

In other words, international criminal law is presented as an alternative to political approaches to conflict resolution, which can succeed when political responses are 'woefully inadequate', and constitutes a 'third way' between military intervention with all of its attendant costs and risks and negotiations that would require appeasing the perpetrators to gain their cooperation.

Yet in Sierra Leone, criminal accountability was not an alternative to diplomacy and force, but rather a reflection of which political approach was chosen. When the international community was pushing Kabbah toward a negotiated solution because of the impending Nigerian withdrawal, amnesty was inevitable regardless of the character of the RUF's crimes. The case for 'peace with justice' – if it was to be meaningful – required someone to replace the Nigerians in pursuit of a military rather than a negotiated solution. Prosecutions only became possible when Britain was willing to assume this role after the hostage crisis through an intervention with some of the characteristics of the 'responsibility to protect' doctrine and UNAMSIL adopted more of an enforcement mandate in line with the recommendations of the Brahimi Report.

---

136) Sikkink, *The Justice Cascade: How Human Rights Prosecutions are Changing World Politics*, (New York: W.W. Norton, 2011) pp. 232, 226.

137) Elise Keppler, 'Grave Crimes', 61(1) *The World Today* (January 2005), p. 18.

138) Luis Moreno-Ocampo, "Keynote Address," The Pursuit of International Criminal Justice: The Case of Darfur, Yale University Law School, New Haven, CT, 6 February 2009. http://www.law.yale.edu/news/darfurconference.htm.

The SCSL experience suggests that in situations of ongoing criminal violence perpetrated by an entrenched regime or an active rebel movement, enforcement-oriented political strategies are a prerequisite for taking international criminal justice seriously – a relationship evident in other tribunals. To illustrate, when the ICTY was an alternative to enforcement during the war in Bosnia, it had little impact on ethnic cleansing as evidenced by the Srebrenica massacre, which took place more than two years after the tribunal's creation. It was only when the ICTY was a complement to NATO's coercive use of force through Operation Deliberate Force – a 17-day bombing campaign against the Bosnian Serbs – and its support for Croatian and Bosnian counter-offensives in the Krajina and in western Bosnia, that ethnic cleansing ended and the prospects for eventual prosecution emerged.[139] The ICTR was able to prosecute the architects of the Rwandan genocide only because the Rwandan Patriotic Army won the civil war and ousted the Hutu *genocidaires* from power.[140] The Special Panels of the Dili District Court (the East Timor Tribunal) exist because the US threatened Indonesia with a cutoff of IMF and World Bank loans during the Asian Financial Crisis if it did not withdraw its forces, and Australia was willing to deploy a peacekeeping mission with robust rules of engagement.[141] In fact, the ICC has been most successful in apprehending suspects when its investigations coincided with enforcement missions. It gained custody of three of the four warlords indicted in the Ituri district in northeast Congo because an EU enforcement mission (Operation Artemis) and a better resourced UN peacekeeping operation with more robust rules of engagement put pressure on the militias to demobilize.[142] And it gained custody of Ivorian President Laurent Gbagbo, who incited violence against his opponents rather than accept his loss in the November 2010 runoff, because France and the UN equated a Security Council mandate to use force to protect civilians with removing Gbagbo from power.[143]

These cases suggest that international criminal justice proponents need to engage the broader normative debate surrounding the 'responsibility to protect' and practical questions regarding its impact in promoting peace and human rights in concrete situations. In Sierra Leone, those questions can be answered affirmatively since the intervention that empowered the SCSL also contributed to a dramatic improvement in human security. A comparable case could also be made for Operation Deliberate Force in Bosnia, which helped end a war whose primary

139) *See* Rodman, *supra* note 95, pp. 532-540.

140) *See* Leslie Vinjamuri, 'Review of Kathryn Sikkink's *The Justice Cascade: How Human Rights Prosecutions are Changing World Politics*', 11(2) *Journal of Human Rights* (2012), p. 287.

141) *See* Sloan, *supra* note 120, pp. 181-191.

142) International Crisis Group, 'Congo: Four Priorities for Sustainable Peace in Ituri', Africa Report No. 140, 13 May 2008, p. 31.

143) Alex J. Bellamy & Paul D. Williams, 'The New Politics of Protection: Côte d'Ivoire, Libya, and the Responsibility to Protect', 87(4) *International Affairs* (2011), pp. 829-838.

targets were civilians, or peace-enforcement in Ituri, which not only enabled the ICC to gain custody of its first suspects, but also helped pacify what had been the most violent region in eastern Congo following the 2002 peace agreement. However, it does not necessarily follow from these cases that comparable interventionist strategies would have been feasible or desirable in Sudan at the time of the Bashir arrest warrant or in Syria today. In fact, where such forcible or coercive options are impractical, international judicial intervention could undercut conflict resolution strategies designed to induce the cooperation of those complicit in criminal violence, which is why accountability was subordinated to expedient bargaining in resolving Liberia's civil war. This was also what US Secretary of State Hillary Clinton probably had in mind when she said that a Security Council referral of the Syrian case to the ICC "can complicate a resolution of a difficult, complex situation because it limits the options to persuade leaders perhaps to step down from power".[144]

A cautionary lesson that should be drawn from the SCSL and experience of other tribunals is that much of the discourse surrounding international criminal justice exaggerates the degree to which it has brought about a paradigm shift in resolving ongoing conflicts and understates the law's dependence on politics. Regardless of the new legal reality, civil wars can only end when one side defeats the other or when there is a negotiated settlement. External actors can influence either outcome through a mix of diplomacy, coercion or force. International prosecution is not a substitute for these choices. Rather, its fate is tied to which strategies are chosen and their impact on the conflict. If national or international forces defeat the perpetrators – or weaken them to the point where their cooperation is unnecessary for a political settlement – the losers can be put on trial though the victors are likely to remain immune unless, as was the case in Sierra Leone, they are weak and dependent.[145] If there is a negotiated settlement – as there was in Liberia after Taylor's departure – this involves a bargaining process in which it is difficult to prosecute those with whom it is necessary to negotiate and maintain a peace agreement. In other words, international criminal law is less an alternative approach to conflict resolution as it is an instrument whose effectiveness is dependent on a particular kind of politics.

---

144) "Calling Assad a War Criminal Could Complicate Things: Clinton," *Agence France Presse*, 28 February 2012.

145) Croatia is another example of a country that defeated Serbia in the war over the Krajina, but ended up surrendering generals considered by nationalists to be war heroes to the ICTY, largely because of its economic dependence on the EU, which linked a road to membership to compliance with the tribunal. *See* Victor Peskin, 'Beyond Victor's Justice: The Challenge of Prosecuting the Winners at the International Criminal Tribunals for the Former Yugoslavia and Rwanda', 4 *Journal of Human Rights* (2005), pp. 213-231.

The Financing of the Special Tribunals for Sierra Leone, Cambodia and Lebanon

Giorgia Tortora[1]
Liaison Officer, Special Tribunal for Lebanon, New York Office, USA

Abstract
The establishment of the hybrid tribunals in Sierra Leone, Cambodia and Lebanon reflected the dissatisfaction of the international community with the criminal tribunals for the Former Yugoslavia and Rwanda. It also represented the attempt to find new models of criminal accountability which could shorten the duration of judicial proceedings, and ensure greater impact on the local societies and greater financial efficiency. This article will provide an overview of how states' opposition to the ICTs model shaped the decision making process on the final financial and administrative arrangements of the Special Court for Sierra Leone, the Extraordinary Chambers in the Courts of Cambodia and the Special Tribunal for Lebanon. It will also highlight the particular financial and administrative features of each of these institutions. Finally, the article will review the financial support received by the hybrid tribunals so far and the specific measures adopted to address recurring funding shortages.

Keywords
Special Court for Sierra Leone (SCSL); Extraordinary Chambers in Courts of Cambodia (ECCC); Special Tribunal Lebanon (STL); funding; management committee

The establishment of the so-called hybrid or mixed tribunals in Sierra Leone, Cambodia and Lebanon reflected the dissatisfaction of the international community with the criminal tribunals created to address the situations of the Former Yugoslavia and Rwanda. It also represented the attempt to find new models of criminal accountability which could shorten the duration of judicial proceedings – while fully respecting the rights of the accused – and ensure greater impact on the local societies, and greater financial efficiency.

The international criminal tribunals established in the wake of the war in the Balkans and the genocide in Rwanda were created as structures under the full administrative and financial responsibility of the United Nations and its member states. Formally brought into being by the Security Council acting under

[1] The views expressed herein are those of the author and do not necessarily reflect the views of the STL.

Chapter VII,[2] they are UN subsidiary organs entirely funded through the UN regular budget and financially accountable to the General Assembly, via the UN Advisory Committee on Administrative and Budgetary Questions (ACABQ) and the Fifth Committee.[3] As such, these tribunals have enjoyed a regular flow of resources and, whilst subject to repeated requests to strive for financial efficiency, they have largely been able to operate without major financial constraints.[4] In addition, the assessed contributions mechanism assured that the Registrar and other senior officials of the international criminal tribunals did not have to divert a significant portion of their time and efforts to the development and implementation of fundraising strategies and could rather concentrate on their day-to-day operations.

Nevertheless, by the end of the 1990s – just a few years into the operation of the international tribunals for the former Yugoslavia (ICTY) and Rwanda (ICTR) – the political will to approve UN funding for additional criminal justice mechanisms had been lost.

The reasons for member states' aversion towards assessed contributions mainly rested with the perceived disproportion between the growth of the tribunals' budgets and the progress made in their proceedings. That is, the cost of the tribunals appeared to be increasing at a rate not justified by the progress of the investigations and prosecutions, whilst, at the same time, concerns regarding the tribunals' financial accountability had started to take hold.[5]

The yearly budget of the ICTY has increased steadily since the beginning of its operations from USD 10 million in 1994 to over USD 150 million in 2011. Similarly, the yearly budget for the ICTR has risen from approximately USD 35 million in 1996 to USD 125 million in 2011. As of August 2011, the international community has spent over USD 1.8 billion and USD 1.6 billion for the ICTY and ICTR respectively. At the same time, confidence in the financial efficiency of the tribunals has been progressively eroded by the criticism of the tribunals' administrative practices

---

[2] The International Criminal Tribunal for the former Yugoslavia was established by UN Security Council Resolution 827 (S/RES/827). The International Criminal Tribunal for Rwanda was established by UN Security Council Resolution 955 (S/RES/955).

[3] The Fifth Committee is the General Assembly's Administrative and Budgetary Committee. It deals with the administration and budget of the United Nations.

[4] In May 2004, because of arrears in payments by member states, a temporary freeze on external recruitment was imposed on the ICTY and ICTR for a year. At that time, the Tribunals were also requested to reduce non-post expenditures.

[5] *See*, for example, Ralph Zacklin 'The Failings of Ad Hoc International Criminal Tribunals', *Journal of International Criminal Law*, 2 (2004); Dominic Raad 'Evaluating the ICTY and its Completion Strategy: Efforts to Achieve Accountability for War Crimes and their Tribunals', *Journal of International Criminal Justice*, 82 (2005), abstract, as well as pp. 88, 96.

articulated in various reports issued by the United Nations Office of Internal Oversight Services (OIOS)[6] and independent experts.[7]

In addition, member states have been disappointed by the international criminal tribunals' perceived resistance to presenting coherent and realistic completion strategies.[8] After time-projections included in the initial completion strategies presented by ICTs proved unrealistic,[9] the UN Security Council eventually

---

6) In June 1996, the UN General Assembly adopted Resolution 213 (A/RES/50/213) requesting OIOS to review the functioning of the ICTR, identify problems and recommend measures to enhance the efficient use of resources. The *Report of the Office of Internal Oversight Services (OIOS) on the audit and investigation of the International Criminal Tribunal for Rwanda* (A/51/789), p. 2 found that:

> In the Tribunal's Registry not a single administrative area functioned effectively: Finance had no accounting system and could not produce allotment reports, so that neither the Registry nor United Nations Headquarters had budget expenditure information; lines of authority were not clearly defined; internal controls were weak in all sections; personnel in key positions did not have the required qualifications; there was no property management system; procurement actions largely deviated from United Nations procedures; United Nations regulations and rules were widely disregarded; the Kigali office did not get the administrative support needed, and construction work for the second courtroom had not even started.

Similarly, the *Annual report of the Office of Internal Oversight Services (OIOS) for the Period 1 July 1995 to 30 June 1996* (A/51/432), para. 78 states that "[a] comprehensive audit of the ICTY showed that it took approximately 18 months [...] before the Tribunal became operational" and identifies a number of areas where more efficient arrangements could have been made. *See* also subsequent reports, including *Annual Report of the Office of Internal Oversight Services (OIOS) for the period 1 July 1996 to 30 June 1997* (A/52/426), and *Report of the Secretary-General on the activities of OIOS, 1 July 2004 - 30 June 2004* (A/59/331).

7) In 1999, for example, having received the ACABQ report on *Revised for 1998 and proposed requirements for 1999 of the International Tribunal for the Former Yugoslavia* (A/53/651), suggesting a review of the management and organizational strategy of the organs of the ICTY, the General Assembly adopted Resolution 651 (A/53/651) requesting the Secretary-General to appoint a panel of independent experts to evaluate the effectiveness of the operation and functioning of the ICTY and the ICTR with the objective of ensuring the effective use of resources of the tribunals. The Report (A/54/634) made several recommendations to improve the efficiency of the tribunals.

8) In 2004, for example, the *Report of the Office of Internal Oversight Services* (A/59/359) observes in para. 93 that:

> [...] there was insufficient information to confirm the Tribunal's contention to the Security Council that the investigation and prosecution mandates of the Office of the Prosecutor would be completed by 2004 and 2008, respectively. There was no coherent documentation of a strategy, and not all seem to have been identified that could have an impact on the two Tribunals' ability to meet their mandate completion dates.

9) In the case of the ICTY, for example, President Jorda took the initiative of first outlining the Tribunal's completion strategy in his *Report on the Operations of the ICTY* presented to the UN Security Council on 20 June 2000, <www.icty.org/sid/7842/en>, 10 September 2012. On that occasion, he noted that the ICTY could be expected to complete all first instance proceedings by 2007. In 2002, he informed the Security Council that the relevant date was now 2008.

decided to take the lead in the implementation of the Tribunals' completion strategy,[10] including with regard to the establishment of a residual mechanism, and the identification of a completion date, requesting the ICTY and ICTR to finalize their operations by 31 December 2014.[11]

It is against this background that decisions were taken by the UN Security Council and General Assembly on the establishment and funding of the so-called hybrid tribunals: the Special Court for Sierra Leone, the Extraordinary Chambers in the Courts of Cambodia and the Special Tribunal for Lebanon. In all cases, member states insisted on de-linking the new institutions from the United Nations, and experimenting with different degrees of separation from its Secretariat, as well as on different voluntary funding and administrative arrangements.

This article will provide an overview of how states' opposition to the ICTs model shaped the decision making process on the final financial and administrative arrangements of the Special Court for Sierra Leone, the Extraordinary Chambers in the Courts of Cambodia and the Special Tribunal for Lebanon. It will also highlight the particular financial and administrative features of each of these institutions – despite the tendency to look at the hybrid tribunals as very similar bodies set apart from the ICTY and ICTR by their source of funding. Finally, the article will review the financial support received by the hybrid tribunals so far and the specific measures adopted to address recurring funding shortages.

1. The Special Court for Sierra Leone

1.1. *Introduction*

As the first international criminal tribunal established outside the system of the United Nations, the Special Court for Sierra Leone (SCSL) was a radically innovative institution and an unprecedented experiment in a number of ways. No other international criminal tribunal had been established before on the basis of a bilateral agreement between the UN Secretary-General and a state, without an 'anchor'

In October 2003, however, the new ICTY President, Judge Meron, stated before the Security Council that first instances proceedings would not finish by 2008, as the Prosecutor intended to submit a substantial number of new indictments.

10) On 23 August 2003, the Security Council seized the initiative on the matter adopting Resolution 1503 (S/RES/1503), and later Resolution 1534 (S/RES/1534), asking the tribunal that any new indictment concentrate only of the most senior leaders suspected of being responsible for war crimes and requested the ICTY to report twice a year on the implementation of its completion strategy.

11) UN Security Council Resolution 1966 (S/RES/1966), para. 3.

in either the United Nations or a domestic jurisdiction. The SCSL was also the first international criminal court to envisage the substantial involvement of judges, prosecutors and staff from the country where the crimes took place, thus challenging the practice of the ICTY and ICTR, which limited the participation of judges and staff from the former Yugoslavia and Rwanda because of security and impartiality concerns. Moreover, contrary to other tribunals, the SCSL was explicitly set up as a focused institution with personal jurisdiction only over those who bear the greatest responsibility for the crimes within its mandate, and subject matter jurisdiction over a mix of international and domestic law. In addition, no tribunal or other international institution of comparable complexity had a voluntary contributions system as its sole source of funding.

The negotiations on the SCSL, therefore, represented a major development in the quest for alternative models of criminal accountability. Moreover, as it will be discussed below, the SCSL experience highlighted the viability of the system of voluntary contributions as well as the long term challenges of such mechanism, past the initial enthusiasm for the establishment of a new institution, and in the presence of extended judicial proceedings. The SCSL experience further proved the effectiveness of an accountability mechanism based on the major donors' direct oversight of the non-judicial functions of the tribunal, in the absence of a UN supervisory role. Finally, it stressed the existence of a direct link between budget levels and the degree of implementation of the UN financial regulations and rules.

1.2. *The Negotiations*

On 12 June 2001, President Kabbah of Sierra Leone sent a formal request[12] to the UN Secretary-General, seeking the assistance of the UN in bringing to justice members of the Revolutionary United Front and their accomplices "responsible for committing crimes against the people of Sierra Leone and for the taking of United Nations peacekeepers as hostages", and in bringing and maintaining "peace and security in Sierra Leone and the West African subregion".

In his letter, President Kabbah explicitly referred to previous "[...] efforts made by the United Nations to respond to similar crimes against humanity in Rwanda and the former Yugoslavia" and asked "that similar considerations be given to this request". The letter also provided in an annex a possible framework for the special court and suggested that the court be established by the UN Security Council, taking into account the specificity of the Sierra Leonean situation. The letter further requested that the special court apply a blend of international and Sierra Leonean

[12] *Letter dated 9 August 2000 from the Permanent Representative of Sierra Leone to the United Nations addressed to the President of the Security Council* (S/2000/786).

law and have a focused mandate, and that a trust fund be created to pay for the investigations, the operations of the court and the enforcement of its sentences.

In formulating its reply to President Kabbah's request, the Security Council considered several drafts of what would later become Resolution 1315 and, with them, different special court models. The early proposals envisaged the establishment of a special court under Chapter VII of the UN Charter, as an organisation funded through assessed contributions. However, in the course of subsequent discussions, a different concept progressively emerged in response to those Council's members that, while ready to accept the establishment of the court, opposed reproducing the model of the international criminal tribunals and/or did not intend to share the financial burden of its operations. In the final version of Resolution 1315 of 15 August 2000,[13] the Security Council agreed that a special court shall be established by an agreement between the UN and the Government of Sierra Leone, rather than a UN resolution. That is, the Security Council decided that the special court was to be created outside the UN system and not as a UN subsidiary body. The court would, however, be an international organization in its own right, completely outside the Sierra Leonean domestic judicial system.

The Agreement establishing the Special Court for Sierra Leone was signed in Freetown on 16 January 2002 and entered into force on 12 April.[14] The Court officially commenced its operations on 1 July 2002.

1.3. *The Funding Mechanism*

The Security Council began its discussions on a court for Sierra Leone at a moment of high dissatisfaction with the financial performance of the United Nations and especially the international tribunals for the Former Yugoslavia and Rwanda. It is therefore of little surprise, in this political context, that the determination of the SCSL financial mechanism was one of the most controversial aspects of the negotiations and the last one to be settled.

The Council's decision not to establish the court as a UN subsidiary body had the immediate implication of depriving it of funding from the regular budget, unless the Council were to explicitly decide otherwise. Resolution 1315 requested the Secretary-General to include in his report to the Council recommendations on "the amount of voluntary contributions, as appropriate, of funds, equipment and services to the special court, including through the offer of expert personnel that may be needed from States, intergovernmental organizations and non-governmental organizations".

---

13) UN Security Council Resolution 1315 (S/RES/1315).

14) No Peace without Justice, *Lawyers' Guide to the Special Court for Sierra Leone,* March 2004, <http://www.npwj.org/sites/default/files/documents/File/NPWJDraftLawyersGuide20040310.pdf>, 10 September 2012.

The Secretary-General's report was submitted in October 2000[15] and included the text of the draft Agreement and Statute of the Court. In his report, the Secretary-General provided, *inter alia*, recommendations on the Court's competences, its structure as well as practical arrangements for its establishment, and a strong objection to the proposed funding mechanism. The Report noted that:

> [a] financial mechanism based entirely on voluntary contributions will not provide the assured and continuous source of funding which would be required to appoint the judges, the Prosecutor and the Registrar, to contract the services of all administrative and support staff and to purchase the necessary equipment. The risks associated with the establishment of an operation of this kind with insufficient funds, or without long-term assurances of continuous availability of funds, are very high, in terms of both moral responsibility and loss of credibility of the Organization, and its exposure to legal liability. In entering into contractual commitments which the Special Court and, vicariously, the Organization might not be able to honor, the United Nations would expose itself to unlimited third-party liability. A special court based on voluntary contributions would be neither viable nor sustainable.

The Report then went on to recommend that, should the Council be opposed to assessed contribution, consideration should be given to a model of 'national jurisdiction', that is to provide some form of international assistance to the Government of Sierra Leone to carry out the trials rather than creating an entirely new institution for the same purpose.

It was as a reflection of the UN concerns over possible financial liabilities for the organisation that early drafts of the Agreement, prepared by the UN Office of Legal Affairs (OLA), included an article on the financial responsibility of the Secretary-General stating that a UN Trust Fund would be created to receive voluntary contributions from the member states and, more importantly, that, should insufficient funds be provided to the Trust Fund, the UN shall be free from its obligations under the Agreement. That is, it was suggested that in case of lack of funding the Agreement would automatically cease to be binding on the UN. That was clearly unacceptable to the Government of Sierra Leone. The provision was later deleted and the matter was left pending until further consultations with the Council.

On 22 December 2000,[16] the President of the Security Council re-stated the Council's decision to establish the Court as an institution based on voluntary contributions. The Council, however, also suggested as a compromise that the Secretary-General proceed with the set up of the court only after receiving funds for at least 12 months and pledges to cover anticipated expenses for a second year

---

15) *Report of the Secretary-General on the establishment of a Special Court for Sierra Leone* (S/2000/915).

16) *Letter dated 22 December 2000 from the President of the Security Council addressed to the Secretary-General* (S/2000/1234).

of the Court's operation. The Council also agreed to explore alternate means of financing the Court, should voluntary contributions be insufficient to implement its mandate. Finally, the Council proposed the creation of a management or oversight committee "which could include representatives of Sierra Leone, the Secretary-General of the United Nations, the Court and interested voluntary contributors"[17] and that "would assist the court in obtaining adequate funding, provide advice on matters of Court administration and be available as appropriate to consult on other non-judicial matters".[18]

In the end, the UN Secretariat endorsed this approach and two new articles (Articles 6 and 7) were included in the Agreement to reflect the compromise.

1.4. *Budget*

The first budget of the Special Court was the outcome of the interaction between OLA and the Group of Interested States (GIS) that started in March 2001.

At that time, the UN Legal Counsel briefed member states on the status of the negotiations for the establishment of the SCSL and suggested the creation of a group of states with a particular interest in the matter, including Sierra Leone, that would convene regularly to consider the practical arrangements required for the actual commencement of the Court's activities, including its budget and administrative arrangements. The Legal Counsel also submitted for the consideration of the GIS a budget proposal drafted by OLA's Executive Office envisaging overall financial requirements of USD 114 million over three years.[19]

Having reviewed the draft budget, key GIS members requested from OLA an explanation of the assumptions at its basis and expressed concern over its size. In the course of subsequent meetings, OLA explained that the SCSL budget was based on parameters similar to the ones used for the first budgets of the ICTY/R, and that it assumed that UN salary packages and procurement rules would apply.

States' determination to move away from the ICTY/R, however, manifested itself also in their opposition to estimates that would essentially duplicate the budgets of those tribunals without questioning their underlying assumptions, or adjusting them to the specific mandate of the court and the costs of operations in Sierra Leone. Eventually, states indicated their intention to work within the framework of a budget in the range of USD 15-18 million per year, and new estimates for an overall amount of USD 56.8 million were preliminary endorsed by the GIS.[20]

---

17) *Ibid.*, para. 2.

18) *Ibid.*

19) The exact figures proposed for the first three years were: USD 30,155,677, USD 42,550,367 and USD 41,896,315 respectively.

20) The revised figures were USD 16.8 million for the first year of operations, USD 20.4 million for the second year and USD 19.5 million for the third year.

As explained by the Secretary-General in his letter to the President of the Security Council dated 12 July 2001,[21]

> [t]he revised budget estimates reflect a scaled-down operation of the Special Court, while maintaining its nature and sui generis character, international standards of justice and the applicable law. A combination of factors including a different basis for calculation of salaries, a reduction in the normal rates of programme backstopping and contingency requirements, as well as a reliance on Sierra Leonean institutions and personnel, and on UNAMSIL administrative and security capacity, at least in the initial start-up phase, resulted in the reduction of the budget estimates.

In November 2001, following two appeals for contributions to the Special Court,[22] the Secretary-General informed the President of the Security Council[23] that "[...] the Secretariat has received contributions in the amount of US$ 14.8 million for the first year — a shortfall of $1.4 million — and pledges in the amounts of $13.0 million and $7.4 million for the two subsequent years — a shortfall of approximately $19.6 million". The Secretary-General further determined that these amounts constituted sufficient funds to start the Court's operations.

Nevertheless, already at the beginning of its second fiscal year, the SCSL budget estimates had to be revised. In presenting the Special Court's budget requirements for the period 1 July 2003 to 30 June 2004, the Court's Registrar indicated that the need to establish a second Trial Chamber, the actual construction costs of the premises and level of staff required, as well as the absence of any substantial support from UNAMSIL to the Court's operational and administrative needs meant that the Court could only achieve its goals with a different level of resources and suggested a figure of USD 34,705,626 versus the initial estimate of USD 20,414,095. The final approved budget amounted to USD 32,534,571.

The approved budgets for the following years amount to: USD 29,963,685 (1 July 2004 to 30 June 2005); USD 25,539,700 (1 July 2005 to 30 June 2006); USD 16,895,900 (this was a six month budget covering the period 1 July 2006 to 31 December 2006); USD 36,003,900 (1 January – 31 December 2007); USD 36,124,200 (1 January – 31 December 2008); USD 28,349,250 million (1 January – 31 December 2009); USD 21,741,200 million (1 January – 31 December 2010); USD 16,013,400 (1 January – 31 December 2011); and USD 9,066,400 (1 January – 31 July 2012).

1.5. *Availability of Funding*

The SCSL has been in many respects a successful organisation. Its indictments were filed less than a year after the arrival of the Prosecutor to Freetown, and trials

---

21) *Letter dated 12 July 2001 from the Secretary-General addressed to the President of the Security Council* (S/2001/693).

22) On 23 March and 18 June 2001.

23) *Letter dated 26 December 2001 from the Secretary-General to the President of the Security Council* (S/2001/1320).

started within two years of the Court's establishment. Sierra Leoneans were recruited at all levels and contributed significantly to the work of the Court and made it a truly mixed institution. In addition, the Court was run on a shoe-string: after almost ten years of operations, the overall cost of the SCSL is about USD 250 million for trials including that of former Liberian President Charles Taylor. Finally, the Court established a unique outreach program and became in that respect a model for other international criminal tribunals. All this, while working under challenging logistical circumstances in a country that had only recently ended a ten year long conflict, and in the midst of security concerns and a lack of basic infrastructure.

Despite its achievements, the horrific nature of the crimes under its jurisdiction and the active role played by the Sierra Leonean Government in advocating in favour of the Court, the SCSL has faced constant and serious financial uncertainty. The international community's continually changing priorities combined with the prolongation of the court's legal proceedings well beyond the initial mandate of three years, together with related questions as to the efficiency of its trials,[24] have made it harder and harder to muster the required level of voluntary contributions and have forced the Court to revert to the UN assessed budget for supplementary resources.

As of 2012, approximately fifty States contributed to the operations of the SCSL. However, the majority of these contributions (approximately 75%) have ranged from few thousand dollars to USD 500,000, and most of the SCSL financial weight (almost two-thirds) has been borne by few states (mainly, Canada, the Netherlands, the UK, and the USA). In addition, contributions have been received on an irregular basis, often leaving the Court with a few weeks worth of funding and creating the need to slow down its expenditures and activities.

On three occasions, the financial situation grew so dire that the SCSL had to make use of Article 6 of the Agreement, and refer the matter to the Secretary-General. In all instances, the Secretary-General wrote to the President of the Security Council seeking the Council's authorization to refer the issue to the General Assembly, and requesting a grant to procure all or part of the funding needed by the Court. The Secretary-General, moreover, suggested that funding was to be provided from the un-earmarked balance of the provisions for his special political missions under section three (Political Affairs) of the UN programme budget.

It should be noted that these initiatives were taken with the understanding that the subvention requests would not affect the independence and structure of the Court, as established by the Agreement between the UN and the Government of

---

24) *See* Antonio Cassese, *Independent Expert Report on the Special Court for Sierra Leone,* 12 December 2006, <www.sc-sl.org/LinkClick.aspx?fileticket=VTDHyrHasLc=&tabid=176>, 10 September 2012.

Sierra Leone. That is, it was clear to all parties that temporarily receiving assessed contributions from the United Nations would not bring the SCSL under the UN administration or alter its legal status.

In 2004, after the submission of a report on the matter from the Secretary-General,[25] and its consideration by the ACABQ and the UN Fifth Committee, the General Assembly adopted Resolution 59/276[26] authorising a disbursement up to USD 20 million to supplement the financial resources of the SCSL from 1 January to 30 June 2005, and Resolution 59/294[27] authorizing the disbursement of an additional USD 13 million for the period 1 July to 31 December 2005.

In 2010, the Secretary-General reported to the General Assembly[28] that because of its financial difficulties, the SCSL did not have resources to operate past the end of that year, and again requested a subvention of up to USD 17,916,560 to cover the period from 1 November 2010 to 29 February 2012, when the SCSL was expected to complete its work.[29]

The decision on the 2010 funding was taken by the General Assembly following a letter of the President of the Security Council that informed the Secretary-General that the Council's members had no objection to further supplementary funding to the SCSL, but also indicated their expectation that there would not be any additional subvention and that the UN Secretariat, the Management Committee and the Registrar and other senior officials of the Court would intensify their efforts to fund future requirements of the SCSL through voluntary contributions.

In 2011, the Secretary-General reverted to the General Assembly once more. He indicated[30] that, due to unforeseen circumstances, the Court would only complete its mandate by July 2012 (rather than by February 2012, as previously estimated). He also informed the Assembly that, despite continued fundraising efforts, as of November 2011, the SCSL had no funds pledged for 2012.[31] The Secretary-General thus requested an additional subvention grant in the amount of USD 9,066,400.

In the meantime, the SCSL completion date has continued to shift. At the end of May 2012, the Taylor's trial ended with his sentencing to 50 years. Appeals are

---

25) *Report of the Secretary General on a Requerst for a subvention grant to the Special Court for Sierra Leone* (A/58/733).

26) UN General Assembly Resolution 276 (A/RES/59/276).

27) UN General Assembly Resolution 294 (A/RES/59/294).

28) *Report of the Secretary General on a Request for a subvention to the Special Court for Sierra Leone* (A/65/570).

29) The General Assembly approved the allocation of USD 15.56 million for the period 1 November 2010 to 31 December 2011, and USD 2.3 million for the period January-February 2012. *See* General Assembly Resolution 259 (A/RES/65/259), Section XII, 2010.

30) *Report of the Secretary General on a Request for a subvention to the Special Court for Sierra Leone* (A/66/563).

31) *Ibid.*, para. 19.

likely to be submitted to the Appeals Chamber by both the Prosecution and the Defence and will require several months before final deliberations take place. At the time of writing, the additional time and funding requirements of the SCSL are not yet know.

In any event, it should be stressed that, despite the recent reliance on assessed contributions, the SCSL has been able to work on the basis of voluntary contributions for two thirds of its life – even if amidst great financial uncertainty. That required the Registrars and other officials of the SCSL to devote substantial part of their time to fundraising, elaborating strategies, holding meetings in New York and various Capitals and targeting states from all regional groups. Since 2007, the SCSL started listing, as part of its Annual Reports, the number of fundraising meetings held every year, and it is estimated that during the period 2009 – 2010 alone, SCSL officials held over 174 fund-raising meetings and 225 fund-raising appeals were addressed to potential donors.[32]

1.6. *Administrative Structure*

The SCSL has been the first international criminal court established outside the UN administration. Nevertheless, when the Security Council considered the funding mechanism of the SCSL, little attention was given to the details of its administrative and oversight structure. As a result, different options were discussed by the Group of Interested states, the Government of Sierra Leone and the UN Secretariat with regard to the creation of an oversight committee, its legal basis and precise functions, and the court's exact administrative arrangements.

The Security Council had first suggested the creation of a Management Committee to the Secretary-General as a way to appease his concerns on the viability of voluntary contributions and to share fundraising responsibility.

Whilst, a few years later, the creation of a Steering Committee for the ECCC and a Management Committee for the STL were considered uncontroversial, at the time of the establishment of the SCSL the idea of a Management Committee was almost 'revolutionary' and it required lengthy negotiations before being implemented.[33] Terms of Reference for the Management Committee were eventually adopted in August 2001. They envisaged the creation of the Committee as an informal arrangement that, nonetheless, had a real decision making authority on all non-judicial matters including providing advice and policy direction on all institutional aspects of its operations; overseeing the Special Court's annual budget

---

32) *Report of the Secretary General on a Request for a subvention to the Special Court for Sierra Leone* (A/65/570), para. 16.

33) *See* Phakiso Mochochoko and Giorgia Tortora, 'The Management Committee for the Special Court for Sierra Leone', in Cesare Romano, Andre Nollkaemper and Jann K. Kleffner (eds.), *Internationalized Criminal Courts and Tribunals* (Oxford University Press, 2004), pp. 141-156.

and other financially related reports; advising the Secretary-General on these matters; and assisting the Secretary-General in ensuring that adequate funds are available for the operation of the Special Court.

In parallel to the discussion on the Management Committee's Terms of Reference, the major donors in the GIS advocated for themselves (and later, for the Committee) the authority to review the Court's administrative arrangements, including its financial regulations and rules, salary packages and the specific responsibilities of the Registrar. Donors assumed that, given the *sui generis* nature of the SCSL, the UN would assist in identifying court-specific financial arrangements that would ensure both cost-effectiveness and accountability. However, after a number of crucial decisions on financial and personnel matters had been taken, the UN Office of the Controller clarified that, because the SCSL funds had been collected in a UN Trust Fund under his responsibility, all UN financial regulations and rules, as well as staff regulations and rules, would have to apply without exception. The states that would constitute the future members of the MC[34] fought to find alternative arrangements. Indeed, they were aware that running the Court as part of the standard UN system would have re-created the same problems faced by the ad hoc tribunals and would have made it impossible for the Court to carry out its mandate within the budgetary limits identified as acceptable by the donor community.

At that point, the viability of other options was discussed, including subcontracting the administration of the Court to other UN agencies and have the Court run as one of their field projects. In the end, six months after the signing of the Agreement between the Secretary-General and the Government of Sierra Leone,[35] the Controller accepted to relinquish control of the Court's administration and transfer the resources in the UN Trust Fund to the Court itself.[36] The SCSL Registrar was thus authorised by the Management Committee to administer the Court's funds directly, and amend the UN regulations and rules in consultations with the Committee. In addition, the Committee confirmed its initial decisions on the SCSL salary packages and the level of the required posts, thus creating a regime different from the one applied throughout the UN system, and entrusted the Registrar with the mandate to implement them. The UN administration in the meantime severed any link with the SCSL and its management.

The administrative structure thus put in place at the SCSL accorded to the Registrar primary responsibility for the correct management of the court's

---

34) In November 2001, the GIS selected as Management Committee members Canada, Lesotho, the Netherlands, Nigeria, the United Kingdom and the United States.

35) The Agreement was signed in Freetown, Sierra Leone, on 16 January 2002.

36) According to the UN Financial Regulations and Rules, the Controller could only transfer the money in the Trust Fund to another UN entity. The post of SCSL Registrar was thus established as UN post in order to make him responsible for the funds' administration.

resources and personnel and its overall efficiency, as well as a strong direct oversight role for the Management Committee – which assumed functions similar to those performed by the ACABQ and the Fifth Committee vis-à-vis the UN. In addition, the Court was to submit to regular internal and external audits by independent institutions. The model – which relies heavily on the competence and skills of the Registrar and the personal commitment of states' representatives on the Committee – has proven in practice to be a well functioning one and was later to be adopted also by the Special Tribunal for Lebanon.

2. The Extraordinary Chambers in the Courts of Cambodia

2.1. *Introduction*

Despite the relevance of its mandate and its important role for the Cambodian society overall, the Extraordinary Chambers in the Courts of Cambodia has surely been, among all the hybrid tribunals, the most troubled one: the negotiations on its establishment took approximately six years; a further two years were needed to adopt its rules of procedure and evidence; its administration has been marred, until recently, by a mix of inefficiency, lack of adequate oversight and corruption; and of late the beginning of cases 003 and 004 has been hampered by allegations of judicial misconduct[37] and interference by the Cambodian Government.

As the SCSL, the Extraordinary Chambers were established through a bilateral agreement between the UN and the Government that requested the tribunal. However, the Extraordinary Chambers is a domestic entity with international assistance. It is part of the Cambodia judiciary, rather than an independent international institution. As in the case of the SCSL, the Extraordinary Chambers are funded through voluntary contributions from member states. However, unlike the SCSL, Cambodia bears the responsibility to finance part of the operations – even if, in practice, Cambodia's contribution has been limited to providing the Chambers' premises and a minimal portion of the costs for the national component of the Chambers.

Moreover, while the SCSL administration operates independently of the UN system, in Cambodia the international component of the Chambers is managed as a UN project. In addition, a UN agency oversees voluntary international contributions made in support of the national component of the Chambers.

This section will review in detail the specific financial and administrative arrangements in place at the Extraordinary Chambers, and the decision making

---

[37] Open Society Justice Initiative (OSI JI), *Recent Developments at the Extraordinary Chambers in the Courts of Cambodia: June 2011 Update,* as well as *Recent Developments at the Extraordinary Chambers in the Courts of Cambodia: November 2011 Update.*

process that brought them into being. It will also consider the circumstances surrounding the financial crises faced by the Extraordinary Chambers and the 'emergency' interventions undertaken, on the one hand, to address its shortcomings and, on the other, to ensure an adequate flow of resources. Finally, this section will argue that most of the Extraordinary Chambers funding difficulties and management problems originated from the intrinsic weaknesses of the Chambers' model, the absence of adequate supervision by both the UN and member states, and the lack of coordination between its international and national components. Indeed, the interaction between Cambodia and the UN in the Extraordinary Chambers did not result in an integrated institution but in a body comprised of two distinct components, hardly coordinating between themselves, and operating under different rules and lines of responsibility.

2.2. *The Negotiations*

On 21 June 1997, the co-Prime Ministers of the Royal Government of Cambodia, Hun Sen and Prince Rannaridh, wrote to the Secretary-General of the United Nations to request the assistance of the UN in bringing to justice those responsible for committing genocide and crimes against humanity during the period of the Khmer Rouge regime from 1975 to 1979.[38] The letter called for the establishment by the UN of an international tribunal similar in character to those for the former Yugoslavia and Rwanda, that is, to a UN subsidiary body with a full international character and mandate. Cambodia, however, later moved away from this model and, on 15 June 1999, requested the UN to provide experts that would assist the country in drafting a law allowing the establishment of a special domestic Cambodian court with the participation of foreign judges and prosecutors.[39]

The General Assembly, rather than the Security Council,[40] first considered the matter in December 1997 and, with Resolution 52/135, accepted Cambodia's request for assistance and mandated the Secretary-General to explore ways of providing it.

The negotiations were eventually concluded in 2004.[41] On 12 June 2004, the UN and the Government of Cambodia signed the Agreement establishing the

---

38) *See Report of the Group of Experts for Cambodia established pursuant to General Assembly resolution 52/135,* (A/53/850 - S/1999/231), para. 5.

39) *See* Statement by the UN Legal Counsel, Hans Corell, at a press briefing in New York, 8 February 2002, <www.un.org/News/dh/infocus/cambodia/corell-brief.htm>, 19 September 2012.

40) The General Assembly considered the matter as part of its wider review of the human rights situation in Cambodia and overall UN support to the implementation of the Paris agreement. In the case of the SCSL, the Security Council – which had already been dealing with the Sierra Leonean conflict – was the UN Secretariat's major counterpart.

41) *See Report of the Secretary-General on Khmer Rouge Trials* (A/57/769).

Extraordinary Chambers in the Courts of Cambodia (ECCC) as a domestic court with international assistance. The Agreement entered into force on 29 April 2005. The ECCC began its operations in February 2006.

2.3. *The Funding Mechanism*

The modalities of the international participation in the ECCC proceedings and the financial responsibility of the parties were spelled out in the Agreement establishing the Extraordinary Chambers.

The Agreement, for example, stated that the Government of Cambodia shall be responsible for providing the premises and related services (Article 14) and for funding salaries and emoluments of Cambodian judges and other Cambodian personnel (Article 15).

The UN shall instead be responsible for a) the remuneration of the international judges, the international co-investigating judge, the international co-prosecutor, the Deputy Director of the Office of Administration and other international personnel; b) costs for utilities and services as agreed separately between the United Nations and the Royal Government of Cambodia; c) remuneration of defence counsel; d) witnesses' travel from within Cambodia and from abroad; e) safety and security arrangements as agreed separately between the United Nations and the Government; as well as f) such other limited assistance as may be necessary to ensure the smooth functioning of the investigation, the prosecution and the Extraordinary Chambers (Articles 16 and 17).

Nevertheless, at the time the Agreement was finalised, the issue of how to fund the ECCC expenses to be borne by the UN was still unresolved, with different options supported by the Secretary-General and the member states respectively. As in the case of the SCSL, the Secretary-General advocated in favour of assessed contributions as a predictable and stable financial mechanism to fund the international staff and judges of the Tribunal and sustain investigations, prosecutions and trials. The member states continued to favour voluntary contributions.

In Resolution 57/228 of February 2003, the General Assembly recorded once again states' widespread opposition to funding any new tribunal through the UN regular budget, and requested the Secretary-General to submit estimates as to the level of voluntary contributions required to support the work of the Extraordinary Chambers.

Responding to such request in his Report of March 2003,[42] the Secretary-General expressed the view that '[...] an operation of this nature, mandated by Member States, would constitute an expense of the Organisation under Article 17 of the Charter of the United Nations and should be financed by assessed

---

42) *Ibid.*, para. 74.

contributions". Nonetheless, the Secretary-General also clarified that, should the General Assembly require that the United Nations assistance to the ECCC be funded through voluntary contributions, the process of establishing the Chambers could only start after sufficient funding was made available for a sustained period of time.

On 13 May 2003, the General Assembly adopted resolution 57/228B approving the agreement concerning the prosecution of crimes committed during the period of the Democratic Kampuchea and deciding, contrary to the recommendation of the Secretary-General, that the expenses to be borne by the UN should be funded through voluntary contributions from member states.

It must be further noted that, soon after the establishment of the ECCC, the UN de facto 'waived' the provisions in the Agreement regarding the Cambodian financial responsibility towards the Extraordinary Chambers. Eager to see the beginning of the ECCC operations after lengthy negotiations, and aware of the conditions of the Cambodian economy,[43] the UN realised that the Cambodian Government could not be expected to mobilize in a useful timeframe the resources necessary to meet their obligations under Article 15. The UN, and member states, thus did not object to donors' interventions to cover the costs of the Cambodian part of the operations. In this context, the issue of Cambodia's non-compliance with its legal obligations was never raised and, contrary to the international community's initial wishes to experiment with a mixed funding system, the ECCC turned into an institution almost entirely funded via voluntary contributions from states other than Cambodia.

2.4. *Budget*

In December 2004, the United Nations announced that an accord had been reached with the Government of Cambodia on a budget of USD 56.3 million for three years of operations. Of this amount, USD 43 million was to be paid by the United Nations and USD 13.3 million by the Government of Cambodia.

A pledging conference was convened by the Secretary-General on 28 March 2005. Thirteen countries pledged contributions totalling approximately USD 38,477,033[44] and the Secretary-General later confirmed that adequate funding had

---

43) Cambodia still belongs to the group of the Least Developed Countries and its economy ranks 187th for per capita income.

44) Contributions were received from: Japan (USD 21, 600,000), France (USD 4,800,00), Australia (USD 2,351,097), Canada (USD 1,612,903), Germany (USD 1,000,000), Holland (USD 1,981,506), Denmark (USD 531,914), Luxembourg (USD 66,050), Austria (USD 360,000), Sweden (USD 150,000), United Kingdom (USD 2,873,563), Norway (USD1,000,000), and Republic of Korea (USD 150,000). *See* ECCC Press release *Pledging conference for the Extraordinary Chambers for the Khmer Rouge Trials at the United Nations Secretariat in New York*, <www.eccc.gov.kh/fr/chronlologies/pledging-conference-extraordinary-chambers-khmer-rouge-trials-united-nations-secretari>, 19 September 2012.

been made available for the purpose of establishing the ECCC.[45] These contributions were supplemented by more than USD 5 million left over from the United Nations Transitional Authority in Cambodia (UNTAC), which the original donors agreed to transfer to the national side of the ECCC.

The initial budget estimates, however, soon had to be reconsidered. According to the Open Society Institute Justice Initiative (OSI JI),[46] already in October 2006 it was evident that the estimates were inadequate. Firstly, as a result of the delay in the commencement of legal activity, the ECCC was not going to be able to complete its work within three years. Second, the original figures had either underestimated the actual needs of certain sections, such as outreach or witness protection, or had omitted a number of crucial items related to the work of the chambers and other units.

In January 2008, the ECCC released a revised budget, requesting approximately USD 113.7 million in addition to the original budget of USD 56.3 million, for a total budget of USD 170 million to cover its operations until March 2011.[47] The revised estimates were ill-received. Donors were already frustrated by the lack of progress in the work of the Chambers, reports of inefficiencies in the administration of the UN side, and mounting allegations of corruption. It was thus made clear by member states that additional financial, and political, support would be forthcoming only if those issues were addressed.

As a consequence of the submission of the new figures, and the reaction they provoked, the UN accelerated its decision to select an independent expert to review the Chamber's trial capacity and planning, as well as the assumptions at the basis of the budget. In March 2008, the UN Secretary-General appointed David Tolbert, the former Deputy Prosecutor for the International Criminal Tribunal for the former Yugoslavia, to act for a three month period[48] as his expert adviser on ECCC issues. Tolbert's mandate included reviewing and streamlining the operations of the UN side of the court as well as the ECCC's overall budget.

Tolbert reported *inter alia* that the ECCC estimates did not reflect a clear and well-thought through action plan, but rather a collection of wish lists from different organs both on the international and domestic side. He introduced a new budget preparation methodology which took into account the projected timeline of the cases, the data on the number of witnesses to be interviewed and documents to be introduced in the proceedings, and the relative complexity of the cases, as well as a comparison with the staffing and resources requirements of other hybrid tribunals, especially the SCSL.

---

45) *See Report of the Secretary-General on Khmer Rouge Trials* (A/60/565) para. 3.
46) *See* OSI JI *Priority Issues for the ECCC*, October 2006.
47) *See* OSI JI *Recent Developments at the Extraordinary Chambers in the Courts of Cambodia*, February 2008.
48) Tolbert's mandate was later extended to almost seven months.

As a result, the financial requirements for the first three years of operations were revised downward, and a new budget in the amount of USD 44.1 million for the period 2005-2009 was adopted.[49] In addition, the budget for 2010-2011 was completely redrafted. On 23 February 2010, donors approved a total amount of USD 92.3 million, including contingency, of which USD 45.5 million was for 2010 and USD 46.8 million was for 2011. A further revised budget, accounting for savings or deferred expenditures in 2010, was approved in January 2011 in the amount of USD 75.4 million, with USD 32.1million requested for 2010 and USD 43.3 million for 2011. The international component of the ECCC accounted for USD 23 million for 2010 and USD 30.8 million for 2011. The national component accounted for USD 7.9 million for 2010 and USD 9.9 million for 2011.[50]

On 25 May 2010, a pledging conference presided by the UN Secretary-General raised USD 17 million and ensured that sufficient resources were granted to the ECCC to continue in its work until the end of 2011.

According to information available on the ECCC website, as of April 2012, about 30 countries have provided funding to the Chambers. Japan donated 52% of all international contributions, with other major donations coming from Australia, France, Germany, the United Kingdom, and the United States of America.

The Government of Cambodia for its part has made available the premises of the ECCC and its detention facilities, and has covered the cost of utilities and other services necessary for their operation. However, the Government has not otherwise been in a position to pay for the salaries and emoluments of Cambodian judges and personnel. In total, the Cambodian Government contributed about 17%, or USD 6.1 million, of the national side's costs of the ECCC. Japan[51] and, to a lesser extent, the European Union[52] are currently the major donors to the Cambodian portion of the budget.

At the time of writing, the ECCC has just begun the trial of case 002, which is unlikely to be completed before 2015.[53] The possibility of bringing case 003 and

---

49) *See* ECCC revised 2005-2009 budget, <www.unakrt-online.org/04_documents.htm#Budget>, 19 September 2012.

50) It should be noted, however, that in 2010 and 2011 the final expenditures were lower than the authorised budgets. For details, *see* ECCC Revised Budget Requirements 2010-11, <www.eccc.gov.kh/sites/default/files/revised_budget_eccc_2010-2011.pdf>, 19 September.

51) Overall, Japan contributed 39%, or approximately USD 12.4 million, to the national side of the budget.

52) The European Union contributed 12%, or approximately USD 3.7 million, to the national side of the budget.

53) On 22 September 2011, the ECCC Trial Chamber issued a *Severance Order pursuant to Internal Rule 88ter* suggesting the separation of the proceedings in case 002 into smaller trials, starting with a consideration of the allegations of forced transfer of the population and related crimes against humanity. It is estimated that case 002 would comprise four trials. A conservative estimate of one year per trial implies that the completion of case 002 may require at least four to five years from its official opening (in November 2011). Note also that the ECCC

004 to trial is also still being discussed. The estimated financial requirements for the next financial cycle of the ECCC (2012-2013) amount to approximately USD 40 million a year for both components. As of June 2012, the ECCC is facing a shortfall of nearly USD 20 million for 2012.

2.5. *Administrative Structure and Oversight Mechanisms*

In order to manage the international assistance to the ECCC, in 2005 the UN established a project (the UN project of Assistance to Khmer Rouge Trials, or UNAKRT), under its Department of Social Affairs (DESA). Subject to the overall authority of the UN Controller, UNAKRT receives and disburses contributions to the ECCC international component, offers technical advice on a range of administrative matters from budgetary issues to human resources, and acts as the main point of contact between the UN Secretariat and the ECCC.

With regard to funds for the national side, in 2006 it was decided that they were to be received and disbursed through a UN entity – the United Nations Development Fund (UNDP) first and United Nations Office for Project Services (UNOPS) later – to address donors' reluctance to contribute directly to the Cambodian Government for this purpose.

The ECCC also established its own administrative apparatus to service the Chambers, the Pre-Trial Chamber, the co-investigating Judges, and the Prosecutor, under the guidance of a Cambodian Director and an international Deputy Director. In accordance with Article 8(2) of the Agreement, the Director is responsible for the overall management of the office of administration except in matters that are subject to UN rules and procedure. The Deputy Director, on the other hand, is responsible for the recruitment of the international staff and the administration of the international component of the ECCC (Article 8(3)). Article 8(4) stipulates that the 'Director and the Deputy Director shall cooperate to ensure an effective and efficient functioning of the administration'.

No ECCC-specific arrangements were, however, envisaged to ensure the Chamber's financial efficiency and accountability. That is, contrary to the case of the SCSL, no arrangements were negotiated to replicate the oversight functions that the ACABQ and General Assembly's Fifth Committee exercise in the case of bodies funded through assessed contributions. No one was given overall oversight authority over the budget preparation and approval processes, the management of the funds provided, and the monitoring of the ECCC's performance.

It appears that this situation resulted from a number of assumptions on the part of states on the safeguards offered by the mere presence of UN administrative staff in Cambodia, the application of UN financial regulations and rules, as well as

2010-2011 budget approved on 23 February 2010 provided in its Annex A (Indicative Court Schedule) that the Court will continue its work until 2015.

the capacity of the UN trust funds to act as a 'filter' and ensure the accountability and transparency of the ECCC's management. In addition, member states seemed initially satisfied with minimal involvement in the work of the ECCC and the informal (and superficial) reporting from the Chambers to representatives of interested states in Phnom Penh, called the 'Group of Friends'.[54]

However, the minimal administrative safeguards and member states' involvement in the management of the ECCC soon proved inadequate. The multiplicity of actors involved from the UN side, the lack of clear reporting lines, and the absence of an oversight mechanism created an environment prone to inefficiencies. This situation was further exacerbated by the almost total lack of cooperation between the ECCC's national and international administrations. Rather than working together, the two administrations developed in isolation, one under the control of the Cambodian Director of Administration and the other under the international Deputy.

In 2007, facing mounting criticism of the inefficiency of the UN component of the administration, the United Nations Office of Legal Affairs appointed Robin Vincent, former Registrar of the Special Court for Sierra Leone, and Steve St. Louis, Chief of Administration for the International Criminal Tribunal for the Former Yugoslavia, to review the ECCC's readiness for trial. As part of their assessment, these experts also considered the administrative structure and its leadership. The summary of recommendations of the experts' report criticized the lack of a clear allocation of responsibilities between the international Director and the Cambodian Deputy Director of administration, the absence of an effective decision making process, as well as insufficient progress in the areas of witness protection, security, media policy, external and internal communications, and reporting to UNHQ (for the international side). In addition, the experts' report recommended undertaking a comprehensive review of the ECCC's budget and staffing table.

In the same period, UNDP conducted an internal audit as a result of concerns regarding human resources practices at the ECCC. The report did not deal with the emerging allegations of widespread kick-back systems[55] and corruption because these allegations did 'not pertain to holders of UNDP letters of appointment but personnel of the Government of Cambodia and therefore fall outside UNDP's jurisdiction'.[56] Nevertheless, it identified a number of issues that had to be addressed, including ineffective monitoring and oversight by the UNDP project's

---

54) The Group of Friends began meeting in August 2006. The meeting was convened jointly by the French and Japanese Missions.

55) The main accusations referred to the existence of a mechanism that would require Cambodian personnel, including judges, to pay back a percentage of their salary (up to thirty percent) to members of the Cambodian government in exchange for their appointment.

56) UNDP Special Report on *Human Resources Management at the Extraordinary Chambers in the Court of Cambodia*, 4 June 2007.

board, poor documentation/justification of recruitments and unjustified (and, according to the budget, unauthorised) staffing levels. Eventually, in July 2010, UNDP closed its ECCC trust fund and UNOPS started providing financial management, monitoring and evaluation services to key donors contributing to the national side.

Despite the Vincent – St. Louis and UNDP reports, steps towards reform were not taken until 2008 when, as discussed above, David Tolbert was appointed as expert and donors urged the UN to implement anti-corruption measures, whilst assuming for themselves a stronger monitoring role over the non-judicial aspects of the ECCC's work.

2.6. *Anti-corruption Measures*

As allegations of corruption at the ECCC continued to spread, international and Cambodian non-governmental organisations started to request publicly an intervention of the United Nations. The United Nations Office of Internal Oversight Services (OIOS) also reviewed complaints received by several Cambodian staff members and, in August 2008, provided a confidential report with its findings to the Cambodian Government. In response, the Government of Cambodia questioned the UN authority to investigate allegations concerning the national side of the Chambers. Nevertheless, the UN – aware that failure to act on this issue would have deprived the ECCC of the support of key states and dramatically reduced its donor base – insisted on starting negotiations with the Cambodians on the establishment of anti-corruption measures.

On 8 April 2009, the UN[57] announced that the Assistant Secretary-General for Legal Affairs had proposed to the Cambodian authorities an ethics monitoring mechanism for the ECCC designed to address 'suggestions' of corruption at the ECCC, and grant to the ECCC staff the ability to approach any ethics monitor on their own and make statements without fear of retaliation. On 12 August 2009, the UN and the Cambodian Government announced that Uth Chorn, a former Auditor General of Cambodia, had been jointly appointed as Independent Counsellor with the mandate to receive future corruption complaints from both the international and national component of the Chambers. The position is equally funded by Cambodia and the UN.

2.7. *Appointment of Special Adviser*

The concerns about the ECCC also led the UN Office of Legal Affairs to advocate for a more direct and regular involvement on the part of the UN in the oversight of

57) <www.un.org/apps/news/story.asp?NewsID=30431&Cr=cambodia&Cr1=.)>, 19 September 2012.

the Chambers, in order to monitor future developments, advise the Secretary-General on issues of significance to the fulfilment of the Court's mandate and take the lead in the implementation of its fundraising strategy. As a result, the UN created the position of 'special adviser' as an effective counterpart for the Cambodian government and donor states.

According to the post's Terms of Reference, the special adviser shall provide assistance on issues regarding the ECCC at the senior level including development of an adequate fundraising strategy, maintaining regular high level contacts with the Cambodian authorities, and monitoring the effectiveness of the Independent Counsellor function. The special adviser reports to the UN Secretary-General through the Controller, while keeping also DESA and the Legal Counsel informed of all matters arising in the course of the discharge of his functions. In effect, this measure sought to remedy the absence of an UN-appointed Registrar in the ECCC.

In July 2010, following a decision by the USA and the Netherlands to finance the position (the post is funded through earmarked voluntary contributions), the Secretary-General appointed as his special adviser Clint Williamson, former US Ambassador for War Crimes. In January 2012, David Scheffer, also a former US Ambassador for War Crimes, was appointed as his successor.

2.8. *The Steering Committee and the Principal Donors Group*

The donors sought to reshape their relationship with the ECCC and provide greater guidance to the Chambers on financial and administrative matters. In 2008, the ECCC's major donors, including representatives of Cambodia, constituted in New York a Group of Interested States (GIS) mandated to review progress reports from the Chambers and provide advice on the ECCC's non-judicial matters. In order to streamline the GIS' decision making progress, a Steering Committee was also formed. It is a more restricted group, which reports to the GIS, and is comprised of states that have made significant monetary contributions to the Chambers and expressed a clear political commitment to supporting the UN in providing technical assistance to the Chambers. According to its Terms of Reference, the Chair of the Steering Committee is to rotate among its members on a quarterly basis and its functions include: a) reviewing the implementation of the Court's work plan, monitoring its progress and providing strategic guidance; b) reviewing budgetary requirements prior to submission to the GIS and review other financial documentation relating to income and expenditures; c) reviewing and considering recommendations emanating from the UNDP/ECCC project board; d) briefing the GIS of the outcome of Steering Committee's meetings, including the recommendations made; and e) assisting the Chambers in its fundraising activities. The Steering Committee presently comprises Australia, Cambodia, France, Germany, Japan, the United Kingdom and the United States, as well as representatives of the UN Office of Legal Affairs, DESA, the Controller's Office, and the Special Adviser to the Secretary-General.

Compared to the Management Committee of the SCSL, the Steering Committee is a more informal arrangement. It has no basis in the Agreement establishing the ECCC. It can make recommendations to the GIS, but it cannot take decisions. In practice, it has also proven a less regular forum for discussing crucial matters – which continued to be raised either by individual states with the UN Secretariat or in smaller unofficial settings. In time, therefore, meetings of both the Group of Friends and the Steering Committee have become sporadic and the major donors have started to meet separately as the Principal Donors Group (PDG) - which includes the major donors (Australia, France, Germany, Japan, the United Kingdom and the United States), but excludes Cambodia.

Overall, the experience of the ECCC confirmed the importance of carefully considering the administrative and oversight structure of tribunals funded through voluntary contributions *before* the commencement of their work. Moreover, it exposed the shortcomings associated with managing a complex institution such as the ECCC as a regular UN technical assistance project. Eventually, the strengthening of the donors' and the UN Secretariat's roles in the ECCC administration addressed many of its initial management problems and improved accountability. Six years into its operations, however, the ECCC continues to face a number of challenges including a critical financial situation, whilst trial 002 is still in its initial stages and possible additional cases are yet to begin.

3. The Special Tribunal for Lebanon

3.1. *Introduction*

The Special Tribunal for Lebanon (STL) is the latest addition to the family of hybrid tribunals. As in the cases of the SCSL and the ECCC, its establishment is the result of an initiative taken by the state in which the crimes under its jurisdiction occurred. Its mandate, jurisdiction and specific features are also outlined in an Agreement negotiated by the UN Secretariat and the Government of the state concerned. Also, as in the case of the SCSL, the Tribunal is a fully international and independent judicial body, which retains a strong link with the country where the crimes under its jurisdiction took place through its subject matter jurisdiction, rules of procedure, and judges' nationality.[58]

58) In accordance with its Statute, the STL has jurisdiction over certain crimes under the Lebanese Criminal Code, its Rules of Procedure and Evidence are guided by the Lebanese Code of Criminal Procedure, and four of its judges are Lebanese nationals (one in the Trial Chamber, two in the Appeals Chamber and one alternate).

The STL, however, is the first instance of a tribunal paid by a mixed system of voluntary contributions from the international community and the country that requested its establishment. While the concept of shared financial responsibility for hybrid tribunals had already been introduced with the ECCC, in fact it is only with the STL that a regular contribution from the requesting state has become a reality. This has been an arrangement implemented thanks to the Lebanese leadership's strong commitment to cooperating with the Tribunal - in spite of the political divisions existing in the country over the institution.

Finally, like the SCSL, the STL operates independently of the UN administration. A Registrar has overall responsibility for its administration and a Management Committee oversees its non-judicial functions. However, unlike the SCSL, it applies most UN staff and financial regulations and rules without departures, and with direct implications for its costs of operation.

3.2. *Background*

In February 2005, the former Prime Minister of Lebanon, Rafik Hariri and 21 other individuals were killed when a bomb was detonated near his motorcade. Over two hundred people were injured in the same attack.[59]

In response to that event, in April 2005, the UN Security Council adopted Resolution 1595,[60] establishing an Independent International Investigation Commission (IIIC) to "assist the Lebanese authorities in their investigation of all aspects of this terrorist act, including to help identify its perpetrators, sponsors, organizers and accomplices". The Commission was created within the UN Secretariat under the responsibility of the Department of Political Affairs and was funded through the UN regular budget, as one of the Secretary-General's special political missions.

Subsequently, faced with a growing wave of political violence,[61] the Prime Minister of Lebanon wrote to the UN Secretary-General[62] on 13 December 2005 requesting *inter alia*[63] that the United Nations establish a tribunal of international character to try those responsible for the killing of Mr. Hariri.

---

59) Indictment in the case of the *Prosecutor v. Ayyash et al.*, para. 2.

60) UN Security Council Resolution 1959 (S/RES/1595).

61) Between March and December 2005, fourteen attacks were perpetrated in Lebanon (*see Third report of the International Independent Investigation Commission established pursuant to Security Council Resolutions 1595 (2005), 1636 (2005) and 1644 (2005)*,(S/2006/161), para. 55). On 12 December, the prominent journalist and member of Parliament Gabran Tueni was killed only a day after returning to Lebanon from Paris, where he had moved because of threats to his life.

62) *See Letter dated 13 December 2005 from the Charge' d'Affaires of the Permanent Mission of Lebanon to the United Nations addressed to the Secretary General* (S/2005/783).

63) On the same occasion, the Government of Lebanon also requested an extension of the IIIC's mandate. *Ibid.*

On 29 March 2006, the UN Security Council authorised the Secretary-General to negotiate, as he had proposed, an agreement with the Government of Lebanon[64] to bring into being an international tribunal which would not remove, however, Lebanon's responsibility for seeing justice done.[65] The Agreement establishing the Special Tribunal for Lebanon was finalised in November 2006, and signed by the Government of Lebanon and the United Nations respectively on 23 January and 6 February 2007. In April 2007, however, the Prime Minister of Lebanon, Fouad Siniora, wrote to the Secretary-General lamenting the refusal of the Speaker of the Lebanese parliament to convene a session to formally ratify the bilateral agreement with the United Nations, despite the presence of an express support by the majority of parliament to do so. The Prime Minister further requested the Security Council to consider overcoming the impasse by bringing the Agreement into force through a binding resolution.

On 30 May 2007, the Security Council adopted resolution 1757[66] and, acting under Chapter VII of the UN Charter, decided that the provisions in the Agreement (and the Statute) would enter into force on 10 June 2007. The Special Tribunal officially commenced its operations on 1 March 2009.

3.3. *The Funding Mechanism*

Following discussions in the Security Council on the STL funding mechanism, the opposition to assessed contribution seemed once again to prevail. Even so, in order to appease some of its members' concern with the sustainability of voluntary funding, the Security Council requested the Secretary-General to report on "options for a funding mechanism appropriate to ensure the continued and effective functioning of the tribunal".[67]

In November 2006, the Secretary-General outlined for the Security Council three possible options for the Special Tribunal's funding mechanism: 1) assessed contributions; 2) voluntary contributions; or 3) a combined funding mechanism.

---

64) UN Security Council Resolution 1664 (S/RES/1664).

65) In his report S/2006/176, para. 5, the UN Secretary-General stated that, after consultations with the Lebanese authorities, it had become clear that:

> "[...] the creation of an exclusively international tribunal would remove Lebanese responsibility for seeing justice done regarding a crime that primarily and significantly affected Lebanon. Therefore, it appears that the establishment of a mixed tribunal would best balance the need for Lebanese and international involvement in the work of the tribunal. That balance would be determined by such important characteristics as the tribunal's founding instrument, jurisdiction, applicable law, location, composition and financial arrangements".

66) UN Security Council Resolution 1757 (S/RES/1757).

67) UN Security Council Resolution 1664, (S/RES/1664) para. 3.

Each of these options took into account Lebanon's willingness to provide for a substantial part of the expenses of the Tribunal.[68]

3.3.1. *Assessed Contributions*

The Secretary-General proposed that 'funding through assessed contributions could be in whole or in part'.[69] Under the first scenario, the expenses of the Tribunal would be considered part of the costs of the UN under Article 17 of the Charter and any voluntary contributions from member states, including Lebanon, would be used to finance extra-budgetary activities. Of course, the extension of Article 17 of the Charter to the STL would have brought the Tribunal under the administrative authority of the General Assembly and the UN financial regulations and rules and UN staff regulations and rules.

In the second instance, that is, if assessed contribution were accepted in part, the Secretary-General suggested that fifty-one percent of the expenses of the Tribunal be borne by the United Nations in accordance with Article 17 of the Charter, and forty-nine percent by the Government of Lebanon.

3.3.2. *Voluntary Contributions*

In case voluntary contributions were to be approved as the funding mechanism of the Tribunal, the Secretary-General suggested dividing its expenses between the international community and the Government of Lebanon, so that fifty-one percent of the expenses of the Tribunal would be borne by voluntary contributions from member states and forty-nine percent by the Government of Lebanon.

3.3.3. *Combined Funding Mechanism*

Finally, the Secretary-General included in his report a mixed funding option, which would have extended to the investigations of the STL the funding arrangements already in place with regard to the IIIC. In brief, the Secretary-General suggested that all expenses incurred for the investigations be covered by assessed contributions – as was the case with the IIIC – while all other expenses would be borne by voluntary contributions from member states (fifty-one percent) and the Government of Lebanon (forty-nine percent).

Among the three options, the Secretary-General clearly expressed support for a mechanism based, at least in part, on assessed contributions and reiterated his concerns about voluntary funding as a means of guaranteeing the viability and regularity of the work of international organisations.

---

68) *Report of the Secretary-General on the Establishment of a Special Tribunal for Lebanon* (S/2006/893), paras. 44-51.

69) *Ibid.*, para. 46.

On 24 November 2006, the President of the Security Council wrote to the Secretary-General[70] to welcome the conclusion of negotiations on the establishment of the Tribunal. With regard to funding, the letter indicated the support of Security Council's members for option two, that is, for voluntary contributions as the sole funding mechanism of the Tribunal with fifty-one percent paid by the international community and forty-nine percent by Lebanon. Further, the Council accepted to include in the Agreement wording similar to Article 6 of the Agreement between the United Nations and the Government of Sierra Leone, clarifying that the Secretary-General would only commence the process of creating the Tribunal, after sufficient funds were made available to finance the first twelve months of its operations.

It should, however, be noted that strictly speaking, the STL is only partially funded through voluntary contributions. Lebanon's contribution is not voluntary but rather mandatory. In so far as it is the result of provisions enshrined in an agreement binding on Lebanon (whether in its own right or as an annex to a Security Council resolution under Chapter VII of the UN Charter), Lebanon's failure to honour the payment of its share would amount to a violation of the obligations assumed under the agreement and it could be construed as a failure to cooperate with the Tribunal. This interpretation of Lebanon's financial responsibility has been confirmed by a number of public statements issued by the UN Secretary-General, donors and the STL itself.[71]

In any event, the Security Council's decision to fund the majority of the Tribunal's expenses through voluntary contributions reflected once more states' broader stance on the ICTY and ICTR, and their 'in principle' opposition to assessed contributions for any new tribunal. In the specific circumstances of the Special Tribunal, the decision in favour of voluntary contributions had also the advantage of insulating its work from external pressure. A decision to fund the STL from assessed contributions would have subjected the STL budget to the approval of the General Assembly and its Fifth Committee, where all states are represented – including those who may have feared the reach of the Tribunal. The controversial nature of the Hariri case might thus have exposed the Tribunal to attempts to limit its operations and delay its progress.

3.4. *Budget*

The first budget of the STL was prepared by Robin Vincent, who had been appointed by the United Nations as interim Registrar and tasked with leading the

---

70) *Letter dated 21 November 2006 from the President of the Security Council addressed to the Secretary-General* (S/2006/911).

71) *See*, for example, the interview of the UN Secretary-General by An-Nahar on 17 September 2011; the interview of the UK Ambassador to Lebanon to the *Daily Star* on 1 November 2011; and the interview of the STL Registrar to the *Daily Star* on 26 June 2011.

'advanced team' responsible for putting in place the logistical and administrative infrastructure necessary for the official beginning of the Tribunal's operations. In November 2008, the final budget was presented for the period 1 January-31 December 2009 in the amount of USD 51.4 million. It was approved by the Tribunal's major donors on 12 December 2008.

The total amount set out in the STL's first budget was significantly higher than the first year allocations for the SCSL and the ECCC, mainly as a result of a number of specific assumptions regarding the Tribunal's first year workload and decisions on its administrative structure. First of all, and contrary to the circumstances of other tribunals, the establishment of the STL followed almost four years of investigations by the IIIC and reports to the Security Council on the progress made and leads followed. There was, therefore, a prevailing sense that given the Commission's work, the likely continuity in the leadership that had conducted such investigations on the ground, and the existence of four individuals in detention in Lebanon in connection to their alleged involvement in the Hariri attack, the Tribunal would be able to quickly issue indictments and move from investigations to trials within its first year of activity. As a consequence, the budget for the Tribunal's first year envisaged a fully operational organisation, with all judges coming on board soon after the official commencement of its operations, and a fully functioning court management unit, detention unit, office of the defence and witness protections services.

Second, decisions taken by the UN, the Government of Lebanon and major donors on the STL's location and administrative arrangements, resulted in overall operating costs 'structurally' higher than those of the other hybrid tribunals. For example, whilst the SCSL and the ECCC were established in the countries where the crimes took place, the STL's headquarters is far from the relevant crime scene. This resulted in the need to devote substantial resources to the investigations and their logistical and security arrangements, and to establish a secondary office in Beirut. Also, locating the STL in Europe inevitably increased its costs in areas such as general operating expenditures, security, procurement, construction, etc. In addition, the decision to use three official languages (Arabic, English, and French) rather than only one like the SCSL, added complexity and significant costs. Finally, the STL is aligned with the United Nations common system of salaries, allowances and benefits. In contrast, the SCSL Management Committee had decided to depart from the UN salary and benefit system to contain fixed expenditures. In the case of the ECCC, a similar outcome was pursued via a decision that staff costs for the Cambodian side should be based on Cambodian salary standards.

Since the approved budget largely corresponded to the level of pledges and contributions already received for the Tribunal, the Secretary-General was in a position to swiftly communicate to the Security Council that sufficient funds had been received to start the operations of the Tribunal.

In subsequent years, the approved budget of the STL has been in the following amounts: USD 55.3 million in 2010, USD 65.7 million in 2011, and Euro[72] 55.3 million in 2012.

3.5. *Availability of Funding*

Despite the inevitable uncertainty linked to voluntary contributions, during its first mandate[73] the STL enjoyed a relatively steady level of funding which allowed it to operate without a major financial crisis. In the period 2009-2011, the STL received contributions from twenty-six states representing five continents. Major donors to the Tribunal have been – besides Lebanon – France, Germany, Italy, the United Kingdom, the United States, the European Union and regional states. In addition, in 2009 and 2010, Lebanon paid its part of the budget within a few months of the budget's approval.

In 2011, the Tribunal faced a more difficult situation because Lebanon did not disburse its share of the budget until the end of the fiscal year. Pending payment of forty-nine percent of the budget, and in order to avoid a liquidity crisis that would have stifled the work of the Tribunal, a number of states intervened in its support. In May 2011, the European Union provided the STL a significant contribution from its Instrument for Stability Fund.[74] Other countries as well provided additional resources to bridge the funding gap. At the same time, the Tribunal controlled tightly its expenditures, postponing incurring certain costs until absolutely necessary and carefully planning its vacancy rates and recruitment of new posts, thus contributing to the international community's increased efforts to support its work in 2011.

In 2012, the Lebanese contribution was received in July.[75] Whilst the STL is confident that Lebanon will continue to pay its share of the budget in future years, the exact timing of the disbursements cannot be predicted. As a consequence, it may be useful for the Tribunal to strengthen further its fund-raising strategy, with a view to building a cash surplus that would ensure the seamless progress of its operations, no matter the timing of the Lebanese contribution in each given year.

---

72) In 2012, the Special Tribunal replaced the US Dollar with the Euro as its official currency.

73) In conformity with Article 21 of the Annex to Resolution 1757 (2007), STL was established with an initial mandate of three years. The three years expired on 1 March 2012. On 22 February, the UN Secretary-General renewed the STL mandate for an additional period of three years <www.dailystar.com.lb/News/Politics/2012/Feb-23/164324-un-extends-stl-mandate-for-3-years.ashx#axzz233xQWF36>, 19 September 2012.

74) *See STL Annual Report* (*2011-12*), pp. 20, 27. *Note* also that, whilst the EU had consistently supported other international criminal tribunals in the past, this was the first instance in which it approved such a substantial contribution and the first time EU funding was directed towards a tribunal's core, rather than extra-budgetary, activities.

75) See STL Media Advisory on the payment of the Lebanese contribution <www.stl-tsl.org/en/media/press-releases/11-07-2012-lebanon-2012-contribution>, 19 September 2012.

3.6. *Administrative Structure and Oversight Mechanisms*

The administrative framework of the STL largely replicates the arrangements in place at the SCSL. The Tribunal operates outside the UN system – even if it applies most of the UN financial regulations and rules - and it is subject to the oversight of a Management Committee, as well as to internal and external audits. The functions of the STL Management Committee are similar to those of the SCSL Management Committee and include the provision of policy direction and advice on all non-judicial aspects of the Tribunal's operation, the review and approval of budget and the assistance to the Secretary-General in ensuring that adequate funds are available for the Tribunal's activities.

Unlike the SCSL Management Committee, however, the STL Management Committee was not established by states interested in the work of the Tribunal but rather by the parties to the Agreement on the establishment of the Tribunal. Indeed, Article 7 of the Agreement establishing the SCSL indicates that "interested states will establish" a management committee to assist the Secretary-General in obtaining adequate funding, etc. Article 6 of the Annex to Resolution 1757 (2007) states that "the parties shall consult on the establishment of a Management Committee". The difference is significant. Whilst the idea of a management committee was debated at length at the time of the creation of the SCSL, within a few years of its inclusion in the administrative structure of the Court, had become mainstream 'concept' and a new financial accountability model for international tribunals.

The STL Management Committee comprises nine members: Lebanon, as well as Canada, France, Germany, Italy, Japan, the Netherlands, the United Kingdom and the United States.

Concluding Remarks

Following the establishment of the ad hoc tribunals for the Former Yugoslavia and Rwanda, the governments of Sierra Leone, Cambodia and Lebanon each approached the UN Secretary-General and the Security Council to request the creation of tribunals of international character to assist them in bringing to justice those responsible for the serious crimes that had occurred in their countries.

In each instance, the Security Council rejected the option of creating a new judicial institution that would be a UN subsidiary body funded through assessed contributions. Instead, the Security Council recommended that the Secretary-General and the concerned state negotiate an agreement to bring to life an international tribunal that would be independent from the UN and funded by voluntary contributions from member states.

The Security Council's approach was indicative of member states' prevailing discontent with the ad hoc tribunals' performance in terms of efficiency, cost-effectiveness and relevance for the populations affected by the crimes under their jurisdiction. By the end of the 1990s, the ICTY and ICTR were no longer considered as viable models for new judicial institutions, and the Security Council's members were eager to experiment with alternate forms of accountability for violations of criminal law.

Whilst it is outside the scope of this article to assess the overall performance of the hybrid tribunals and whether they have been able to improve on the judicial efficiency and effectiveness of the ICTs, it seems reasonable to argue that the combination of their funding mechanism and oversight structure has resulted in greater confidence among donor states about their cost-effectiveness. It has also offered states greater means to intervene in instances of (alleged or actual) mismanagement.

The reliance on voluntary funding has unquestionably made it harder for the hybrid tribunals to muster the resources needed to sustain their work during a protracted period of time, and financing their budget every year requires great efforts on the part of the tribunals' leadership and main supporters. Nevertheless, the reliance on voluntary funding has 'forced' the hybrid tribunals to enhance their cost-effectiveness and withstand regular scrutiny of their spending decisions. The participation of steering/management committees in the oversight of the tribunals, on the other hand, has contributed to a 'vested interest' in their success. It has also promoted a stronger sense of ownership of the tribunals among the states concerned and the major donors. Finally, the constant need to expand their donor base has led the hybrid tribunals to pro-actively reach out to as large a pool of states as possible, regularly sharing information about their progress and their financial performances, and enhancing their transparency.

In conclusion, the experience of hybrid tribunals in terms of cost-effectiveness, relations with the countries affected by the crimes under their jurisdiction, and partnership with major donors, can prove useful not only to other potential new tribunals but also to those already operational, such as the International Criminal Court.

State Cooperation with the International Criminal Tribunal for Rwanda

Cedric Ryngaert
Associate Professor of International Law, Leuven University; Leuven, Belgium
Utrecht University, Utrecht, The Netherlands

Abstract
This contribution discusses the mismatch between States' duties to cooperate with the International Criminal Tribunal for Rwanda (ICTR) and the reality of State non-cooperation. It focuses on two issues of cooperation which have been particularly important to the Tribunal: the arrest of fugitives by States, and the referral of cases to national jurisdictions under the Tribunal's completion strategy. The articles demonstrates how Rwanda has used cooperation - which it knows is indispensable for the Tribunal's functioning - as a bargaining chip to obtain certain concessions from the Tribunal, but argues that also the ICTR itself and the international community should receive a portion of the blame for State non-cooperation.

Keywords
state cooperation; International Criminal Tribunal for Rwanda (ICTR); case referrals; arrest; Security Council

Pursuant to Article 28 of the Statute of the International Criminal Tribunal for Rwanda (ICTR), 'States *shall* cooperate with the [ICTR] in the investigation and prosecution of persons accused of committing serious violations of international humanitarian law' and 'States *shall* comply without undue delay with any request for assistance or an order issued by a Trial Chamber'.[1] Thus, in hardly ambiguous terms, the ICTR Statute *requires* all States to cooperate with the ICTR.[2] If States fail to cooperate with the ICTR, in accordance with Rule 7*bis* of the ICTR Rules of Procedure and Evidence (RPE), the Trial Chamber or a Judge may request the President of the Tribunal to report the matter to the Security Council, or the Prosecutor may request the President to notify the Security Council.

In reality, States have not scrupulously complied with their statutory obligation to cooperate with the Tribunal. But never has the Tribunal referred a case of non-cooperation to the Security Council, apparently out of fear of deterring State

[1] Article 28(1) and (2) ICTR Statute (emphasis added).

[2] The binding effect of this provision finds its legal roots in UN Security Council Resolution 955 (1994), which established the ICTR, and was adopted under Chapter VII of the UN Charter.

cooperation.[3] Instead, the ICTR has typically attempted to solve problems of State cooperation through diplomatic channels. This has not always been successful. In his excellent book on the subject, Victor Peskin describes how Rwanda – the State with which the ICTR has had the bulk of cooperation problems – has consistently managed to counter-shame the Tribunal (by besmirching the Tribunal's record), if attention was drawn to Rwanda's lack of cooperation (*e.g.*, regarding the travel of defense witnesses or the production of documents).[4] As a result, Rwanda could often get away with blatant violations of its duty to cooperate with the Tribunal, or used the threat of non-cooperation to cajole the Tribunal into taking decisions favourable to Rwanda.

We will not repeat Peskin's analysis of the 'virtual trials of cooperation' between Rwanda and the ICTR here. Nor will we analyze the legal minutiae of State cooperation regarding the production of documents or the summoning of witnesses; Charmaine de los Reyes has provided a very fine overview of ICTR case-law regarding these issues and has usefully drawn attention to the difficulties which the Defense faces in having documents produced by States or having witnesses travel from States.[5] Instead, apart from discussing the *Barayagwiza* case, which cannot be dispensed with given its status as a classic case of successful Rwandan blackmailing of the Tribunal (Section 2), we will focus on two issues of cooperation which are particularly important to the Tribunal: the arrest of fugitives by States (Section 1) and the referral of cases to national jurisdictions under the Tribunal's completion strategy (Section 3). In a 2011 report to the Security Council, the ICTR President identified these issues of cooperation as the most pressing, alongside the transfer of convicts for the enforcement of their sentence, and the relocation of acquitted persons and persons who have served their sentence.[6]

1. Arrests[7]

International criminal tribunals, and the ICTR is no exception, do not have the power of arrest: to obtain custody of indicted persons, they are dependent on

---

3) Charmaine de los Reyes, 'State Cooperation and its Challenges for the International Criminal Tribunal for Rwanda', in Emmanuel Decaux, Adama Dieng and Malick Sow (eds.), *From Human Rights to International Criminal Law / Des droits de l'homme au droit international pénal* (Nijhoff, Leiden, 2007) 55, 80.

4) Victor Peskin, *International Justice in Rwanda and the Balkans: Virtual Trials and the Struggle for State Cooperation* (Cambridge University Press, Cambridge, 2008) 179.

5) Reyes, *supra* note 3.

6) Report on the completion strategy of the International Criminal Tribunal for Rwanda (as of 12 May 2011), UN Doc. S/2011/317, para. 59.

7) As far as Sections 1 and 2 are concerned, the author has drawn on his previous work, but has added updates. See Cedric Ryngaert, 'The International Prosecutor: Arrest and Detention', in

States. Under the ICTR *régime*, as already noted in the introduction, States have a duty to cooperate with the ICTR, including with its requests for arrest and surrender. Despite the binding character of the ICTR Statute in this respect, State cooperation regarding arrest has not always been forthcoming – not so much from Rwanda, but mainly from other States. Many *génocidaires* had fled from Rwanda to neighbouring African States after Paul Kagame's Rwandan Patriotic Front (RPF) took power. Many of those States dragged their feet after receiving requests for arrest and surrender from the ICTR, because either they had been on friendly terms with the previous Rwandan regime or they lacked the resources to track and arrest the fugitives.

Kenya and Zaire/Democratic Republic of Congo (DRC) in particular failed to cooperate satisfactorily,[8] a problem that had not yet fully been remedied by 2011. In a 2011 progress report on its completion strategy, the ICTR called again on the DRC and Kenya to support the ICTR in tracking and arresting fugitives, and denounced a Kenya/ICTR joint task force for failing to make effective progress in tracking fugitives.[9] Cooperation from Kenya, which supported the genocidal Hutu regime, has indeed come in fits and starts. A major Kenyan police operation (operation NAKI) managed to locate seven indicted persons, among whom the former Rwanda prime minister, in Nairobi in 1997, but this happened only after a tracking team set up at the ICTR had located them – which in turn convinced the Great Powers to exert pressure on Kenya. By and large, however, the relative pacification of the Great Lakes region has had a beneficial effect on the number of arrests of ICTR fugitives in the region.[10] Still, as of 2012 nine individuals remained on the run from the ICTR.[11] One of them, Félicien Kabuga, one of the masterminds of the

---

Luc Reydams, Jan Wouters, Cedric Ryngaert (eds.), *The International Prosecutor from Nuremberg to The Hague* (Oxford University Press, Oxford, 2012) 647-699.

8) See Kingsley C. Moghalu, *Rwanda's Genocide: The Politics of Global Justice* (Palgrave Macmillan, New York, 2005), 161-165.

9) Report on the completion strategy of the International Criminal Tribunal for Rwanda (as of 12 May 2011), *supra* note 6, paras. 54-56.

10) Steven D. Roper and Lilian A. Barria, 'State Co-operation and International Criminal Court Bargaining Influence in the Arrest and the Surrender of Suspects', 21 *Leiden Journal of International Law* (2008) 457, 461. As recently as 30 June 2010, for instance, Jean Uwinkindi was arrested in Uganda. Uwinkindi would become the first individual to be referred to Rwanda under Rule 11*bis* of the ICTR Rules of Procedure and Evidence (see below).

11) Also the international community's interest in tracking down the remaining Rwanda *génocidaires* in the Great Lakes region after 2002 (when the international community's attention shifted more towards the events in the Middle East, Iraq and Afghanistan, and the war on terror) is partly to blame for the lacklustre cooperation with the ICTR regarding arrest and surrender. Cf. Moghalu, *supra* note 8, 174. U.S. President Obama's decision in October 2011 to send U.S. military advisers to Uganda to help battle the Lord's Resistance Army, and arrest its leaders, may however signal renewed international interest in the region. See White House, Letter from the President to Congress, 14 October 2011.

Rwandan genocide and according to Forbes Magazine one of the ten most wanted man on earth,[12] is believed to be (still) hiding in Kenya.

Because few ICTR fugitives were present on Rwandan soil, few cooperation problems concerning arrest arose in the ICTR-Rwanda relationship. However, quite soon, the ICTR and Rwanda collided with each other in a case where they both wanted to have a fugitive present abroad arrested and surrendered: the *Karamira* case. Theoretically, the ICTR (unlike the ICC) has primacy over national courts.[13] This implies that the international tribunal may formally request States to defer to the competence of the tribunal.[14] Requested States are under an obligation to comply with the request of the tribunal.[15] Accordingly, when a State has received a request for surrender from the ICTR *and* an extradition request from another State, such as Rwanda, it should honour the former request. The *Karamira* case has shown, however, that, in practice, the primacy of the ICTR may be a paper tiger only. Karamira was amongst those believed to be most responsible for the 1994 Rwanda genocide. After the atrocities, he had fled to India, where he was tracked down by Rwandan agents in 1996. During his transit to Rwanda at the Ethiopian airport of Addis Ababa, he fled. The Ethiopian police managed to immediately re-arrest him, but the publicity that had been given to the case lifted the veil of secrecy in which the transfer of Karamira was cloaked:[16] upon learning of Karamira's presence in Ethiopia, the ICTR Prosecutor swiftly acted to request his surrender to the ICTR. This caused particular headaches for the Ethiopian Government, which was a political ally of the new Rwandan regime, and had apparently offered Rwanda transit through Ethiopia to move Karamira to Rwanda. Like in the case of Barayagwiza (see below), Rwanda thereupon started to apply pressure on the ICTR Prosecutor, threatening to no longer cooperate with the ICTR (e.g., the ICTR would no longer have access to witnesses in Rwanda). The pressure was so fierce that the OTP eventually decided to give in: Ethiopia transferred Karamira to Kigali rather than Arusha. He was executed in Rwanda in 1998.[17]

The *Karamira* case teaches us that blackmail by States competing with the tribunal for the surrender of an individual may well work: in case threats by the competing State may put the very functioning of the tribunal at risk, there may be no other option for the tribunal than to waive its right of primacy over national

12) See for this list: http://www.forbes.com/2011/06/14/most-wanted-fugitives_slide_9.html.

13) Article 8.2 of the ICTR Statute.

14) *Ibid.*

15) Article 28 of the ICTR Statute.

16) Other secret Rwanda transfers were successful, however, such as the kidnapping of the former Rwandan minister of Justice in Zambia. Cf. Thierry Cruvellier, *Le tribunal des vaincus* (Calmann-Lévy, Paris, 2006) 28.

17) *Ibid.*, 25-33.

courts.[18] The ICTR Prosecutor had to balance the different interests involved, also with an eye on the future and legacy of the court. At times, it could withstand State pressure – as is illustrated by the transfer of Colonel Bagosora from Cameroon to the ICTR in the face of intense Rwandan pressure –[19] but at other times, as is illustrated by *Karamira*, caving in to pressure was apparently the only viable option for the Prosecutor.

It is noted, of course, that Rwanda presents a rather unique situation. The genocidal government had been deposed by the RPF, which had formed a new regime intent on bringing the former regime to justice. In most situations, the State on whose territory the atrocities occurred will *not* be interested in prosecuting the culprits, rather on the contrary (e.g., Serbia). It is not excluded, however, that such a State will, in spite of not being interested in genuine prosecution, request extradition, for the sole purpose of shielding the person from *international* prosecution. Obviously, in this situation, the requested State may be exposed to international criticism when extraditing the person to the requesting State rather than to the international tribunal. The lack of international protest against Karamira's transfer to Rwanda instead of to the ICTR was, in the final analysis, informed by the knowledge that Rwanda would truly mete out justice (the harsh manner in which justice was eventually meted out was taken for granted), although it may also have been attributable to the accommodative stance of the major powers towards the 'victimized' Rwandan Tutsi regime.

2. *Barayagwiza*

Many problems of cooperation between the ICTR and Rwanda have their roots in Rwanda's perception that the ICTR does not dispense justice. Rwanda, and Rwandan victims' groups, have often threatened to suspend, or have actually suspended, cooperation with the tribunal when they did not agree with ICTR proceedings (*e.g.*, regarding witness protection), or with the outcomes of ICTR trials. Such problems arose at various junctures in history, but the 1998-1999 *Barayagwiza* saga can probably be considered as the lowest point in the ICTR-Rwanda relationship. The ICTR has hardly forgotten this experience:[20] in the 2008 *Munyakazi* decision, the ICTR Referral Chamber cited the reaction of Rwanda to the ICTR's

---

18) Cf. the statement of Prosecutor Richard Goldstone in this sense, quoted in Cruvellier, *supra* note 16, 31.

19) Peskin, *supra* note 4, at 172-177.

20) *Contra* William A. Schabas, in André Klip & Göran Sluiter (eds.), *Annotated Leading Cases of International Criminal Tribunals* (Antwerp, Intersentia, Vol. VI) p. 262 ('It is perhaps significant that the final Barayagwiza decision of the Appeals Chamber of 3 November 1999, seems to have been entirely forgotten in subsequent case law, as if it were a bad dream.').

decisions in *Barayagwiza* as evidence of the absence of sufficient guarantees against outside pressures in Rwanda.[21] This in turn informed its decision *not* to refer the *Munyakazi* case to Rwanda (as will be set out in more detail below, the ICTR has now started referring cases to Rwanda, however, citing progress regarding fair trial guarantees).

Barayagwiza was transferred from Cameroon to the ICTR on 19 November 1997, nineteen months after his initial detention on 17 April 1996 by Cameroon at the request of the ICTR. Upon arrival at the detention unit of the ICTR, a ninety-six-day interval elapsed before he made his initial appearance on 23 February 1998. The delays appeared at least partly attributable to the ICTR. Believing that his rights were violated, Barayagwiza filed a *habeas corpus*-like motion with the Court, which was dismissed by the Trial Chamber (1998).[22] But on appeal (1999), the Appeals Chamber ruled that the case was so egregious as to warrant a remedy under the abuse of process doctrine because of 'the combination of delays that seemed to occur at virtually every stage of the Appellant's case'.[23] Thus, in the tribunal's view, it was the cumulative character of the violations of the OTP in relation to Barayagwiza's arrest and detention that led to a finding of abuse of process. The tribunal observed starkly that 'the Appellant was simply forgotten about'.[24] Citing the duty of prosecutorial diligence, it concluded that 'the Prosecutor failed in her duty to take the steps necessary to have the Appellant transferred in a timely fashion',[25] and that, in addition, she should have taken prudent steps so as to ensure that 'the accused is brought before a Trial Chamber "without delay" upon his transfer to the Tribunal'.[26] The Appeals Chamber then ordered the most extreme possible measure to remedy the prosecutorial inaction and the resultant denial of Barayagwiza's rights: the release of the appellant and the dismissal of the charges against him.[27]

The release of Barayagwiza immediately caused serious political problems for the ICTR, since Rwanda – who wanted to see Barayagwiza convicted for the role

---

21) *The Prosecutor v. Yussuf Munyakazi*, Case No. ICTR-97-36-R11bis, Decision on the Prosecutor's Request for Referral of Case to the Republic of Rwanda, 28 May 2008, para. 40 ('[T]he Chamber is of the view that sufficient guarantees against outside pressures are lacking in Rwanda. In particular, the Chamber notes the Rwandan Government's interrupted cooperation with the Tribunal following a dismissal of an indictment and release of an Appellant [*Prosecutor v. Barayagwiza*, Case No. ICTR-97-19, Appeal Chamber, Decision, 3 November 1999] as well as its negative reaction to foreign judges for indicting former members of the Rwandan Patriotic Front ("RPF") [footnote omitted]. The Chamber is concerned that these actions by the Rwandan Government, as will be explained in more detail below, show a tendency to pressure the judiciary, a pressure against which a judge sitting alone would be particularly susceptible.').

22) Trial Chamber, *Barayagwiza*, ICTR-97-19-AR72, Decision of 17 November 1998.

23) Appeals Chamber, *Barayagwiza* I, ICTR-97-19-AR72, 3 November 1999, para. 109.

24) *Ibid.*, para. 96.

25) *Ibid.*, para. 98.

26) *Ibid.*, para. 99.

27) *Ibid.*

he played in the 1994 genocide – announced the suspension of all cooperation with the tribunal until the Chamber would reverse its decision: Rwanda barred the ICTR Prosecutor from her office in Kigali, and denied permission to leave the country to sixteen witnesses scheduled to testify in the trial of Bagilishema at the ICTR.[28] From then onwards, politics took over.[29] Pressure mounted on the Tribunal to reconsider its ruling.[30] In its pleadings before the Appeals Chamber, the ICTR Prosecutor did not shy away from highlighting the political dimension of the *Bayaragwiza* case: in her characteristically blunt style, in the face of an imminent shutdown of the ICTR, she urged the Appeals Chamber to give in to Rwanda and reconsider its earlier ruling:[31]

> Let me just say a few words with respect to the government of Rwanda. The government of Rwanda reacted very seriously in a tough manner to the decision of 3 November 1999. It was a politically motivated decision, which is understandable. It can only be understood if one is cognisant with the situation, if one is aware of what happened in Rwanda in 1994. I also notice that, well, it was the Prosecutor that had no visa to travel to Rwanda. It was the Prosecutor who was unable to go to her office in Kigali. It was the Prosecutor who could not be received by the Rwandan authorities. In November, after your decision, there was no co-operation, no collaboration with the office of the Prosecutor. In other words, justice, as dispensed by this Tribunal was paralysed and it was the trial of Bagilishima which had to be adjourned because the Rwandan government did not allow 16 witnesses to appear before this Court. In other words, they were not allowed to leave the territory of Rwanda. […] However, your Honours, due account has to be taken of that fact. Whether we want it or not, we must come to terms with the fact that our ability to continue with our prosecution and investigations depend on the government of Rwanda. That is the reality that we face. What is the reality? Either Barayagwiza can be tried by this Tribunal, in the alternative; or the only other solution that you have is for Barayagwiza to be handed over to the state of Rwanda to his natural judge, *judex naturalis*.
>
> Otherwise I am afraid, as we say in Italian, *possiamo chiudere la baracca*. In other words we can as well put the key to that door, close the door and then open that of the prison. And in that case the Rwandan government will not be involved in any manner…"

Given the political importance of the case, on 31 March 2000, the Appeals Chamber rendered a new decision, which, not wholly surprisingly, reversed the 1999 decision. Observing 'that the violations suffered by the Appellant and the omissions of the Prosecutor are not the same as those which emerged from the facts on which the [1999] Decision is founded', the Chamber ordered that the initial remedy – the dismissal of the indictment and the release of the appellant,

---

28) *Munyakazi*, *supra* note 21, para. 41; Peskin, *supra* note 4, 179.

29) See also at length Moghalu, *supra* note 8, 111-123.

30) Peskin points out in this respect that '[ICTR Prosecutor] Del Ponte remained in Arusha for two weeks until the Appeals Chamber announced its decision to hold a hearing to reconsider its initial ruling.' Peskin, *supra* note 4 181.

31) *See Prosecutor v. Barayagwiza*, Case No. ICTR-97-19-AR72, Appeals Chamber, Decision: Prosecutor's Request for Review or Reconsideration", 31 March 2000, Declaration of Judge Raphael Nieto-Navia, para. 2. See also *Munyakazi*, *supra* note 21, para. 41.

must be altered:[32] if he were found not guilty, he would receive financial compensation, and if he were found guilty, his sentence would be reduced.[33]

As expected, the Appeals Chamber's second decision was severely criticized: the 'new' facts identified by the Chamber were actually known to the Prosecutor (the moving party),[34] and the decision was thus considered to be politically inspired.[35] Nonetheless, criticism was also levelled at the Appeals Chamber's *first* decision,[36] so that, in the final analysis, the second decision may well represent good law.

The *Barayagwiza* episode demonstrated that the Tribunal does not operate in a political vacuum. After *Barayagwiza*, both the Prosecutor and the Chambers realized that they should tread cautiously so as not to antagonize Rwanda, whose cooperation with the Tribunal was indispensable. This also meant not applying the law on State cooperation to its fullest extent, *e.g.*, by not seeking a referral to the UN Security Council in case of Rwandan-non-cooperation. As Charmaine de los Reyes observed in this respect: 'As the [ICTR] applies the rules to secure State cooperation, it risks attracting politically motivated embargos on assistance as well as criticism regarding its impartiality.'[37] That being said, obviously, the ICTR organs will almost never openly admit that they do not function independently and have succumbed to sustained political pressure in the face of potential non-cooperation by Rwanda.[38]

---

32) Appeals Chamber, *Barayagwiza* II, ICTR-97-19-AR72, 31 March 2000, para. 74.

33) *Ibid.*, para. 75. See also the ICTR's judgment in *Prosecutor v. Nahimana, Barayagwiza, Ngeze*, ICTR-99-52-T, 3 December 2003, para. 1107 (reducing Barayagwiza's sentence to thirty-five years of imprisonment).

34) E.g., Schabas, *supra* note 20, 261-262.

35) Cf. Peskin, *supra* note 4, 184 (noting that 'among many ICTR staff members, doubts emerged about the autonomy of the tribunal from Rwandan pressure').

36) A tribunal judge interviewed by Peskin, *ibid.*, 180, confided that '[i]f you have these kinds of allegations, I don't see how you can let [Barayagwiza] walk away on a technicality ... You can't just let him walk away, that's not justice.'. Another tribunal judge, interviewed by Peskin, *ibid.*, 184, also stated that it is inadvisable to render 'a legal decision that is wrong in the reality of the world'. Smeulers, an academic commentator, has deemed it 'unacceptable that such a man gets off the hook because of perceived small procedural mistakes ...' (Alette Smeulers, in André Klip and Göran Sluiter (eds.), *Annotated Leading Cases of International Criminal Tribunals* (Intersentia, Antwerp, Vol. XI) 111). Schabas, for his part, has observed that the judges 'found themselves adopting a position that was simply too extreme, too shrill, entirely disproportionate ... the remedy proposed, namely a permanent stay of proceedings, was quite excessive ... The 3 November 1999 decision was quite simply bad law, and the Appeals Chamber had to do something to fix it.' (Schabas, *supra* note 20, 261-262). And Swart has commented that 'the violations of the Appellant's rights, although serious, were considerably less egregious and numerous than the Appeals Chamber believed' (Bert Swart, in André Klip and Göran Sluiter (eds.), *Annotated Leading Cases of International Criminal Tribunals*, (Intersentia, Antwerp, Vol. II) 206).

37) Reyes, *supra* note 3, 55.

38) *Barayagwiza* II, *supra* note 32, para. 34 ('"The government of Rwanda reacted very seriously in a tough manner to the decision of 3 November 1999." Later, the Attorney General of Rwanda appearing as representative of the Rwandan Government, in his submissions as 'amicus curiae' to the Appeals Chamber, openly threatened the non co-operation of the peoples of Rwanda

3. Case Referrals to States under Rule 11*bis*

One may gather from the above-mentioned account of Rwandan cooperation with the ICTR, that the Tribunal has adopted a particularly – and perhaps overly – accommodative stance towards Rwanda. However, accommodation was not, at least not initially, the strategy espoused by the ICTR Trial Chamber when it decided on the Prosecutor's requests for referral to Rwanda, under Rule 11*bis* of the Tribunal's Rules of Procedure and Evidence, of various cases pending before the ICTR: these requests were dismissed on the ground that the rule of law quality of Rwanda's justice system was insufficient. Only in 2011, with the closure of the ICTR imminent, did an ICTR Referral Chamber refer the first case to Rwanda (*Uwinkindi*).

The Prosecutor's referral policy implemented the ICTR completion strategy and hinged on the ability and willingness of States to cooperate with the ICTR in bringing intermediate- and lower-rank ICTR accused to trial in national jurisdiction. State acceptance of referred ICTR cases is an important, although non-obligatory, aspect of State cooperation with the ICTR, and warrants a detailed discussion, all the more so given the recent evolutions in ICTR case-law.

3.1. *Early Attempts at Referral to Third States (2005-2007)*

In 2003, the UN Security Council urged the ICTR to formalize a completion strategy which would involve the transfer of 'cases involving intermediate- and lower-rank accused to competent national jurisdictions, as appropriate, including Rwanda, in order to allow the ICTR to achieve its objective of completing investigations by the end of 2004, all trial activities at first instance by the end of 2008, and all of its work in 2010.'[39] To allow the transfer of such cases as part of its completion strategy, the ICTR judges (as did their ICTY counterparts) added Rule 11*bis* to the ICTR Rules of Procedure and Evidence.[40]

---

with the Tribunal if faced with an unfavourable Decision by the Appeals Chamber on the Motion for Review. The Appeals Chamber wishes to stress that the Tribunal is an independent body, whose decisions are based solely on justice and law. If its decision in any case should be followed by non-cooperation, that consequence would be a matter for the Security Council.'). See however the ICTR Prosecutor pleadings in *Barayagwiza*, quoted above.

39) Eighth *Preambular* Paragraph of Security Council Resolution 1503 (2003). See also para. 6 of Security Council Resolution 1534 (2004), requesting the Tribunal 'to provide the Council, by 31 May 2004 and every six months thereafter, assessments by its President and Prosecutor, setting out in detail the progress made towards implementation of the Completion Strategy of the Tribunal, explaining what measures have been taken to implement the Completion Strategy and what measures remain to be taken, including the transfer of cases involving intermediate and lower rank accused to competent national jurisdictions'.

40) Rule 11*bis* RPE: Referral of the Indictment to another court:

On the basis of Rule 11*bis*, from 2005 onwards the Prosecutor filed requests with the ICTR Trial Chambers to refer a number of cases, initially not to Rwanda, but to other States that were willing to try the accused under the universality principle. While it appeared logical to send the cases to Rwanda – the State where the atrocities had occurred – the Prosecutor pointed out that Rwanda still imposed the death penalty and could not guarantee a fair trial; as a result, the requirements of Rule 11*bis* (C) would not be met in the Prosecutor's view.[41] But interestingly, the Prosecutor added that, even if those requirements were met, 'strong public policy reasons favour the involvement of other countries in the prosecution of the Accused because it would be a manner of educating people in other countries on the lessons to be learned from the Rwandan genocide and would promote the development of ideas to prevent future similar tragedies.'[42] Accordingly, prosecuting Rwandan *génocidaires* was considered as a joint endeavour of the ICTR and the entire community of States, even if the latter had no nexus with the Rwandan genocide.[43]

This ideal of a joint endeavour was however short-lived. Only France, Norway and the Netherlands declared themselves able and willing to take over ICTR cases. Ultimately, the Trial Chambers only granted the Prosecutor's request for a referral of two cases to *France* (*Bucyibaruta* and *Munyeshyaka*, 2007),[44] and even then, as

---

'(A) If an indictment has been confirmed, whether or not the accused is in the custody of the Tribunal, the President may designate a Trial Chamber which shall determine whether the case should be referred to the authorities of a State:
(i) in whose territory the crime was committed; or
(ii) in which the accused was arrested; or
(iii) having jurisdiction and being willing and adequately prepared to accept such a case,
so that those authorities should forthwith refer the case to the appropriate court for trial within that State.
(B) The Trial Chamber may order such referral *proprio motu* or at the request of the Prosecutor, after having given to the Prosecutor and, where the accused is in the custody of the Tribunal, the accused, the opportunity to be heard.'
[...]

41) Rule 11*bis* (C): 'In determining whether to refer the case in accordance with paragraph (A), the Trial Chamber shall satisfy itself that the accused will receive a fair trial in the courts of the State concerned and that the death penalty will not be imposed or carried out.'

42) *The Prosecutor v. Michel Bagaragaza*, Case No. ICTR-2005-86-R11*bis*, 19 May 2006.

43) Even before 2005, however, States had exercised universal jurisdiction over Rwandan *génocidaires* who were not indicted by the ICTR. See Luc Reydams, 'Belgium's First Application of Universal Jurisdiction - the "Butare Four" case', 1 *Journal of International Criminal Justice* (2003) 428. Other States, such as the Netherlands, found that they did not have jurisdiction over crimes of genocide committed in Rwanda in 1994. See Cedric Ryngaert, 'Universal Jurisdiction over Genocide and Wartime Torture in Dutch Courts: an Appraisal of the Afghan and Rwandan cases (2007)', 2 *Hague Justice Journal* (2007:2) 13.

44) *The Prosecutor v. Laurent Bucyibaruta*, Case No. ICTR-2005-85-I, Decision on Prosecutor's request for referral of indictment to France, 20 November 2007; *The Prosecutor v. Wenceslas Munyeshayaka*, Case No. ICTR-2005-87-I, Decision on Prosecutor's request for referral of indictment to France, 20 November 2007.

of 2011, France had not made notable progress regarding the prosecution of these cases.[45] The Prosecutor's request for a referral of the *Bagaragaza* case to *Norway* was declined on the grounds that Norway did not have jurisdiction *ratione materiae* over the crimes charged (genocide, conspiracy to commit genocide, and complicity in genocide).[46] The Prosecutor thereupon filed a request for a referral of the same case to the Netherlands, which was granted by the Trial Chamber[47] - but then, when push came to shove, Dutch courts, hearing the referred case, ruled that they did not have jurisdiction to hear the case. A brief discussion of the Dutch proceedings in the *Bagaragaza* case is warranted as it illustrates well the difficulties plaguing the ICTR's referral policy to 'third' States.[48]

At first instance, in 2007, a Dutch District Court found that Dutch courts could not entertain 'original' or 'derivative' jurisdiction over the case of Bagaragaza. In the Court's view, original jurisdiction did not lie since, at the time of the Rwandan genocide in 1994, Dutch law did not provide for universal jurisdiction over genocide. The Court observed that such universal jurisdiction may now apply pursuant to the Dutch International Crimes Act of 2003, but it added that such new legislation cannot apply retroactively, nor can customary international law (provided that it allowed the exercise of universal jurisdiction over genocide back in 1994) – custom being an unwritten source of law – expand the jurisdictional rules of the Dutch code. Derivative jurisdiction, in the sense of jurisdiction derived from the jurisdiction of the ICTR over the case, did not lie either, according to the Court. In order for Dutch law to be applicable to persons against whom the prosecution has been transferred from a foreign State to the Netherlands, a treaty is required pursuant to Article 4a of the Dutch Penal Code. Applying the criteria listed in the provision to the case of Bagaragaza, the Court ruled that, while the ICTR could be equated with a foreign State (if a functional interpretation of the legal provision were espoused), no treaty that listed arrangements for the transfer of cases from the ICTR to the Netherlands could be identified. The criteria of the said Article 4a were therefore not met, and the Dutch Prosecutor's request regarding Bagaragaza was held to be inadmissible.[49]

---

45) See Statement by Justice Hassan B. Jallow, Prosecutor of the ICTR, to the United Nations Security Council, 6 June 2011 ('I am also hopeful that the two other cases referred to France (*Laurent Bucyibaruta* and *Wenceslas Munyeshaka*) will receive greater attention in the course of this year in the French courts.').

46) *The Prosecutor v. Michel Bagaragaza*, Case No. ICTR-2005-86-R11*bis*, Decision on the Prosecution motion for referral to the Kingdom of Norway, para. 16. Norway had stated that it would lay charges against the accused under the domestic law of homicide, which did however not require the specific intent of genocide.

47) *The Prosecutor v. Michel Bagaragaza*, Case No. ICTR-2005-86-R11*bis*, Decision on the Prosecution motion for referral to the Kingdom of the Netherlands, 13 April 2007.

48) The author draws on a previous note he published as 'The Failed Referral of Michel Bagaragaza from the ICTR to the Netherlands', 4 *Hague Justice Journal* (2009) 237-243.

49) The reasoning of the District Court is reprinted in the Supreme Court judgment in *Bagaragaza*, LJN: BD6568, Hoge Raad, 08/00142, Section 5.1.

On appeal, in late 2007, the Appeals Court upheld the inadmissibility of the case, yet it did so on other grounds. It concurred with the District Court's finding that there was no treaty between the ICTR and the Netherlands in the sense of Article 4a of the Penal Code. In this context, the Court held, relying on an expert advisory opinion, that the correspondence between the Prosecutor of the ICTR and the Dutch Minister of Justice relating to the transfer of Bagaragaza could be qualified as an informal treaty, but that such an informal treaty was not contemplated by the drafters of the Penal Code amendment resulting in Article 4a of the Penal Code.[50] The Appeals Court's decision differed from the District Court's decision, however, in that it refused to equate the ICTR with a *State* for purposes of Article 4a, thereby rejecting the District Court's flexible, teleological statutory interpretation: the Court pointed out that equating an organ of the United Nations (the ICTR, established by the UN Security Council) did not satisfy the requirement of cognizability (*kenbaarheid*) of the law.[51] On this point, the Supreme Court added that the terminological distinction between a 'State' and an 'international tribunal' was commonly accepted, and that accordingly there was no reason to construe 'State' as also implying 'international tribunal'.[52]

After the District Court of The Hague had held that it did not have jurisdiction over the acts committed by Bagaragaza, the ICTR swiftly revoked its transfer order on 17 August 2007. Bagaragaza himself was subsequently transferred, on 20 May 2008, to the ICTR, where, on 24 June 2008, he pleaded guilty with the Prosecutor. After Bagaragaza's transfer to Arusha, the Dutch Supreme Court (*Hoge Raad*) eventually upheld the Court of Appeals's decision on 21 October 2008. The ICTR convicted Bagaragaza to 8 years' imprisonment on 17 November 2009.[53]

The Dutch courts' inflexible application of Dutch criminal procedure law on judicial cooperation may appear regrettable. This sort of legal nicety indeed seriously compromises the ICTR's completion strategy. Jurisdictional and substantive obstacles to a successful prosecution in the State to which cases are referred under Rule 11*bis* render referrals problematic, and oblige the ICTR, which struggles which a huge caseload anyway, to again take up cases which it could possibly have gotten rid of. Dutch courts should not come in for too much criticism, however. After all, they simply applied Dutch law, and as is common in criminal

---

50) The reasoning of the Appeals Court is reprinted in the Supreme Court judgment, Section 5.2, para. 29.

51) *Id.*, para. 16. The Appeals Court argument relating to the presence/absence of a treaty for purposes of Article 4a of the Penal Code appears superfluous, as the criteria of Article 4a are cumulative. If the transferring entity is not a State, Article 4a cannot come into play anymore, irrespective of the 'treaty' condition being fulfilled. Nevertheless, the argument was apparently made in the interest of the law.

52) Supreme Court judgment, Section 6.5.1.

53) *The Prosecutor v. Michel Bagaragaza*, Case No. ICTR-05-86-S, Sentencing Judgment, 17 November 2009.

cases, rather strictly.[54] Those who are really to blame for the failing Completion Strategy resulting from the aborted Rule 11*bis* referrals are those who devised and implemented the completion strategy in the first place: the United Nations and the ICTR. The Dutch Appeals Court in *Bagaragaza* observed incisively in this respect that it might have reached a different conclusion if the United Nations and the Netherlands had entered into a treaty which would have clarified the transfer of cases of ICTR indictees to the Netherlands in the framework of the completion strategy, even in situations where the Netherlands did not have original jurisdiction.[55] Such a treaty would have satisfied the requirements of Article 4a of the Dutch Penal Code, and have allowed for a smooth transfer of ICTR cases to the Netherlands. The *Bagaragaza* saga shows that the architects of the ICTR Completion Strategy paid insufficient attention to the legal details of its implementation.

3.2. *The Attempts to Refer Cases to Rwanda*

The Prosecutor, realizing that the route of referring cases to third States may prove to be a dead end, changed course rather early on, in 2007, when it started filing requests (five in 2007) for case referrals to *Rwanda*.[56] The Prosecutor had come round to believing that the accused would receive a fair trial in the courts of Rwanda, and that the death penalty would not be imposed or carried out.

---

54) A cynic may contend that the Dutch courts' rigid interpretation of the statute was informed by policy considerations rather than accepted techniques of statutory interpretation. The courts may have been concerned about Dutch judicial authorities being overburdened by cases which bear almost no relation with the Netherlands. The Dutch Government's acceptance of the ICTR Prosecutor's request to have Bagaragaza's case transferred to the Netherlands, and its reasoning that the transfer *was* covered by Article 4a of the Penal Code, appears to belie this, however.

55) Appeals Court judgment, reprinted in Supreme Court judgment, Section 5.2, para. 29.

56) The Prosecutor's Request for the Referral of the Case of Gaspard Kanyarukiga to Rwanda Pursuant to Rule 11 *bis* of the Tribunal's Rules of Procedure and Evidence, 7 September 2007 (below referred to as the "Prosecution Request"); *The Prosecutor v. Fulgence Kayishema*, The Prosecutor's Request for the Referral of the Case of Fulgence Kayishema to Rwanda Pursuant to Rule 11 *bis* of the Tribunal's Rules of Procedure and Evidence, 11 June 2007; *The Prosecutor v. Yussuf Munyakazi*, The Prosecutor's Request for the Referral of the Case of Yussef Munyakazi to Rwanda Pursuant to Rule 11 *bis* of the Tribunal's Rules of Procedure and Evidence, 7 September 2007; *The Prosecutor v. Idelphonse Hategekimana*, The Prosecutor's Request for the Referral of the Case of Idelphonse Hategekimana to Rwanda Pursuant to Rule 11 *bis* of the Tribunal's Rules of Procedure and Evidence, 7 September 2007; *The Prosecutor v. Jean-Baptiste Gatete*, The Prosecutor's Request for the Referral of the Case of Jean-Baptiste Gatete to Rwanda Pursuant to Rule 11 *bis* of the Tribunal's Rules of Procedure and Evidence, 28 November 2007.

See also Statement by Justice Hassan B. Jallow, Prosecutor of the ICTR, to the United Nations Security Council, 6 December 2010 ('Referral of all but three of the ten fugitives to national jurisdictions for trial remains a key element of the completion strategy of the ICTR. In the absence of acceptance of these cases by other member states, Rwanda continues to be the focus of the ICTR referral strategy.').

The efforts of the Prosecutor were however swiftly rebuffed by the Trial Chambers, which, in a string of judgments rendered in 2008, refused to honour the Prosecutor's requests for referrals on the ground that Rwandan courts failed to live up to adequate due process standards.[57] The Chambers held in particular that the accused would face difficulties in calling witnesses residing outside Rwanda and obtaining witnesses residing in Rwanda because they would be afraid to testify before Rwandan courts. They added that a conviction to life imprisonment could mean solitary confinement in violation of international detention standards, and that Rwanda's legal framework may not criminalize command responsibility.[58] In so doing, the Trial Chambers passed harsh judgment on the quality of the Rwandan court system, and appeared to set the ICTR again on a collision course with Rwanda. This occurred at as crucial a time as the end of the ICTR's lifespan: without referrals of a substantial number of cases on its docket to States, and Rwanda in particular, the ICTR would face serious difficulties in terminating its trials on time. The ICTY, in contrast, had been quite successful in referring cases back to the States where the atrocities had taken place, and thus seemed set to meet the targets set in its completion strategy.[59] Therefore, the ICTR Prosecutor stated ominously in a December 2010 statement at the UN Security Council:

> In the absence of a transfer of these cases and with the probable arrest of fugitives in the near future, the work of the Tribunal could increase significantly, thus extending the projected completion date for trials. The transfer of such a workload to the proposed residual mechanism would expand the size of such an interim institution substantially. On the other hand the referral of these cases now to national jurisdictions could possibly see the end of trials at the Tribunal by the end of 2011.[60]

To avert the danger of the ICTR not meeting the completion deadline, the Prosecutor did not relent in his efforts to have genocide cases tried in Rwanda. He handed over to Rwanda the case files of 25 suspects who had been investigated

---

[57] See at length on these decisions: Inge Onsea, 'The Legacy of the ICTR in Rwanda in the Context of the Completion Strategy: The Impact of Rule 11*bis*', in Cedric Ryngaert (ed.), *The Effectiveness of International Criminal Justice* (Intersentia, Antwerp, 2009) 173-194.

[58] *The Prosecutor v. Yussuf Munyakazi*, Case No. ICTR-97-36-R11*bis*, Decision on the Prosecutor's request for referral of case to Rwanda, 28 May 2008; *The Prosecutor v. Jean-Baptiste Gatete*, Case No. ICTR-2000-61-R11*bis*, Decision on Prosecutor's Request for Referral to the Republic of Rwanda, 17 November 2008; *The Prosecutor v. Ildephonse Hategekimana*, Case No. ICTR-00-55B-R11*bis*, Decision on Prosecutor's Request for Referral to the Republic of Rwanda, 18 June 2008; *The Prosecutor v. Fulgence Kayishema*, Case No. ICTR-01-67-R11*bis*, Decision on Prosecutor's Request for Referral to the Republic of Rwanda, 16 December 2008; *The Prosecutor v. Kanyarukiga*, Case No. ICTR-2002-78-R11*bis*, Decision on Prosecutor's Request for Referral to the Republic of Rwanda, 6 June 2008.

[59] Cf. Jens Dieckmann and Christina Kerll, 'UN Ad Hoc Tribunals Under Time Pressure – Completion Strategy and Referral Practice of the ICTY and ICTR from the Perspective of the Defence', 8 *International Criminal Law Review* (2008) 87.

[60] Statement by Justice Hassan B. Jallow, Prosecutor of the ICTR, to the United Nations Security Council, 6 December 2010.

but not indicted by the ICTR (and thus did not qualify for the Rule 11*bis* referrals) in 2010,[61] and - encouraged by the following *dictum* of the Trial Chamber in the *Munyakazi* referral case - he continued to engage with Rwanda regarding the referrals:

> The Chamber would like to emphasise that it has taken notice of the positive steps taken by Rwanda to facilitate referral. The Chamber is of the view that if Rwanda continues along this path, the Tribunal will hopefully be able to refer future cases to Rwandan courts.[62]

And indeed, Rwanda took steps with a view to meeting the concerns voiced by the Trial Chambers in the negative referral decisions of 2008, in particular concerning the insufficiency of witness protection (the imposition of the death penalty or life imprisonment with special conditions was no longer an issue).[63] In 2010, the Prosecutor took the view that the changes brought about by Rwanda satisfied the criteria of Rule 11*bis* as construed by the Trial Chambers. Again entering into a judicial alliance with Rwanda, it filed a request for the referral of the *Uwinkindi* case to Rwanda.[64] Various non-governmental organizations swiftly countered the Prosecutor's positive characterization of legal reform in Rwanda by filing *amicus curiae* briefs with the Trial Chamber.[65] The Government of Rwanda and the Kigali Bar Association supported the referral.

In a decision rendered on 28 June 2011, that must have surprised many an observer, the ICTR Trial Chamber ordered the case of *Uwinkindi* to be referred to Rwanda, citing, indeed, the progress made by Rwanda.[66] Any progress, however,

---

61) Report of the International Criminal Tribunal for Rwanda to UNGA (2010), UN Doc. A/65/188–S/2010/408, para. 53.

62) *The Prosecutor v. Yussuf Munyakazi*, Case No. ICTR-97-36-R11*bis*, Decision on the Prosecutor's request for referral of case to Rwanda, 28 May 2008, para. 67.

63) *Prosecutor v. Jean Uwinkindi*, Case No. ICTR-2001-75-R11*bis*, Decision on the Prosecutor's request for referral of case to Rwanda, 28 June 2011, para. 47.

64) *Prosecutor v. Jean Uwinkindi*, Case No. ICTR-2001-75-R11*bis*, Prosecutor's request for the referral of the case of Jean-Bosco Uwinkindi to Rwanda pursuant to Rule 11*bis* of the Tribunal's Rules of Procedure and Evidence ("Motion"), 4 November 2010. Jean Uwikindi, an indicted fugitive, was arrested in Uganda on 30 June 2010 and transferred to the Tribunal on 2 July 2010.

65) Human Rights Watch, International Criminal Defence Attorneys Association, the International Association of Democratic Lawyers. See *Prosecutor v. Jean Uwinkindi*, Case No. ICTR-2001-75-R11*bis*, Decision on Prosecutor's request for referral to the Republic of Rwanda, 28 June 2011, paras. 7-14.

66) *Id.*, para. 223 ('This Chamber notes that, in the intervening period, Rwanda has made material changes in its laws and has indicated its capacity and willingness to prosecute cases referred by this Tribunal. This gives the Referral Chamber confidence that the case of the Accused, if referred, will be prosecuted consistent with internationally recognised fair trial standards enshrined in the Statute of this Tribunal and other human rights instruments.'). This decision was confirmed on appeal by the ICTR Appeals Chamber, which did not find an error of law in the Trial Chamber's reasoning. *Jean Uwinkindi*, Case No. ICTR-01-75-AR11bis, Decision on Uwinkindi's appeal against the referral of his case to Rwanda and related motions, 16 December 2011.

was often merely made on paper, as a number of *amici* pointed out. This was not lost on the Chamber, but it observed that the issues which concerned the previous Referral Chambers 'had been addressed to *some* satisfaction' by Rwanda.[67] As becomes clear throughout the decision, the Chamber was willing to take risks when referring cases to Rwanda, whose legal system still left to be desired, and which had only taken some steps to remedy the defects identified in the 2008 (non-)referral decisions.[68] In a later referral decision of June 6th, 2012, in the case of *Munyagishari*, the Referral Chamber was somewhat more cautious, however.[69] While in principle ordering the transfer of this case to Rwanda, the Chamber nevertheless imposed a number of conditions, relating to the monitoring process, the assignment of a lawyer, and the protection of defense witnesses, to be met by Rwanda before the case could also practically be referred.[70] This may be seen as a minor correction of the *Uwinkindi* referral decision. This decision may, in particular as far as the monitoring of referred cases was concerned, have been taken too hastily: the Referral Chamber appeared to accept at face value that the African Commission on Human and People's Rights (ACPHR) would be willing to send court monitors to Rwanda.[71] In reality, however, as of April 2012, no agreement with the ACPHR or another suitable organization had materialized, as a result of which the President of the ICTR had to issue a decision instructing the appointment of two ICTR legal staff as interim monitors (April 5th, 2012). Only after this decision could Uwinkindi be transferred to Rwanda (April 19th, 2012).[72] Negotiations with the ACPHR were still on-going as of June 2012; only after an agreement has been reached, will Munyagishari be transferred, provided that the other conditions imposed by the Chamber are met.[73]

---

67) *Id.*, para. 224 (emphasis added).

68) See, *e.g.*, paras. 96, 102, 103, 146.

69) *The Prosecutor v. Bernard Munyagishari*, Case No. ICTR-2005-89-R11*bis*, Decision on Prosecutor's request for referral to the Republic of Rwanda, 6 June 2012.

70) *Id.*, para. 220 (emphasizing 'that it is persuaded to refer this case only subject to the conditions that an independent organisation is appointed as monitor before, or shortly after the transfer of the Accused; the President of the Kigali Bar Association confirms to the President of the Tribunal that the Accused will be assigned a lawyer with previous international experience and the Prosecutor General of Rwanda provides a written Assurance satisfying the President of the Tribunal or the Residual Mechanism that witnesses who testify in the present case and who are then compelled to testify in subsequent domestic genocide cases shall not risk prosecution that would otherwise be prohibited by the Transfer Law as an indirect consequence of appearing as witnesses in this transfer case.').

71) Note that Rule 11*bis* D(iv) of the ICTR RPE was amended to enable not only the Prosecutor to appoint monitors, but also to enable the Chambers to request the Registrar to send observers, even observers of another institution (the African Commission) (para. 209).

72) *Id.*, para. 211.

73) *Id.*, para. 220.

3.3. *Assessing the Referrals to Rwanda*

Especially the *Uwinkindi* referral decision, and *Munyagishari* to a lesser extent, have – again – been a major judicial victory for Rwanda in its tug-of-war with the ICTR. Unless the quality of the rule of law in Rwanda is drastically reduced, it is expected that the Trial Chambers will soon refer even more cases involving low- or mid-level perpetrators to Rwanda,[74] while the chances that the ICTR will ever consider revocation are low, as the Chamber noted itself in the *Uwinkindi* case.[75] The decision will also please the ICTR's political overlords at the UN Security Council, who would like to have the ICTR terminate its mandate as agreed. In fact, the Trial Chamber seems to be informed by this political imperative, where, unlike in 2008, it assesses Rwanda's legal practice with a particularly light touch.[76]

When reading the decision, sometimes it appears that the referral was a foregone conclusion for which *ex post* some legal arguments had to be found. In practical terms, referral decisions can be considered as *faits accomplis*. It is striking in this respect that the Referral Chamber, in the last paragraph of its decisions in *Uwinkindi* and *Munyagishari*, '*expresses its solemn hope* that the Republic of Rwanda, in accepting its first referral from this Tribunal, will actualise in practice the commitments it has made in its filings about its good faith, capacity and willingness to enforce the highest standards of international justice in the referred cases.'[77] Although this hope would be underpinned by the existence of ACPHR trial monitors – who would provide 'robust monitoring' – and the possibility of

---

[74] In early 2012, two cases concerning two accused still at large were referred to Rwanda: *The Prosecutor v. Fulgence Kayishema*, Case No. ICTR-01-67-R11bis, Decision on the Prosecutor's request for referral of case to Rwanda, 22 February 2012; *The Prosecutor v. Charles Sikubwabo*, Case No. ICTR-95-1D, Decision on the Prosecutor's request for referral of case to Rwanda, 26 March 2012. It is noted that the *Uwinkindi* decision has not henceforth made referrals automatic. A referral decision continues to be based on the merits of each case. See *Munyagishari* referral decision, para. 41 ('The Chamber is obligated by Rule 11 *bis* to satisfy itself that Munyagishari, specifically, will receive a fair trial in the courts of Rwanda. The referral of one accused does not necessitate that all subsequent requests under Rule 11 *bis* must be automatically granted. The facts pertaining to each request vary and the Chamber shall consider the merits of the Accused's arguments, particularly those that have not previously been advanced. Nonetheless, the Chamber is bound by the Appeals Chamber interpretation of the law.') (citation omitted).

[75] *Uwinkindi* referral, para. 217 ('the Referral Chamber will only consider the revocation mechanism as a remedy of last resort'). See also *Munyagishari* referral, para. 216. Rule 11*bis* E provides for revocation: 'At any time after an order has been issued pursuant to this Rule and before the accused is found guilty or acquitted by a court in the State concerned, the Trial Chamber may *proprio motu* or at the request of the Prosecutor and upon having given to the authorities of the State concerned the opportunity to be heard, revoke the order and make a formal request for deferral within the terms of Rule 10.'

[76] *Id.*, para. 90 ('the Chamber recalls that its role is not to assess whether the fears of the individual potential witnesses are legitimate or not'); para. 103 ('relevant Rwandan laws must be given a chance to operate before being held to be defective').

[77] *Id.*, para. 225. See also *Munyagishari* referral, para. 222 (emphasis added).

the revocation of the accused's referral,[78] one cannot fail to note the sense of surrender which the Referral Chamber's words ooze. Without credible sanctions, one can only – almost helplessly – *hope* that Rwanda lives up to the expectation that defense counsel or witness will not be prosecuted for contempt or perjury when making statements amounting to a denial of genocide, that no measures of retaliation are taken against defense witnesses, and that the courts will function independently and impartially.[79]

That being said, one may want to give the Referral Chamber credit for its recent referrals, as it seems to have departed from its previous stringent requirement that Rwanda have fully developed rule of law safeguards in place at the time of the prosecutor's application for referral. One may indeed wonder whether it is reasonable that an international criminal tribunal providing a high degree of rule of law protection, based on Western conceptions of the rule of law, should require exactly the same guarantees, to be realized here and now, from a country in transition, such as Rwanda. Arguably, an imperfect rule of law should pass the test, as this would allow for democratic learning (it is indeed hoped that in *Uwinkindi* and *Munyagishari* Rwanda will truly implement its commitments), and allows trials to take place in the very territory where the atrocities took place, thereby encouraging local ownership and contributing to national reconciliation. Viewed from this perspective, the Trial Chamber's decision in *Uwinkindi* should not, or at least not in the first place, be viewed as caving in to Rwandan pressure or as a hurried political decision informed by the ticking clock of the tribunal's completion strategy.

Nonetheless, more ethnographically oriented authors such as Nicola Palmer believe that even in *Uwinkindi* (and one would assume, *a fortiori*, in *Munyagishari*), the ICTR has relied too heavily on its own understanding of rule of law standards (and the understanding of international NGOs) instead of 'critically engaging with concurrent judicial practice inside [Rwanda].'[80] Palmer argues, on the basis of semi-structured interviews which she conducted with various protagonists at the ICTR and Rwanda, that ICTR judges are mainly interested in the development of the tribunal's own body of legally consistent case-law, whereas Rwandan legal practitioners rather emphasize the building of judicial capacity.[81] It is precisely the difference between these objectives that informs the ICTR Rule 11*bis* referrals

---

78) *Uwinkindi* referral, paras. 207-217. See on 'robust monitoring' *Munyagishari* referral, para. 211.

79) In this respect, 'Rwanda has expressed its intention to introduce new legislation that would allow the panel for any case referred for trial in Rwanda to include judges from foreign or international courts. The Chamber expects this to happen upon referral of this case and finds that this measure would further enhance the Accused's fair trial rights.' *Id.*, para. 114.

80) Nicola Palmer, 'Transfer or Transformation?: a Review of the Rule 11*bis* Decisions of the International Criminal Tribunal for Rwanda', in 20 *African Journal of International and Comparative Law* (2012) 1, 20.

81) *Id.*, at 7-16.

vaudeville, with the Tribunal since 2007 requiring that Rwanda push through legal reforms before any case could be referred, Rwanda obeying, and the Tribunal subsequently requesting new reforms. The conditions imposed by the Tribunal in *Munyagishari* clearly fit this mould, although it remains no less true that by nevertheless ordering the transfer of cases in both *Uwinkindi* and *Munyagishari*, the Tribunal has taken a leap of faith in Rwanda's rule of law potential, as compared to the pre-2011 decisions that simply dismissed the Prosecutor's applications for referral to Rwanda.

Having evaluated the ICTR referrals to Rwanda, let us now briefly return to the initial idea of referring cases to third States (see section 3.2). As the Prosecutor now seems to have secured the referral of cases to Rwanda, will he still pursue negotiations with third States (in particular European States) to accept cases from trial from the ICTR?[82] As discussed earlier, such referrals have not been particularly successful in the past. But in addition, the willingness of European States to accept these cases may have diminished. Recent practice regarding alleged Rwandan perpetrators who were not indicted by the ICTR shows that European governments are hardly enthusiastic about trying Rwandan *génocidaires* in their own courts.[83] The Swedish government, for instance, decided to extradite a Rwandan (Ahorugeze) to Rwanda who had been arrested in Stockholm in 2008.[84] Admittedly, European *courts* have so far refused to extradite individuals to Rwanda, citing exactly the due process concerns cited by the ICTR Referral Chambers in 2008.[85] However, the Referral Chamber's decision in the *Uwinkindi* decision may give fresh ammunition to governments to convince their courts to grant

---

82) See Statement by Justice Hassan B. Jallow, Prosecutor of the ICTR, to the United Nations Security Council, 6 June 2011 ('In a further attempt to implement the referral strategy of the ICTR and whilst continuing our focus in Rwanda, I visited a number of European states in April this year and held discussions with senior officials to encourage their governments to consider accepting cases for trial from the ICTR. I wish to record my appreciation for the warm reception by the member states concerned. I sincerely look forward to their positive consideration of our requests.').

83) But see the conviction of François Bazaramba in a Finnish court in 2010. Rwanda had requested Finland to extradite Bazaramba, but Finland refused to honour the request on the grounds that the defendant might not be assured of a fair trial there. Finland subsequently went on to try Bazaramba. See *International Justice Tribune* (IJT 108), 16 June 2010.

84) The Swedish Supreme Court ruled on 26 May 2009 that the Swedish Government had final authority to grant the extradition of Rwandan nationals. The Court dismissed the arguments of Ahorugeze that he was in danger of persecution in Rwanda, or that his fair trial rights would be violated. The decision (in Swedish) is available at http://www.haguejusticeportal.net/Docs/NLP/Sweden/Ahorugeze_SupremeCourt_26-5-2009.pdf.

85) See, *e.g.*, *R (Brown) v. Governor of Belmarsh Prison (DC)* [2007] 2 WLR; *Vincent Brown and others v. the Government of Rwanda and the Secretary of State for the Home Department* [2009] EWHC 770 (Admin) (ruling that there was a 'real risk' that the individuals would suffer a 'flagrant denial of justice by reason of their likely inability to adduce the evidence of supporting witnesses' if they were extradited to Rwanda, and fearing interference in the judiciary by the government of Rwanda).

extradition to Rwanda,[86] and to clear their docket of Rwandan genocide cases. This policy has been bolstered even further by the 2011 decision of the European Court of Human Rights in the already mentioned case of *Ahorugeze*. In this decision, the Court relied heavily on the ICTR Trial Chamber's considerations in the *Uwinkindi* case, and considered itself unable to conclude that substantial grounds existed for believing that Ahorugeze, if extradited to stand trial in Rwanda, faces a real risk of treatment proscribed by Article 3 or would face a real risk of a flagrant denial of justice' in violation of Article 6 ECHR.[87]

Ultimately, if the goal of the completion strategy is to prevent impunity, it does not really matter *where* presumed perpetrators of the Rwandan genocide are tried. What is relevant is *that* they are tried somewhere, whether it is at the ICTR, in Rwanda, or in Europe. If Rwanda is willing to try them all, impunity is certain not to ensue, all the more so because Rwanda considers presumed *génocidaires* as enemies of the State who will not get away with a lenient sentence. However, the fact that Rwanda precisely treats those individuals as such is reason for concern: will Rwanda sufficiently protect their due process rights? The ICTR has given Rwanda the benefit of the doubt, and it will now be up to the monitors of the African Human Rights Commission to remove all remaining doubts in the years to come. But then, if the Commission attests to rights violations, it remains to be seen what remedies can realistically be pursued. In the past, Rwanda has demonstrated abundantly its capacity to deflect criticism of its own behaviour by drawing attention to the failures of the ICTR, and by highlighting the shameful role (or absence of any role) of the Western powers in the Rwandan genocide. As far as the failures of the ICTR are concerned, the extremely long duration of the ICTR trial in the recently finished *Government* case may be cited. In this case, a judgment was rendered only on 30 September 2011 after a trial of eight years. This trial, which even resulted in the acquittal of two accused who were in custody since 1999, is sure to raise eyebrows in Kigali and further undermine the ICTR's image in Rwanda. Reflecting on this case, Schabas has even gone as far as to state that 'the Rwandan justice system compares well to the International Tribunal in this

[86] Note however that the Referral Chamber in *Uwinkindi*, para. 43, has held that 'the nature of extradition and referral proceedings is materially different': 'Extradition is a bilateral arrangement between two States wherein upon extradition the extraditing State transfers the custody of the accused to the receiving State and the former exercises no control over the trial of the extradited person. Referral, however, is a *sui generis* mechanism wherein the referring Tribunal retains the power to revoke its decision if fair trial rights are not ensured. Referral is also ordered pursuant to a stringent monitoring mechanism that keeps the Tribunal informed of the receiving State's adherence to the conditions of referral.' It is not fully clear, however, whether this fine legal distinction should have consequences for State-to-State transfer cases. After all, the human rights concerns that may impede referral are exactly the same concerns that may impede extradition.

[87] ECtHR, *Ahorugeze v. Sweden*, Appl. No. 37075/09, Judgment of 27 October 2011, paras. 95 and 129.

respect.'[88] As far as the failures of Western powers are concerned, it is of note that a Belgian judge recently attributed (December 2010) the evacuation of a UN compound where Rwandans had taken refuge in the early days of the genocide, to Belgium, and found a causal link between the evacuation and the subsequent death of the Rwandans at the hands of the Interahamwe militia.[89] Realizing their own mistakes, the international community will quite possibly refrain from voicing fierce criticism of Rwanda's trial record in the referred cases, let alone calling for a revocation by the ICTR. In fact, referrals, as well as extraditions, to Rwanda appear as *faits accomplis*.

4. Concluding Observations

This contribution has described the mismatch between States' duties to cooperate with the ICTR and the reality of State non-cooperation. States have a statutory obligation to cooperate with the Tribunal when it comes to locating and arresting fugitives, allowing witnesses to travel freely to the ICTR, or handing over documents to the Tribunal. In addition, they have at least a moral duty to accept cases for referral from the ICTR in the framework of the Tribunal's completion strategy if their laws allow for genocide trials and comply with international human rights standards, and similar duties to offer detention facilities to enforce ICTR convicts' sentences and to help the Tribunal relocate acquitted persons who have served their sentence. Reality, however, shows that States have not always complied with these legal and moral obligations. Few States have offered to accept cases for referral, to enforce sentences or to relocate persons. Rwanda has even used cooperation – which it knows is indispensable for the Tribunal's functioning – as a bargaining chip to obtain certain concessions from the Tribunal.

That being said, the ICTR should not escape its fair share of criticism for the failures of cooperation between the Tribunal and States, Rwanda in particular. Peskin has for instance argued that ICTR Prosecutor Del Ponte should not have abandoned her plans to indict RPF officers, but instead should have used any leverage that she had to ensure international cooperation with these plans.[90] More importantly perhaps, due to the slow pace of trials before the ICTR, and the Tribunal's failures during investigations, prosecutions, and trials, as exemplified by the *Barayagwiza* case, the Tribunal has lost the moral high-ground and made itself vulnerable to Rwandan counter-attacks of its record, consisting, *inter alia*, of

---

88) William A. Schabas, 'Justice Delayed at the International Criminal Tribunal for Rwanda', available at http://humanrightsdoctorate.blogspot.com/, 1 October 2011.

89) Court of First Instance (civil), *Mukeshimana and others v. Belgian State and others*, R.G. n° 04/4807/A et 07/15547/A, ILDC 1604 BE 2010, 8 December 2010.

90) Peskin, *supra* note 4, 222-225.

(unlawful) cooperation boycotts or boycott threats. Finally, apart from non-cooperative States and the ICTR itself, also the international community should receive a portion of the blame for State non-cooperation: the major powers – out of shame for the genocide or for strategic reasons – have failed to exert strong pressure on recalcitrant States (Rwanda in particular).

The end-goal of cooperation with the ICTR should however not allow for all possible means. This applies in particular to non-obligatory cooperation mechanisms, such as the referral of cases to national jurisdictions under Rule 11*bis* RPE. In this respect, it is arguable that the international community, by imposing a very tight completion schedule on the ICTR, has contributed to a prosecutorial practice of requesting premature case referrals to States that were not able or willing to prosecute ICTR indictees. Whether the very first ICTR Trial Chamber referral of an ICTR case to Rwanda will prove to be premature remains to be seen, however.

A Tale of Two Institutions: The United Nations Security Council and the International Criminal Court

Rosa Aloisi
Teaching Fellow, University of North-Texas, Denton, TX, USA

Abstract
The International Criminal Court (ICC) is a judicial body that has been created as a politically independent judicial institution to prosecute the most serious international crimes. However, the political independence of the Court has been questioned considerably in the past decade because of the relationship between the United Nations Security Council (UNSC), which has the power to refer or defer situations to the Court, and the ICC. In this work, I argue that in analyzing the relationship between the UNSC and ICC it is evident that clashing political and judicial interests have done a disservice to the implementation of international justice. I will focus on the two instances of referrals so far approved by the UNSC and highlight some of the political aspects that seem to be hindering and delaying, in spite of international pressures for UNSC attention, a referral of the situation in Syria.

Keywords
United Nations Security Council (UNSC); International Criminal Court (ICC); International Criminal Court jurisdiction

1. Introduction

The International Criminal Court (ICC) is a judicial body that has been created as a politically independent judicial institution to prosecute the most serious international crimes, including genocide war crimes, and crimes against humanity. In the words of former ICC Chief Prosecutor Luis-Moreno Ocampo, the job of the ICC is "to conduct investigations [concerning the most serious violations of international humanitarian law] fairly, impartially, and present it to the judges."[1] According to Article 13 of the ICC statute, the Court can initiate an investigation if

> a) A situation in which one or more of such crimes appears to have been committed is referred to the Prosecutor by a State Party in accordance with article 14; (b) A situation in which one or more of such crimes appears to have been committed is referred to the

[1] Louis Moreno Ocampo, with Al-Arabya News, 4 November, 2011. <http://english.alarabiya.net/articles/2011/11/04/175443.html>.

> Prosecutor by the UNSC acting under Chapter VII of the Charter of the United Nations; or (c) The Prosecutor has initiated an investigation in respect of such a crime in accordance with article 15.

The negotiations preceding the formulation of Article 13 of the ICC Statute were surrounded by considerable controversies. The final version of Article 13 of the ICC Statute, as we read it today, was the result of profound compromises and intense bargaining between those that wanted a judicial body completely independent from any political influence, and those espousing the idea of a judicial institution subordinated to some form of political control.

In particular, one of the key issues of the negotiations was the role the UNSC would play in the initiation, development, and enforcement of ICC investigations, including the type of political, social, and financial support the UNSC would provide to the ICC. The initial negotiations for the creation of a permanent international criminal court taking place within the UN International Law Commission (ILC) had envisioned a court that was perfectly subordinated to the UNSC and operating within the Charter of the United Nations.[2] Specifically, the five permanent members of the UNSC had envisioned a 1) strong role for the UNSC vis á vis the ICC and, 2) a considerably circumscribed jurisdiction of the Court.[3] Opposed to this vision were all the other countries that were extremely suspicious of the intentions of the UNSC, whose record of being an impartial and fair institution was, to say the least, questionable. Thus, as time passed and pressures to create a politically independent institution grew,[4] the ILC opted for a solution that would compromise between the two sets of expectations standing at the opposite ends of the bargaining spectrum between political independence and political subordination. In fact, the Rome Treaty, while recognizing the power of the UNSC to refer a situation to the Court, and leaving the evaluation of the admissibility of the case to the investigation of the Prosecutor, gives to the UNSC the power to defer investigations. Specifically, amid concerns raised by the permanent members of the UNSC, which opposed the political independence of the Court and the discretionary power of the ICC Chief Prosecutor, the ICC Statute recognized the power of the UNSC to defer the initiation of an investigation for 12 months, given the

---

2) Mahnoush H. Arsanjani, 'The Rome Statute of the International Criminal', *The American Journal of International Law* (1999) 22-43. William A. Schabas, 'United States Hostility to the International Criminal Court: It's All About the Security Council', *European Journal of International Law* (2004) 701-720.

3) Philippe Kirsch and John T. Holmes, 'The Rome Conference on an International Criminal Court: The Negotiating Process', *The American Journal of International Law* (1999) 2-12.

4) In one very critical editorial, Cherif Bassiouni, Chairman of the Drafting Committee of the Rome Diplomatic Conference to Establish an International Criminal Court suggested "better not to have an ICC, than to have it in the service of a political body that has hardly distinguished itself by adherence to the rule of law." Cherif Bassiouni, 'Where is the ICC Heading? The ICC – *Quo Vadis?' Journal of International Criminal Justice* (1999) 4: 421-427.

presence of peace talks, peace operations, and security concerns. This solution was largely accepted by both the legal and political parties to the negotiation of the Treaty. On the deferral power, the strict vote requirements for a resolution of the UNSC to pass – nine vote majority and the concurrence of the five permanent members of the UNSC – was a considerable guarantee that the power to defer a situation was not going to be abused.[5] On the referral power, the political authority of the UNSC could empower international justice, by de facto extending its jurisdiction to non-member states.

However, the compromised solution included in the ICC Statue has created over time operational problems in the administration of international justice. On paper, the UNSC referral mechanisms established by the Rome Treaty seemed a very good idea at the time that the Court was established. In fact, it is worth noting that the UNSC referral power extends the court's jurisdiction over states that are not members to the ICC statute and it creates obligations for member states and non-member states that go beyond the obligations descending from the Statute. However, in reality the UNSC referrals have been less than adequate in supporting the investigations of the ICC. The prospect of a referral by the UNSC to the ICC, once thought of as one of the most likely mechanisms through which the ICC would initiate investigations, has become particularly difficult because of the UNSC's political composition; the technical and financial support to the Court has been non-existent; and lastly the UNSC has been accused of dispensing referrals selectively. These considerations require a thorough assessment and reconsideration of the relationship between the ICC and UNSC, specifically of the referral power and its consequences, and of the political influence that the UNSC has over the ICC.

I argue that the referral power given to the UNSC has come at a high cost for the legitimacy and functioning of international justice. In this work, I will first give a brief overview of the relationship between the UNSC and ICC as established in the Rome Treaty. Then, I will specifically address two aspects of the UNSC referral procedures: 1) the type of enforcement mechanisms and cooperation requirements that the UNSC referral triggers and whether these enforcement mechanisms have been fully implemented; and 2) the political aspects of the referrals, which have in turn and to some extent politicized the work of the ICC. I argue that in analyzing the relationship between the UNSC and ICC as it has unfolded in the past decade, it is evident that clashing political and judicial interests have done a disservice to the implementation of international justice. I will focus on the two instances of referrals so far approved by the UNSC and highlight some of the political aspects that seem to be hindering and delaying, in spite of international pressures for UNSC attention, a referral of the situation in Syria. Lastly, I will address some of the solutions that could improve the relationship between the

5) Schabas, *supra* note 2.

ICC and the UNSC, as well as create enforcement mechanisms that might provide a better system of international justice.

2. The UNSC in the ICC Treaty

As mentioned above, within the jurisdictional preconditions of the ICC Statute (Articles 12-19) there are two specific provisions that deal with the relationship between the UNSC and the ICC. The first of these provisions, Article 13 Section (b) establishes that the UNSC may refer to the ICC a situation in which crimes that are under the jurisdiction of the ICC have been committed. The UNSC operates its functions under Chapter VII of the UN Charter and, in referring the situation to the ICC, *de facto* extends the jurisdiction of the ICC to crimes committed in territories of states that are no party to the ICC Treaty or by nationals of non-member states.

Article 16, is the second article of the ICC Statute dedicated to the UNSC, and it establishes that

> No investigation or prosecution may be commenced or proceeded with under this Statute for a period of 12 months after the Security Council, in a resolution adopted under Chapter VII of the Charter of the United Nations, has requested the Court to that effect; that request may be renewed by the Council under the same conditions.

Under these two provisions the UNSC seems to be something in between a "triggering institution" and a "gatekeeper institution". On the one hand, it promotes investigations and, on the other, can stop them based on concerns of security. The deferral power, in particular, was based on the need to reconcile peace and justice in situations in which the presence of peace talks or security concerns makes justice a secondary goal to the international community.

As mentioned above, the two articles are the result of extensive bargaining leading to the Rome Conference of 1998, during which the final Statute of the ICC was adopted. The result is a mixed jurisdictional system in which, court authority is recognized by the consent of states, but also where the UNSC has two different functions: 1) extending ICC jurisdiction and thus overcoming the requirement of "state consent" and imposing obligations that go beyond the ICC Statute; and 2) blocking ICC operations when the pursuit of peace and security and the pursuit of justice are at odds.

In spite of extensive work on the definition of the relationship between the ICC and the UNSC, the two articles leave much more work to be done in order for the ICC to be fully operative and for the UNSC to appear as unbiased as possible and driven by the magnitude of the crimes rather than political relations. There are two major concerns that Articles 13(b) and 16 present to the international community. First, the UNSC referral under Chapter VII of the Charter has the power to impose obligations on all member states of the Charter, regardless of their status as members of the ICC. However, it has been noted that once the UNSC refers a situation of a non-member state to the ICC, the latter has no power to enforce cooperation on that state under Part 9 of the Rome Treaty.[6] Thus, the UNSC itself should be in charge of enforcing cooperation. Secondly and more importantly, the practice of referral and deferral by the UNSC has been governed by political motives, thus diminishing in the eyes of the international community the legitimacy of the ICC's work. The questions to examine are two: 1) how has the UNSC fared in helping the ICC to enforce cooperation on non-member states;? and 2) How much have the UNSC referrals (Darfur and Libya) and the decision not to yet discuss the situation in Syria been dictated by political concerns rather than the magnitude of the crimes? I suggest that the UNSC has not been particularly helpful in enabling the ICC to dispense international justice and that the ICC has willingly compromised some important requirements which characterized the legitimacy of law, in order to achieve that little international political support it could gather from the UNSC.

3. Enforcing and Providing Cooperation

There has been an increasing debate as to the type of obligations the UNSC referral imposes on non-member states to the ICC. As appropriately noted by Cassese (2006), the ICC is equipped with enforcement measures in the event that relevant member states under the ICC attention fail to cooperate with the investigation of the Court. In fact, Article 87(7) of the Rome Treaty establishes that

> Where a State Party fails to comply with a request to cooperate by the Court contrary to the provisions of this Statute, thereby preventing the Court from exercising its functions and powers under this Statute, the Court may make a finding to that effect and refer the matter to the Assembly of States Parties or, where the Security Council referred the matter to the Court, to the Security Council.

However, given the principle of "state consent", Article 87(7) is only "dead letter" to non-member states. Thus, the UNSC referral of states that have not accepted the jurisdiction of the Court, while giving the ICC a considerable extension of its jurisdiction, must also be enforced to some extent with the help of the UNSC itself. Once a referral takes place and a relevant state fails to cooperate the ICC should have the full support of Chapter VII of the UN Charter and any refusal to redress a specific behaviour by a state should trigger the full enforcement mechanisms of

[6] Dapo Akande, 'The Effects of Security Council Resolutions and Domestic Proceedings on State Obligations to Cooperate with the ICC', *Journal of International Criminal Justice* (2012) 299-324.

Chapter VII, including the use of military force. However, there is much debate with regard to the cooperation of non-member states to the ICC and the collaboration of the UNSC following a referral. Scholars have extensively analyzed the content of the obligations that non-member states face following the UNSC referral.[7] Specifically, first the referral by the UNSC definitely triggers a full cooperation responsibility on states; second the UNSC has a certain freedom in imposing specific responsibilities, not necessarily descending from the statute of the ICC; third, it can use its political power to devise sanctions and consequences otherwise not available to the ICC enforcement machinery.

That being said, up to this day the UNSC has referred two cases to the ICC (Sudan on Darfur and Libya) and listened to several reports of the ICC Chief Prosecutor on the development of the investigations. However, given the enormous difficulties faced by the ICC in accessing the countries under investigations, the lack of arrests of major criminals indicted, and the lengthy proceedings through which cases are built, we must wonder whether the UNSC has supported the investigations and procedures of the situations referred to the ICC. In particular, we need to assess the UNSC performance on three different grounds: 1) the amount of actual cooperation the UNSC has requested from relevant states; 2) the amount of cooperation given to the ICC following the referral; and 3) the technical and financial support necessary to the ICC to perform its investigations.

3.1. *The Request of Cooperation*

The UNSC has, at the time of writing, referred two situations to the ICC; The Sudan situation on Darfur and the situation in Libya. While I will subsequently examine these situations more extensively, they are important at this point of the analysis to understand how the UNSC has signalled to the relevant states the importance of the referral and the gravity of the consequences for the lack of cooperation. The two referrals approved with two different UNSC Resolutions,[8] bear some considerable problems associated with the wording of the requested cooperation which limits considerably the subjects that can fall under the attention of the ICC and restricts the type of activities investigators can embark upon while performing their duties.

The resolutions pertaining to the referral of the Darfur and Libya situations are similar both in their terms and wording. While obliging the states to cooperate

---

7) Akande, *supra* note 6. Carsten Stahn, 'Libya, the International Criminal Court and Complementarity – A Test for Shared Responsibility', *Journal of International Criminal Justice* (2012)325-349. Lawrence Moss, 'The UN Security Council and the International Criminal Court – Towards a More Principled Relationship', *UN Security Council in Focus* (March, 2012) 1-13.

8) Security Council Resolution 1593 (UN/SC/RES 1593) 31 March, 2005. Security Council Resolution 1970 (UN/SC/RES 1970) 26 February, 2011.

with the ICC, the resolutions have clearly recognized that other non-state parties have no obligations under the statute, and invite organizations or other parties involved in the conflict to only "cooperate". Paragraph 6 of both Resolutions indicates that

> nationals, current or former officials or personnel from a State outside the (Sudan) or (Libyan Arab Jamahiriya) which is not a party to the Rome Statute of the International Criminal Court, shall be subject to the exclusive jurisdiction of that State for all alleged acts or omissions arising out or related to operations in (Sudan) or (the Libyan Arab Jamahiriya) established or authorized by the UNSC, unless such exclusive jurisdiction has been expressly waived by the State.

Some UNSC member states were particularly concerned regarding the wording of the resolutions that limited the ICC jurisdiction to the relevant state under investigation, thus jeopardizing the achievement of universal justice and suggesting a hierarchy of crimes based on the individuals that perpetrated them. These provisions created concern among some of the States sitting at the UNSC; In spite of approving the referral in order to let the ICC exercise its jurisdiction on the cases, Argentina and Brazil manifested their disapproval of the limitation of jurisdiction included in UNSC resolution 1593 referring the situation in Sudan, while Brazil voiced its regret in the UNSC Resolution 1970, referring Libya. The main concern about the limitations imposed on the ICC jurisdiction by the UNSC concerns the fact that such limitations could become a standard practice of the UNSC referrals. The consequences of the wording of the UNSC resolutions considerably diminish the potential effectiveness of the referral as a mandatory enforcement mechanism, while at the same time justifying pockets of impunity. In establishing the above limitation of the ICC jurisdiction, the UNSC is shielding from prosecution individuals who may have committed crimes in light of their personal capacity, thus creating a jurisdiction *ad personam* in clear violation of legal principles of equality and impartiality.

We should also note that there are considerable differences between the practices the UNSC is endorsing within the ICC and the support given by the UNSC to the ad hoc tribunals for the former Yugoslavia and Rwanda. Under the statutes of the ad hoc tribunals the UNSC imposed a general obligation of cooperation upon all member states. Ultimately this led to considerable facilitation in the execution of arrest warrants for those indicted by the two ad hoc tribunals. In this regard, the ICC is still facing considerable difficulties in arresting President Al-Bashir of The Sudan in spite of the fact that he has travelled extensively through Africa and to countries that are members of the ICC. Interestingly, one particular issue the UNSC has neglected to address is the execution of arrest warrants, in particular of head of states, such as Al-Bashir in the Sudan situation. Given the extension of jurisdiction provided by the UNSC referral, it is still unclear whether Article 98 of the Rome Treaty, which regulates the "Cooperation with respect to waiver of immunity and consent to surrender" allows states to claim the immunity of head of states or the request of full cooperation and obligations descending from the Chapter VII of UN Charter overcomes Article 98.

In the specific case of Al-Bashir confusion arose given the firm resistance of the African Union to interpret the referral of the UNSC as lifting President Bashir's immunity. The absence of such specification in the UNSC referral and the tentative terms with which it delimited the ICC jurisdiction weakened considerably the position of the ICC and its personnel in trying to access the country and asking other state members to the ICC to arrest Al-Bashir. President Al-Bashir has been travelling freely throughout Africa and each and every country, including Malawi, Chad, and Kenya have adamantly refused to arrest him, suggesting that the UNSC referral or its request of cooperation with the ICC does not in any way mean that Al-Bashir immunities have been lifted. It could have been sufficient in order to enhance the ICC position in the Darfur case that the UNSC had expressly mentioned the removal of Article 98 and the full application of Article 27 of the Rome Treaty, which establishes the "irrelevance of the official capacity" for those indicted of the crimes under the ICC jurisdiction. This is just an example showing how the lack of specifications regarding the exact terms of the obligations imposed by the referral, creates enormous difficulties for the exercise of the ICC jurisdiction.

Additionally, compared to the ad hoc tribunals the ICC faces extensive resistance from many nations of the world that portray the ICC as a politically and geographically biased institution. This, and the lack of enforcement mechanisms in cases referred by the UNSC, not only weakens the ability to improve the application of universal justice, but creates disincentives for other states to ratify the ICC statute or implement legislation that could favour the apprehension and prosecution of war criminals.

3.2. *Giving Cooperation*

It has been noted that the UNSC has been particularly passive and absent in giving support to the ICC after the referral of a specific situation. The relationship between the ICC and the UNSC has been limited to the periodic reports the Chief Prosecutor has presented concerning the evolution of the investigation. On its side the UNSC has done very little to participate or support the investigations launched following its referrals. However, on this point, two considerations are necessary. On the one hand, there is without a doubt a deep responsibility by the UNSC from not acting, even following instances of non-cooperation duly reported by the Prosecutors. The UNSC has been doing very little to acknowledge the difficulties through which the ICC has worked and has not threatened the enforcement of mechanisms under Charter VII of the UN Charter following clear instances of non-cooperation. On the other hand, the ICC prosecutor has been accused of moving at "leisurely pace", thus delaying measures that the UNSC could have undertaken following non-cooperative behaviour. Scholars noted that the ICC Prosecutor considerably delayed sending requests to the Sudanese authorities to enter the country with investigators.[9] The requests would have been met by a firm denial, at which point the prosecutor could have asked the UNSC to take into consideration the refusal to cooperate and implement the appropriate measures to secure compliance.

There is also little cooperation when it comes to the imposition of sanctions against individuals who are indicted by the Court. The UNSC has at its disposal a lengthy list of sanctions that run from the freezing of foreign assets, to travel bans that could help the ICC to pursue its quest for justice. The most recent case of the referral of the situation in Libya has been one that shows how the UNSC has been particularly reluctant in giving assistance to the ICC. The Court has been having problems collecting evidence, accessing sites where crimes have been committed, and even talking to those indicted,[10] which inevitably hinder any possibility of securing fruitful proceedings in The Hague. The UNSC has not exerted any kind influence, remaining mostly silent on the consequences its referral is having on the implementation of justice.

The main problem remains one of cooperation and assistance from a political body such as the UNSC, which has the means to enforce cooperation, to a judicial body that lacks completely this kind of enforcement mechanisms. Whether the responsibility for the lack of cooperation lies in the inability of the ICC to move at a faster pace or in the unwillingness of the UNSC to give effective cooperation to the Court, the dynamics of the relationship between the two institutions remain particularly complicated. Member states of the UNSC have suggested that if there is a lack of political will, especially by the five permanent members of the UNSC, three of which, Russia, China, and U.S. are not even party to the ICC, to create stronger ties with the ICC in the investigation of cases referred by the UNSC itself, then a solution might be that of creating committees of support. Such committees might follow up on the cases referred by the UNSC together with the ICC and provide the necessary assistance and back up enforcement mechanisms which a referral entails.

3.3. *Technical and Financial Support*

International investigations are costly and demanding. Courtroom proceedings are also expensive and time consuming in which a full array of experts,

---

[9] Antonio Cassese, 'Is the ICC Still Having Teething Problems?' *Journal of International Criminal Justice* (2006) 434-441.

[10] For example, as of today it is not clear under which conditions Al Islam Gaddafi is detained. As well, the ICC has not had any access to the place where he is detained.

interpreters, psychologists, and victims assistants is necessary to ensure the correct functioning of international justice. The ICC has been facing many difficulties in dealing with the lack of resources and time consuming procedures. From a financial point of view the UNSC has made a common practice to mention in the referrals that member states to the ICC bear the costs of the investigations. This situation is particularly new when it comes to the relationship between the UNSC and international judicial institutions. Indeed, the UNSC and General Assembly have borne most of the expenses of the investigations taking place at the International Criminal Tribunals for the former Yugoslavia and Rwanda.

Even more, the UNSC referrals have prevented any financial help that might be given to the ICC by the UN and thus, for example, in paragraph 8 of the Resolution 1970 regarding the Libya situation, it establishes that

> none of the expenses incurred in connection with the referral, including expenses related to investigations or prosecutions in connection with that referral, shall be borne by the UN and that such costs by the parties to the Rome Statute and those States that wish to contribute voluntarily.

The obstacles the ICC faces in embarking upon complex investigations with limited financial support have been additionally complicated by the lack of any technical or administrative support by the UNSC. Once again the UNSC lacks the political will to come to the aid of the ICC investigations. In the midst of the ICTY investigations, the UNSC created a Commission of Experts whose investigations and reports were used by the ad hoc Tribunal to investigate numerous violations of humanitarian law in the former Yugoslavia as well as initiate several important prosecutions. In the case of the ICC, the first referral of the situation of Darfur had been preceded by a Commission of Inquiry, which had followed several assessments of the situation by UN human rights bodies. However, in a swift decision to refer the situation of Libya, the UNSC did so before there were valid grounds that would support the existence of case on which the ICC would then initiate a Trial. Only after the referral did the UN Human Rights Council decide to create a commission of inquiry to help the ICC.

This is, in reality, a controversial issue. Certainly it could be suggested that waiting for a Commission of inquiry to initiate and conclude an investigation which would give ground to the ICC to proceed with its own legal assessment of the crimes, could further deteriorate the already precarious situation in countries facing escalation of violence. However, it is worrisome that following the referral the UNSC only relies on the reports of the Chief Prosecutor to become informed of the ongoing investigations, while waiting for other bodies of the UN, such as the Human Rights Council to assess the gravity and developments of crises, and indicate the necessary measures and programs to follow to redress violations of humanitarian law. It has become particularly evident that the Rome Treaty, while establishing a principle of cooperation between two institutions of different nature, has relied considerably on the development of praxis through the referral of cases—praxis that should address the unspecified procedures through which the two institutions should cooperate. What the participants to the Rome Treaty forgot to ask was: what happens after the UNSC refers a situation outside the jurisdictional realm of the ICC? How much involvement and responsibility should the UNSC have in the case? Most likely, these and many more questions about the relationship between the UNSC and the ICC were left unanswered because of their political implications and the unwillingness of the permanent members of the UNSC to commit to a judicial institution that could alter political relationships.

3.4. *General Considerations on the UNSC Cooperation*

Experts and international lawyers participating at the Rome Conference and bargaining the terms of the UNSC involvement with the ICC in the years preceding 1998, had already anticipated that the UNSC could hardly gather the political will to refer cases to the ICC. The composition of the UNSC, the fact that three of its five permanent members had shown signs of prejudice toward the Court, and thus the difficulty of achieving a necessary majority to refer a case, were all signs of a considerable lack of alignment between a heavily politicized organ and a permanent international judicial body. However, even after welcoming as a sign of improved cooperation the two referral cases of Darfur and Libya, the ICC seems to be doomed to struggle in its investigations by the lack of political will in the UNSC.

As cogently noted by international relations analysts,[11] if the Darfur and Libya situation taught us something about the enforcement and cooperation mechanisms within the ICC operations, we should know that for an international judicial body to be successful some fundamental prerequisites must be in place: political, technical and financial support, together with the enforcement of arrest warrants. As we have seen from the analysis above, the UNSC has been unwilling or politically constrained, thus delimiting its support to the ICC. Inadequate support of the UNSC to the ICC has been particularly evident in the Sudan case. Even after the Prosecutor reported to the UNSC that Sudan was not cooperating under the terms of Chapter VII of the UN Charter, the UNSC failed to take any concrete step to secure Sudan' s cooperation. Additionally, the presence of China and Russia among the five permanent members of the UNSC has basically worked as an informal guarantee that Al-Bashir or any other subject indicted by the UNSC will ever be apprehended by the ICC. Both states have placed great emphasis on

---

11) Till Papenfuss, 'What If Syria was Referred to the ICC?', *Global Observatory, Analysis on Global Issues*, 20 June 2012, <http://www.theglobalobservatory.org/analysis/309-what-if-syria-was-referred-to-the-icc.html>.

non-interference in the affairs of other states due in part to both sovereignty concerns and fear of external interference in their own affairs. The economic and political interests that China and Russia have in the region create considerable protection against any infringement of Al-Bashir's immunity, and many other states for that matter. The failure to cooperate with the ICC now extends to the parties to the ICC Treaty, which independently of the UNSC referral are bound to cooperate with the ICC under Part 9 of the treaty. As mentioned above, both Malawi and Chad are members of the ICC that have hosted President Al-Bashir, but refused to arrest him, with the additional support of the African Union, which constantly calls for a deferral of the Sudan situation and Bashir's arrest warrant.

The referral of the Libya situation comes with additional problems. In an attempt to promptly react to the escalation of violence the UNSC adopted the Resolution 1970 very quickly, but in doing so and to garner the consensus of its members, copied most of the sections of the Darfur situation, including sections in which the jurisdiction of the court was considerably limited and focused specifically on "crimes against humanity" following the narrow investigation of events that had taken place in Benghazi. As well as for the Sudan case, the referral of the situation in Libya left a considerable number of problems unresolved, including "duties of arrest and surrender or the applicability of immunity provisions."[12] In addressing the situation in Libya at a much faster pace than the situation in Darfur, the Prosecutor quickly issued arrest warrants and, as quickly, the Pre-Trial Chamber gave its approval. Criticism followed considering that the UNSC did not really support the ICC operations and as per today, the ICC has not arrested anyone considered responsible for the violations of humanitarian law in Libya. The Libya situation is particularly complex as the National Transitional Council, Libya's temporary government, asserts Libya's ability and willingness to prosecute those indicted by the ICC. Problems of complementarity, jurisdiction, and admissibility of the case ultimately have created a stalemate between the ICC and Libya, with a largely silent and unresponsive UNSC.

4. Politics vs. Justice

> …international justice cannot be sheltered from political consideration when they are administered by the quintessential political body: the Security Council. I have long advocated a separation of the justice and political agendas, and would prefer to see an ICC that had no connection to the Security Council. But this is neither the case nor the trend. (Louis Arbour)[13]

---

12) Stahn, *supra* note 7, p. 330.

13) Louise Arbour, 'The Rise and Fall of International Human Rights' British Museum, 27 April 2011, Lecture <http://www.crisisgroup.org/en/publication-type/speeches/2011/the-rise-and-fall-of-international-human-rights.aspx>.

The political dimension of international justice is undeniable. The creation of international criminal courts, ad hoc and special tribunals has been the result of political will and, whether they have been more or less successful, has depended upon political support. International judicial institutions do not possess their own enforcement mechanisms; they do not have a police force to arrest indicted individuals and must rely either on the cooperation of sovereign states or on the only organ that can enforce orders made under Chapter VII of the Charter of the UN, which is the UNSC. The political and legal compromises of which I spoke above are particularly evident in the referrals, but especially in the non-referrals of situations by the UNSC to the ICC. Many feared that the legal functions of the ICC could interfere with the political functions of the UNSC. The UNSC feared that an investigation might interfere with ongoing efforts of conflict resolution, while the ICC feared that situations could remain pending before the UNSC, under Article 16 of the Rome Treaty without ever being resolved.[14]

There is also a political-judicial paradox affecting the relationship between the ICC and the UNSC. It is a common belief that in order for international justice to be legitimate, independence from political will is a necessary requirement. However, the ability of the UNSC referral to extend the jurisdiction of the Court has been considered an important aspect of the achievement of universal justice. In the absence of the UNSC referrals some of the worst cases of international humanitarian law could go unpunished. Given the presence of this intricate relationship the points that remain to analyze are a) whether the ICC can maintain fairness and impartiality in situations referred by the UNSC; b) and whether the UNSC can debate and refer situations based on the gravity of crimes, rather than on the political considerations of its permanent members. These points can be analyzed by assessing the two referrals of the UNSC on Sudan and Libya, but also by looking into other cases, such as Yemen, Sri Lanka, and more recently Syria, which in spite of international pressures for UNSC referral, have not received the attention of the UNSC.

Former Chief Prosecutor of the ICC, Luis Moreno Ocampo, clearly implied that the UNSC's inertia is negatively affecting the implementation of international justice by ignoring the spread of violence in several regions of the world. In an interview with the *Al Arabiya News*, when asked about Yemen and Syria, Ocampo answered "...talk to the Security Council, they can do it, they can decide to refer the case to the ICC; it is their decision, it is their responsibility, not mine [...]. Without a referral I have no jurisdiction, I can do nothing."[15] It is evident that the main problem linked with the inertia of the UNSC lies in the fact that without a referral the ICC cannot intervene where its jurisdiction is needed the most, where violence, violation of humanitarian law and political persecution are rampant.

---

14) Arsanjani, *supra* note 2.

15) Ocampo, *supra* note 1.

Through the present, the UNSC has assessed potential ICC referrals with a political lens. It seems that considerations of power politics, typical of international relations, have created a world of first and second class crimes, as well as a list of sovereignties that can be or cannot be breached by the investigations of the ICC. Ultimately, the ICC is not a truly independent institution, but significantly influenced by the five Permanent Members of the UNSC, which can defer or not-refer a valid case.

4.1. *The UNSC Referral of the Darfur Situation: Politically Tolerated*

When the UNSC referred the Sudan case on Darfur to the ICC with UNSC Resolution 1593 adopted on 31 March 2005, leaders and supporters of the Court were speaking of a breakthrough in the relationship between the two institutions.[16] However, the referral was approved following the abstentions from voting by China and the United States, which could have vetoed the decision. The abstentions signalled more a "tolerance" toward the decision following the report of the Commission of Inquiry into the situation, which unveiled the dramatic events taking place in Darfur, rather than a political commitment to the prosecution of crimes by the ICC. The need to avoid a veto of two of the permanent members of the UNSC, prompted some of its member states to tailor a referral that made some forms of concessions to the US and China and did not simply consist of a blank referral to the ICC. Indeed, the US was particularly keen to point out that the only reason why it did not veto the Resolution was due to the need for the international community to work together in order to end impunity in Sudan. The US also wanted certain guarantees to be given to protect US nationals from prosecution and to shield the UN from the costs associated with the operation of the ICC. The US made sure that the resolution referring the case to the ICC recognized the existence of Article 98 agreements with many states assuring that these states would not surrender US nationals to the ICC for prosecution. In a similar fashion, paragraph 6 of the referral also established that

> nationals, current or former officials or personnel from a contributing State outside Sudan which is not a party to the Rome Statute of the International Criminal Court shall be subject to the exclusive jurisdiction of that contributing State for all alleged acts or omissions arising out of or related to operations in Sudan established or authorized by the Council or the African Union, unless such exclusive jurisdiction has been expressly waived by that contributing State.

Paragraph 6 of the resolution represents a particular problematic statement for the performance of international justice. It seems to indicate that the UNSC does not abide by the principles of equality and impartiality that should govern the

---

[16] Cassese, *supra* note 9.

administration of international law. As well, it compromises the independence and legitimacy of the ICC by according a permanent immunity from prosecution to a long list of individuals.

China also abstained, and it has considerable political and economic interests at stake in The Sudan, as noted by several news agencies[17] and scholars.[18] From oil extracting firms, to the export of arms, China has been a close ally of the Sudanese government since the early 1990s. China has kept buying oil from the Sudanese government, thus helping finance Sudan's politics of repression in Darfur. Arms made in China have been used to perpetrate the genocidal policies of the Sudanese government.[19] The opposition that China plays inside the UNSC has been particularly strong. While the UNSC could have played a firmer role in imposing sanctions, introducing economic embargos, and enforcing travel bans, it has submitted its will to the political interests of and veto threats by China.[20] Lastly and more generally the UNSC made another statement that substantially limits the support the ICC would receive in its investigation of the Darfur situation. Paragraph 2 of the UNSC 1593 established that "…States not party to the Rome Statute have no obligation under the Statute, [and] urges all States and concerned regional and other international organizations to cooperate fully."

Contrary to the resolutions that created the ad hoc tribunals for the former Yugoslavia and Rwanda, Resolution 1593 seems to imply no particular urgency for states to cooperate with the ICC. The main problem with the statement however, was not only that of limiting the responsibility of cooperation, but that of limiting the legitimacy of the Court in the eyes of non-member states and state parties to the ICC. If a judicial institution cannot ask for the full support of the international community to perform its duties, and this situation is also enabled by the organ of the UN that has the power to enforce such cooperation, then the ICC seems to be doomed to be a weak institution facing insurmountable challenges and opposition to its jurisdiction.

All these considerations are a clear indication that, although welcomed as sign that the world would not tolerate heinous crimes going unpunished, the referral of the Darfur situation was *de facto* approved because of specific political compromises that have been limiting the power of the investigation of the ICC and level of collaboration of the UNSC in securing information, access to sites, and arrest

---

17) Peter S. Goodman, 'China Invests Heavily in Sudan's Oil Industry', *Washington Post Foreign Service*, December 23, 2004. *See also*, BBC News Africa, 'Darfur Arms Report that Angered China Goes to the UN', 12 November 2010.

18) Paul D. Williams and Alex J. Bellamy, 'The Responsibility to Protect and the Crisis in Darfur', *Security Dialogue* (2005) 27-47. Erica Downs, 'The Fact and Fiction of Sino-Africa Energy Relations', *China Security* (2007) 42-68.

19) Kristof, Nicholas D. "China and Sudan, Blood and Oil", *New York Times*, 23 April 2006.

20) Richard Goldstone, 'Holding Heads of State Accountable for Crimes against their Peoples: The Al-Bashir and Gaddafi Cases', *International Judicial Monitor* (2011) <http://www.judicial-monitor.org/archive_fall2011/sectorassessment.html>.

warrants. As Goldstone has cogently pointed out,[21] when the UNSC refers a case to the ICC, its political will to enforce the consequences descending from the referral are tested against the relevant state. I argue that its political will is also tested against the political standing of the members of the UNSC. Sudan has consistently questioned, together with the African Union, the legitimacy of the ICC actions following the UNSC referral, by refusing to arrest President Bashir. However, the UNSC has also failed to start the full enforcement machinery of Chapter VII of the UN Charter, by simply choosing not to impose sanctions and restrictions on Bashir and Sudan, but also on those countries that have hosted Bashir and that should be cooperating with the ICC as state parties to the ICC Treaty.

4.2. *The UNSC Referral of the Libya Situation: A "Swift" Decision*

As suggested by scholars,[22] UNSC Resolution 1970, with which the situation of Libya was referred to the ICC, reflected many of the shortcomings of the Sudan referral and additional problems due to the time frame within which it was approved. Indeed, in an attempt to quickly respond to the violence escalating in Benghazi and to the failure of Gaddafi's government to protect its population, the UNSC resolution was approved with an unprecedented unanimous decision to refer the case to the ICC. The referral occurred before the International Commission of Inquiry into the escalation of violence in Libya had concluded its work and before a solid ground for prosecution had been established. Certainly there was widespread evidence of violations of humanitarian law and crimes against humanity being committed in Libya, which prompted the immediate referral.[23] The ICC immediately issued an arrest warrant for Gaddafi, one of his sons, Saif Al-Islam Gaddafi, and a senior member of its government Abdullah Al-Senussi. The African Union quickly reacted by asking African countries to not cooperate with the Court, while some of the non-permanent members of the UNSC, although voting in favour of the referral, manifested their concerns regarding the possibility that the ICC investigation could hinder attempts at finding a negotiated exit from power by Gaddafi and his supporters.

In its entirety, Resolution 1970 of the UNSC was better structured than the Sudan referral and, as suggested by scholars,[24] better supported by the UNSC's

---

21) *Ibid.*

22) Stahn, *supra* note 7. Leslie Vinjamuri, 'The ICC and Conflict Zone' interview appeared on Canadian International Council, May 6, 2012. <http://www.opencanada.org/features/leslie-vinjamuri/>.

23) Report of the International Commission of Inquiry to Investigate All Alleged Violations of International Law in the Libyan Arab Jamahiriya. UN Doc. A/HRC/17/44, 1 June, 2011.

24) Ivo H. Daalder and James G. Stavridis, 'Nato's Victory in Libya – The Right Way to Run an Intervention', *Foreign Policy* (2012) 2-7.

actions. The resolution imposed arms embargo, travel bans, and froze the assets of Gaddafi and his supporters. However, the rapidity of its approval created two different sets of problems for the operations of the ICC. First, there was a general problem of information about the facts that had justified the referral. The ICC stepped into a conflict situation without adequate knowledge of the events that had unfolded up to February 2011 and, although the Pre-Trial Chamber issued the arrest warrants only a week after the referral, there was a long list of Gaddafi's supporters who were simply unknown to the ICC investigators. Second, Resolution 1970 did not provide any bargaining strategy with Gaddafi's government and its supporters signalling that, in spite of a long list of sanctions intended to shape Gaddafi's behaviour, the real intention of the Resolution was to force Gaddafi out of power and create a new regime.[25] This situation most likely triggered an additional escalation of violence, which then prompted the UNSC to approve Resolution 1973 asking all UN member states to discuss measures, including the use of force, to enforce security in Libya.

In addition to these problems, the UNSC referral contains some ambiguous provisions that still speak, in spite of its unanimous approval, of the worries about ICC universal jurisdiction. Like the Sudan resolution, Resolution 1970, excludes non ICC parties from the possibility of cooperation or prosecution by the Court, once again violating the principle of equality before the law and impartiality of its application. The referral also establishes a limitation on the temporal jurisdiction of the Court, asking the ICC to investigate crimes under its jurisdiction that have occurred after February 11, 2011. Although the Court jurisdiction on state members to the ICC is temporarily limited from the date they have ratified the Rome Treaty, one of the advantages of the UNSC referrals is its ability to tailor such resolutions in a way that would provide the most encompassing form of justice. Paragraph 4 of the Resolution establishing the temporal limitation of the Court is a suspicious sign to the international community about the real intentions of the UNSC limitation. Western countries had long-term political and economic relationships with Gaddafi's regime, and their affairs will never come under the scrutiny of the ICC investigation. Lastly, the referral, while not mentioning Article 13(b) of the ICC Statute, mentions Article 16 with regard to the deferral power of the UNSC. Given the approval of Resolution 1973, after which NATO forces were deployed in Libyan air space to enforce security and protect humanitarian interests, the reference to Article 16 in Resolution 1970 looms as a potential hindrance to the ICC investigation that could happen at any time when peace talks or security concerns rise.

Ultimately, as with the Sudan referral, the above considerations lead to the conclusion that Resolution 1970 is as much political, as was Resolution 1593. Although welcomed as an opportunity for the ICC to investigate crimes that would have

---

25) Vinjamuri, *supra* note 22.

otherwise remained outside its jurisdiction, the UNSC referral has *de facto* helped create the basis for the enforcement of a selective justice—one in which individuals may not be indicted, states may not cooperate, and crimes may not be investigated. A more general concern lies in the fact that the repetition of limitations to the ICC jurisdiction in both Resolutions 1593 and 1970 could signal praxis that the UNSC is establishing to politically control the ICC's investigations. The ICC has already been attacked as an institution in the hands of western powers. The limitations imposed on the investigations by the UNSC resolutions, which practically shield UN member states and nationals from the ICC prosecution, are a clear signal of political power working through a judicial institution. Under these conditions the ICC is not only limited in the impact that it may have on the promotion of justice, deterrence of crimes, and establishment of peace, but its legitimate standing as an impartial and fair judicial institution may also be questioned.

4.3. *Cases Non-Referred: A Missing Opportunity*

As much as an analysis of the UNSC referrals tells us about its commitment to the ICC and its political interests, a true understanding of the delicate balance between these institutions and the clash of justice and politics comes from the analysis of the many situations which, although carrying the same characteristics of the referred cases, have not been receiving the attention of the UNSC. Some have suggested that the political nature of the referrals of the Darfur and Libya situations is evident in that the gravity of the crimes committed in those situations are not any greater than violations of humanitarian law occurring elsewhere, but overlooked by the UNSC.[26] Some have argued that the growing influence of the ICC can be jeopardized by further involvement of the UNSC in the investigations of the ICC.[27] Among scholars and practitioners there is lively debate as to whether it is better not to have a universal justice, than to have it at the expenses of judicial independence.[28]

These concerns are well founded. Up to this day the UNSC has been avoiding inquiries and potential discussions about referrals regarding many other cases in which the intervention of the Court might be necessary. In 2009 the UNSC failed to take into serious consideration crimes against civilians in Sri Lanka and Gaza. A report by the UN had brought to light that tens of thousands of civilians had lost their lives between January and May 2009 in the fight between the government of

26) Simon Jennings, 'Playing Politics with the ICC: The Security Council's Referral of Libya to The Hague Court Highlights the Limitations of International Justice', *Institute for War and Peace Reporting* (2011) < http://iwpr.net/report-news/playing-politics-icc>.

27) Richard Dicker, 'A Flawed Court in Need of Credibility', *OP-ED, The New York Times*, May 21, 2012.

28) Bassiouni, *supra* note 4.

Sri Lank and Tamil rebels, with crimes committed most likely by both sides to the conflict.[29] More recently a report by Amnesty International to the 21st session of the UN Human Rights Council,[30] established that after years of conflict, Sri Lanka has failed to account for the crimes committed by government and rebels thereby creating a climate of impunity "where arbitrary detentions, torture and other ill-treatment, enforced disappearances, and custodial killings continue unchecked."[31] Although such assessments of the Sri Lanka situation might trigger the complementary jurisdiction of the ICC, it has become very clear that Sri Lanka will never be taken into consideration by the UNSC, given Russia's firm opposition to even discuss the case and China's strong support for the Sri Lankan government.

The "Arab Spring" highlighted even greater problems with the political standing of the UNSC and the enforcement of international justice. The events unfolding in Yemen, violations of human rights in Bahrain of unarmed protesters asking for the end of Al Khalifa regime's brutality, and the violence currently escalating in Syria have not been addressed by the UNSC in the framework of international justice. Although adopting various resolutions regarding the Yemen situation condemning human rights violations by Yemeni authorities and urging the initiation of investigations according to international standards, the UNSC never mentioned the Rome Treaty or the ICC.[32] The close ties of the Yemeni regime to and the strategic interests of the US in the region have been identified as the primary obstacles to a UNSC referral. While Bahrain protesters and human rights organizations have asked the ICC to intervene by issuing arrest warrants for the regime leaders inflicting torture and persecution on civilians, the UNSC has remained mostly silent. There are significant political interests in maintaining a friendly regime in a strategic section of the Middle East rather than seeing the rise to power Shiite-led government which, according to scholars, "could increase Iran's influence and lead to the loss of U.S. use of Bahrain's military facilities."[33]

More recently much debate has occurred around the UNSC's failure to consider a referral of the current situation in Syria. In August 2011 the Human Rights Council established an international commission of inquiry into the situation in Syria and

---

29) Report of the Secretary General's Panel of Experts on Accountability in Sri Lanka. 31 March, 2011. http://www.un.org/News/dh/infocus/Sri_Lanka/POE_Report_Full.pdf.

30) "No Real Will to Account: Shortcomings in Sri Lanka's National Plan of Action to Implement the Recommendation of the LLRC" Amnesty International Written statement to the 21st session of the UN Human Rights Council (10-28 September 2012). <http://www.amnesty.org/en/library/asset/ASA37/010/2012/en/b2a6a558-1da8-4de7-a9a0-650ef5732b9cb/asa370102012en.pdf>.

31) *Ibid*, p.1.

32) UNSC Resolution 2014, 21 October, 2011. (UN/SC/RES/2014). <http://daccess-dds-ny.un.org/doc/UNDOC/GEN/N11/559/61/PDF/N1155961.pdf?OpenElement>.

33) Kenneth Katzman, 'Bahrain: Reform, Security, and U.S. Policy', *Congressional Research Service Report* (2012) p. 16.

urged the UNSC to refer the situation to the ICC.[34] When states on the UNSC started drafting a referral it was done with a clear reference to the ICC jurisdiction over the crimes committed, but the reference was removed given the immediate reaction of China and Russia, which feared an escalation of rapid events as in Libya. Following many reports of the Human Rights Council and the Office of the High Commissioner for Human Rights, the UNSC was repeatedly briefed to take action so that international criminal responsibility could be addressed. However, a referral seems particularly unlikely in the near future.

On this point, scholars and practitioners are divided between those calling for an immediate referral of the situation to the ICC[35] and those believing that a referral may create a backlash and further escalate violence.[36] However, before considering a referral, the main problem to address remains a political one—the viability of a referral to the ICC of the Syria situation must go through the political evaluation of the permanent members of the UNSC, simply because Syria is not a party to the ICC. The ties that Russia and China have with the Bashar al-Assad government make a referral of the UNSC to the ICC unlikely. Furthermore, it is feared that a veto by Russia and China regarding ICC intervention could be interpreted by the Syrian regime as a source of impunity, which further complicates the matter.

Scholars[37] have suggested, however, that a referral by the UNSC is not altogether impossible. The UNSC has shown a unanimous condemnation of the events taking place in Syria. If anything can be learned from the previous referrals and the reaction of the permanent members of the UNSC, a referral might be possible given the achievement of a political compromise that would guarantee a safe exit to Bashar al-Assad and his supporters to countries willing to host them. Thus, while a blank referral to the ICC seems quite impossible at this moment, given the UNSC's power to tailor the referral to China and Russia's economic and military interests in the region, a compromise is not out of the question.

However, two major concerns would develop if the UNSC were to issue a tailored referral to appease China and Russia. On the one hand a referral guaranteeing a safe exit and immunity to some suspected war criminals would send the wrong message that justice is not equal for all individuals. It would offend the memory of thousands of Syrian civilians who have died demanding the end of a

---

34) UN Human Rights Council Special Report 19th special session on the "deteriorating human rights situation in the Syrian Arab Republic and the recent killings in El-Houleh" - 1 June 2012. <http://www.ohchr.org/Documents/HRBodies/HRCouncil/SpecialSession/Session19/A-HRC-RES-S-19-1_en.pdf>.

35) David Scheffer, 'Fanning the Flames of Justice in Syria' in *Project Syndicate September 9 2012*, *<http://www.project-syndicate.org/commentary/fanning-the-flames-of-justice-in-syria>*.

36) Vinjamuri, *supra* note 22. Mark Lynch 'Can the ICC Take on Syria?' *Foreign Policy* (4 March, 2012) *<http://lynch.foreignpolicy.com/posts/2012/03/04/syria_and_the_icc>*.

37) Scheffer, *supra* note 35.

violent regime. On the other hand, such a political compromise would defeat the same purpose of the ICC investigation and prosecution. Limiting the jurisdiction of the Court with regard to the individuals to prosecute damages enormously the legitimacy of the ICC, especially when those immune from the jurisdiction are the most responsible for the persecutions and violations of humanitarian law. The use of a political tool to shield political leaders, who are friends of the permanent members of the UNSC, if applied, would undermine the same purpose of an international court and allow leaders to "get away with murder."[38]

5. Discussion

As the analysis above shows, the lack of commitment to ICC operations following referrals, the heavily politicized language of the UNSC Resolutions 1593 and 1970, and the "power politics" discourses surrounding talks of future referrals of situations to the ICC, severely compromises the pursuit of international justice. It seems unlikely we will be seeing a referral by the UNSC in the near future. The Resolutions on Sudan and Libya were surrounded by extraordinary circumstances in which an unusual and united international support on Libya and strong indignation over the humanitarian crises in Darfur made the UNSC more willing to muster the political will to refer the situations. However, even those referrals are affected by the political games played at the UNSC. The limitation of jurisdiction, the lack of economic and technical support, and recognition of privileges for special categories of individuals seems to indicate a biased justice, which the ICC has accepted in the name of advancing universal jurisdiction.

The solutions to such a situation might be hard to find and even harder to enforce given the resistance of the UNSC to recognize the complete independence of the Court and the desire of the ICC to investigate cases that would not otherwise fall under its jurisdiction. The preferable solution would be that of pressuring states into accepting the jurisdiction of the Court, eliminating therefore a need for the referral of the UNSC. However, it is doubtful that leaders who could fall under the scrutiny of the ICC investigation will willingly submit their nations to the Court's jurisdiction. An enlargement of the ICC membership, including countries whose humanitarian crises have made headlines, is unlikely.

In reality, what is most needed is a redesign of the relationship between the UNSC and the ICC, including increasing pressures by the ICC members on the UNSC to align the aims of its resolutions with its behaviour, and a reconsideration of the way the UNSC addresses issues of international justice. In order to improve the relationship between these institutions it is necessary to reach a mutual understanding of the role each one of them plays in the international arena.

---

38) Dicker, *supra* note 27.

Political interests are paramount to the UNSC and the implementation of international justice is of pivotal importance for the growing influence of the ICC. However, resolutions and acceptance of referrals must be driven by coordination and cooperation of the two different paramount interests governing these institutions. The UNSC should recognize that international justice cannot always bow to political considerations and that, if its ultimate goal is that of enforcing peace and security throughout the world, then the ICC could be an additional instrument in doing so. The ICC's mission to promote universal international justice does not comport well with the desire to accept constraints that ultimately do more harm than good to justice. The extension of its jurisdiction following the referral of the UNSC may damage what is more important—the legitimacy and fairness of its operations. Ultimately, what is important is the perception that justice delivered by the ICC is fair, impartial, and legitimate. These are the instruments through which compliance with international justice can grow, more than the occasional limited referral of the UNSC. That is to say, there has been a certain complicity between the ICC and the UNSC. Both institutions seek to improve peace, security, and justice in the world, while in reality both are intimately concerned with their credibility and international standing.

Member states to the UN should also be more active in pressuring the UNSC to stop the evaluation of situations to be referred to the ICC based on the political relationships with leaders, rather than the gravity of the crimes committed. Aside from a general condemnation of the inertia of the UNSC, leaders sitting at the UN have done little to determine specific criteria through which the UNSC should assess the cases and then make a decision to refer it to the ICC. The UNSC has no responsibility to justify or explain its decisions and it is mostly immune from criticisms. It has no criteria to follow and it assesses each situation according to the country under scrutiny. Ideally, in the absence of consensus, the Permanent Members of the UNSC should abstain from vetoing resolutions referring cases, rather than becoming accomplices in the bloodshed of rampant human rights violations and humanitarian crises.

One last consideration must be made. While former Chief Prosecutor Moreno-Ocampo called for the UNSC to exercise its duty and responsibility in referring the case of Syria to the Court, the ICC might soon "regret what it is wishing for". If the record of support to the Court and cooperation between the two institutions has taught us anything, it is that we should know that the UNSC is applying a "limited involvement" principle, in which neither financial, nor technical assistance is provided to the Court, while at the same time prejudicing the freedom of the ICC. Further referrals may become cumbersome for the limited personnel, resources, and enforcement mechanisms at the Court's disposal and ultimately negatively affect the work of the ICC.

Justice, Power and Peace: Conflicting Interests and the Apprehension of ICC Suspects

James Meernik
Professor of Political Science, University of North Texas, Denton, TX, USA

Abstract
The International Criminal Court (ICC) has the legal power to issue arrest warrants, but not the political power to arrest. Rather, it must rely on other national and international actors to enforce these requests. All the actors—the ICC, the suspected war criminals, and the key state actors—in these high stakes dramas involving the apprehension of suspected war criminals have distinct interests that guide their actions. Typically, as I argue, these contending interests lead to political disputes. I will argue that the principal interest of the International Criminal Court is justice; the principal interest of the actors indicted by the ICC is power; and the principal interests of international actors are peace and justice. Further, I contend that the ability of the ICC to gain custody of suspects will be determined by its ability to induce the international community to privilege justice over peace.

Keywords
International Criminal Court (ICC); apprehension; indictments; violence

The International Criminal Court (ICC) is an international criminal justice system without the law enforcement support necessary to carry out its mandate. It has the legal power to issue arrest warrants, but not the political power to arrest. Rather, it must rely on other national and international actors to enforce these requests to apprehend those who have been indicted of violations of international law, just as the ad hoc tribunals such as the International Tribunal for the Former Yugoslavia has done. The apprehension of suspects is the one absolutely vital interest that must be realized in order for the ICC to fulfil its mission to provide judicial accountability for violations of international humanitarian law. Yet, like other recent international tribunals, the ICC is a superordinate body with some statist trappings (e.g., it is responsible to the Assembly of States parties) in a Westphalian world seeking to try cases against state citizens. It is a delicate mixture that requires ICC leadership with substantial diplomatic skill and tact to lead an institution whose lodestar is the law, not politics. It is precisely the outcome of this intersection of law and politics that will ultimately determine whether the ICC is successful in the quest for international justice.

All the actors—the ICC, the suspected war criminals, and the key state actors—in these high stakes dramas involving the apprehension of suspected war criminals have distinct interests that guide their actions. Typically, as I argue, these contending interests lead to political disputes. To explain and predict the outcomes of these disputes one must begin by identifying the interests of those involved. I will argue that the principal interest of the International Criminal Court is justice; the principal interest of the actors indicted by the ICC is power; and the principal interests of international actors are peace *and* justice. Further, I contend that the ability of the ICC to gain custody of suspects will be determined by its ability to induce the international community to privilege justice over peace. Conversely, the success of those indicted by the ICC in avoiding apprehension will depend upon their ability and that of their state (if it so chooses) to induce the international community to prefer peace over justice. Both the ICC and those indicted have tools and resources they can utilize to alter the perceived costs and benefits for those in the international community who must decide the weight to be placed upon the achievement of peace and justice.

In the analysis that follows I begin by outlining the powers and procedures of the ICC in its efforts to secure custody of those it indicts. Subsequently I assess in depth the interests of each of the three, principal actors in the apprehension process and the strategies available to them to achieve their interests. Finally, using this framework of interests and strategies I evaluate the likelihood that the ICC will gain custody of suspects. I conclude by suggesting the types of changes in actor preferences that might increase the capacity of the ICC to gain greater compliance with its arrest warrants.

1. Indictment and the Mechanics of Apprehension

The Treaty of Rome provides for the ICC's jurisdiction only when the state in which an alleged crime takes place is a party to the treaty; the suspect is a national of a state that is a party to the treaty or the case is referred to it by the United Nations Security Council. The Court may then exercise jurisdiction if a situation is referred to it by a state party, the United Nations Security Council, or the Prosecutor initiates an investigation on his own authority. The Prosecutor must seek the approval of a pre-Trial chamber in order to conduct an investigation.

The Rome Treaty provides for legal challenges to the admissibility of a case or the jurisdiction of the Court in a particular situation. Relevant grounds for challenges to the admissibility of a case, which are found in Article 17 of the Treaty of Rome, may be justified if 1) the case is already being investigated or prosecuted by the state that would normally possess jurisdiction; 2) the case has already been investigated and the state with jurisdiction has elected not to prosecute; 3) the person(s) concerned have already been tried; and 4) the situation is not of sufficient gravity to justify action by the ICC. The Prosecutor can contest such state challenges on the grounds that the state with jurisdiction is genuinely unable or unwilling to carry out the investigation or prosecution. This may be demonstrated by showing that a state's proceedings were used for the purpose of shielding those responsible; there has been an unjustified delay in the initiation of proceedings or the proceedings were not conducted in an impartial or independent manner.[1]

A challenge to the admissibility of a case to the ICC would unfold in the following manner. First, as found in Article 18 (section 1):

> When a situation has been referred to the Court pursuant to article 13 (a) and the Prosecutor has determined that there would be a reasonable basis to commence an investigation, or the Prosecutor initiates an investigation pursuant to articles 13 (c) and 15, the Prosecutor shall notify all States Parties and those States which, taking into account the information available, would normally exercise jurisdiction over the crimes concerned. The Prosecutor may notify such States on a confidential basis and, where the Prosecutor believes it necessary to protect persons, prevent destruction of evidence or prevent the absconding of persons, may limit the scope of the information provided to States.

Subsequently:

> Within one month of receipt of that notification, a State may inform the Court that it is investigating or has investigated its nationals or others within its jurisdiction with respect to criminal acts which may constitute crimes referred to in article 5 and which relate to the information provided in the notification to States. At the request of that State, the Prosecutor shall defer to the State's investigation of those persons unless the Pre-Trial Chamber, on the application of the Prosecutor, decides to authorize the investigation.

Challenges may also be made to the jurisdiction of the ICC in a particular case. Challenges to either the admissibility of a case or the jurisdiction of the ICC can be brought by the accused who has been named in an indictment; by the state that would normally possess jurisdiction on the grounds that it is already investigating or prosecuting, or by a state from which jurisdiction is required under Article 12. The states at issue in Article 12 are those nations on whose territory the crimes are alleged to have been committed, or those nations whose citizens are alleged to have committed the crimes.

States may choose to pursue these international legal options to demonstrate they have exhausted such remedies, if they genuinely believe that the Prosecutor's indictment is in error, or to seize the opportunity to demonstrate the innocence of the accused. Such situations are unlikely to occur or be of any political significance if they do in the types of cases on which we are focusing. If a state itself has referred the case in the hopes that non state actors would be investigated, they are

---

1) *Rome Statute of the International Criminal Court*, Article 17(2) a, b & c.

unlikely to challenge indictments concerning their opponents. If the investigations commenced on the basis of a Security Council resolution or the Prosecutor's own authority, state leaders and non-state actors will possess few incentives to engage fully in legal challenges. Their appearance in Court may well result in their detention. Those leaders from states that have not signed and ratified the Treaty of Rome are more likely to adopt the Slobodan Milosevic position at the ICTY and assert the Court has no authority over them. Ultimately, when regime leaders or non state actors genuinely are resistant to the ICC's exercise of authority, any legal challenges are likely to be a sideshow to the larger challenges that occur in the political realm.

An investigation by the Office of the Prosecutor can take place on the territory of the state in question if authorized by the pre-Trial Chamber or through a request for such cooperation as outlined in Part 9 of the Rome Treaty. State parties are to fully cooperate with all such requests. Such investigations may involve the collection of evidence, interviews with witnesses locally or via a summons from the Prosecutor to appear before the ICC, and requests for assistance from states involved in the situation under investigation. The Prosecutor must seek the approval of the pre-Trial Chamber, which in reality may be a single judge, to issue orders and warrants for arrest. More importantly the pre-Trial Chamber may:

> Authorize the Prosecutor to take specific investigative steps within the territory of a State Party without having secured the cooperation of that State under Part 9 if, whenever possible having regard to the views of the State concerned, the Pre-Trial Chamber has determined in that case that the State is clearly unable to execute a request for cooperation due to the unavailability of any authority or any component of its judicial system competent to execute the request for cooperation under Part 9.[2]

The Prosecutor may then request that the pre-Trial Chamber issue a warrant for the arrest of persons for whom a prima facie case has been developed, or request that the pre-Trial Chamber issue a summons if it is believed this would be a more effective method to insure the cooperation of the accused, and which leaves open the possibility that the accused will continue to remain at liberty subject to the conditions imposed by the ICC. This, in fact, is what has occurred in the investigation of the violence in Kenya surrounding its contested elections where those accused of fomenting the violence were brought to the ICC in April 2011. State parties that receive an arrest warrant from the ICC are required to take immediate action. Once local legalities have been observed the individual(s) is to be turned over to the ICC. States parties are obliged to carry out these directives as a result of their acceptance of the treaty. Other states may enter into temporary arrangements with the ICC to facilitate cooperation. The ICC may refer such matters to

---

2) *Ibid.*, Article 57:3: (d).

the Assembly of States Parties or the United Nations Security Council when that body is the source of the referral.[3]

Ultimately the International Criminal Court, although in theory able to utilize the political muscle of the Assembly of States Parties or the United Nations Security Council in instances where that body refers a situation, possesses *de jure* power, albeit not *de facto* power to see that its orders are carried out. Despite the legal modalities set up in the Treaty of Rome to facilitate the cooperation of states, such assistance cannot be expected, but rather must be negotiated and earned on a case by case basis.

1.1. *The Interests of the ICC: Justice*

The *raison d'etre* of the International Criminal Court is to prosecute those suspected of violations of international law. Without suspects in its detention unit and trials in its courtrooms, not only does the ICC become incapable of realizing its mission, such failures would set back the cause of international justice more generally. Therefore, I argue that the principal interest of the ICC is justice. The manifold meanings and ambitions associated with 'justice' make a thorough exegesis of the ICC's justice mission better suited to a book-length treatise. Here I will confine myself to identifying the ICC's interest in justice, in the context of the apprehension of suspects, from two different vantage points—the perspectives of the victims and the development of a system of international law.

1.2. *The ICC, Justice and the Victims*

Justice for the victims of international criminal behaviour—both those directly and indirectly affected—involves most fundamentally a re-balancing of the scales of right and wrong. When a community's laws are broken and its social fabric and morals destroyed, the community must find a way to either return to an equilibrium in which previously held conceptions of right and wrong are once again the 'norm', or to put the past behind it. A return to the ante bellum understanding of justice may be advanced by any number of transitional justice mechanisms such as truth commissions, trials, lustration, reparations, etc.[4] Justice for the victims is likely best served if there is popular acceptance of the transitional justice mechanism(s) as legitimate and effective.[5] Absent a return to community norms regarding the kinds of criminal actions taken during wartime, societies, or their

---

3) *Ibid.*, Article 87:5(b).

4) Tricia Olsen D., Leigh G. Payne, and Andrew G. Reiter. *Transitional Justice in Balance: Comparing Processes, Weighing Efficacy* (United States Institute of Peace, Washington, DC, 2010).

5) Mark Drumbl. *Atrocity, Punishment and International Law* (Cambridge University Press, Cambridge UK, 2007); James Gibson. *Overcoming Apartheid* (Russell Sage Foundation,

governments, may instead choose to deliberately forget and seek to place the past in a corner of the collective memory and politics from which it cannot interfere with other national goals. The International Criminal Court can provide one type of justice to these victims—the dispassionate pursuit of an objective and legal truth of the criminal actions and the legal liability of those charged with responsibility for carrying out these crimes.

Whether this type of international justice is best suited to local needs has been the subject of a fascinating debate among scholars and practitioners.[6] The question I address here does not pertain to the impact of the ICC on local communities, but rather the meaning of the ICC's mission to deliver justice to these afflicted peoples. Legal justice for the direct and indirect victims of criminal actions implies the prosecution of those believed responsible. It is a form of justice with roots in the just deserts tradition and the goal of retribution. Though international jurists may protest that modern, international justice is rooted, by tradition and necessity in *lex talonis*, the act of prosecution and the division of the trial into victims and villains demonstrate the resilience and relevance of this ancient conception of justice. More importantly, the ultimate goal of international justice is to end the culture of impunity surrounding war crimes, crimes against humanity and genocide. Without apprehension, prosecution and punishment, the credibility of international justice is undermined and the very purpose of the ICC would be called into question. The ends of justice for the International Criminal Court are centred on righting the scales of justice to provide meaningful retribution to acknowledge the suffering of today's victims and help prevent the suffering of tomorrow's would-be victims.

What does this mean in practice? If there is to be justice for the victims at the International Criminal Court, it will require trials and this, in turn necessitates that the ICC accord primacy to the capture of suspects over other interests, such as peace, stability or sovereignty. The ICC cannot issue findings or reports regarding culpability for violations of international law. It cannot take matters of individual criminal liability to the United Nations to demand sanctions or punishment for those it believes are guilty. And while compensation for the victims is permitted under ICC rules, this is an auxiliary enterprise that is independent of its criminal justice enterprise. Trials are the only mechanism by which the ICC can

New York, NY, 2004); James Gibson. 'Does Truth Lead to Reconciliation? Testing the Causal Assumptions of the South African Truth and Reconciliation Process', 48 *American Journal of Political Science* (2004) 201-217.

6) Drumbl, *supra* note 5; Kimi King and James Meernik, 'A Distant Court: Assessing the Impact of the International Criminal Tribunal for the Former Yugoslavia', in Göran Sluiter, Bert Swart, and Alexander Zahar, (eds.), *The Legacy of the International Criminal Tribunal for the Former Yugoslavia* (Oxford University Press, Oxford, 2011); David Mendeloff, 'Truth-Seeking, Truth-Telling, and Postconflict Peacebuilding: Curb the Enthusiasm?', 6 *International Studies Review* (2004) 355–380; Jack Snyder and Leslie Vinjamuri, 'Trials and Errors: Principles and Pragmatism in Strategies of International Justice', 28 *International Security* (2003/2004) 5-44.

ultimately fulfil its mandate to, "...to put an end to impunity for the perpetrators of these crimes and thus to contribute to the prevention of such crimes". Hence, if as the Treaty of Rome asserts, that the ICC, "shall have the power to exercise its jurisdiction over persons for the most serious crimes of international concern",[7] it will require defendants on trial.

1.3 *Justice, Deterrence and the Development of an International Criminal Law System*

After the early successes of the Nuremburg and Tokyo tribunals, the dreams of an international judicial system that would give teeth to the Geneva Conventions and the Genocide Convention were trumped and trampled by the zero sum politics of the Cold War. There remained little likelihood that any state or non state actor that committed violations of international law would ever wind up on an international docket. Although the Cold War was not the only factor inhibiting the development of the prosecution of international humanitarian crimes, nonetheless the norm of impunity remained and, if anything gathered strength as millions perished through repression, civil war and other forms of violence. In the shadow of these atrocities and the re-emergence of ethnic violence in Europe in the former Yugoslavia, the return to international justice in the 1990's presaged a belief that prosecution of international crimes could help deter their occurrence. Scholars have extensively analyzed the (potential) deterrent impact of international tribunals.[8] As Ku and Nzelibe write, "...contemporary justifications for these tribunals stress their potential to deter future humanitarian atrocities".[9] Indeed, the charters of the ICTY, ICTR and the ICC all make reference to the deterrent function of international justice either in the expectation or hope that an international judicial system would alter the decision making calculus of would-be violators. The ICTY's authorizing statute asserts that the, "establishment of an international

---

[7] *Rome Statute of the International Criminal Court*, Part 1, Article 1.

[8] Payam Akhavan, 'Beyond Impunity: Can International Criminal Justice Prevent Future Atrocities', 95(1) *American Journal of International Law* (2001) 7-31; Drumbl, *supra* note 5; Martha Minnow, *Breaking the Cycle of Hatred* (Princeton University Press, Princeton, 2002); Robert D. Sloane, 'The Expressive Capacity of International Punishment: The Limits of National Law Analogy and the Potential of International Criminal Law', 43 *Stanford Journal of International Law* (2007) 39-94; Snyder and Vinjamuri, *supra* note 6; Eric Stover and Harvey Weinstein, 'Introduction: Conflict, Justice and Reclamation', in Eric Stover and Harvey Weinstein, (eds.), *My Neighbor, My Enemy: Justice and Community in the Aftermath of Mass Atrocity* (Cambridge University Press, Cambridge, UK, 2004) pp. 1-26; Ruti Teitel, 'Bringing the Messiah Through the Law', in Carla Hess and Robert Post, (eds.), *Human Rights in Political Transitions: Gettysburg to Bosnia* (Zone Books, New York, 1999) pp. 177-194.

[9] Julian Ku and Jide Nzelibe, 'Do International Criminal Tribunals Deter or Exacerbate Humanitarian Atrocities?', 84 *Washington University Law Review* (2006) 777-833, pp. 779.

tribunal and the prosecution of persons responsible for the above-mentioned violations of international humanitarian law *will contribute to ensuring that such violations are halted* and effectively redressed" (emphasis added).[10] The ICTY, ICTR and the Special Court for Sierra Leone have each arrested nearly all their indicted suspects, which we might suspect (hope) contributed to ending the culture of impunity locally and perhaps internationally.

Given the longstanding impunity enjoyed by nearly all war criminals throughout history and the recognized need to end the suffering inflicted by these individuals, the long-term prospects for international criminal justice depend substantially on demonstrating that such actions will no longer be tolerated.[11] Akhavan argues that the removal from power or the ostracizing of former political and military leaders diminishes the perceived need for individuals to engage in acts of revenge; leads to greater levels of cooperation among formerly warring groups and promotes specific and general deterrence.[12] Akhavan also writes, "... the international community's policy of using the ICTY as an instrument to remove from power indicted leaders has contributed to post conflict peace building by creating incentives for political parties to behave in a more conciliatory manner",[13] and that the ICTR, "...has palpably improved the post conflict situation by impeding resurrection of the former government and enhancing the political attraction of criminal justice as an alternative to Hutu violence".[14] The removal of suspected war criminals from their area of operations achieves the immediate deterrent effect of ending their ability to commit violations of international law, and may also have the practical effect of hindering such actions by others whom they organized. More importantly, the arrest of the suspect should not only hamper the commission of such crimes, it may also help dissuade the suspect's compatriots from engaging in such behaviour in the future.

The nascent International Criminal Court, however, with a global and permanent jurisdiction can build upon these successes, but will also seek to establish a successful record of apprehension and demonstrate that it will brook no exceptions to ending the culture of impunity. To not insist upon the apprehension and trial of those the Court indicts would risk serious damage to the legal and political precedents that have built up over the last 20 years. Politics still does play a role in the international judicial system as many of the situations before the Court have arisen from self-referrals by member states as well referrals by the UN Security

---

10) Statute of the International Tribunal, adopted by United Nations Security Council Resolution 827, U.N. SCOR, 48th Sess., 3217th mtg. at 6, U.N. Doc. S/RES/827 (1993), 32 I.L.M. 1203 (1993).

11) Mark Harmon and Fergal Gaynor, 'Ordinary Sentences for Extraordinary Crimes', 5 *Journal of International Criminal Justice* (2007) 683-712.

12) Akhavan, *supra* note 8.

13) *Ibid.*, p. 16.

14) *Ibid.*, p. 26.

Council (e.g., Uganda, Congo). I contend that once the indictments have been issued, however, the International Criminal Court will not open these decisions to political negotiation nor withdraw them in the face of political pressure. To do so would be to open the entire judicial process to political negotiation, undermine the purposes of the Court, and damage the prospects for deterrence of future crimes. We should expect that the ICC, most especially the Office of the Prosecutor, will insist upon the implementation of its decisions in order to preserve its power and to further erode the culture of impunity. This does not mean that the Prosecutor will not sometimes delay action or refrain from taking certain steps in an investigation and accept short term losses to preserve long term interests. Indeed, the Treaty of Rome does permit the Prosecutor to refrain from investigation when he believes such action, "would not serve the interests of justice".[15] However, my focus is on those situations that have resulted in an investigation where the failure to follow through would entail significant loss of credibility and harm deterrence. Therefore, I argue that the ICC's principal interest in situations where individuals have been indicted will be to serve the cause of justice and demand apprehension and trial.

2. The Interests of the Accused

When the ICC issues an indictment and arrest warrant for individuals residing in a particular nation, we must consider several elements of a likely decision tree such individuals would utilize when considering their interests and options. First, the individual must determine whether to comply with the arrest warrant and either surrender or acquiesce to arrest. At first glance this might seem like a simplistic question. Why would anyone, particularly someone with the ambition and drive to run a nation, willingly surrender himself to an international tribunal? Nonetheless, there are a number of important factors that might make surrender a better option than several other potential outcomes. First, some individuals may view an indictment as either a badge of honour or an insult against their honour and welcome the chance to defend their actions in court. Even some of the most brutal war criminals can be exceptionally delusional and believe they are truly innocent or that the other side committed far worse atrocities, which would excuse their conduct. Second, we have the example of the Serbian government that has made surrender an attractive option financially for suspected war criminals:

> Serbia passed legislation last year to provide pensions to its indicted war criminals. The law gives indictees a full salary, plus unspecified "compensation" for family and legal expenses. In the Republic of Srpska, the Serb-controlled part of Bosnia, benefits are even

[15] *Rome Statute of the International Criminal* Court, *supra* note 1, Article 53 1(c).

> more generous: a full salary to the indictee himself, a double salary paid to his family, plus 80 euro a month to each of his school-age children. (A typical Bosnian Serbian salary is only 200 euro a month.) Family members also get four expense-paid trips a year to The Hague to visit indicted loved ones. And last year Srpska added a cash bonus of 25,000 euro for anyone who surrenders.[16]

Especially when such governments are under pressure from their financial and political supporters to comply with the demands of international tribunals, a 'surrender reward' can be an attractive option for all parties. Third and finally, it is quite possible that the comforts of detention in The Hague are much more appealing to some than the prospect of falling into the hands of their enemies, or life on the lam. Ku and Nzelibe show those who are most likely to commit violations of international humanitarian law (operationalized as leaders of coups in African nations from 1956-2003) are quite likely to eventually be killed or imprisoned by their political opponents.[17] In fact, the majority of coup leaders meet with such fates. While Ku and Nzelibe sought to demonstrate that international tribunals were unlikely to affect deterrence, one can also speculate that for some suspected war criminals, on balance, a trip to The Hague would be more attractive than a trip before the firing squad.

I argue that not only are those indicted by the ICC likely to adopt a strategy of confrontation, there are substantial incentives to utilize the resources at their disposal to threaten unrest and violence. First, indictments and arrest warrants send signals to a wide audience of opponents, supporters and fence-sitters that the individual's power and position are being challenged. Even though these audiences may have little knowledge or concern for the International Criminal Court, they may well recognize that the ICC has many influential and powerful supporters that could turn the screws on their nation if they chose to do so. Hence, the suspect has strong reason to both challenge the legitimacy of the ICC's actions and rally supporters to his cause to avoid any perception that his power is being undermined and open to challenge. Accordingly, this creates substantial incentives for the leader to rally his supporters to harangue against the ICC and its 'interference'; to threaten or commit acts of violence against those who may be considering defying the leader's authority; or to engage in other acts that demonstrate the individual's potency and the costs of challenging his position. Such tactics were used on numerous occasions in Croatia and Serbia (ICTY), and more recently in The Sudan.

Second, those indicted by the ICC are likely keenly aware of the international community's desire to serve the ends of justice *and* peace. If the leader's challenge to the ICC is framed in legal terms, the individual is less likely to prevail on these grounds where the playing field is so uneven. Rather, the more obvious strategy is

---

16) Rod Nordland, 'Pensions for War Criminals', *Newsweek*, 25 July 2005 U.S. Edition, p. 44.

17) Ku and Nzelibe, *supra* note 9.

to engage the international community's interest in creating or sustaining peace (e.g., Slobodan Milosevic's insistence that he was a partner in peace with the West during the 1990's). Since these indictments occur either during or after violent conflict, the likelihood of war re-emerging is substantial. And for many in international inter-governmental and non-governmental organizations, the avoidance of war and the care of civilians will be of paramount concern. Threatening to unleash violence may inspire such organizations and states to caution against placing the interests of abstract justice above the real harm that will come to peace efforts, as some have argued as recently as the indictment of Muammar Qaddafi.[18] It is difficult to downplay such threats as leaders of international organizations may not wish to call their bluff. If the international community insists upon justice and apprehension and the leader's threats are discovered to be mere bluster, there will be a collective sigh of relief as the indictee is sent packing to The Hague. On the other hand, if the threat is real and violence and perhaps renewed war do result, the consequences will be deadly. Since few observers are likely to truly understand the interests and mind of the indicted leader, the risk averse course of action is to counsel caution. We should expect that calculating leaders will have every incentive to make such threats for there is little to lose and much to gain. Indeed, such claims and the possibility of renewed violence as a result of ICC indictments are difficult to counter and have been employed to criticize the very notion of an international criminal justice enterprise.[19] Eager to exploit these very real and recurrent divisions between those who insist on either justice or peace at any price, suspected war criminals can help deter their apprehension by engaging the peace versus justice debate and forcing a more favourable calculation of the costs and benefits of pursuing either strategy. Thus, suspected war criminals have substantial internal and external incentives for aggressively challenging their indictments. Ultimately these interests centre on maintaining their power.

3. The Interests of the International Community

It is impossible to speak of the 'international community' as a single actor with clear, consistent and readily identifiable interests. Rather this entity is made up of numerous states, governmental organizations, non-governmental organizations, and other private actors with many, disparate and often conflicting goals. In the context of the emerging international criminal justice system, however, there are far fewer, key actors, though their interests are no less variegated. There are those

---

18) *See* Howard LaFranchi, 'Libya's Qaddafi charged with war crimes: a help or a hindrance to NATO?', *The Christian Science Monitor*, 27 June 2011 <www.csmonitor.com/USA/Foreign-Policy/2011/0627/Libya-s-Qaddafi-charged-with-war-crimes-a-help-or-hindrance-to-NATO>, 24 August 2012, which quotes human rights experts on the impact of the Qaddafi indictment.

19) Mendeloff, *supra* note 6; Snyder and Vinjamuri, *supra* note 6.

states which are active proponents of the ICC, including many in the Assembly of States Parties, and in the United Nations. Other prominent actors that must be factored into analyses of the likely response of the international community would include the permanent members of the UN Security Council (including the United States, which while not an ICC supporter, by virtue of its overwhelming power, must necessarily factor into major international actions in support of the ICC), the European Union, certain human rights organizations (e.g., Amnesty International, Human Rights Watch), and states contributing troops to peacemaking missions, if any, in the affected nations. To avoid using any cumbersome terms or lengthy lists, I will simply refer to these actors as the 'international community' with the understanding that such a term does not do justice to their diverse interests and actions. While many of the national actors may have their particular political and economic interests in the affected nations, the goals that must be reconciled by these actors in order to take action to facilitate their realization are peace and justice.

The members of the international community demonstrate a greater or lesser affinity for the abstract and subjective term 'justice' that will determine whether they prefer justice over peace. It is the price that must be paid for justice that really determines the commitment to it. The price entails, inter alia, the cost of apprehension (i.e., as determined by its political and practical feasibility), the support or acquiescence of key actors that are critical to apprehension; and the likelihood that apprehension will lead to further violence or instability. All such costs must then be weighted by other factors such as the extent of the crimes committed, the prima facie case regarding the responsibility of the accused, and the likelihood that other national, regional or international interests may be implicated. For example, if the indicted individual were bereft of supporters; his state possessed little of value; the crimes committed were horrendous and the feasibility and cost of capture were insignificant, then the price of justice would be quite low and hence the willingness to pay for such a bargain would be commensurately high. On the other hand, if the indicted individual enjoyed strong support among powerful states; the actions of his state implicated the interests of other nations; and his involvement in the crimes committed was not clearly obvious, the increased price of justice might very well deter concerted international action to achieve apprehension. The price of justice, however, is generally high as the ICC is not likely to confine its investigations to 'unimportant' events and issue indictments without clear evidence implicating the accused. Thus, we should expect that ICC indictments will generally test the commitment of the ICC's supporters to pursue justice—there will likely be few 'easy' cases.

Therefore, because of the high cost of international justice and the normal difficulties involved in obtaining any kind of international consensus on tough issues, especially when the United States can generally be expected to be unsupportive of an assertive ICC, the 'interest', by default, of the international community will tend toward peace. In reality, we can expect that when international support for apprehension is lacking, it is the status quo that will persist, albeit justified in the name of preventing further violence. The avoidance of intrusive efforts at apprehension also comport with the high value many states, especially China and Russia, place on sovereignty. Pursuing peace through diplomacy rather than justice through apprehension also is the less risky and expensive strategy, especially in the short-run. Given an international environment in which there are almost always multiple problems or crises calling for attention and funding, we should find little stomach for such controversial actions. The status quo, disguised in the garbs of peace and diplomacy, will persist until a critical mass of support for apprehension and justice is obtained. Just how this might come about I describe below.

4. Peace versus Justice: Who Wins and what Happens

A decision tree is the clearest method for describing the events that are likely to unfold as a result of an investigation by the Office of the Prosecutor at the International Criminal Court. Assuming a situation in which there is reason to believe that violations of international law have occurred in some state; the Office of the Prosecutor has conducted an investigation into these allegations; and that the ICC has issued a public indictment naming one or more individuals in this state, the first decision node lies with the government of the state in which the alleged violations occurred. The government, or in some cases a rebel movement, which may well be led by an individual named in the indictment, must decide whether to challenge the indictment or not. I define a challenge as a statement or action that questions the authority of the ICC to issue the indictment, asserts the sovereignty of the state or other actors as superior to any international legal obligation, or seeks to undermine the ability of the ICC to conduct its operations in the present case. Such challenges do not have to be grounded in any recognized or relevant legal basis. Indeed, many of those who have been indicted and even apprehended by international tribunals have asserted that these institutions lack proper authority, such as Slobodan Milosevic who called the ICTY a "false tribunal" and who through efforts large and small (e.g., refusing to refer to the justices by their titles) continually sought to challenge the tribunal's authority.

Figure 1 outlines the various decision or action nodes for the three actors. The beginning point in this decision tree is the issuance of an indictment by the ICC. The first choice in Figure 1 is made by the government in question, or a rebel movement whose leader(s) have been indicted by the ICC. These are the individuals who would decide whether to carry out this request and attempt to apprehend the individual(s) in question or challenge the indictment. If the target of the indictment is a government leader, the actor and the target are one and the same. Either

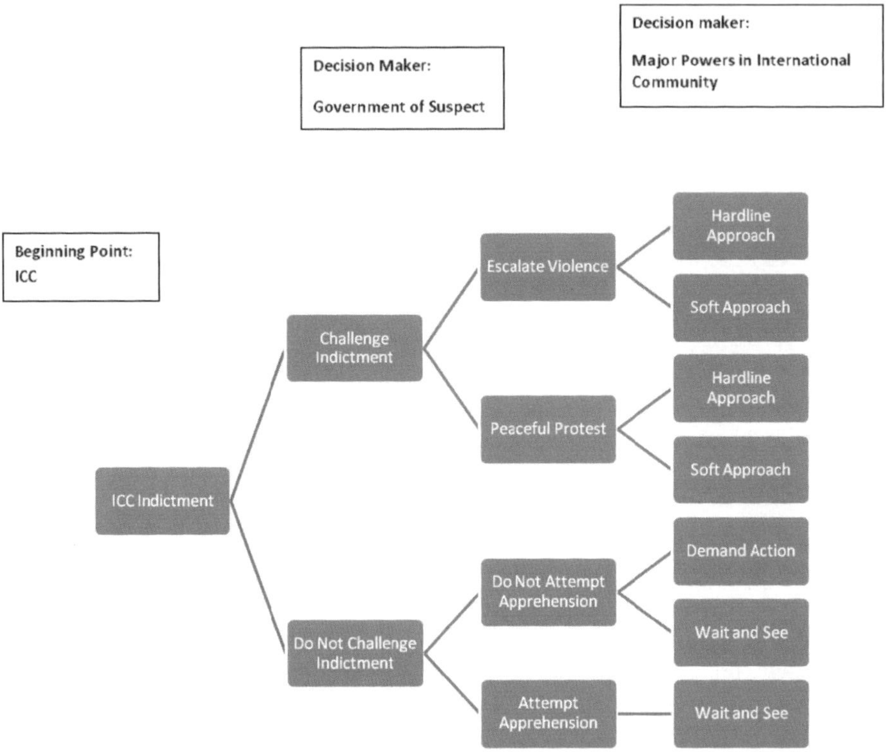

Fig.1. Decision making tree involving ICC indictment.

the target must decide whether to surrender himself, or other government leaders must determine if their colleague(s) should be arrested and sent to The Hague. On the other hand, if the target is part of a non-governmental force fighting for control of the state, more than likely the government does not possess the capability to arrest the individual. Presumably, if the government had the means of apprehension, it would have already done so given the threat posed to the security of the regime. If the choice is made to genuinely attempt to execute the warrant, the decision tree largely ends. If the attempt is successful, then legal proceedings at the ICC commence, while if the attempts do not result in capture, a confrontation between the ICC and the regime actors is likely avoided as long as good faith efforts are being applied. If the regime's or rebel movement's sincerity and credibility regarding the apprehension efforts are undermined by an unwillingness to take concerted action, it is possible the major actors in the international community will become more assertive in their efforts to gain compliance. However, we will set aside those situations of apparent compliance to examine the more confrontational outcomes.

4.1. *State Leaders: Comply or Contest?*

Here I focus on regime leaders and save for later a discussion of the choices confronting non state actors under indictment. Should the regime leaders choose to challenge the indictment their options are numerous, and range from verbal protestations and expressions of concern all the way to an escalation of violence. We would expect these leaders to conceal their true willingness to undertake apprehension, which may also vary over time in response to changing domestic conditions and the actions taken by the international community. Rather, we would expect that the regime leaders would make a public display of their concerns and refusal to comply in order to signal that the costs may be substantial if the international community were to aggressively pursue apprehension through military force or impose costly sanctions on the regime. By concealing their sincere preferences while often signalling their most hard line position, leaders expect to extract concessions from the international community to modify or drop the indictment (maximalist position) or secure some form of support or concessions that would sustain their hold on power (e.g., foreign assistance; support for the regime's position in peace talks). In short, there is every incentive for these leaders to challenge the indictment and approach the situation as a political battle rather than legal dispute. The former represents a more encompassing strategy involving multiple actors occurring on a political field of play familiar to the leaders and contains within it the possibility of regime gains. The latter scenario unfolds in a legal setting, generally unfamiliar to leaders and which is mostly a bilateral process (the ICC and the target) without the possibility of a negotiated and mutually beneficial settlement.

Therefore, I expect that the dominant decision choice for leaders will be to contest indictments.[20] Indeed, those indicted by international tribunals, such as

---

[20] Nonetheless, there are circumstances in which the Prosecutor and the ICC can take actions that do not privilege apprehension of suspects over other, possible objectives. First, prior to launching an investigation, the Prosecutor shall consider whether, "Taking into account the gravity of the crime and the interests of victims, there are nonetheless substantial reasons to believe that an investigation would not serve the interests of justice" [*Rome Statute*, Article 18(1)]. Presumably then, if the ICC were to privilege other objectives over apprehension of those suspected of violating international law, it would do so prior to the initiation and completion of investigations and the indictment of suspects. Second, the Prosecutor can request that the pre-Trial Chamber issue a summons that certain individuals appear before the Court if there is reason to believe that a summons will be sufficient to compel individuals to come forward. The summons may or may not contain restrictions on the individual's liberty, other than detention (*Rome Statute*, Article 58(7)). Third, states may choose to grant interim release of those arrested in the execution of an ICC warrant. Such states are to report on the ongoing status of these suspects to the ICC, but shall determine when surrender to the Court is to occur (*Rome Statute*, Article 59). Thus, there are narrowly tailored circumstances in which the ICC may consent to actions that fall short of apprehension and prosecution for violations of international law, but in general its mandate and its mission would likely

Slobodan Milosevic, Radovan Karadzic, Ratko Mladic at the ICTY, the major figures at the ICTR, Charles Taylor at the Special Court for Sierra Leone, and nearly all those indicted by the ICC, have chosen to contest their indictment in some manner. As well, I would expect that non state actors contesting for control of the state would also challenge indictments for the same reasons outlined above. Whether it is the leadership of the Lord's Resistance Army in Uganda, several of those indicted by the ICC in connection with crimes committed in the Congo or the leader of the Janjaweed militia in The Sudan, few individuals have willingly surrendered to the Court. The more fundamental question for these regime and non-state actors is whether to contest the indictment(s) forcibly or in a more restrained fashion.

4.2. *Methods of Contesting Indictments*

Beyond the legal options described previously, states, their leaders and non state actors may pursue a variety of strategies for contesting indictments and seeking to achieve their political objectives. The international crimes that the Prosecutor alleges occur in a political context. Leaders authorize the commission of such crimes to achieve political objectives, such as to eliminate or reduce the power of political opponents, or, to achieve strategic or tactical advantages over their opponents on the battlefield. The ultimate goal guiding both their domestic political and military actions and their challenge to the ICC indictment is grounded in their quest for political survival. They contest the ICC indictment to maintain power against domestic and international threats. They commit international crimes to maintain or augment their power to survive in command. Hence, an understanding of their reactions to ICC indictments must be understood in this context. The type, scope and severity of their response will be guided by their assessment of what is necessary to maintain power and thwart challenges to their authority.

As I argued previously, state political and military leaders have every incentive to contest indictments by the ICC. However, given the low probability of their apprehension by external forces, it is unlikely they would perceive a compelling need to engage in intense, widespread or prolonged activities to challenge the international community. The resources required to sustain a high level of organized street protest or an escalation of military activity would tax what may often be a modest or meagre level of state resources. Indeed, if such leaders are being challenged by non-state actors, their energies will likely remain focused on staving off threats to their power. Therefore, we would expect that the most likely visible response by state leaders to an ICC indictment would be actions such as street

flounder on a sea of politics were the Court given broad discretion to allow politics to explicitly influence its actions.

protests, damage to or destruction of institutions associated with foreign and international powers, the expulsion of some of the less important foreign NGO's, IGO's and other external actors, and similar actions. We should expect these actions to be brief, but intense to communicate to the ICC and the international community that there will be substantial costs to pay if attempts are made to apprehend the leader and to quickly signal to domestic regime opponents that the leaders still maintain their grip on power and control over state resources and the means of coercion.

Non state actors seeking control of the state confront rather dissimilar incentives. The likelihood of their capture would likely be significantly higher given that their statist opponents and the international community possess strong incentives to secure their detention. First, apprehension of non state actors may well be undertaken or facilitated by regimes that have every reason to capture their opponents. Indeed, most of those individuals who are in custody in The Hague are individuals whose indictments resulted from a state referral. And while they may enjoy some degree of mobility in remote areas and across state borders, their movements also risk detection by other adversaries and by those attracted to the prospects of a reward for capture. These actors, however, armed with the tools of war and often willing to commit the most horrific of atrocities to intimidate friends and enemies alike, can threaten a high level of violence against the most vulnerable populations the government may be unwilling or unable to protect. Their response is unlikely to be confined to media-friendly demonstrations and the occasional destruction of a symbol of Western power, but rather to the extent such leaders perceive a need to act to thwart any apprehension efforts or challenges to their power, their responses are likely to involve an escalation of their ongoing conflict.

As a result, we are likely to see something of the stalemate that characterizes efforts to arrest state and non state leaders. The major actors from the international community are likely to look upon attempts at pursuit and apprehension of rebel leaders into the bush or the mountains with an aversion equal to if not surpassing their reluctance to aggressively enforce arrest warrants on state leaders. Rather, we might expect the international community to work through the local government and local forces to secure their apprehension. It must also be pointed out that most of the situations under investigation by the ICC involve referrals by states where rebel forces have committed atrocities. Governments, like that of Uganda, however, have asked the international community to refrain from seeking the capture of these rebels for fear of undermining peace negotiations. Thus, even when the conditions might appear to be ripe, or at least better than average, to bring these suspected war criminals into custody, it is still possible that they enjoy the protection of more powerful actors. Once again, most roads lead to stalemate.

4.3. *The Choice of the International Community: Justice or Peace*

I argue that the key actors of the international community will espouse the values of justice, but will prefer the risk averse strategy of avoiding aggressive efforts at apprehension because of the relative peace it buys. The costs of apprehension will generally outweigh the benefits of justice and may increases the costs of peace. Thus, I take a utilitarian perspective on these interests and argue that for the international community the apprehension of suspected war criminals is a political issue and not a purely legal matter. As such, when the diplomatic, financial and peace-sustaining costs of apprehension increase, the political costs, both internationally and domestically increase for those who must ultimately shoulder these burdens. Therefore, the critical question to ask in assessing the likelihood the international community will take action to apprehend those indicted by the ICC is, "what is the cost?" The price of justice is set largely by the accused.

Should major powers determine to back efforts at enforcement of ICC indictments, peace processes and other types of international negotiations involving external actors, such as the United Nations, and local actors may be undermined or disrupted. Given the types of states that are likely to come under scrutiny by the Office of the Prosecutor, we can expect there to be issues of war, ethnic strife, regime transition or major human rights violations that have generated international attention and investigation. Once the ICC begins identifying the local, negotiating partners as suspects in war crimes or crimes against humanity, the neutrality and good offices of international actors become suspect. The international actors involved in negotiations may seek to distance themselves from ICC actions, and some may even express displeasure and disapproval, but for the UN and many other major powers, outright disavowal of ICC actions will not be possible. Those under investigation and especially those indicted by the Office of the Prosecutor may question their sincerity and credibility as negotiating partners. They may assume that these states are behind the ICC efforts and walk out of negotiations. They may even believe such negotiations are a trap and that to appear with these international partners is to risk arrest. Therefore, we should expect that many international actors would perceive significant costs and risks to peace in the event of ICC indictments and arrest warrants. Indeed, the very fact that with the exception of a few figures wanted by the ICTY, international (e.g., UN) forces have played little role in the apprehension of suspected war criminals.

The conflicts and issues that result in both peace negotiations and ICC indictments also involve neighbouring states, whose support may be lost if the neutrality of international negotiators is called into question. Such states may have vested interests in these conflicts; harbour rebels fighting the government; be expected to take part in policing sanctions, such as preventing the flow of arms; and may even be involved in the violence themselves. If the international community is relying upon such states to bring peace and stability to the region, and should such states call into question the neutrality and credibility of international actors involved in negotiations and perceived as supporters of the ICC, the prospects for peace may be significantly jeopardized. There are significant, potential downsides to ICC indictments for peace and stability and thus good reason to expect that major powers in the international community will be reluctant to throw their full support behind apprehension efforts.[21]

I argue that the members of the international community whose political, military and economic support will be called upon to pay the price of justice will therefore privilege peace over justice. When the accused can make a credible threat that efforts at apprehension will be met with resistance, if not outright escalation to violence and war-waging, there will be little stomach to interfere in the internal affairs of another state to such a degree. Witness the extreme reluctance of NATO forces to arrest members of the Bosnian Serb government in the 1990's. Furthermore, if the state actors and organizations that are responsible for capturing the indicted individual view the losses suffered or the peace jeopardized as a result of a successful or unsuccessful attempt at apprehension as unacceptable, it is quite likely they will be reticent or reluctant to pursue further efforts. For example, the unsuccessful US attempt to capture Somali warlord Muhammad Farah Aided in 1993 that led to the deaths of 18 American soldiers, one Malaysian solder and somewhere between 500 and 1500 Somalis may have contributed to the American reluctance to use its troops in the former Yugoslavia to arrest those suspected of war crimes by the ICTY. Apprehensions are fraught with tremendous political and military dangers that, if realized by the principal supporters, could quickly dampen enthusiasm for future efforts. Rather, we would expect diplomatic and legal efforts at crisis resolution to continue as the major actors seek to find a solution to the ICC indictment that will not entail such difficulties. As well, accustomed as these players are to the give and take of international diplomacy, we should expect that they would prefer to operate in this realm as long as there is some prospect of success and in order to exhaust all such non-intrusive remedies. Therefore, I hypothesize that the dominant strategy of

21) It is possible, however, that all parties involved in peace processes and political negotiations may be able to compartmentalize these efforts and separate them from ICC actions. The situation in The Sudan is instructive. ICC indictments against Sudanese leaders for the atrocities in the Darfur region elicited defiance and protest from the regime. Indeed, the situation in Darfur was referred to the ICC by the UN Security Council, which might have been expected to further jeopardize efforts at peace in Darfur as well as in south Sudan where separate fighting had been ongoing for years. Yet, despite the political disputes over Darfur between the Sudanese government and those international actors concerned about Darfur, negotiations regarding the future of south Sudan continued. And recently that area declared independence from the central government and was welcomed into the community of nations. Hence, it may well be possible for confrontation and cooperation to coexist in states whose leaders are under ICC indictment when all parties share a compelling interest in peace, and when such efforts can be separated from the more contentious issues surrounding the ICC indictments.

the international community will be to bargain for peace and hope for justice. In combination with the preferred strategy of the target state and the accused to contest the ICC indictment, the predicted outcome will be stalemate. Apprehension, if it is to occur, will result from the efforts of local, not international actors.

Discussion

I argue that because of the interest of the ICC in holding fast to the pursuit of justice; the interests of those indicted for international crimes in holding onto power, and the interests of the international community in avoiding actions that might jeopardize peace or lead to violence, the initial outcome of most ICC indictments will be stalemate, particularly when state leaders are the target of the ICC. We see this illustrated best in the case of The Sudan, where indicted leaders have refused to surrender and have actively challenged the actions of the ICC. This type of outcome is also more likely to occur in the context of state leaders as the international community and the state in question will share incentives to arrest non-state actors contesting for power. I argue that the initial reaction is likely to be stalemate, but precisely how long such an outcome will last is difficult to estimate. We would expect that all the principals in this international drama—the ICC, the target states and the international community—will update their assessment of the costs and benefits of apprehension over time. If those indicted continue to violate international law, pressure to arrest may increase, while if leaders appear to have ceased such activities, the demand for apprehension may wane. Similarly, if it appears that diplomatic and economic actions and sanctions are weakening the suspected war criminals' grip on power, the key international actors may redouble their efforts. Thus, although the first stage in this international test of wills is stalemate, it does not imply that such stalemates cannot be broken through the strategic use of carrots and sticks designed to promote cooperation with the instruments of international justice.

Indeed, there are examples from the histories of the ICTY and ICTR that show that sustained economic and diplomatic pressure, coupled with a realization that the accused were doing more to undermine rather than sustain the peace, can facilitate apprehension of suspects. In the case of both the ICTY and the ICTR, many of the most powerful among those indicted eluded capture for many years during which they were able to continually undermine efforts at a wider peace (in the case of Rwanda) or political transition in the case of Bosnia, Croatia and Serbia. The capacity of many (although certainly not all of them as elements of the former Hutu regime continue to this day to wreak havoc in the Congo) of the former Rwandan *genocidairres* to foment violence in central Africa was only halted once the international community, chiefly the United States and Great Britain threw their weight behind efforts to force the surrender of these individuals.

Similarly in the former Yugoslavia, Franjo Tudjman in Croatia and Slobodan Milosevic in Serbia prevented the emergence of leaders who would modernize their nations and surrender war crimes suspects all the while arguing their efforts were indispensible to peace. In fact, Milosevic continued to make such claims after he was in the dock at the ICTY as a defense against his charges. Such leaders are often given substantial latitude and forbearance by the international community for fear of the havoc they could unleash. Yet, once it became apparent that these leaders were doing more damage than good for the peace process, their threats to spoil the peace became less meaningful and credible. And in the end, their departure from power smoothed the transition in these states to cooperation and integration with the international community.

One of the conundrums of building peace is that often the very people who appear to be important in the peace process are, in fact, those who are most responsible for holding it up, if not damaging it. While many leaders will claim they are indispensible participants in the peace process, their arguments tend to be rooted in a desire to share in the spoils of power rather than the responsibilities of peace. In fact, research has shown that these 'spoilers' are among the most critical threats facing nations that are seeking a way out of violence. Stedman contends that the greatest danger to post-conflict societies, "...comes from spoilers—leaders and parties who believe that peace emerging from negotiations threatens their power, worldview, and interests..."[22] When the ICC is able to gain the apprehension of those spoilers who have been indicted, their absence facilitates post-conflict peace building by giving local actors the political space needed to reconstruct society.[23] When the key actors in the international community in these cases—chiefly the US, Great Britain, France and key allies in NATO came to understand that apprehension would help sustain rather than jeopardize the peace, their efforts at apprehension became much more vigorous. These efforts eventually resulted in the arrest of every individual who was left on the ICTY's indictment list, and nearly all of those indicted by the ICTR. This rationale for apprehension, rooted in a more instrumentalist view of its purposes, rather than a normative commitment, is likely necessary in the short term until the international norms supporting the ICC grow stronger.[24]

Thus, the initial outcome of the decision tree outlined above is most likely to be a stalemate with the indicted leaders seeking to hold onto power by contesting ICC indictments. The international community can be expected to play a 'wait and see' strategy to assess the likely fallout with regard to peace negotiations and political transitions, as well as regional repercussions stemming from the ICC

---

22) Stephen. J. Stedman, 'Spoiler Problems in Peace Processes', 22 *International Security* (1997), 5.

23) Minow, *supra* note 8; Akhavan, *supra* note 8, pp. 16-26.

24) *See also* Leslie Vinjamuri, 'Deterrence, Democracy, and the Pursuit of International Justice', 24(2) *Ethics and International Affairs* (2010) 191-211.

actions. This has happened in The Sudan and Uganda, while those indicted by the ICC with regard to events in the Congo, the Central African Republic and the Ivory Coast have mostly been apprehended. The situations regarding Kenya and Libya continue to play out at the time of writing. The stalemate scenario seems most likely to play out in the case of state leaders who have a stronger power base and claim to legitimacy both domestically and internationally. Rebel leaders, as I have described earlier, must contend with both an international community and state leaders who would prefer to see them in detention rather than out fighting.

The ICC has chosen a mixed strategy of going after both office holders and non state actors. The Prosecutor has indicted three former or current heads of state including President Bashir of The Sudan, former President Laurent Gbagbo of the Ivory Coast and the late Colonel Qaddafi of Libya. President Bashir continues to refuse to cooperate with the ICC, while former President Gbagbo was ousted from power, captured and eventually sent to The Hague. Colonel Qaddafi died shortly after his indictment (although it would seem safe to assume he too would have refused to go gently to the ICC). The ICC issued summonses for several Kenyan politicians to appear before the Court in connection with the violence surrounding the Kenyan elections of 2007. It appears, at the time of writing, that trials involving several of the Kenyan politicians that were under investigation will take place. That these trials are set to commence does tend to call into question the idea expressed here that leaders will vigorously contest such accusations and refuse to surrender. Further, in-depth research into this situation is necessary, however, before any firm conclusions can be reached. The case of the former President of the Ivory Coast, Laurent Gbagbo is something of an anomaly as he is the only former head of state in detention. After he refused to concede defeat in the presidential elections of November 2010, fighting began between his forces and those of his election opponent, Alassane Outtara. Gbagbo was later captured and remained under local arrest for several months before the ICC issued its indictment and he was sent packing to The Hague in late 2011. The remainder of the indictments have been issued against non state actors who are often contesting for control of power, resources or land, although some have been affiliated with governments.

In all these cases the ICC has waded into ongoing civil and even international conflicts. The resolution of these conflicts is likely to be the most critical element of all in determining who is apprehended and who defies the Court. When government leaders lose, as in Libya and the Ivory Coast, the possibility of their detention in The Hague increases dramatically. Those who remain in power can be expected to continue their defiance. The fate of rebel leaders is similar. Once local fighting and politics have reached some sort of resolution, the fate of these leaders can be addressed more purposefully. Until then, international justice will likely have to wait its turn.

The International Criminal Court: A Pipe Dream to End Impunity?

Dawn L. Rothe[a] and Victoria E. Collins[b]
[a]Department of Sociology and Criminal Justice, Old Dominion University, Norfolk, VA, USA
[b]School of Justice Studies, Eastern Kentucky University, Richmond, KY, USA

Abstract
The prospects of the emerging international criminal justice system, namely the International Criminal Court, serving as a catalyst to end impunity of those most responsible for crimes against humanity, war crimes, genocide, and massive violations of human rights, remains bleak given four underlying factors: the ideology of deterrence that undergirds the system, jurisdictional limitations, the backlash of its involvement in and issuance of arrest warrants during highly contentious conflicts. This article offers some insight into these issues and the obstacles they present to the success of the International Criminal Court in ending impunity and future cases of such criminality. We begin by discussing the International Criminal Court followed by the ideology of deterrence and issues associated with the Court's jurisdiction. We then draw on two case examples, namely Uganda and Columbia, to discuss the challenges to involvement in ongoing conflicts and post-conflict situations.

Keywords
state crime; international criminal justice; social control; International Criminal Court (ICC); deterrence

> If [the twentieth century trend of wars, war crimes, misery and hardship] is not to continue into the twenty-first century, then the international community will have to take positive steps to arrest it. One effective deterrent would be an international criminal justice system, sufficiently empowered to cause would-be war criminals to reconsider their ambitions, knowing that they might otherwise be hunted for the rest of their days and eventually be brought to justice.[1]

1. Introduction

As of 1 June 2002 the Rome Statute of the International Criminal Court went into effect, creating a court whose purpose is the prosecution of those most responsible for the commission of war crimes, genocide and crimes against humanity. As

[1] Richard J. Goldstone. *For Humanity: Reflections of a War Crimes Investigator.* (New Yale University Press, Haven, 2000).

established, the Court is a complementary court designed to investigate and prosecute cases when states are unwilling or unable to do so themselves. It can only try cases dealing with crimes that have occurred since the Rome Statute's entry into force on 1 July 2002 and after a state's ratification of said statute. Further, in order for a case to fall under its jurisdiction, one of three conditions must be met in terms of location of the crimes.[2] The first geographic criterion is that the crimes in question must have occurred within the territory (or territory controlled by), vessel, or aircraft of a State Party, or have been committed by nationals of a State Party (i.e., uniformed military). Secondly, a state may agree to accept the jurisdiction of the Court, without being a state party. Thirdly, the United Nations Security Council can recommend a case to the Court and authorize the Court's jurisdiction in the matter if neither of the above conditions are met (e.g., the situation in the Sudan-Darfur case).[3]

Once a case or situation comes to the Prosecutorial branch's attention, an investigation is carried out to see the viability of the situation as a crime covered under the jurisdiction of the Court and subsequent successful prosecution. The Office of the Prosecutor is currently conducting investigations on crimes committed in seven states: Sudan (for the situation in Darfur), the Democratic Republic of the Congo, Uganda, the Central African Republic, Kenya, Libya and Côte d'Ivoire. The case *The Prosecutor v. Joseph Kony, Vincent Otti, Okot Odhiambo and Dominic Ongwen* is currently being heard before Pre-Trial Chamber II. In this case, five warrants of arrest have been issued (with the death of Lukwiya, the proceedings against him were terminated) and four suspects remain at large.[4] In the Democratic Republic of Congo situation four cases have been brought before the relevant Chambers: *The Prosecutor v. Thomas Lubanga Dyilo*;[5] *The Prosecutor v. Bosco Ntaganda*;[6] *The Prosecutor v. Germain Katanga and Mathieu Ngudjolo Chui*;[7] and *The Prosecutor v. Callixte Mbarushimana*.[8] Dyilo, Katanga, and Ngudjolo Chui are in the custody of the ICC while Ntaganda remains at large. There are four cases in

---

2) *Article 12 of the Rome Statute*, 2002, <http://www.icc cpi.int/Menus/ICC/Legal+Texts+and+Tools/Official+Journal/Rome+Statute.htm >, 21 June 2012.

3) Christopher, W. Mullins and Dawn L. Rothe, 'The Ability of the International Criminal Court to Deter Violations of International Criminal Law: A Theoretical Assessment', 10 *International Criminal Law Review* (2010) 771-786; Dawn L. Rothe and Isabel Schoultz, 'International Criminal Justice: A Deterrent for Crimes of the States?', *The Journal of Studi Sulla Questions Criminale: Nuova Serie dei Delitti e Delle Pene* (2012) forthcoming.

4) International Criminal Court: *Prosecutor v. Joseph Kony, Vincent Otti, Okot Odhiambo and Dominic Ongwen*, Case No.ICC-02/04-01/05.

5) The International Criminal Court: *Prosecutor v. Thomas Lubanga Dyilo*, Case No. ICC-01/04-01/06.

6) The International Criminal Court: *Prosecutor v. Bosco Ntganda*, Case No.ICC-01/04-02/06.

7) The International Criminal Court: *Prosecutor v. Germain Katanga and Mathieu Ngudjolo Chui*, Case No.ICC-01/04-01/07.

8) The International Criminal Court: *Prosecutor v. Callixte Mbarushimana*, Case No. ICC-01/04-01/10.

the situation in Darfur, Sudan: *The Prosecutor v. Ahmad Muhammad Harun ("Ahmad Harun") and Ali Muhammad Ali Abd-Al-Rahman ("Ali Kushayb")*;[9] *The Prosecutor v. Omar Hassan Ahmad Al Bashir*;[10] *The Prosecutor v. Abdallah Banda Abakaer Nourain and Saleh Mohammed Jerbo Jamus*;[11] and *The Prosecutor v. Abdel Raheem Muhammad Hussein*.[12] Banda and Jerbo appeared voluntarily on 17 June 2010, the other two suspects remain at large. In the situation in the Central African Republic, *The Prosecutor v. Jean-Pierre Bemba Gombo*, trial started on 22 November 2010.[13] Likewise, in the situation in Kenya, six Kenyan citizens voluntarily appeared before Pre-Trial Chamber II on 7 and 8 April 2011. *The Prosecutor v. William Samoei Ruto and Joshua Arap Sang*[14] and *The Prosecutor v. Francis Kirimi Muthaura and Uhuru Muigai Kenyatta*[15] remain active. In the situation of Libya, three warrants of arrest for *Muammar Mohammed Abu Minyar Gaddafi, Saif Al-Islam Gaddafi and Abdullah Al-Senussi*[16] were issued. On 22 November 2011, the case against Gaddafi was dropped due to his death and the other two suspects remain at large. In the situation of the Côte d'Ivoire, only one case is going forward *The Prosecutor v. Laurent Gbagbo*[17] to wit he is in custody.

While the Court may request a warrant for or subpoena an individual, the Prosecutor and the Court lack an empowered policing agency to ensure the fulfillment of either request.[18] The Prosecutor is limited to requesting the presence of persons being investigated, victims, and witnesses. It must rely on the compliance of a state or state party to relinquish any evidence, suspects, or witnesses that are relevant to the ongoing investigations carried out by the prosecutorial branch.

Additionally, given the infancy of the Court, the structure of the international system that remains grounded in sovereign state rule, the ICC continues to promote and be attentive to its perceived legitimacy and its mission: the "State Parties

---

9) The International Criminal Court: *Prosecutor v. Ahmad Muhammad Huran ("Ahmad Harun") and Ali Muhammad Ali Abd-Al-Rahman ("Ali Kushayb")*, Case No.ICC-02/05-01/07.

10) The International Criminal Court: *Prosecutor v. Omar Hassan Ahmad Al Bashir*, Case No.ICC-02/05-01/09.

11) The International Criminal Court: *Prosecutor v. Abdallah Banda Abakaer Nourain and Saleh Mohammed Jerbo Jamus*, Case No.ICC-02/05-03/09.

12) The International Criminal Court: *Prosecutor v. Abdel Raheem Muhammad Hussein*, Case No.ICC-02/05-01/12.

13) The International Criminal Court: *Prosecutor v. Jeran-Pierre Bemba Gombo*, Case No.ICC-01/05-01/08.

14) The International Criminal Court: *Prosecutor v. William Samoei Ruto and Joshua Arap Sang*, Case No.ICC-01/09-01/11.

15) The International Criminal Court: *Prosecutor v. Francis Kirimi Muthaura and Uhuru Muigai Kenyatta*, Case No. No.ICC-01/09-02/11.

16) The International Criminal Court: *Prosecutor v. Muammar Mohammed, Abu Minyar Gaddafi Saif Al-Islam Gaddafi and Abdullah Al-Senussi*, Case No.ICC-01/11-01/11.

17) The International Criminal Court: *Prosecutor v. Laurent Gbagbo*, Case No.ICC-02/11-01/11.

18) *Articles 54–58 of the Rome Statute*, 2002, <http://www.icc-cpi.int/Menus/ICC/Legal+Texts+and+Tools/Official+Journal/Rome+Statute.htm>, 22 June 2012.

to this Statute... [are] *Determined* to put an end to impunity for the perpetrators of these crimes and thus to contribute to the prevention of such crimes".[19] However, there are many challenges to the Court's ability to fulfill its mission to end impunity and to serve as a deterrent[20] that we argue result mainly from the following four factors: the ideology of deterrence that undergirds the system, jurisdictional limitations, the backlash of its involvement in highly contentious conflicts, and similar adverse reactions resulting from the issuance of arrest warrants during said conflicts. Drawing on the case examples of Uganda and Colombia, we illustrate how the latter challenges the Court's legitimacy as an international control mechanism in ongoing conflict and post-conflict situations. Consider first, the basics of the Court structure followed by the issues associated with deterrence.

2. Research on Deterrence

Nearly all extant criminological research on deterrence has been at national levels and on 'street' crime in general. This body of research has shown mixed results, at best, for a deterrent effect. One of the major issues highlighted in the literature is the assumption that actors are rational (including bounded rationality) in their decision-making prior to and during crime commission. It assumes that human nature, are rational which is subject to debate, especially so in the context of certain crimes such as homicide that has been shown empirically to be committed more emotive than calculating, thus, failing to allow for consideration of irrational decision-making. Considering that social theorists and philosophers have long contemplated the nature of man, as both rational and irrational, any underlying assumption as an a priori starting point fails to consider the alternative. For example, Vilfredo Pareto suggests that humans are not rational beings producing action.[21] However, humans have a need to espouse their actions as logical and rational so they invent a posteriori logical reasons to justify their acts. They "wish to represent involuntary acts as voluntary and non-logical actions as logical ones, conjure up strangely imaginary reasons, which they try to use to deceive themselves as well as others about the true motives of their actions". In other words, humans rationalize their behaviors after irrational action.

---

19) *The Preamble to the Rome Statute*, 2002 (A UN DOC /CONF.1833/51. 1999), <http://untreaty.un.org/cod/icc/statute/romefra.htm>, June 12, 2012.

20) Dawn L. Rothe and Christopher W. Mullins, 'Beyond the Juristic Orientation of International Criminal Justice: The Relevance of Criminological Insight to International Criminal Law and its Control', 10 *International Criminal Law Review* (2010) 97-110; Dawn L. Rothe and Isabel Schoultz, 'International Criminal Justice: A Deterrent for Crimes of the States?', *The Journal of Studi Sulla Questions Criminale: Nuova Serie dei Delitti e Delle Pene* (2012) forthcoming.

21) Vilfredo Pareto, *The Rise and Fall of Elites: An Application of Theoretical Sociology* (Transactions Publishers, New Brunswick, 1991).

Additionally, such a strict assumption of human nature as rational beings ignores the structural and contextual factors of individual decision-making (e.g., organizational or cultural pressures).[22]

If on the other hand, we set aside the broader debate of human nature and accept that humans are rational beings that perform a calculus to avoid pain or cost avoidance, there is reason to believe that rational calculus thought is affected by social location.[23] As criminological research has shown, those in positions with more at stake to risk are more likely to desist and or refrain from crime. This coincides with the life-course perspective as well that highlights that it is not merely aging out of crime that is a factor by itself, but that changes in ones' life course, where having more to lose serves as a form of inner-control, as a deterrent: marriage, relationships, and employment. As such, this could then be carried over to assume that some of those actors most likely to be involved in international law violations would seem to be those who are most susceptible to legal sanctions given 'what they have to lose'—social/political position as applied to those in positions of power that are believed to orchestrate the crimes.[24] On the other hand, leaders of insurgency groups may well feel they have more to lose politically and economically by ceasing the criminal activity in the grand scheme. Rationality and the impact of social location can be overshadowed by deeper internal commitments. Simply, assuming a high level of rationality, may not be so straight forward or resemble what is often thought of as a binary situation, as it is impacted

---

22) Mullins and Rothe *supra* note 3; Dawn L. Rothe and Christopher W. Mullins, 'Beyond the Juristic Orientation of International Criminal Justice: The Relevance of Criminological Insight to International Criminal Law and its Control', 10 *International Criminal Law Review* (2010) 97-110; Ronald C. Kramer and Raymond J. Michalowski, 'The invasion of Iraq as state-corporate crime', in Raymond J. Michalowski Ronald C. Kramer, (eds.), *State-Corporate Crime: Wrongdoing at the Intersection of Business and Government* (Rutgers University Press, Piscataway, 2006) pp.199-214; Raymond J. Michalowski and Ronald C. Kramer (eds.), *State-Corporate Crime: Wrongdoing at the Intersection of Business and Government* (Rutgers University Press, Piscataway, 2006); Alette Smeulers, 'Perpertrators of international crimes: towards a typology', in Alette Smeulers and Roelof Haveman, (eds.), *Supranational Criminology: Towards a Criminology of International Crimes* (Intersentia, Mortsel, 2008) pp.233-265; Katharine A. Marshall, 'Prevention and Complementarity in the International Criminal Court: A Positive Approach', 2 *Human Rights Brief* (2010) 21-26.

23) Alex Piquero and Raymond Paternoster, 'An application of Stafford and Warr's reconceptualization of deterrence to drinking a choice theory of corporate crime', in Neal Shover and John P. Wright, (eds.), *Crimes of Privilege – Readings in White-collar Crime* (Oxford Press, New York, 1992) pp.194-210; Raymond Paternoster and Alex Piquero, 'Reconceptualizing Deterrence: An Empirical Test of Personal and Vicarious Experiences', 32 *Journal of Research in Crime and Delinquency* (1995) 251-86; Mark C. Stafford and Mark A. Warr, 'Reconceptualization of General and Specific Deterrence', 30 *Journal of Reearch in Crime and Delinquency* (1993) 123-135.

24) Dawn L. Rothe and Christopher W. Mullins, 'Beyond the Juristic Orientation of International Criminal Justice: The Relevance of Criminological Insight to International Criminal Law and its Control', 10 *International Criminal Law Review* (2010) 97-110.

by individual moral considerations grounded in specific situations and structures: culture, ideology, and religion as well as the immediate conflict situation.[25]

Scholars have noted that mass violence and conflicts give rise to situations where individuals behave differently than as seen in street crime contexts. In situations of conflict, the law can be seen as necessarily negotiable and its meaning seen as invalid given the circumstances. This is especially the case when individual morality is influenced by the on-going situation or the individual ideology guiding their behaviour. Here, the fighting and subsequent crimes committed can be believed as legitimate, just, or as the only means to defend or advance the interests of the group or the individual's situation or status, making the crimes necessary, if they are even viewed as 'crimes'. This can be impacted further by the greater sense of fear an individual feels in terms of the potential loss if they did not choose the behaviour that is cast as 'illegal' under international law (i.e., liberation movements or to dispose a regime). Simply, environments affect the moral choices made by individuals where behaviour is contextual.

As such, immediate needs in a conflict situation may change expected cost-benefit analysis where more weight is given to the costs of not committing the crimes than to 1) the cost of committing the crimes, or 2) any real or perceived cost of being held accountable. Here fear, not of punishment, but loss of power and or a broader goal a militia, insurgency group, or government leaders may have could far outweigh any potential costs associated with international criminal law.

If we assume the costs of committing these crimes would be greater than the potential benefits, given all contextual considerations, there are other means in which deterrence can be negated at the individual level: through utilizing common techniques of neutralization to ensuring plausible deniability.[26]

Other factors that have had empirical support for a deterrent effect include certainty, legitimacy of the law, both of which are tied to the most important variable, individual perception. Simply, when offenders do not perceive a punishment as likely to be imposed, then there will be little disincentive toward offending, no matter the celerity or the proportionality of the punishment in question. This relates to both, certainty of being caught and punished as well as legitimacy. If an offender has absolute knowledge that someone else committed the same act and is not 'caught' or punished, there is a disjuncture and certainty is lost. This is especially important at the international criminal justice level. Additionally, the issue of legitimacy is highly relevant for international criminal law and criminal justice as both the law and the institution of social control must be perceived as legitimate.

25) Dawn L. Rothe and Isabel Schoultz, 'International Criminal Justice: A Deterrent for Crimes of the States?', *The Journal of Studi Sulla Questions Criminale: Nuova Serie dei Delitti e Delle Pene* (2012) forthcoming.

26) Dawn L. Rothe, *State Criminality: The Crime of all Crimes*, (Lexington Books, Lanham, 2009).

After all, criminological theories, dating back to the 1930s and Edwin Sutherland's Differential Association have long noted that individuals' definition of the law as favorable or unfavorable have a bearing on the decision-making processes to offend or not offend. While unfavorable definitions of the law are not referred to as issues of legitimacy by Sutherland, they are one and the same: not viewing a particular law as legitimate is viewing it unfavorably. If one feels a law should not be followed, individuals will not see it as a right and proper restriction of behavior.[27] Research on white collar crime has shown that the best statistical predictor of deterrence (not committing an action) is the individual belief that legal restriction in question is legitimate and morally valid. If a combination of law as unfavorable and the *perception* of the risks of being caught and potential punishment are nigh, the impact of general deterrence is negated.[28]

The rule of law can be said to only be a general deterrent when the law is viewed favorably by those under its authority and when it is *perceived* at the individual level that there is a certainty of being caught and being held accountable.[29] If, for example, the perceived threat of being caught is strong, the particular law need not be viewed as legitimate. On the other hand, if law is viewed as legitimate, the perception of being caught holds less impact as the internalized belief in legitimacy, which can serve as a self-controlling mechanism. This has been referred to as legitimacy based deference. When both are absent, deterrence holds no effectiveness.[30] The following section delves into these issues.

3. The Jurisdictional Limitations of the ICC and Deterrence

The presence of national and/or international criminal trials have not prevented suicide bombers from committing atrocities, illegal activities by guerrilla members in Colombia, the Lord's Resistance Army's systematic attacks against civilians or the use of child soldiers, the United States' acts of aggression against Iraq, or Israel's continued use of targeted assassinations and illegal occupation. At core, as

---

27) Edwin H. Sutherland, *Principles of Criminology*, (4th edition), (J.B. Lippincott Company, Chicago, 1939).

28) Christopher, W. Mullins and Dawn L. Rothe, 'The Ability of the International Criminal Court to Deter Violations of International Criminal Law: A Theoretical Assessment', 10 *International Criminal Law Review* (2010) 771-786; Rothe and Mullins, *supra* note 24.

29) Richard Wright and Scott H. Decker, *Burglars on the Job: Streetlife and Residential Break-ins* (Northeastern University Press, Boston, 1994); Neal Shover and David Honaker, 'The socially bounded decision making of persistent property offenders', 31 *The Howard Journal of Criminal Justice* (1992) 276-293; Neal Shover and Belinda Henderson, 'Repressive crime control and male persistent thieves', in Hugh D. Barlow, (ed.), *Crime and public policy: putting theory to work* (Westview Press, Boulder, 1995).

30) Rothe and Schoultz, *supra* note 25.

previously noted, a deterrent effect is hindered by certainty, legitimacy, and individual perception.[31]

Certainty is at odds with the ICC due to its very structure as a complementary court. For example, having absolute knowledge that similar crimes, crimes against humanity and war crimes, have been committed by other states where there has been no accountability or enforcement of the law defies any real or perceived level of certainty. Here the issue of selective enforcement of international criminal law is at issue. This is not something new as history has shown that international law has not equally taken into account all extraordinary events. Consider the Nuremberg trials and the way in which the atrocities of World War II were dealt with in relation to prosecuting Nazi commanders while ignoring Dresden, Hiroshima and Nagasaki or even the Gulags under the former Soviet Union.[32] The sensitive selection of extraordinary cases is particularly questioned under the ICC, which has mainly focused on African conflicts at the expenses of others.

The ICC, as we previously noted, is founded on complementarity. The limitation on the Court's jurisdictional powers weakens certainty.[33] Consider the cases that are 1) not covered due to jurisdictional limitations, but also 2) the selectivity of cases that result from the complementarity of the Court as well as the discretion of cases selected by the prosecutor, and 3) the role of the United Nations Security Council in forwarding specific situations and cases to the Court. Recall that the United Nations Security Council can recommend a case to the Court and authorize the Court's jurisdiction in the matter if neither other jurisdictional conditions apply as in the case of Sudan and Darfur. Even with the ability of the Security Council to suggest an investigation, parties with veto powers or with strong alliances with such a state, face little risk in their situation being forward to the Court. This reduces the court's ability to deter when state parties and their operatives are not under the court's jurisdiction.[34]

Even when cases are forwarded, such as Sudan, the limited powers of enforcement severely weaken a deterrent effect, directly and through the individual perception that is a needed component for effective deterrence. The inability to apprehend a suspect weakens the Court's credibility, legitimacy, and perceived certainty of capture and punishment. Consider the 're-election' of Sudan's President al-Bashir for another term as President, the first head-of-state to be reelected while facing an international arrest warrant, and the ongoing violence and crimes committed against the civilian population does not lend well to the idea of deterrence. Beyond the domestic level, the relationships and welcoming of

---

31) *Ibid.*

32) Nils Christie, 'Answers to atrocities, restorative justice in extreme situations', in Ezzat Fattah and Stephan Parmentier, (eds.), *Victim Policies and Criminal Justice on the Road to Restorative Justice* (Leuven University Press, Leuven, 2001) pp. 379-392.

33) Rothe and Schoultz, *supra* note 25.

34) Mullins and Rothe, *supra* note 28.

al-Bashir by other African heads of state to their countries as well as an overwhelming welcome to China by China's President Hu Jintao in the face of the outstanding arrest warrant issued by the ICC highlights the weaknesses of perceived certainty or legitimacy in the eyes of other African Countries, China and al-Bashir. Furthermore, here, not only is lack of cooperation by these countries to hand him over to the ICC a negation to the perceived certainty of enforcement of law violations, but serves as a case of direct knowledge of a violator of international criminal law receiving continued impunity. The direct knowledge that these laws are selectively applied and enforced further negates any deterrent effect.[35]

Consider also the domestic issues that result from selectivity as in the case of Kenya and the post-elections violence aimed at civilians. The Court issued arrest warrants for six Kenyan executives (dubbed 'The Ocampo Six')[36] for their involvement in the Kenyan post-election violence in 2007-2008, yet there are others who are believed to have orchestrated and participated in the post-election violence that are glaringly absent from the Court's attention. Likewise, in the situations of the Congo and Uganda, the Prosecutor has focused only on militias, and in the case of Uganda first announced the taking of the situation alongside the Ugandan President, regardless of the abundance of evidence that the governmental armies committed grave human rights violations as well. Consider also the case of the Congo where the Court has only addressed the crimes of the militia groups despite the fact that the Forces Armées de la République Démocratique du Congo (FARDC) are claimed to be one of the most notorious violators of international law within the Congo conflict. Amongst these violations is the use of child soldiers. Between October 2008 and December 2009, the FARDC was documented to be responsible for recruiting 42% of the 1,593 children,[37] yet no army official has yet stood trial for these transgressions. Not only does this affect the perceived legitimacy of the Court in the eyes of the militia leaders,[38] but significantly reduces the potential of a general deterrent outcome for other militias and heads of state. Furthermore, it creates additional resentments within the domestic population and further impacts the overall perceived legitimacy of the Court.[39]

---

35) Rothe and Schoultz *supra* note 25.

36) William Ruto, Henry Kosgey and Joshua Arap Sang are alleged to have prepared and implemented a plan to attack the civilian population in Rift Valley. The Prosecutor also claims that there were reasonable grounds to believe that Uhuru Kenyatta used the Mungiki, in agreement with Francis Muthaura, to retaliate against ODM supporters, and that Muthaura instructed Mohammed Hussein Ali, then Commissioner of Police, not to intervene to prevent the attacks. The suspects appeared before the Court on 7 and 8 April (Case no. ICC-01/09-01/11), see International Criminal Court, supra note 15.

37) United Nations Security Council, *Report of the secretary-general on children and armed conflict in the Democratic Republic of the Congo* (S/2010/369).

38) Mareike Schomerus, 'A terrorist is not a person like me': An interview with Joseph Kony', in Tim Allen and Koen Vlassenroot, (eds.), *The Lord's Resistance Army: Myth and Reality* (Zed Books, London, 2010) pp.113-131.

39) Rothe and Schoultz, *supra* note 25.

As noted, individual perception is central to a deterrent effect. Given the ongoing resistance to the legitimacy of international criminal law and the Court by several states, insurgency groups, and militaries, the Court is further weakened in its ability to serve as a general deterrent. Consider the case of Libya where the ICC issued arrest warrants for Muammar Gaddafi, the second sitting head of state to be indicted by the ICC, his son Saif al-Islam and his military intelligence chief General Abdullah al-Sanoussi. The issue of the perceived lack of legitimacy of the law was reflected in a statement by Gaddafi's spokesperson, Moussa Ibrahim "The ICC has no legitimacy whatsoever. We will deal with it".[40] Whether a symbolic or defiant statement, it does reflect an ongoing issue of the Court's perceived legitimacy. Further, the Court's apprehension record offers little reason to consider the risk/threat of the prosecution a perceived certainty for regimes, high ranking government officials, and military or militia leaders to be handed over to the Court.

Regardless of the difficulties of any real deterrent effect presented here, the ICC continues to defend the universal and impartial belief in such an outcome. This is problematic because the approach and its discourse are not grounded in political realities of the international legal order and/or situations of violent conflict and post-conflict peace processes.

3. The ICC Involvement in Conflict and Post-Conflict Situations and the Unintended Backlash

> All of us who are concerned for peace and triumph of reason and justice must be keenly aware how small an influence reason and honest good will exert upon events in the political field.[41]

In addition to the core issues hindering a deterrent effect, criticisms have been levied against the Court in relation to its involvement in conflict situations from the issuance of arrest warrants during peace negotiations to its exertion of political pressures on states in processes of conflict resolution and restoration.[42] This is what Evans refers to as the justice versus peace problem.[43] After all, there can be a

40) Vivienne Walt, 'A Gaddafi Arrest Warrant Raises the Stakes in Libya.', *Time*, 27 June 2011.

41) Albert Einstein, *Miscellaneous*, <www.websophia.com/faces/einstein.html#miscellaneous>, June 24, 2012.

42) Isabella Bueno and Andrea Diaz, 'Retributive and restorative justice in Colombia: Challenges in the time of the ICC and the ongoing conflict', in Michael Bohlander, Thordis Ingadottir, James Meernik, Dawn L. Rothe, Wolfgang Schomburg, (eds.), *The Reality of Modern International Criminal Justice* (Martinus Nijhoff Publishers, UK, 2012) forthcoming; Marco Fanara, *Prosecution or impunity? Is there an alternative?* <www.monitor.upeace.org/ar-chive.cfm?id_article=799>, 18 April 2011.

43) Gareth Evans, 'Peace versus Justice', *Guest Lecture at The University of Melbourne and President Emeritus of the International Crisis Group*, <www.gevans.org/speeches/speech418.html>, 27 July 2010.

clash between the demands for peace and bringing an end to a conflict and efforts to hold accountable those responsible in a court of law. The "problem arises when there is an ongoing conflict, and a peace negotiation is attempting to reach agreement between parties capable of perpetuating it" as in the case of Uganda for example. Likewise, such a clash can occur with competing demands of justice versus those of reconciliation as in the case of Columbia.

Uganda serves as an example, where despite the claims of the Achioli community that the intervention of the ICC would obstruct peace efforts, the prosecutor of the ICC issued arrest warrants against the Lord's Resistance Army (LRA) leadership (a militia group), conducing the LRA to respond by a rejection of ending the war in presence of the arrest warrants.[44] With the case of Columbia, the ICC Prosecutor Ocampo's investigation found that over thirty members of the Congressional body and President Uribe were involved either directly or through financial support of the paramilitaries in carrying out atrocities on Columbian civilians. Upon the ICC's exertion of pressure, the Government responded, however, the pressure had additional and unforeseen consequences related to disarmament and peace which will be discussed in more detail below.

3.1. *The Situation with Uganda*

Since independence in 1962 Uganda has been mired in political conflict and civil war that has produced continuous and widespread atrocities, war crimes and crimes against humanity. The nearly four decades of crimes against humanity and violence that have plagued Uganda's vulnerable populations are the result of the actions of a militia group, the Lord's Resistance Army, political party factions attempting to gain power and control of the state, and the Ugandan military force practicing sporadic banditry and violence.[45]

In December 2003, the President of Uganda, Yoweri Museveni referred the ongoing conflict with the LRA and their crimes against humanity to the International Criminal Court.[46] In October 2005, the Court announced arrest warrants for Joseph Kony and four of his top deputies. The charges ranged from the mutilation of civilians to the forced abduction of, and sexual abuse of children.

---

[44] Rosalind Shaw, Lars Waldorf, Pierre Hazan (eds.), *Localizing Transitional Justice: Intervention and Priorities after Mass Violence* (Standford University Press, Palto Alto, 2010).

[45] Mullins and Rothe, *supra* note 28.

[46] This caused outrage among Ugandans, NGO's, and militia groups calling into question the legitimacy of the Court. Knowing that Museveni and the Uganda Peoples Defence Force (UPDF) were deeply involved in crimes against humanity including child abductions, torture, rape, indeterminate detentions, and civilian displacement, the public announcement appeared as if the Court was providing additional impunity to the regime. The court failed to effectively communicate its mandate and impartiality to the civilians of northern Uganda which undermined the court's credibility and impartiality in the eyes of many there.

The involvement of the Court, however, did not serve the processes of peace or conflict resolution in Uganda. Rather, the Juba peace talks ceased and the LRA stepped up the levels of violence as well as relocated across the border in Sudan. Beyond continued violence, the LRA, after ICC involvement, stepped up its campaign to engage child soldiers through increased abductions and inductions into the militia group. Kony immediately stated his refusal to continue in the ongoing peace negotiations unless the ICC withdrew its arrest warrants. Consequentially, the Juba Peace Accords broke down in 2008 due to the LRA leaders' refusal to take part in the 2008 round of talks. This was based largely on the threat posed by the ICC's indictments of the LRA commander as well as the Court's Prosecutor's refusal to drop the indictments.[47]

After the initial referral and the end of peace negotiations, Museveni had requested that the Court drop the charges against the LRA leaders. However, under the Rome Statute, there is no condition where a government can withdraw a request once it has been accepted and in process.[48] Consequentially, the arrest warrants facilitated, what many in Uganda believe to be, another barrier to the conclusion of peace talks that had already seen many obstacles.

Additionally, controversy remains over the role of amnesty in national settings once the ICC has become involved. Specifically, there is a tension between allowing amnesty for peace and cessation of a conflict and what the Court, and some proponents of the ICC view as impunity.[49] As Clark, suggests "...to give amnesty to individuals indicted by the ICC over the most serious crimes of concern to the international community as a whole would compromise the effectiveness of the ICC and bring questions about whether the ICC can really carry out its mandate."[50] This relates specifically to the case of Uganda and its 1999 amnesty law, which was designed as a tool to enhance peace negotiations and end the violence by allowing LRA fighters to confess and demobilize in exchange for amnesty.[51] Uganda's right to utilize the Amnesty Act of 2000 does not, however, void their referral to the ICC or the Court's jurisdiction.[52] Clark insists, "peace must

[47] See this journal and Steven Roach, 'Multilayered Justice in Northern Uganda: Reconciling Mato Oput with ICC Intervention', in Michael Bohlander, Thordis Ingadottir, James Meernik, Dawn L. Rothe, Wolfgang Schomburg, (eds.), *The Reality of Modern International Criminal Justice* (Martinus Nijhoff Publishers, UK, 2012) forthcoming.

[48] Tom Ginsberg, *The Clash of Commitments at the International Criminal Court'*, (The Law School The University of Chicago, Chicago, 2008) <www.law.uchicago.edu/files/files/pl251.pdf>, 12 June 2012.

[49] Roach, *supra* note 47.

[50] Janine N. Clark, 'The ICC, Uganda and the LRA: Re-framing the debate', 69 *Journal of African Studies* (2010) 141-60.

[51] Justice and Reconciliation Project, *Agencia Colombiana para la reintegración, desmovilización*, <www.reintegracion.gov.co.>, Jan 10 2012.

[52] Marco Fanara, *Prosecution or impunity? Is there an alternative?* <www.monitor.upeace.org/ar-chive.cfm?id_article=799>, 18 April 2011.

come before justice and that the ICC's arrest warrants undermine prospects for peace in Uganda".[53]

Furthermore, as history has shown in the case of Uganda, prosecution offers no incentive to end hostilities[54] rather it may well be a major factor in the continuation of and displacement of the conflict.[55] After all "it will be more difficult for the members of illegal armed groups to sit at the negotiations table if they know they will be strictly punished".[56]

The ICC's intervention in Northern Uganda has raised concerns about the role of international justice in conflict and post-conflict situations. Such interference has called increasing attention to not only the political tensions between the ICC and state governments, but also the legitimacy of the Court's goals for justice at what may be the expense of peace.[57] Furthermore, as noted by Bill Oketch,

> It's true that justice should prevail, but we should not forget that justice delayed is justice denied. And there is no doubt that it has been delayed.... Anyone campaigning for Kony's arrest should beware of reopening old wounds inflicted by the LRA. Those wounds are deep enough. Northern Uganda has lost more than 20 years to the LRA insurgency and we cannot afford to lose one more day. We need to concentrate on peace-building, redevelopment, reconciliation, and educating our children.[58]

3.2. *The Situation with Columbia*

For more than five decades Colombia was involved in an armed conflict that has resulted in millions of victims of serious violations of human rights including but not limited to torture, massacres, kidnapping, forced displacement, and child recruitment into paramilitary and guerrilla groups. Roughly three million Columbians have been internally displaced (IDP), making it the world's second largest population of IDPs.[59] Thousands of individuals have been involved in committing these atrocities, most notably government forces and paramilitary,

---

53) Clark, *supra* note 50.

54) Fanara, *supra* note 52; Dinah E. Shelton and Gale Cengage, 'Genocide and Crimes Against Humanity Amnesty', in Marco Fanara, *Prosecution or impunity? Is there an alternative?* <www.monitor.upeace.org/ar-chive.cfm?id_article=799>, 18 April 2011.

55) Mullins and Rothe, *supra* note 28; H. Abigail Moy, 'The International Criminal Court's Arrest Warrants and Uganda's Lord's Resistance Army: Renewing the Debate over Amnesty and Complementarity', 19 *Harvard Human Rights Journal* (2006) 267-73.

56) Natalie Riveros, 'Peace vs. Accountability in Colombia', *University for Peace* <www.monitor.upeace.org/NRIVEROS.pdf>, 12 March 2012.

57) Roach, *supra* note 47; Ginsberg, *supra* note 48.

58) Bill Oketch, 'Kony 2012 Campaign Too Late in North Uganda', *Institute for War and Peace Report ICC – Africa update* (2012) p.316.

59) Andrés Quintero, Tegan A. Culler, 'IDP Health in Columbia: Needs and Challenges', *Reproductive Health Access Information and Services in Emergencies*, <www.fmreview.org/FMRpdfs/FMR33/70-71.pdf>, March 20 2012.

guerrilla groups (i.e., the United Self-Defense Forces of Colombia (AUC), the Revolutionary Armed Forces of Colombia (FARC), the Ejército Popular de Liberación (EPL), the Partido Revolucionario de los Trabajadores (PRT), the Movimiento Armado Quintín Lame (MAQL), and the Army of National Liberation (ELN))- many of whom have demobilized either collectively or individually.[60]

The role of the International Criminal Court, in relation to Columbia, concerns its jurisdiction for crimes committed given the Country's efforts to address them through restorative justice mechanisms, legislation, and implementation of new laws. Specifically, the involvement of the ICC has raised considerable concerns surrounding its jurisdictional role and national mechanisms of justice given the Court has established limitations regarding other national approaches to justice. Additionally, and perhaps most concerning is that, not unlike Uganda, the threat of being prosecuted by the ICC, has hindered local processes for reconciliation and restoration as well as the willingness of paramilitary groups to surrender and reintegrate. Prior to discussing these issues, it is important to have an understanding of the history of the Court and Columbia.

Less than four months after the Rome Statute entered into force in 2002, Colombia came under its jurisdiction for the crimes of genocide and crimes against humanity. Since November 1, 2009 the moratorium that had been in effect for war crimes, requested by President Uribe, was lifted, leaving the Court with jurisdiction for all crimes listed in the Rome Statute (save for crimes of aggression which remains undefined). The Court's jurisdiction, however, is contingent upon the failure of the national justice system to 'address' and those that committed the crimes and to impart justice. Simultaneously, in 2002, the Colombian government began implementing local transitional justice mechanisms to bring to an end the conflict that had lasted for more than 50 years. This included Columbia's Law 975, known as the Justice and Peace Law (JPL) which was enacted to facilitate peace negotiations between the regime and the various armed factions. This law was in part, also a response to the pressure and influences of the international retributive model of justice.[61]

Given the relationship between the Court and Columbia, there are multiple relations and effects. Consider that since 2005 when the Court claimed it would maintain a permanent evaluation of the situation in Columbia and then in 2006 when it opened its preliminary examination, Columbia has actively and symbolically reacted to the Court and subsequent pressures from the Prosecutor, including adjusting and creating domestic policy responses to appease the international

---

60) See this journal and Isabella Bueno and Andrea Diaz, 'Retributive and restorative justice in Colombia: Challenges in the time of the ICC and the ongoing conflict', in Michael Bohlander, Thordis Ingadottir, James Meernik, Dawn L. Rothe, Wolfgang Schomburg, (eds.), *The Reality of Modern International Criminal Justice* (Martinus Nijhoff Publishers, UK, 2012) forthcoming.

61) *Ibid.*

system of control. For example, JPL replaced other laws used to enhance peace negotiations through the use of amnesty and pardons, and states that ex-combatants who committed grave crimes and agree to demobilize must be prosecuted in exchange for reduced sanctions.

The effects of the Court's involvement and self-proclaimed jurisdiction, while having had some positive impacts, have also resulted in secondary consequences. Recall that the Court's jurisdiction is regulated by the principle of complementarity where priority is given to States to provide accountability for the crimes encoded in the Rome Statute. Thus, the Court is not supposed to take an active role save a state "is unwilling or unable genuinely to carry out the investigation or prosecution." As noted, the Court remains overseeing the matter in Columbia and

> continues to exert pressure on the Government to increase the punitive models and accountability at what may well be expense of the surrender and reconciliation of militia and paramilitary members as well as the success of national measures to address the conflict and subsequent crimes committed.[62]

The significance of this needs to be considered in light of Columbia's long history of using amnesties to address the demobilization of guerrilla members and some paramilitary groups in an effort to achieve peace and reconciliation, which has now been replaced with the inclusion of a more retributive response. Through pressure to disallow amnesty and increase the retributive component of justice, many individuals within the various factions have continued in hiding and/or with arms to avoid potential prosecution, prolonging the conflict and violence.

As stated by Sriram in the interviews she conducted in Colombia, "all armed groups feared prosecution before the ICC, but were split as to whether it would encourage them to keep fighting or to lay down their arms."[63] Likewise Bueno's[64] research and extensive interviews revealed that one of the main reasons why offenders from the guerrilla groups have not demobilised is precisely the fear of being locked up in prisons and or extradited to the United States.

The following quotes are from low-level FARC offenders[65] who are not covered by the Justice and Peace Law, but by Law 1106 of 2006 (absence of prosecutions) and show the tensions between the desire to demobilize and fear of prosecution or extradition. "Imagine that you come here [demobilisation site] to be free and

---

62) *Ibid.*

63) Chandra L. Sriram, *The ICC Africa experiment: the Central African Republic, Darfur, northern Uganda, and the Democratic Republic of the Congo*, <www.humansecuritygateway. com/documents/ISA_ ICCAfricaexperiment.pdf>, June 12, 2012.

64) The following quotes were responses from various faction groups in extensive interviews conducted by Isabella Bueno and have been provided to the authors for use.

65) Names have been removed and interviewees were assigned numbers to protect their identity, save for any that have requested their names be given.

you end up in prison; one prefers to remain free *en el monte*; always running but at least having a space where to run".[66] Another FARC member stated that the threat of punishment and extradition would stop offenders from demobilising: "there should be opportunities for everyone. If I were asked in extradition, I would never demobilise. That person (asked in extradition) should be given an opportunity. Even if the person has to work to pay for his/her faults..." Another FARC member states that prison sentences are discouraging many combatants from FARC from demobilising: "If they promise you freedom and therefore you demobilise and then they put you in jail, how would the others demobilise? That's why there are many people who do not come here, they see all that in the news." Another FARC member discusses his own fearful experience of demobilisation, "I was so scared the day I demobilised, I said to myself 'where would they take me? Would they lock me up, tie me up'?" Offenders are often afraid of being obliged to go to prison, "thinking that they're going to rot in jail makes them hesitate and stops them from taking the decision we took (to demobilise)".[67]

Other FARC members note that punitive measures such as prison are counter-productive and lend to victimization of offenders. As stated by FARC 99;

> The government should give psychological assistance to a demobilised chief commander. Over there things are done because you are obliged to, not because you mean to, so I think it won't be fair to put an offender in jail, no matter what his rank is. We are talking about a person who regrets and wants to be free; instead of sending him to prison he should receive therapeutic education. There are chiefs who have never been educated; some of them don't even know how to sign.

FARC 202 states, "I think that 50 or 40 or 2 or 3 years is the same; they shouldn't do it because it doesn't solve anything. It would be difficult to go to jail for 40 years, but in any case one doesn't repair what has been done." This sentiment was repeated in many interviews, noting that "spending long time in prison won't repair anything".[68]

The situation in Columbia with the ICC highlights the tenuous nature between the push for an international criminal justice system and a retributive model of accountability and the most feasible means to achieve peace and demobilisation of various factions. As the quotes above highlight, there are secondary effects of international threats of prosecution where various members of militias, guerrilla groups, and paramilitary that will not demobilize or surrender their cause in the face of such a threat.

---

66) FARC interviews The quotes contained here were responses from various faction groups in extensive interviews conducted by Isabella Bueno and have been provided to the authors for use.

67) *Ibid.*

68) *Ibid.*

3.3. *Summary of the ICC's Involvement in these Cases*

Due to the involvement of the ICC, we have seen that other issues arise, lending to additional cycles of violence where crimes against civilians continue, groups move across another border and continue to victimize vulnerable populations, as well as the refusal of various factions to demobilize or surrender. As noted by Lambourne,

> the efforts of international lawyers and human rights advocates to fairly and justly prosecute those responsible for perpetrating crimes against humanity, and to ensure a future respect for the rule of law and human rights principles, are juxtaposed against the efforts of international peace negotiators and conflict resolution practitioners who prioritize the establishment of peace and security and a climate of reconciliation between former enemies.[69]

In the case of Uganda, Joseph Koney and the LRA immediately stepped up violence, moved across borders and victimized others there, especially young children with the ICC intervention. Moreover, moving to another country and stepping up efforts using different means, not only continued the cycle of violence on vulnerable populations, but served to negate peace negotiations with the group and the Ugandan government. In an interview with the United Nations under-secretary general for humanitarian affairs and emergency relief, Jan Egeland in November 2006, Kony emphatically stated that he would never surrender as long as he faces the risk of being arrested.[70] The long impasse between the LRA and the ICC has frustrated many Ugandans as they are sick of conflict and have far greater concerns of illness and starvation and have stated they would prefer the ICC charges be dropped to stop the ongoing conflict that has now extended into other bordering states. Similarly, in the case of Columbia, we see various members of insurgency factions that have refused to participate in negotiations or demobilize under the threat of prosecution and the removal of any amnesty or pardons.

Beyond the general continuation of violence and crimes against humanity, there are levels of secondary victimization of both victims and perpetrators. As some of the FARC members have noted, after demobilisation many realize that they have been 'used' by chief commanders: "they are the ones who rule, in a very relaxed way, drinking whiskey, while one risks one's life...they are the ones who order"[71]... if we don't do it (execute the order), we risk our lives, we have to do it for A or B reason. They are responsible".[72] While obeying orders is not a legal

---

69) Wendy Lambourne, 'Transitional Justice and Peacebuilding after Mass Violence', *Proceedings of the Centre for Peace Research and Strategic Studies* (KU Leuven, 2006).

70) Jan Egeland, 'United Nations under-secretary general for humanitarian affairs and emergency relief', in Jeffrey Gettleman, (ed.), *UN envoy meets with Ugandan rebel* (New York Times, New York, 2006), < www.nytimes.com/2006/11/13/world/africa/13uganda.html>, (12 June 2012).

71) FARC, *supra* note 66.

72) *Ibid.*

defence, such a deep seated belief impacts not only the belief in the fairness of punishments, but the long term efforts towards restoration. This is especially so when high ranking state officials and military personal have committed their share of crimes against humanity and or war crimes and receive complete impunity while the focus remains on the insurgency groups, paramilitary, and militias.

In the case of Uganda, as the cycle of violence and the kidnapping of children continue, those children that have escaped or rescued from the LRA continue to be victimized in many cases by not being allowed to return or accepted back into their local communities. Moreover, female child soldiers continue to be victims as they have been raped, many impregnated, and suffer from psychological disorders and Sexually Transmitted Infections as a result of the violence. Though many have been 'freed', they have returned to impoverished communities where they are rejected and "verbally and physically harassed by the community, called "killers," "Kony's wives," and "prostitutes," and often beaten and stoned".[73] Moreover, children remain in hiding, afraid to wander in the streets or walk to school, for fear of being abducted again into the LRA.

As we have highlighted here, there is a fine line between ending a long history of impunity and achieving peace in conflicts where crimes against humanity, genocide, and war crimes are committed. The cases discussed above merely highlight the potential of the ICC to serve as a barrier to peace negotiations when the threat of prosecution at the international level is introduced. In these cases, one must carefully balance the goal of peace and cessation of conflict with prosecutions. As noted by Grono, ICC prosecution or peace through amnesty and impunity should only be traded off against the other when there is no other viable alternatives and when the benefits of peace outweigh the harm that may be caused by involvement of the international criminal justice system.[74]

4. Discussion

The international criminal justice system, the International Criminal Court in particular, has made significant progress, given its infancy; yet, the Court has its challenges and contradictions. The cases drawn on here have paid particular attention to the role of the Court in ongoing conflicts and the challenges of peace negotiations in light of the threat of arrest and prosecution. Having said this, it should be

---

[73] United Africans for Womens and Childrens Rights, *United Africans for Women's and Children's Rights: What We Do*, <www.africanwomenrights.org/what_we_do/scholarships.php>, May 12 2012.

[74] Nick Grono, *The role of the International Criminal Court in peace processes: mutually reinforcing or mutually exclusive?* (Institute of Public Policy Research, London, 2006), <www.crisisgroup.org/en/publication-type/commentary/the-role-of-the-international-criminal-court-in-peace-processes.aspx> 29 May 2012.

noted that the continuation of this violence and crimes is not solely due to the ICC involvement, but one should not discount the role it has played.

As with domestic level criminal justice systems, there is always a level of politics involved. This is enhanced at the international level given state sovereignty and a complementary system, leaving the Court in a "gray zone between the judicial and political".[75] In the case of the ICC, there are issues of sovereignty and an ambiguous definition of what is a country's acceptable level of addressing the crimes committed versus allowing impunity before the Court intervenes. This is especially important in discussing the role of amnesty in peace negotiations which is the issue at heart of the justice versus peace debate.

There are the concerns surrounding certainty, perceived legitimacy of the law and the Court, as well as individual level barriers that include the context of the violations (i.e., conflict in most cases), plausible deniability, individual perceptions and inner moral decision-making influences that impact the success of the ICC as a deterrent mechanism. Additionally, one cannot ever know who actually is deterred from due to the existence of ICJ or the ICC; we can only know who was not deterred.[76]

Until the gap between an ideal belief in a potential deterrent effect and the reality of empirical research on deterrence and the extant conditions of the Court can come closer together, the achievement of deterrence will remain marginal at best and unlikely in the future. This suggests that, in order for the ICC to remain a legitimate institution, the advocates of the international criminal justice paradigm must come to terms with the limits of international prosecution, in terms of both, general and specific deterrence.

[75] Carla Del Ponte Madame Prosecutor, *Confrontations with Humanity's Worst Criminals and the Culture of Impunity* (Other Press, New York, 2008) p.7.

[76] Rothe and Schoultz, *supra* note 25; William Schabas, in Mark Kersten, *Engaging John Bolton on Libya and the ICC* (Blogpost on justice in conflict blog 201), <www.justiceinconflict.org/2011/03/08/a-response-to-john-bolton-on-libya-america-and-the-icc/>, March 8 2011.

Which Approach to Justice in Colombia under the Era of the ICC

Isabella Bueno and Andrea Diaz Rozas
KU Leuven, Leuven, Belgium

Abstract

How could Colombia deal with the overwhelming cruelty of mass atrocities committed during its ongoing conflict? This article intends to thoroughly explain the strategies implemented in Colombia to deal with the issues of transitional justice in an ongoing conflict and to illustrate the state of the art of the approaches to justice. In order to do so, we will show the limits of the retributive justice approach at both the national and the international level and propose the applicability of the restorative justice approach in dealing with mass victimisation. This debate becomes even more complex due to the shadow of the International Criminal Court (ICC), which has exerted great influence in implementing a dominant retributive oriented approach to the expenses of other ways of doing justice.

Keywords

retributive justice; restorative justice; Colombia; transitional justice; International Criminal Court (ICC)

1. Introduction

For more than five decades Colombian society has experienced a devastating conflict that has implied millions of victims of serious violations of human rights such as torture, massacres, kidnapping, forced displacement, child recruitment, among others. Behind these atrocities are thousands of offenders, many of whom have already demobilized either collectively or individually.[1] Despite the ongoing conflict, and for the first time in its history,[2] Colombia implemented State organized

[1] Agencia Colombiana para la Reintegración, *Desmovilización*, <www.reintegracion.gov.co>, 10 January 2012.

[2] In the words of Gómez, "in previous peace processes in Colombia, crimes against humanity have never been prosecuted, the victimizers have never been required to confess, even negligibly, to the truth of their crimes, nor have the victims and their right to reparations been taken into consideration". Felipe Gómez, 'Challenges for Transitional Justice in Contexts of Non-transition: The Colombian Case', in Michael Reed and Amanda Lyons, (eds.), *Contested Transitions: Dilemmas of Transitional Justice in Colombia and Comparative Experience* (International Center for Transitional Justice, Bogota, 2010).

transitional justice mechanisms to deal with the consequences of mass atrocities; Law 975, better known as the Justice and Peace Law (JPL), was enacted into law by the president on 25 July 2005 to "ease the peace negotiations with the armed groups and the individual and collective reincorporation of the members into civil life, guaranteeing that the victims will have the right to truth, justice and reparation".[3]

This law, which did not go without thorny controversy,[4] established the legal framework for members of paramilitary and guerrilla groups responsible for the violations of human rights, who were not granted amnesties and pardons through Law 1106 of 2006.[5] Unlike the ordinary Colombian penal code, which prescribes prison sentences that could go up to 60 years, the JPL offers a reduced alternative prison sentence. In sum, as Lyon notes, the JPL establishes "a confessional criminal justice model that offers willing candidates significant reduced sentences (five to eight years in prison) in exchange for satisfaction of several conditions, including cessation of criminal activity, full confession to past crimes, and submission of all personal assets for victim reparation".[6]

Besides these criminal proceedings, the JPL created a particular commission, the National Reparation and Reconciliation Commission (CNRR), whose main guiding principle "is to take care of yesterday's victims so as to prevent tomorrow's victims".[7] Furthermore, reparative procedures such as the administrative reparation and the historical Victims' Law, as well as a consolidated disarmament, demobilization and reintegration (DDR) process have also been implemented in Colombia.

Certainly, the overwhelming cruelty and massive scale of the crimes committed in the conflict has posed various obstacles to the effective administration of these mechanisms, which raises the question of the adequate approach to deal with past crimes. In its effort to find a balance between justice and peace, Colombia has implemented various transitional justice mechanisms that have been influenced by the retributive approach, following the current paradigms of justice at the international level. In fact, these paradigms have laid so much emphasis on retributive justice that they prevented other ways of dealing with mass atrocities, like the one offered by the restorative justice approach.

---

3) Article 1 of the Justice and Peace Law, Law 975 of 25 July 2005.

4) Eduardo Pizarro and León Valencia, *Ley de Justicia y Paz* (Cara & Sello, Grupo Editorial Norma, Bogota, 2009).

5) Law 1106 of 2006, which extended the effects of Law 782 of 2002, granted amnesty to the demobilized members of illegal armed groups who did not have criminal charges.

6) Amanda Lyons, 'For a Just Transition in Colombia', in Michael Reed and Amanda Lyons, (eds.), *Contested Transitions: Dilemmas of Transitional Justice in Colombia and Comparative Experience* (International Center for Transitional Justice, Bogota, 2010).

7) Eduardo Pizarro 'Justice, truth and reparation law and its impact on the peace processes in Colombia', in *Colombia: Peace Processes and their Legal Framework* (EPP-ED Group in the European Parliament, Brussels, 2005), p. 18.

As a matter of fact, the role of the International Criminal Court (ICC or the Court) in Colombia has made this debate even more complex due to the delicate correlation between national mechanisms of justice and the jurisdictional role of the ICC. In fact, since the court is one of the main representatives of the retributive justice approach when dealing with past crimes, it has established limitations regarding other approaches to justice like the restorative one.

This article intends to illustrate the state of the art of the retributive and the restorative approach to justice in Colombia. In order to do so, we will first of all give a brief overlook of the Colombian conflict and its legal tradition. Secondly, we will explain the strategies that have been used to deal with the crimes of the ongoing conflict, showing the limits of the retributive justice approach at both the national and international level, and finally, we will explore the applicability of the restorative justice approach in dealing with mass victimisation under an era governed by the shadow of the ICC.

2. The Colombian Conflict

Colombia is currently on the process of establishing the grounds of its transition after more than 50 years of violence. In fact, it is one of the three more extended ongoing conflicts in the world, in which "violence has become the reference point for Colombian politics, society, and economy".[8]

One of the first landmarks of this long lasting conflict is the period known as *"La Violencia"* (1946-1953): an episode of Colombian history marked by regional clashes between two political parties, the Liberals and the Conservatives, and symbolized by the murder of the liberal leader Jorge Eliécer Gaitán which took place on the unforgettable 9 April 1948. It is estimated that between 1946 and 1953, 200,000 persons were killed in the confrontations between liberal self-defense groups and counter-insurgent Conservatives militias.[9] The inability of the civilian leaders to deal with rural violence and their own political disputes allowed General Rojas Pinilla to lead a *coup d'état* in 1953. Four years later, a pact was signed between these two traditional parties, removing Rojas Pinilla and giving rise to the National Front (1958-1974): an alliance that lasted 16 years during which Liberals and Conservatives intercalated the presidency and other governmental positions.

---

[8] Gonzalo Sánchez, 'Problems of Violence, Prospects for Peace', in Charles Bergquist et al. (eds.), *Violence in Colombia, 1990-2000: Waging War and Negotiating Peace* (Scholarly Resources Inc., Wilmington, 2001) pp. 1-38.

[9] Fernán González, *Conflicto Violento en Colombia: Una perspectiva de largo plazo*, <www.google.com/url?sa=t&rct=j&q=la%20violencia%201946%201953%2C%20200%2C000%20muertos%20colombia&source=web&cd=4&ved=0CD8QFjAD&url=http%3A%2F%2Fcmap.upb.edu.co%2Frid%3D1144355653250_1241055914_694%2FConflictoViolentoColombiaFernanGonzalez.doc&ei=ydtDT8H6LozvggeEy92nCA&usg=AFQjCNGLUV8mog9SHD4GAE-NUFUQYg9CKw&sig2=BfMvkz4PiRegyJdkta-OUw>, 15 December 2011.

However, in spite of the general stability triggered by the National Front, various parties felt excluded from the political scenario. In addition to such exclusion, the emergence in the 60s of Cuban-style communism and social revolutionary ideologies contributed to the consolidation of left-wing revolutionary guerrillas groups such as the National Liberation Army (ELN-1964), the Revolutionary Armed Forces of Colombia (FARC-1966), the Popular Liberation Army (EPL-1967) and the 19th of April Movement (M19 – 1970), among others.

During the 1970s, Colombian society went through diverse processes of transformations that made evident the obsolescence of official institutions. The weak Colombian State was ineffective to deal with these social changes and the emergent popular claims for land distribution and social justice continued being ignored by the government.

The fight of guerrilla groups against the government and civilians triggered the emergence of the paramilitaries in the 80s. These groups emerged initially in Antioquia, the Caribbean Coast and the Valle and particularly expanded after the year 1984. Lately, in 1997, under the leadership of Carlos Castaño, they became a structured and extensive organization known as the *Autodefensas Unidas de Colombia* (United Self-Defense Forces of Colombia, AUC).[10]

The decades of the 1980s and the 1990s were marked by relevant processes of negotiations and peace accords with guerrilla groups. As a result, various demobilized *guerrilleros* were offered the opportunity of participating into society in a democratic way, particularly in the National Constituent Assembly, which resulted in a new Colombian Constitution promulgated on 4 July 1991. But still, in spite of this fruitful sequence of peace events, Colombia missed a historical opportunity to achieve peace through the assassinations and disappearances of the members of the Patriotic Union, a coalition of communist-socialist tendency product of previous guerrilla's demobilizations. Undoubtedly, this tragic event compromised further negotiations with the guerrillas,[11] notably with the FARC and the ELN, that are still operating today.

The attempt of achieving peace was also intended by President Pastrana (1998-2002) when offering an area of 42.000 km2 to the guerrilla of the FARC: a demilitarized Colombian territory, known as "El Caguán", totally submitted to the rules of the illegal organization. Despite this generous presidential effort, the FARC continued committing mass atrocities on a daily basis. As a result, in February 2002, Pastrana announced the definitive breaking off of the peace process with the FARC and put an end to the demilitarized region.

It was in this context marked by profound disillusionment and even rage that Colombians elected President Álvaro Uribe Vélez (2002-2012) on a military

10) Fernán González, 'The Colombian Conflict in Historical Perspective', 14 *Accord, An International Review of Peace Initiatives* (2004) 10-17.

11) Sánchez, *supra* note 8.

platform. Uribe changed the dynamic of the negotiations combining it with a hard-line militaristic approach,[12] characterized by the implementation of the "democratic security" policy, which involved an intensification of the military response against the guerrilla groups.[13] In fact, unlike the FARC and the ELN, the AUC did not take long to initiate a peace agreement with the Uribe administration that led to the signing of the San José de Ralito agreement in 2003, and according to which the members of the AUC accepted to demobilize in exchange of appropriate mechanisms designed to deal with their legal status and processes of reintegration. This peace agreement, whose exact terms and conditions remain unknown, led to the demobilization of more than 30,000 paramilitaries. However, the number of demobilized ex-combatants increments on a daily basis due to the individual demobilizations of ex paramilitary and guerrilla members.

In addition to the complexity triggered by the illegal armed groups, the Colombian conflict has been terribly affected by the traffic of drugs; the economy produced by this profitable business has transformed the conflict, consolidating different forms of power that involves both paramilitary and guerrilla members, but also regional and national political and military authorities.[14]

It is in this complex context of ongoing conflict that Colombia implemented State organized transitional justice mechanisms.

3. Transitional Justice

Transitional justice implies rethinking the way to end conflicts and the type of strategies for post-conflict or post-authoritarian reconstruction. It refers, in fact to "the full range of processes and mechanisms associated with a society's attempts to come to terms with a legacy of large-scale past abuses, in order to ensure, accountability, serve justice and achieve reconciliation".[15] This definition involves a number of elements, such as, truth seeking, accountability, reparation and reconciliation, which scholars have considered relevant when analysing transitions.[16]

---

12) Cynthia Arnson et al., *Los procesos de paz en Colombia: Múltiples negociaciones, múltiples actores* (Woodrow Wilson International Center for Scholars, Washington, D.C, 2007).

13) Marc Chernick, *Acuerdo Posible. Solución negociada al conflicto armado colombiano* (Ediciones Aurora, Bogota, 2008).

14) This phenomenon known as "Parapolítica" (Parapolitics) showed its real dimension when in 2005 the existence of these connections was disclosure and investigations against 102 members of the Congress began. Claudia López, "'La Refundación de la Patria", De la Teoría a la Evidencia', in Claudia López, (ed.), *Y refundaron la patria... De cómo mafiosos y políticos reconfiguraron el Estado colombiano* (Debate, Bogota, 2010).

15) Report of the Secretary-General to the Security Council of the United Nations, *The rule of law and transitional justice in conflict and post-conflict societies* (S/2004/616).

16) Ruti Teitel, *Transitional Justice* (Oxford University Press, New York, 2000). Also see: Stephan Parmentier, 'Global Justice in the Aftermath of Mass Violence. The Role of the International

From the Nuremberg trials to the creation of the ICC, the question of "transitional justice" has been shaped by various approaches and mechanisms. In fact, the complexities and unique characteristics of each war-torn society encourage a rich variety of mechanisms to the expenses of a unique globalized mechanism of transitional justice.

By dealing with such wide-ranging human issues, transitional justice is by nature a multidisciplinary field of study. In the words of Kritz,

> projects on justice and reconciliation in the aftermath of mass abuses have proliferated at universities and think tanks. It has become a topic of inquiry in a variety of disciplines, including law, philosophy, sociology, political science, theology, anthropology and the arts.[17]

Interestingly though, despite the important role played by TRC and local-level mechanisms, amongst others, the field of transitional justice has been mainly tainted by a legalistic vision of justice, particularly at the international sphere. In fact, as Liwerant rightly notes, "with the exception of juridical and historical works, social sciences barely considered collective murders until the turn of the 21st century".[18] This pre-eminence of the legal dimension is also evident in the configuration and development of the field,[19] especially if we take into account that it is based on the idea of introducing legal constraints to transitions.

The dominant role of international law in the literature and practice of transitional justice has not gone without controversy and disputes with other disciplines that share different interests than those promoted by law. For example, Lambourne explains how "the efforts of international lawyers and human rights advocates to fairly and justly prosecute those responsible for perpetrating crimes against humanity, and to ensure a future respect for the rule of law and human rights principles, are juxtaposed against the efforts of international peace negotiators and conflict resolution practitioners who prioritize the establishment of peace and security and a climate of reconciliation between former enemies".[20] The duel between international lawyers and conflict resolution practitioners deeply touches the very particular transitional process of Colombia. As we will

---

Criminal Court in Dealing with Political Crimes', 41 1-2 *International Annals of Criminology* (2003) pp. 203-224.

17) Neil Kritz, 'The Legacy of Abuse: Confronting the Past, Facing the Future' in Alice H. Henkin (eds.), *Where We Are and How We Got Here: An Overview of Developments in the Search for Justice and Reconciliation* (New York University School of Law, New York, 2002).

18) Sara Liwerant, 'Mass Murder: Discussing Criminological Perspectives', 5 *Journal of International Criminal Justice* (2007), pp. 917-939.

19) Ruti Teitel, 'Transitional Justice Genealogy', 16 *Harvard Human Rights Journal* (2003), pp. 69-94.

20) Wendy Lambourne, 'Transitional Justice and Peacebuilding after Mass Violence', Seminar Presentation, Centre for Peace Research and Strategic Studies (K.U. Leuven, Leuven, 2006).

see, retributive approaches, particularly the threat of being prosecuted by the ICC, may pose serious obstacles to the peace and reconciliation process in Colombia.

In addition, this legal dimension of transitional justice is not yet fully consolidated; there is in fact an ongoing tension between legal standards coming from international law and the practices of States during transitions.[21] On the one hand, international legal standards came from the development of different branches of international law, in what Bell calls a "regime merge" of international human rights law, international humanitarian law and international criminal law.[22] On the other hand, the national practice is characterized by practical considerations when governments have to deal with dilemmas in these periods.

The product of this tension is a range of possibilities between two extremes, where it is possible to find a discourse of "human rights respect as a synonym of retribution" and more "alternative measures related to the seeking of truth". These two "models" are often presented as the unique alternatives for transitional measures.[23]

The "human rights respect as retribution" discourse places significant emphasis on accountability as a synonym of criminal procedures.[24] The relevance it has acquired can be seen by the large institutionalisation and widespread legal and economic support for retributive mechanisms worldwide. This trend is influenced by the experience of the Nuremberg and Tokyo trials, the Ad-Hoc International Criminal Tribunals for Rwanda and the Former Yugoslavia, the International Criminal Court, the internationalised courts of Sierra Leone, Kosovo, Timor-Leste and Cambodia and the domestic trials that have taken place in different parts of the world.[25]

On the other side we find "other alternative measures" to respond to past abuses which involve a broader understanding of justice and the possibility of using diverse mechanisms to deal with the past. Consequently, it is possible to introduce a certain degree of flexibility to the common belief that criminal prosecutions are the only way to obtain accountability.

Thus, as we have previously explained, there is not only a preeminent legalistic understanding of transitional justice but also a retributive view of it. The criminal and prosecutorial character that transitional justice has adopted can be observed

---

21) Christine Bell, *On the Law of Peace. Peace Agreements and Lex Pacificatoria* (Oxford University Press, Oxford, 2008).
22) *Ibid.*
23) Kieran McEvoy, 'Letting go of legalism: Developing a "Thicker" version of Transitional Justice', in Kieran McEvoy and Lorna McGregor (eds.), *Transitional Justice from Below: Grassroots Activism and the Struggle for Change* (Hart Publishing, Oxford, 2008).
24) Luc Huyse, 'The Process of Reconciliation', in David Bloomfield et al. (eds.), *Reconciliation after Violent Conflict. A Handbook.* (IDEA, Stockholm, 2003).
25) Rachel Kerr and Eirin Mobekk, *Peace and Justice. Seeking Accountability after War,* (Polity Press, Cambridge, 2007).

in the multiplication of international bodies in charge of prosecuting grave human rights violations, the international community's pressure for the application of international human rights standards and the consolidation of international crimes as a consequence of the ICC's creation.[26] At the national level, there have been cornerstone cases like the judgment of the former Peruvian president Alberto Fujimori and the numerous national prosecutions in Colombia.

Since the retributive approach has dominated the transitional justice field, Colombia has considered mandatory to comply with its legal international obligations. However, as previously noted, there are other visions of justice, such as the restorative one, that really questions the assimilation of justice to the retributive approach.

4. The Legal Framework for Dealing with Massive Crimes in Colombia

The Rome Statute that created the International Criminal Court entered into force in 2002. In fact, such creation was the more visible effort of the international community towards prosecuting international crimes. The beginning of its operations showed that the Court was a reality and it made imminent for many States the necessity of adapting their criminal policies to comply with the Court's standards.

Also in 2002 the Colombian government started to implement transitional justice mechanisms as an effort to bring to an end a conflict that has lasted for more than 50 years and that has caused thousands of victims of the most atrocious crimes. The Colombian government began peace negotiations with the AUC and started to design the legal framework for their demobilization.

These two events intersected each other generating multiple relations and effects between them. On the one hand, since 2005 the ICC has maintained a permanent evaluation of the Colombian situation, which became even stronger with the opening of the preliminary examination in 2006. On the other hand, the Colombian government has actively reacted to the Court's claims, implementing a national policy to respond to these demands.

These two interrelated normative levels constitute the framework of retributive justice in Colombia that we will analyze, making a critical assessment of its achievements and deficiencies.

4.1. *The National Level: Pardons and Trials*

Colombia has an old legacy of solving conflicts through negotiations and amnesties. It has involved solutions based only on political considerations, generally

---

26) Naomi Roht-Arriaza, 'Mass Murder: Discussing Criminological Perspectives State Responsibility to Investigate and Prosecute Grave Human Rights Violations in International Law'. 78 *California Law Review* (1990).

conferring pardon to the conflictive parts.[27] However, the influence of criminal justice on the international scene has changed this tendency. There are in fact, other considerations that prevent general and unconditional pardons to achieve peace and a requirement to prosecute the gravest crimes.

In the next part we will analyze the Colombian legal tradition, how it has changed in the last decade and the current situation of the implementation of retributive–criminal justice mechanisms.

4.1.1. *The Colombian Legal Tradition*

By the end of the 1980s and during the 1990s, the government engaged in many negotiations with the illegal armed groups. The majority of these agreements did not include any obligation regarding reparations to victims, the search of truth and the administration of justice. In fact, they only considered judicial benefits for those who decided to demobilize.[28]

Thus, in 1989, the government reached an agreement with the M-19, offering them an amnesty through Law 77 of 1989. In the same line, during the first years of the 1990s, the Colombian government established a set of norms to cover the demobilization of different armed groups. Based on that framework, in 1991 the *Ejército Popular de Liberación* (EPL), the *Partido Revolucionario de los Trabajadores* (PRT) and the *Movimiento Armado Quintín Lame* (MAQL) decided to demobilize after a peace accord with the government.[29]

After this process the new Constitution of 1991 was enacted, including important social reforms brought forward by ex members of these groups. The Constitution also included the power of the Executive and the Legislative branches to grant pardons and amnesties. In 1992 the *Comandos "Ernesto Rojas"* signed a peace accord under Decree 1943 of 1991. In 1993, the government enacted Law 104 that established the extinction of the action and the criminal penalty, as a background for the demobilization in 1994 of the *Corriente de Renovación Socialista* (CRS), the *Milicias Urbanas de Medellín* and the *Frente Francisco Garnica de la Coordinadora Guerrillera* (FFG). Finally, in 1998 the government reached an agreement with the MIR-COAR armed group under Law 418 of 1997 that established grounds for the extinction of the criminal action and penalty in political and related crimes.[30]

As it is possible to observe, the general pattern of these agreements was not the prosecution of perpetrators. These norms usually ended or prevented any type of prosecution against the demobilized and excluded some crimes, known in Colombia as acts of "ferocity and barbarity", which involved crimes such as

---

27) Carlos Alberto Mejía, 'Aproximación a los instrumentos jurídicos aplicados a los procesos de "negociación de la paz" en Colombia', 2 *CES Derecho* (2011) pp. 58-71.

28) *Ibid.*

29) Decree 213 of 1991 also covered their disarmament.

30) Report on the demobilization process in Colombia. OEA/Ser.L/V/II.120, Doc. 60, 13 December 2004.

kidnapping, murder committed outside combat or crimes committed putting the victim in a defenceless situation.[31] However, it is not clear until which point investigations were conducted to establish whether or not the beneficiaries of pardons committed those crimes.

In the last years the possibility of granting pardons have suffered limitations with the arising of transitional justice and what some have called the "new humanitarian conscience", which makes a pure negotiated solution impossible.[32] According to this new scenario, it is not possible to confer pardon to perpetrators of grave crimes (mainly international crimes).

Colombia has accommodated to this scenario by gradually introducing international law into its national legal culture. In the last years, and probably as a consequence of the expansion of the "global transitional justice" discourse,[33] governmental and non-governmental actors in Colombia have learnt the transitional justice and International Law paradigms and have started to apply them in their institutions and mechanisms. The interviews conducted in Colombia with representatives of the executive and the judiciary brands showed their high level of knowledge of transitional justice theory and terminology.[34] Such knowledge was also manifested on the way in which the government introduced transitional justice as an instrument to deal with mass victimization committed in the country. Furthermore, the transitional justice language was also used by opposing groups to challenge the government's discourse.

In this particular context, which was the product of diverse legal transformations, began the negotiations between the Colombian government and the AUC, leading to the necessity of creating a new legal framework.

4.1.2. *The Current Legal Framework for the Demobilization*

The legal framework of the demobilization has its origins in the processes of negotiation, demobilisation and reinsertion of the armed actors of the conflict. It is based on two legal regimes that clearly reflect the mixture of the pardon and retributive-criminal approaches, as a result of the influence of the transitional justice discourse.

The first legal framework is the one of Law 1106 of 2006 and its decrees. This legal regime is applicable to members of the illegal groups who have declared not

---

31) These crimes are included in the text of article 127 of the Colombian Criminal Code that has ruled the exclusion of atrocious crimes from political crimes.

32) Ivan Orozco, *Sobre los Límites de la Conciencia Humanitaria. Dilemas de la Paz y la Justicia en América Latina* (Editorial Temis - Universidad de los Andes, Bogota, 2005).

33) Ruti Teitel, 'Global Transitional Justice', *Working Paper Nº 8* (Center for Global Studies, George Mason University, Fairfax, 2010).

34) These interviews were conducted with representatives of the government during the fieldwork developed in Colombia between October 2010 and March 2011. Andrea Diaz's doctoral thesis (unpublished work).

to have committed grave crimes. Given the absence of prosecutions, we could assimilate this legal framework to the Colombian pardon tradition previously exposed.

The second legal regime is the one of the Justice and Peace Law of 2005, read in conjunction with the Constitutional Court rulings C-370 and C-570 from 2006 and the decrees created for its application. According to this law, those ex combatants who committed grave crimes and accord to demobilize must be prosecuted in exchange of reduced sanctions. This legal framework is influenced by the new trend of transitional justice and international criminal law that require prosecution for international crimes.

Both regimes have been applied in the current process of demobilization in Colombia, offering a complex legal framework that shows the interrelation of different visions of justice.

4.1.2.1. The Legal Regime of Law 1106

This first legal framework is composed by a set of norms created on the basis of Law 418 of 1997, and whose effects have been extended through Law 548 of 1999, Law 782 of 2002 and Law 1106 of 2006 (with effects until December 2010).[35] These norms establish administrative measures that should be taken under the supervision of the Executive power and applied to the demobilization process of ex combatants who are not under prosecution and have not been convicted, or declared not to have committed crimes that "according to the Constitution, the law, or international treaties signed and ratified by Colombia are ineligible for this class of benefits".[36]

Law 418 of 1997, whose effects were extended by Law 548 of 1999, opened the possibility for a dialogue between the State and members of illegal groups having a political status. In fact, this legal framework was applied to the peace negotiations that took place in the 90s between the government and the FARC, but which unfortunately failed.

Furthermore, the Uribe administration extended the effects of this legal framework through Law 782, promulgated on 23 December 2002, only two days after the paramilitary groups decided the unilateral cessation of hostilities. However, this new regulation did not require the recognition of a political status of the illegal groups to begin a negotiation.

Law 782 prescribed an official pardon for those who had been part of an illegal group but who were not involved in the commission of grave crimes.[37] In fact, the

35) These laws have been implemented through the following decrees: 128 of 2003, 3360 of 2003 and 2767 of 2004.
36) Article 21 of Decree 128.
37) This norm was regulated by Decree 128 of 2003. It offers detailed information regarding the proceedings and organisms to carry on the demobilization and reintegration of those individuals who agree to demobilize.

crimes covered by this legal framework were rebellion, treason and riot and the benefits included freedom of prosecution (amnesty or pardon) and access to the social and reintegration programs of the government.[38]

However, the absence of meaningful testimonies and deep investigations allowed an important percentage of the demobilizations to take place without establishing whether those persons had committed or not grave crimes[39] Since the verification was done only considering the absence of criminal imputations on the official records and a personal statement declaring so, there is no certainty if the demobilized were involved or not in the commission of grave crimes.[40] Some critics consider that this process produced de facto and general amnesties. In addition, the lack of real control has also allowed many persons, who didn't belong to the demobilized groups, to participate in the process and many real combatants of these groups to be excluded.[41]

In that regard, the Inter-American Commission on Human Rights (IACHR) has affirmed that these norms,

> should not by themselves pose a legal obstacle to investigating crimes against humanity or grave violations of human rights, and the waiver of prosecution contained in that legislation does not have the effect of *res judicata* with respect to criminal investigations that may be opened in the future.[42]

4.1.2.2. The Justice and Peace Law Regime

The second element of the Colombian demobilization legal framework is based on the Justice and Peace Law – Law N° 975 of 25 July 2005. In contrast to Law 1106's

---

38) The effects of this law were later extended through Law 1106 of December 2006 until 21 December 2010. To cover the extent number of demobilizations that took place out of this period, the Colombian government enacted Law 1424 of 2010, which gives legal benefits to people who were demobilized from illegal armed groups, so they can preserve their freedom, if they comply with the commitments of their reintegration process (stop committing crimes, tell the truth to contribute to the historical clarification and to specific facts and participate of the reintegration activities). According to the director of the Colombian Agency for Reintegration, almost 21500 ex-paramilitary members had applied for benefits under this law. This law was in force until 28 December 2011.

39) Some data mentioned that 87% of the 35000 demobilizations took place under this regime. Other sources consider that it has covered almost the 92% of the total number of demobilizations. FIDH, *Colombia, la desmovilización paramilitar, en los caminos de la Corte Penal Internacional* (FIDH, Paris, 2007) pp. 17-18.

40) According to Decree 128, the criteria required to be included under this legal framework were the absence of criminal records and a certificate issued by the Weapons Surrender Committee (CODA), Article 13 of Decree 128.

41) Report on the implementation of the Justice and Peace Law: Initial stages in the demobilization of the AUC and first judicial proceedings. OEA/Ser.L/V/II.129, Doc 6, 2 October 2007, para. 39.

42) *Ibid.*, para. 42.

regime, this norm called for criminal prosecutions, clearly showing the influence of retributive justice in the implementation of transitional justice in Colombia.[43]

Basically, the Justice and Peace Law granted significantly reduced prison sentences to members of illegal armed groups who have agreed to demobilise and who were involved in grave human rights violations. The law conditions the grant of these benefits to the disclosure of the full truth about past crimes, the devolution of illegally obtained goods to compensate the victims and the compromise to not commit new crimes.[44]

As we mentioned before, this norm was designed in the context of a society trying to pass from conflict to peace; consequently, the process was carried out without a clear legal framework. In fact, Law 975 was drafted and discussed while the government was negotiating the ceasefire and demobilization process of the AUC. At the same time, the ICC was starting its operations, a situation that imposed serious considerations and limits to the content of the future norm.

The first draft of the law presented by the government in August 2003 was the *Ley de Alternatividad Penal* (The Alternative Sanction Law). This draft did not guarantee the rights to reparation, truth and justice of the victims and contained an evident unbalance between the lenient punitive benefits for the perpetrators and the lack of protection and effective mechanisms to protect the victims' rights. As a result, the proposal was hardly criticized by the Congress and the civil society, and finally, withdrawn by the government.

Nevertheless, the core of this first draft was maintained in the future debates on the law: the possibility of giving disproportionately reduced sanctions to perpetrators of grave crimes, an idea that combined plea bargain/pardon and retributive models of justice. In fact, whereas the bargain/pardon model was already part of the Colombian legal culture to end conflicts and negotiate peace, the retributive one was reinforced by the international trend that supports the use of retributive criminal justice for mass victimization.[45]

---

43) Felipe Gómez, 'Global Transitional Justice Justicia, Verdad y Reparación en el Proceso de Desmobilización Paramilitar en *Colombia*', in Felipe Gómez (eds.), *Colombia en su laberinto. Una mirada al conflicto* (Catarata, Madrid, 2008).

44) Comisión Colombiana de Juristas, Anotaciones sobre la ley de justicia y paz. Una mirada desde los derechos de las víctimas (Comisión Colombiana de Juristas, Bogotá, 2007).

45) This approach is supported by the Inter-American system of human rights, of which Colombia is part, since it deems criminal prosecution as the way to comply with State obligations under the American Convention on Human Rights. See: Inter-American Court of Human Rights: *The Case of Velasquez-Rodriguez v. Honduras*, 29 July 1988, Inter-Am. Ct. H.R., Series C, No. 4, para. 134; Inter-American Court of Human Rights: *The Case of Godinez-Cruz v. Honduras*, 20 January 1989, Inter-Am. Ct. H.R., Ser. C, No. 5, para. 175; Inter-American Court of Human Rights: *The Case of Paniagua-Morales v. Guatemala*, 8 March 1998, Inter-Am. Ct. H.R., Ser. C, No. 37, T I; Inter-American Court of Human Rights: *The Case of Barrios Altos v. Peru*, 14 March 2001, Inter-Am. Ct. H.R., Ser. C, No. 75.

Law 975 needs to be read in association to the Constitutional Court's decision of 18 May 2006 (C-370/06) that changed the interpretation of many of its articles, the jurisprudence of the Supreme Court and the Decrees[46] that implement the law. However, the application of the law to nearly 4 346 ex members of illegal groups who had applied to the process should also be taken into account in order to fully understand it.[47]

On the one hand, The Constitutional Court's jurisprudence included parameters of interpretation to protect victims' participation in the process and their access to full reparations. Furthermore, Decision C-370/06 also clarified the obligation to enforce the sanction, established the consequences inflicted if the applicants kept information from the authorities and better regulated the deadlines to complete judicial proceedings.[48] On the other hand, the Supreme Court ruled about the lack of political status of paramilitary groups,[49] it also established the procedural requirements for the incidental issue of reparation,[50] it banned from handing out partial charges derived from incomplete confessions[51] and it established victims' rights as the core of the whole process.[52]

These modifications transformed the Justice and Peace Law, showing how check and balances work in the Colombian society. Even though this is a positive feature that reflects a dynamic democracy, it also shows the lack of a clear strategy and single objective on the law's application. In fact, on the one hand, during the process of creation of the norm, different actors added diverse, and sometimes contradictory elements to the law and, on the other hand, during its application each institution understood and implemented different modus operandi, according to their particular understanding of the law and their own goals and interests.

The lack of consensual strategy has posed a lot of problems on the application of the law and has caused the delay on the achievement of results. Furthermore, it has taken a long time to establish a coordinated and linked response on the way the law had to be applied.

The overturning of Wilson Salazar's (aka "*el Loro*") sentence, showed how different the National Prosecutor's Office, the Justice and Peace Tribunals and the Supreme Court understood the objectives and procedural considerations of

---

46) These are Decree 4760 of 2005, Decree 2898 of 2006, Decree 3391 of 2006, Decree 4417 of 2007, Decree 315 of 2007 and Decree 23 of 2007.

47) Presidencia de la República, *La desmovilización y la Ley de Justicia y Paz en cifras*, <www.web.presidencia.gov.co/sp/2010/julio/24/16242010.html>, 12 February 2012.

48) Case D-6032, Judgment C-370/06, July 13 2006, Constitutional Court of Colombia.

49) Case Orlando César Caballero Montalvo, desmobvilizado del Bloque Élmer Cárdenas de las AUC, Case No. 26.945, Decision N° 26.94511, July 2007, Supreme Court.

50) One of the cases that established the regime of reparations of the JPL was Case 28.769, 11 de diciembre de 2007, modified by on 23 May 2008, Supreme Court.

51) Case 29.560, 28 May 2008, Supreme Court.

52) Case 31.539, 31 July 2009, Supreme Court and Case 28.040, 23 August 2007, Supreme Court.

the law.[53] This problem was solved only after the Justice and Peace Tribunals, following the Supreme Court's considerations on the overturning decision, created a protocol to be used by all these organisms involved in the judicial process. The protocol changed the strategy, and required to obtain and analyze both the background and the specific information of each case to establish a macro and a micro understanding of them. This new strategy and the burden of handling a significant number of cases with insufficient institutional resources, have caused serious delays on the proceedings.[54] According to official data, in 31 December 2011 there were only 9 cases already adjudicated.[55]

Additionally, there are doubts about the efficacy on the application of the law when analyzing the level of achievement of two of its main objectives: peace and reparation. At the theoretical level, peace was the main justification for the detriment of justice when justifying the law. However, after six years of the law's operation the achievement of this objective is less than clear. The rearmament of previously demobilized groups and the emergency of new criminal organizations in the regions and spaces left by the paramilitaries, show the insufficient accomplishment of this goal.[56]

Regarding reparations, the recent promulgation of the Victims' Law, a broad framework of administrative reparations, can also be seen as the failure of the reparations' scheme of the Justice and Peace Law. The slowness of the judiciary process has delayed reparations and the scarcity of resources to cover the demand allow to affirm that the rights of the victims to reparation have not been effectively guaranteed under the Justice and Peace Law scheme.[57]

In addition to reparations, victims have also been integrated and acknowledged through their participation in the proceedings. According to official data, there are

---

53) Case Wilson Salazar (*aka* El Loro), 18 August 2009, Criminal Chamber of the Supreme Court of Colombia. In this sentence the Supreme Court annulled the first JPL conviction, of Wilson Salazar, considering that conspiracy to commit a crime was a "vital and essential" part of belonging to the AUC and must be part of a conviction.

54) Interviews conducted during the fieldwork developed in Colombia between October 2010 and March 2011. Diaz, *supra* note 34.

55) Unidad Nacional de Fiscalías para la Justicia y la Paz, Gestión Unidad Nacional de Fiscalías para la Justicia y la Paz, <http://www.fiscalia.gov.co/justiciapaz/index.htm>, 18 January 2012.

56) These 'emerging' groups are known as BACRIM. The CNRR has researched this issue and documented a large amount of information on these groups. Comisión Nacional de Reparación y Reconciliación, *Disidentes, Rearmados y Emergentes: ¿Bandas Criminales o Tercera Generación Paramilitar?* (CNRR, Bogotá, 2007).

57) Catalina Díaz y Camilo Bernal, 'El diseño institucional de reparaciones en la Ley de Justicia y Paz: una evaluación preliminar', in Catalina Díaz et al. (eds.) *Reparar en Colombia: los dilemas en contextos de conflicto, pobreza y exclusión* (Centro Internacional para la Justicia Transicional y Centro de Estudios de Derecho, Justicia y Sociedad, Bogota, 2009). Also see: International Crisis Group, *Corregir el Curso: Las Victimas de la Ley de Justicia y Paz en Colombia. Informe sobre América Latina N°29–30* (International Crisis Group, Bogotá, 2008).

more than 54 000 victims who have participated in the process.[58] However, some NGOs have said that although the official data show great figures, it is minimal in relation to the real number of victims that should have been involved in the process.[59] They also mentioned the lack of coordination among official institutions and the limited access to information for their effective participation.[60]

With regards to the main achievements of the JPL law, defenders argue that without the implementation of the law and the revelations given by the applicants in the free depositions, it would have been impossible to obtain all the information provided to the victims. In fact, there are nearly 33 499 facts confessed by ex members of paramilitary groups that have allowed to find the location of mass graves and the fate or whereabouts of thousands of disappeared persons.[61]

It has also facilitated the "visibilization" of victims (Pizarro, 2009), since the environment created by the law has generated the emergence of many victims' organizations and the consolidation of the existing ones. However, some sectors have pointed out that this is not a consequence of the law, but an international trend consolidated by the work of NGOs and national victims' organizations.[62]

The analysis of the national legal framework shows that Colombia has combined pardon (Law 1106) and criminal-retributive approaches (Justice and Peace Law) to deal with past crimes. In both cases, we have seen the limitations of an excessive focus on one paradigm to the expenses of other approaches to justice. This trend is reinforced by institutions with high symbolic value, as the ICC, a role that we will analyze in the next part.

4.2. *The International Level: the International Criminal Court*

The ICC is one of the main representatives at the international level of the retributive justice approach and one of the main influences at the national level on the implementation of transitional justice mechanisms in Colombia. As a matter of fact, the Rome Statute created the ICC in 1998 to prosecute perpetrators of war

---

58) Unidad Nacional de Fiscalías para la Justicia y la Paz, Gestión Unidad Nacional de Fiscalías para la Justicia y la Paz, <http://www.fiscalia.gov.co/justiciapaz/index.htm>, 16 January 2012.

59) International Crisis Group, *supra* note 57.

60) *Ibid.* Also during the direct observation of the process in Colombia, we observed some difficulties on the effective participation of victims, such as the limitations in the way they communicated and made questions during the hearings and also on the access of victims to the place where the proceedings were taking place due to economic, geographical and time constrains.

61) Unidad Nacional de Fiscalías para la Justicia y la Paz, Gestión Unidad Nacional de Fiscalías para la Justicia y la Paz, <http://www.fiscalia.gov.co/justiciapaz/index.htm>, 17 January 2012.

62) Michael Reed, 'Transitional Justice Under Fire: Five Reflections on the Colombian Case', in Michael Reed and Amanda Lyons, (eds.), *Contested Transitions: Dilemmas of Transitional Justice in Colombia and Comparative Experience* (International Center for Transitional Justice, Bogota, 2010) pp. 87-114.

crimes, crimes against humanity and genocide (since the crime of aggression has not been defined yet). In Colombia it has jurisdiction since November 2002[63] for crimes against humanity and genocide and since November 2009 for war crimes, when the deadline of the delay declaration for this crime ended.[64]

The ICC's jurisdiction is regulated by the principle of complementarity, laid down under article 17 of the Rome Statute, and according to which, priority is given to the States to assure accountability for the crimes over which the ICC has jurisdiction. Nonetheless, the latter may turn out operative if the state "is unwilling or unable genuinely to carry out the investigation or prosecution". The Statute has developed in fact specific criteria to determine whether there is unwillingness and inability behind a national prosecution.[65]

The relationship between the ICC and Colombia is meaningful for both parties. On the one hand, Colombia represents a difficult case for the ICC, since this country has implemented a criminal policy to deal with past crimes, in contrast to the other cases under the ICC's evaluation where prosecutions were not even proposed. On the other hand, for Colombia, the ICC represents the most compelling institution to trigger criminal prosecutions. These factors, together with the ongoing conflict, made the relation between Colombia and the ICC even more complex.

As previously noted, in 2002, when the ICC was starting to operate as an international judicial body, Colombia began a peace process with the AUC. After a period of initial contacts the ICC decided to open the Preliminary Examination of

---

63) Law 742 of 5 June 2002 was enacted to introduce the Rome Statute to the national legislation. Also see the Constitutional Court decision on the matter C-578, 2002.

64) Rome Statute of the ICC, Ratification (with Declarations), Colom., para. 5, 5 August 2002, 2194 U.N.T.S. 523, <www.treaties.un.org/pages/ViewDetails.aspx?src=TREATY&mtdsg_no=XVIII-10&chapter=18&lang=en>, 17 December 2011.

65) Such criteria are regulated by Article 17 (2) (3) of the Rome Statute, which states as follows:

2. In order to determine unwillingness in a particular case, the Court shall consider, having regard to the principles of due process recognized by international law, whether one or more of the following exist, as applicable:
   (a) The proceedings were or are being undertaken or the national decision was made for the purpose of shielding the person concerned from criminal responsibility for crimes within the jurisdiction of the Court referred to in article 5;
   (b) There has been an unjustified delay in the proceedings which in the circumstances is inconsistent with an intent to bring the person concerned to justice;
   (c) The proceedings were not or are not being conducted independently or impartially, and they were or are being conducted in a manner which, in the circumstances, is inconsistent with an intent to bring the person concerned to justice.
3. In order to determine inability in a particular case, the Court shall consider whether, due to a total or substantial collapse or unavailability of its national judicial system, the State is unable to obtain the accused or the necessary evidence and testimony or otherwise unable to carry out its proceedings;

the Colombian case in 2006. Currently, the ICC keeps the examination at that stage and maintains a permanent monitoring of the situation.[66]

To understand the influence of the ICC in the Colombian process, and the decisions made by the government to deal with past crimes, it is necessary to analyze the way in which the ICC has related to Colombian actors. In fact, there are historical milestones of this relation that can be classified as direct and indirect contacts between both actors. In the first group we can find all the official and public contacts between the ICC and the Colombian representatives, and in the second group, there are all the non-official and informal contacts. This distinction is meaningful because it reflects the problem of the inconsistency and lack of clarity of the messages of the ICC and its effects at the national level.

On the one hand, it is possible to establish a link between the direct contacts and a prudent but at the same time, ambiguous message. In this first group we can include the Colombian negotiation and posterior ratification of the Rome Statute, the Prosecutor's Office monitoring of the Colombian situation,[67] the decision to open the Preliminary Examination, the official visits and communications of the Prosecutor to Colombia[68] and the Colombian responses to the Prosecutor's demands. All these contacts have been official and generally have been made public.

In contrast to the direct contacts, it is difficult to make a list of indirect contacts because usually they were not public. As examples we can mention, the meetings of the Prosecutor with judges, prosecutors and representatives of the executive branch, as well as non-public speeches of the Prosecutor during his visits. In these

---

66) International Criminal Court, *Communications, Referrals and Preliminary Examinations*, <http://www.icccpi.int/Menus/ICC/Structure+of+the+Court/Office+of+the+Prosecutor/Comm+and+Ref/>, 21 February 2012.

67) The first direct approach was on March 2005 when the Prosecutor sent a letter to the Colombian government requesting information about the draft law that was going to be considered by the Parliament. Letter from Luis Moreno Ocampo to the Colombian Ambassador in The Hague, Francisco Jose Lloreda, transcribed in El Nuevo Siglo of 15 2008, *Corte Penal Internacional Hace Requerimientos a Gobierno Uribe*, <www.elnuevosiglo.com.co/noticia.php>, 12 December 2011.

68) The ICC Prosecutor has visited the country in two opportunities. In the first visit on October 2007, he asked about the steps taken by the authorities to investigate and prosecute those most responsible for crimes against humanity committed in Colombia since 2002. International Criminal Court, *ICC, Prosecutor Visits Colombia, Media Advisory ICC-OTP-20071018-254-En of 18 October 2007*, <http://www.icccpi.int/menus/icc/press%20and%20media/press%20releases/2007/otp%20media%20advisory_%20icc%20prosecutor%20visits%20colombia?lan=en-GB>, 20 December 2011. During this visit the Chief Prosecutor had meetings with government officials, judges and prosecutors. In the second visit in August 2008 the Prosecutor investigated the extraditions of 15 former paramilitaries being tried under the Justice and Peace Law to the United States of America in May 2008 and the parapolitics scandal. The Spanish prosecutor Baltazar Garzón joint him and they participated in an exhumation by the Technical Investigations Corps of the General Prosecutor's Office in Uraba. He also met with senior officials from the Government, the Prosecutor's Office and the Supreme Court of Justice as well as representatives of Colombian civil society. International Criminal Court, *ICC prosecutor visits*

contacts, the Prosecutor has shown a complacent attitude regarding the situation in Colombia.[69] Even though there are no records or documents of some of the informal interchanges that took place during those meetings, we have obtained information from the interviews we conducted in the fieldwork. According to the information gathered, the ICC's Prosecutor has been clear stating that Colombia is making an overwhelming effort, even beyond what the Court would expect. Besides, the ICC's representatives advised national judges to avoid conducting extensive and deep judicial proceedings, and to better focus on specific crimes to issue the maximum number of sentences.[70]

The differentiation between direct and indirect contacts is important to explain why actors in Colombia have constructed completely different interpretations of the ICC's perception of the Colombian situation and consequently, why they have different expectations about the ICC's role. On the one hand, the Colombian government believes that Colombia has made more than what is expected by the ICC and that it even constitutes an example for other countries when implementing a "positive complementarity" approach. According to the government, thus, it would not be possible to consider an intervention of the ICC in Colombia. On the other hand, some human rights activists and victims' organizations believe that the ICC's intervention is possible and even imminent, considering that Colombia has failed to address accountability during the process of demobilization and has perpetuated impunity.

In both cases, we can observe an overemphasis on the ICC's role and the model it represents. Different authors have considered the potential positive effects of the ICC's intervention in Colombia,[71] idealizing the ICC and dismissing

---

Colombia, Press Release of 21 August 2008, <www.icc-cpi.int/press/pressreleases/414.html>, 27 December 2011.

69) In contacts not directly related to Colombia, the Prosecutor has made a comparison to other cases where they have opened an investigation, showing that are not comparable to the Colombian situations where an institutional framework has been created to address violations:

> "When I took office, Colombia and the DRC were the gravest situations under our jurisdiction. The difference between the two was that Colombia was and is conducting national proceedings against guerrilla leaders, paramilitaries and their political supporters, and in some cases against members of the Police, the Army and Congress, which required further analysis by my Office."
>
> "We are regularly visiting Colombia to follow the progress of proceedings. The Colombian authorities have committed to genuinely investigating and prosecuting the crimes themselves in order to avoid our intervention. We continue to assess domestic proceedings."

Luis Moreno-Ocampo, 'The International Criminal Court - Some Reflexions', 12 *Yearbook of International Humanitarian Law* (2009) pp. 3-12.

70) Interviews conducted during the fieldwork developed in Colombia between October 2010 and March 2011. Diaz, *supra* note 34.

71) Jennifer Easterday, 'Deciding the Fate of Complementaity: A Colombian Case Study', 26 *Arizona Journal of International & Comparative Law* (2009) pp. 50-111.

the great potential of national actors to change their own system. Accordingly, there is an overestimation of what the ICC can do for Colombia, and as an indirect consequence there is also an overrepresentation of retributive justice as the only way to deal with past crimes.

As we have noted before, the over emphasis on the retributive approach is evident not only in the interpretations of the ICC's role, but also in the approaches to justice and the strategies that the government has chosen to implement transitional justice.[72]

It should be mentioned, though, that the emphasis on international criminal law is not only due to the ICC, but to the large institutional structure at the international level that supports this trend. In Colombia, the adaptation of national legislation to the new trends of international criminal law, took place even before the adoption of the Rome Statute.[73] However, this concern about complying with international standards has become even deeper after the creation of the ICC.

The ambiguity generated by the unclear position of the ICC and the limitations of the retributive model at the national level pose the problem of the limits of retributive criminal justice to deal with exceptional situations, involving mass victimisation. These scenarios require more complex and refined strategies that include a broader spectrum of approaches to justice.

4.3. *Problems and Difficulties of this Approach*

The question remains though whether the national Colombian prosecutorial process, with its reduced alternative sentences, is respectful enough of the Rome Statute's interests and standards. Despite some theoretical assumptions and scarce practical experiences, today, many questions remain without answer, and only the historical trajectories of the ICC will draw the path towards a better understanding of correlative dynamics between national mechanisms, like the Colombian one, and the ICC. However, as some have noted, given the normative and factual existence of mechanisms in Colombia, it would be difficult to conclude that Colombia lacks of will and ability to prosecute, and therefore, justify an eventual intervention of the ICC.[74] In fact, unlike some African cases that lack of a normative framework to prosecute the most responsible of mass atrocities, Colombia counts with a consolidated normative process, though a particular one.

---

72) Aponte mentioned about the implementation of the Rome Statute to the national legislation that there is not a problem regarding the length of the legislation. Alejandro Aponte, 'Colombia', in: Kai Ambos and Ezequiel Malarino (eds.), *Persecución penal nacional de crímenes internacionales en América Latina y España* (Konrad-Adenauer-Stiftung, Montevideo, 2003.

73) *Ibid.*

74) Kai Ambos, *Procedimiento de la Ley de Justicia y Paz (Ley 975 de 2005) y Derecho Penal Internacional. Estudio sobre la facultad de intevención complementaria de la Corte Penal Internacional a la luz del denominado proceso de «justicia y paz»* (GTZ, Ed Temis, Bogotá, 2010).

This being said, the ICC keeps an eye open on the actual implementation of the JPL process and its intervention remains a possible outcome.

But still, even if the case has been admissible under article 17, the provision on "interest of justice" provides the Prosecutor with discretionary decision to evade an investigation that "would not serve the interests of justice".[75] As Valinas rightly notes, "cases of ongoing conflict as in Colombia have a special resonance in the question of the interpretation of Article 53. The urgent need to end the conflict for, above all, humanitarian reasons lends a special weight to the perception of the role of the ICC in such situations".[76] The peace vs. justice debate comes into light when thinking of the eventual intervention of the ICC during the ongoing Colombian conflict. How would the remaining illegal armed groups in Colombia react towards the intervention of the ICC? As Pizarro notes, disarming to be prosecuted, without being military beaten, has not been a common historical feature; in fact, the paramilitaries constitute the first example of an illegal armed group that gave up weapons in such circumstances to enter into a peace process which included a prosecutorial process involving prison sentences, although alternative lowered ones.[77] Undoubtedly, finding a negotiated solution with the remaining illegal armed groups in Colombia under the era of the ICC, will definitely nurture the complex debate on justice vs. peace, and notably raise significant questions on the meaning and interpretation of the concept of justice, which takes us to foresee the applicability of "alternative ways of doing justice", such as restorative justice, under the unpredictable shadow of the ICC.

5. Beyond Retribution; Any Space for a Restorative Approach in Colombia?

After having attempted to analyse the complex correlation between traditional criminal justice and the Colombian transitional justice process, we consider appropriate to go further this exercise and question ourselves, relevant and indispensable questions regarding the very meaning of justice, which has been already designed and oriented by the international community towards a narrowly legal and retributive understanding. Despite the dominant character of retributive justice at the international sphere, there are many arguments against the eventual intervention of the ICC, particularly in sensitive and challenging contexts of ongoing conflicts involving illegal armed groups, like the Colombian one.

---

75) Article 53 of the Rome Statute.

76) Marta Valinas, 'Interpreting complementarity and interests of justice in the presence of restorative- based alternative forms of justice', in Carsten Stahn and Larissa van den Herik (eds.), *Future Perspectives on International Criminal Justice* (T.M.C. Asser Press, The Hague, 2010).

77) Pizarro, *supra* note 4.

In our opinion, before thinking of a possible intervention of the ICC in the Colombian transitional justice process, we should reflect on vital questions such as: what would the international retributive vision of justice constructively achieve in the midst of an ongoing conflict? To what extend would international justice meet the needs and interests of suffering Colombia? Is the ICC giving priority to the needs and interests of Colombians and its peaceful future over the interests of the legal international network, or vice versa? Would the ICC contribute to better deal with the issues of transitional justice: truth, accountability, reparation and reconciliation?[78] Is there any space for "alternative forms of justice", such as restorative justice under the era of the ICC?

Although restorative justice has been particularly developed in contexts that exclude large-scale mass abuses, this vision of justice has progressively, albeit scarcely, drawn the attention of intellectuals and practitioners working in the field of transitional justice.[79] Restorative justice, an emerging approach within the criminological sciences that intends to find solutions to the dominant conventional justice system, offers a consistent and innovative vision of justice based on the substantive goal of restoring the harm that has been caused by an offense without the intention of inflicting punishment,[80] whether applied to common crimes in times of peace or to serious violations of human rights during transitional justice contexts.

Colombia has certainly developed great interest in restorative justice as a tool to improve and complement the traditional retributive criminal system; not only the concept has been introduced in the Colombian Political Constitution and in the Code of Criminal Procedure, but it has been thought as a better way of dealing with the issues of mass victimization caused by the internal ongoing conflict. The attempt towards introducing a restorative approach into the Colombian transitional justice framework was clearly seen through the government's draft bill on alternative sentencing, which intended to replace prison sentences for other forms of accountability. Nevertheless, as we have previously explained, the law on alternative sentencing was rapidly withdrawn since it was somehow assimilated to a form of impunity. Along these lines, Gómez considers the alternative sentencing law "a bill that, with vague references to restorative justice, in reality sought to guarantee impunity for the demobilized paramilitaries".[81]

---

78) Parmentier, supra note 16.

79) Elmar Weitekamp et al., 'How to Deal with Mass Victimization and Gross Human Rights Violations. A Restorative Justice Approach', in Uwe Ewald and Ksenija Turkovic (eds.), *Large-Scale Victimization as a Potential Source of Terrorist Activities - Importance of Regaining Security in Post-Conflict Societies* (IOS Press, Amsterdam, 2006) pp. 242-252.

80) Lode Walgrave, 'Restorative Justice: An Alternative for Responding to Crime?', in Shlomo G. Shoham *et al.* (eds.), *International Handbook of Penology and Criminal Justice* (Taylor & Francis, CRC Press, Oxford, 2008) pp. 613-689.

81) Gómez, *supra* note 2.

Moreover, a Colombian civil society initiative, accompanied with the political support of the previous government, expressed its interest on restorative justice by organizing an international symposium on "Restorative Justice and Peace in Colombia" that took place in Cali, on February 2005. During the symposium an extraordinary South African delegation exposed their transitional justice process, and notably, their experience with the famous South African TRC. Surprisingly, though, and despite such interest on restorative justice, this vision of justice did not receive the acceptance and reception one could have expected.

Although the JPL and the global Colombian transitional justice process do have restorative justice elements,[82] the presence and shadow of the ICC, as well as the strong lobbying activity of the advocates of retributive justice, amongst other reasons, must have had a great impact in the decreasing role of restorative justice in Colombia. However, this vision of justice remains of great importance to the Colombian transitional justice process whose future might be brightened.

Since the ICC constitutes a legal-retributive approach we will analyse on the one hand, some limitations of retributive approaches in dealing with the issues of mass victimization in Colombia, and on the other hand, some possible advantages of applying instead "alternative forms of justice", such as restorative justice, which takes us to reflect on the possible dialogue between the ICC and alternative ways of doing justice.

5.1. *Limits of a Retributive Approach in Dealing with the Issues of Mass Victimization in Colombia*

Despite the big difference between dealing with common or ordinary crimes and serious violations of human rights, the way in which national and international criminal tribunals deal with the issues of mass abuses is very much based on the system used by national criminal trials to deal with ordinary crimes.[83] Such structural "transplant", which is also applied by the ICC, does not go without difficulties.

Firstly, criminal trials are frequently subject to widespread critics such as being too long, expensive, inhospitable, exclusive, complex and above all, unable to meet the needs of victims, offenders and the communities. In fact, as restorative justice advocates argue, criminal trials have somehow taken the conflict away from the people involved in it[84] and failed "to engage and empower those most

---

[82] Pizarro, *supra* note 4.

[83] As Drumbl notes, "the structure, rules, and methodologies of the process and punishment of extraordinary international criminality constitute a transplant of the structure, rules and methodologies of ordinary criminal process and punishment in those states that dominate the international order. Certain adaptations have taken place along the way". Mark A. Drumbl, *Atrocity, Punishment and the Law* (Cambridge University Press, Cambridge, 2007).

[84] Nils Christie, 'Conflicts as Property', 17 *British Journal of Criminology* (1977) pp. 1-15.

directly affected by crime".[85] Such criticisms could be the consequence of a justice system that has been particularly conceived to inflict punishment to offenders; a justice system that has somehow left behind the reparation and reintegration of the traumatic harm of victims and offenders.[86] Surprisingly enough, the victim case scenario does not ameliorate in cases of massive crimes, principally in processes before ad hoc international criminal tribunals.[87]

As to the issue of accountability, a vital question arises: who and how should be held accountable for mass atrocities? In the mist of conflicts, national or international conventional justice systems will hold accountable for past atrocities a number of select guilty perpetrators, leaving behind many individuals who massively contributed to the boost of violence. As Fletcher and Weinstein note "trials do not address the complicity of those who stood by or cheered a vicious leader or who elected a war criminal to represent them".[88] Undoubtedly, accountability is one of the most controversial issues of the transitional justice process in Colombia. As Bueno demonstrates in her thesis, victims and offenders of the Colombian conflict consider that massive atrocities wouldn't have taken place without the collaboration and support of thousands of human beings working directly or indirectly, and for various different reasons, towards the development of the conflict. According to them, the Colombian conflict is not limited to the illegal armed groups, but covers a vast range of variables and indirect offenders without whom the conflict would have never reached such dimensions.

Interestingly, some members of the Colombian indigenous communities argue that the roots of the conflict could be based on a disrespectful Western mentality. Correspondingly, Eliécer, a member of the Arhuacan indigenous community, explains in his own words the way in which they have been brutalized for more than 500 years by this mentality,

---

85) Jennifer L. Sawin and Howard Zehr, 'The Ideas of Engagement and Empowerment', in Gerry Johnstone and Daniel W. Van Ness, (eds.), *Handbook of Restorative Justice* (Willan Publishing, Devon, 2007) pp. 41-58.

86) Isabella Bueno's doctoral thesis (unpublished work), which deeply illustrates the opinions and perceptions of victims and offenders about the traumatic experience of the conflict and the difficulties implied to heal the harm and reintegrate into society;

87) According to Llewellyn and Howse, "[c]riminal prosecutions, particularly of the kind being undertaken at The Hague, in fact offer very limited opportunity for victims to tell their stories and be heard with respect and sympathy". Jennifer Llewellyn and Robert Howser, 'Institutions for restorative justice: The South African Truth and Reconciliation Commission' 49 *University of Toronto Law Journal* (1999) pp. 355-388. As a matter or fact, both ad hoc international criminal tribunal for the Former Yugoslavia and for Rwanda didn't offer a space for the victims to heal their harms and respectfully participate in the process. However, fortunately, the ICC put an end to these limitations; henceforth, besides being able to participate in their personal capacity, victims are allowed to claim reparation before the ICC.

88) Laurel E. Fletcher and Harvey M. Weinstein, 'Violence and Social Repair: Rethinking the Contribution of Justice to Reconciliation', 24 *Human Rights Quarterly* (2002) pp. 573-639.

> For more than 500 years we have been victimised physically and mentally by various actors, call them Catholic missionaries, colonizers, settlers, peasants, guerrillas, paramilitaries and delinquents, all of them inflamed by their needs, in one way or another ended with the peace in our territory, amputating our rights as a community.[89]

In addition, victims and offenders of the Colombian conflict consider the Colombian state responsible for its institutional absence and inability to offer economic and social opportunities to the poor, and for being unable to fight against the corrupted politicians who haven't ceased from stealing the nation's public funds, and who have collaborated and financed the phenomenon of paramilitarism, together with chief generals, policemen and business men. According to paramilitary chief, Freddy Rendón Herrera, known as "*El Alemán*", the Colombian state should assume its responsibility for having participated hand by hand with the paramilitaries during the conflict. In his words,

> for 46 years the politicians of this country haven't been able to find a solution to a conflict that pushed me to take weapons and break the law and the constitution, and be here today assuming a responsibility that I must assume. But today, that institution that has been unable to find a solution to the problem, pretends to prove to the world and to the Colombian society that we are responsible for everything,

ironically, Freddy continues,

> today, the police agents, the soldiers, the politicians are not aware for example that Freddy was a member of the *Autodefensas* present in the north of Chocó, in the Caribbean; the policemen didn't see me, the soldiers didn't see me, the politicians were not aware, the mayors didn't realise, the town councillors never met us. But I saw them all, I met them all, I spoke to all of them, I worked with all of them jointly...[90]

Moreover, Colombians have a strong opinion against the role of some NGOs that have financed and defended the actions of guerrillas, and the international community, particularly the developed countries, that have financed the Colombian drug business. Along these lines, a victim of kidnapping by the ELN, argues that

> the drug consumers, mainly the social ones, the NGOs defending these groups –guerrilla groups -, the weapon producers who gain so much money and cause so much prejudice, are equally responsible; they are active actors that consciously cause harm because they want to cause it. And there are passive guilty ones, like the local authorities that allow this to happen and corruption; corrupted authorities are guilty for omission, the other ones are guilty for action. I am amazed by the tolerance towards the consumption of drugs, it's amazing, amazing, you see it everywhere, it's amazing; each person that consumes drugs is killing someone, is killing someone physically![91]

89) Bueno, *supra* note 86.
90) *Ibid.*
91) *Ibid.*

In fact, the international dimension of the conflict frustrates Colombians. Not only they consider developed countries guilty for the damages occurred in the Colombian territory, but this international dimension makes Colombians very pessimistic with regards to an eventual solution to the conflict.[92] In the words of a victim of displacement, "the conflict of drugs goes beyond Colombia; it has been brought by other countries, they are the ones with the financial resources and the negotiators; they are the main source of the problem. They should accept that they are guilty of our country's harm".[93]

As a result, exclusive retributive accountability may leave behind an unpleasant perception susceptible of affecting many transitional justice processes.[94] Although today there is a widespread agreement according to which conflicts are made of massive invisible forces that have benefited from the conflict and encouraged it, criminal trials still work on the basis of exclusive retributions that can only increment division to the expenses of unification, and may therefore hamper the path towards reconciliation.

Further, those exclusively chosen perpetrators would be held individually accountable for massive collective crimes.[95] In the words of Fletcher and Weinstein, "because the criminal justice system addresses only individual accountability for criminalized acts, the evidence from social psychologists forces us to rethink the question of collective responsibility".[96] Surprisingly, international retribution, which is practically limited to imprisonment, doesn't take into account the collective dimension of conflicts.

And still, even when prosecutions have been chosen to deal with mass atrocities, one must be sure if they are really feasible and/or worth it. Besides the abovementioned political difficulties prosecutions may imply, there are additional barriers such as the huge number of eventual defendants and the excessive cost of international trials. Even at the international level that counts with financial support, prosecutions do not go without further logistical, and even ethical, complications; in addition to the difficulties related to "catching up" the offenders, and the barriers *due process* may pose, the experience of both the ICTY and the ICTR has proven to be exorbitantly expensive and long. This critical situation has triggered some to consider the reconstruction of national legal systems a better choice than

---

92) *Ibid.*

93) *Ibid.*

94) Drumbl, *supra* note 83. The negative effects of exclusive retributive forms of accountability are well described by Drumbl's strong statement according to which "for many Rwandans and Bonsian Muslims, retribution might well include accountability for the UN and foreign governments, whose peacekeepers were ineffective while genocidal massacre occurred in their midst".

95) This principle of individual responsibility for collective crimes has been applied by international criminal law and reaffirmed by article 25 of the ICC statute.

96) Fletcher and Weinstein, *supra* note 88.

the expensive prosecution of some offenders.[97] Along the same lines, according to the report of the Secretary General:

> [u]nfortunately, the international community has not always provided rule of law assistance that is appropriate to the country context. Too often, the emphasis has been on foreign experts, foreign models and foreign-conceived solutions to the detriment of durable improvements and sustainable capacity.[98]

Frequently, advocates for prosecution argue that criminal trials aim at preventing future human rights violations, constitute a historical memory and encourage peace and reconciliation. In our opinion, though, meeting such goals in an ongoing conflict seems far from being a reality; paradoxically, criminal trials may even pose obstacles to achieving these goals.

Regarding deterrence, we argue that although criminal trials may have a censure effect over gross violations of human crimes, they do not necessarily deter offenders from committing these crimes. As Aukerman rightly notes, "it is virtually impossible to assess whether or not the threat of prosecution has ever prevented genocide and war crimes".[99] Certainly, the presence of national and/or international criminal trials has not prevented suicide bombers from committing atrocities, neither actual guerrilla members in Colombia to continue their illegal activities.

Even in cases of eventual deterrence, we join Aukerman's point of view according to which "it is unlikely that post-atrocity prosecution is the most effective way to prevent future atrocities".[100] According to the victims and offenders of the Colombian conflict, mass atrocities will continue to occur as long as they do not find a solution to the causes of the conflict, particularly corruption, the lack of social and economical opportunities to all citizens, and above all, the drug business. In sum, national and international prosecutions may have the positive effect of censuring an atrocity and set a precedent, but, on the one hand, they do not constitute the unique censuring instrument, and on the other hand, they do not necessarily deter from committing mass atrocities, particularly in cases of ongoing conflict, like the Colombian one, in which criminal structures are so well consolidated and the conflict *per se* has become such a profitable business.

As to the key issue of truth, in our opinion, since prosecutions intent to inflict punishment over the guilty offender, the concept of truth would be particularly used to achieve this goal. In other words, prosecutorial truth would aim at

---

97) Naomi Roth-Arriaza, 'The New Landscape of Transitional Justice', in Naomi Roht-Arriaza and Javier Marriezcurrena, (eds.), *Transitional Justice in the Twenty-First Century; Beyond Truth versus Justice* (Cambridge University Press, New York, 2006) pp. 1-16.

98) Report of the Secretary General, *supra* note 15.

99) Miriam J. Aukerman, 'Extraordinary Evil, Ordinary Crime: A Framework for Understanding Transitional Justice', 39 *Harvard Human Rights Journal* (2002) pp. 39-97.

100) *Ibid.*

unveiling the truth behind a crime to determine the offender's degree of culpability, and therefore, leave behind the truth containing the explanations of the occurrence of mass atrocities. We join therefore the vision of some authors who argue that "the truth that is revealed in court trials, international and national, is a fragmented fact finding process to serve as evidence in proving or refuting guilt, but never to bring out the truth of the conflict as a social phenomenon. Trials do not allow perpetrators or survivors to produce a story that might coincide and lead to an explanation of the causes of the conflict".[101] Moreover, according to many offenders of the Colombian conflict, despite the calming and healing effect telling the truth may have, the threat of punishment has deterred many offenders from telling the truth about the crimes they have committed.[102]

With regards to the issue of reconciliation it seems doubtful to consider that prosecutions can positively contribute to a process of reconciliation in a torn-apart society. In fact, "there have been virtually no studies that systematically have attempted to examine or measure the contribution of trials to reconciliation and social reconstruction".[103] We could even go further to consider that prosecutions could hamper the road towards reconciliation, at least in situations of ongoing conflict. As Bueno has thoroughly demonstrated in her thesis, one of the main reasons why offenders from the guerrillas haven't demobilised is precisely the fear of being locked up in prisons.[104]

Uganda also provides an example of such difficult case scenario; despite the claims of the Achioli community according to which the eventual intervention of the ICC would obstruct peace efforts, the prosecutor of the ICC issued arrest warrants against the LRA leadership, conducing the LRA to respond by a rejection of ending the war in presence of the arrest warrants.[105] In fact, the delicate and even undesirable consequences of an eventual intervention of the ICC in situations of ongoing conflicts raises relevant questions regarding its legitimacy and real utility, which, in our opinion, shouldn't be ignored by the field of transitional justice. In fact, as Shaw and Waldorf rightly note, "as the heated public controversy over the International Criminal Court's involvement in Uganda indicates, the current phase of transitional justice is frequently marked by disconnections between international legal norms and local priorities and practices".[106] Moreover, although we believe reconciliation between victims and offenders shouldn't be forced by

---

101) Weitekamp et al., *supra* note 79.

102) Bueno, *supra* note 86.

103) Fletcher and Weinstein, *supra* note 88.

104) Bueno, *supra* note 86.

105) Sverker Finnstrom, 'Reconciliation Grown Bitter? War, Retribution, and Ritual Action in Northern Uganda', in Rosalind Shaw *et al* (eds.), *Localizing Transitional Justice: Interventions and Priorities After Mass Violence* (Stanford University Press, Stanford, 2010) pp. 135-156.

106) Rosalind Shaw and Lars Waldorf, 'Introduction: Localizing Transitional Justice', in Rosalind Shaw *et al* (eds.), *Localizing Transitional Justice: Interventions and Priorities After Mass Violence* (Stanford University Press, Stanford, 2010) pp. 3-26.

any transitional justice mechanism, we do not consider convenient to incite negative and even hatred emotions susceptible of further bridging the gap between the parties. Accordingly, Llewellyn and Howse argue that

> the paradigmatic, isolating, or alienating methods of retribution seem totally self-defeating – for one cannot restore a relation of equality between the members of society by removing one party in the relationship (the perpetrator) from society altogether, whether by execution, banishment, or imprisonment.[107]

Further, such excluding process may pose great barriers for the proper reintegration of the offender and therefore for his/her personal and family reconciliation.

Additionally, what about traditional mechanisms integrating culturally based ways of doing justice? According to some,

> [w]e cannot assume that legal justice is desired or the highest priority in all countries after periods of repression or violence. Culture and history may lead to different definitions of justice and to different paths for achieving it; justice can be defined broadly, and retributive justice is only one part of that definition.[108]

Since transitional justice at the international level has been almost exclusively focused on a legal approach, particularly with the creation of the permanent ICC, countries going through transitional processes may be tempted to avoid implementing their culturally based mechanisms in order to align to the standards of international criminal justice, and therefore, avoid an eventual request of the ICC on the basis of the principal of complementarity. Consequently, the inconvenience is twofold: on the one hand, countries may lose interest in studying and probably implementing a rich variety of indigenous and local-level mechanisms that may serve for inspiration to the western world and provide cultural richness to the country, and on the other hand, the legal approach would gain force at the expenses of other ways of doing justice.

Moreover, history has shown an international community that has not always equally taken into account all extraordinary events. As Christie explains while referring to the Nuremberg trials and the atrocities of World War II, "by hanging commanders, and while the judges in Nuremberg focused on finding personal guilt for atrocities, other phenomena were left in peace, left to grow. Three themes were not discussed in Nuremberg: - Dresden – Hiroshima and Nagasaki – The

107) Llewellyn and Howser, *supra* note 87.

108) Harvey M. Weinstein, Laurel E. Fletcher, Patrick Vinck and Phuong N. Pham, 'Stay the Hand of Justice: Whose Priorities take Priority?', in Rosalind Shaw *et al* (eds.), *Localizing Transitional Justice: Interventions and Priorities after Mass Violence* (Stanford University Press, Stanford, 2010) pp. 27-48.

Gulags".[109] The sensitive selection of extraordinary cases is particularly questioned nowadays under the era of the ICC, which has mainly focused on African conflicts to the expenses of others.

So retributive approaches, either national or international, do not seem to have a very clear and coherent purpose; according to Drumbl, even "judges still remain unsure, and often divided, about the purpose of the punishment they mete out".[110] One could even ask if the justice practitioners are not being dominated by the system itself. In fact, as national trials have been criticized for being unable to meet the needs and interests of the parties involved in the process, "[s]imilar problems will arise if transitional justice reflects only the priorities of the international community and not those of the affected country".[111] All these critical aspects leads us to consider prosecutions a simple way of avoiding exploring the real truth and complexities behind a conflict; it may be easier to point out the "bad" guys than assuming a broader concept of responsibility; a concept that may rightly involve the massive number of individuals, states, political groups, NGOs, national and international organizations that, massively, participated in the occurrence of mass victimization.

5.2. *Restorative Justice; an Option in Dealing with an Ongoing Conflict*

Whether applied to ordinary crimes during times of peace, or to crimes of serious and massive nature in transitional justice contexts, restorative justice offers a vision of justice that pretends to elucidate the way in which criminality should be dealt with; restorative justice, thus, by means of a critical analysis on the weaknesses of existing visions of justice, particularly on the dominant retributive-oriented approach, offers solutions susceptible of being applied during times of peace and/or war. Although it has been particularly developed in relation to ordinary crimes, this vision of justice has progressively entered the discourse of transitional justice. But still, despite the blooming growth of restorative justice and transitional justice as independent fields of study, little has been said about the coalition of both. Nevertheless, advocates of restorative justice seem to agree upon the potential significant role it could play in addressing severe cases. Along these lines, Stovel argues that approaching transitional justice from a restorative perspective would be beneficial since

> [i]t is the form of justice most directly concerned with reconciliation. It addresses the reintegrative needs of both victims and most perpetrators. In poor countries with weak

---

109) Nils Christie, 'Answers to Atrocities. Restorative Justice in Extreme Situations', in Ezzat A. Fattah and Stephan Parmetier (eds.), *Victim Policies and Criminal Justice on the Road to Restorative Justice – Essays in Honor of Tony Peters* (Leuven University Press, Leuven, 2001) pp. 379-392.

110) Drumbl *supra* note 83.

111) Aukerman *supra* note 99.

> judicial systems, it offers an alternative to lengthy and expensive trials. And in much of Africa, it draws on pre-existing restorative justice traditions and institutions.[112]

The question of the application of restorative justice in cases embracing systematic political violence has been raised largely as a result of the influential work of the renowned South African Truth and Reconciliation Commission and Rwandan "*gacaca courts*"; Nonetheless, although both mechanisms have been originally tainted with restorative overtones, they do also comprise non restorative-oriented elements, and even retributive shades, like *gacaca's* accountability measures.[113] In fact, the scarce literature on the coalition of restorative justice and transitional justice refers to the existing mechanisms of transitional justice, but hasn't gone further to build a solid framework about this fusion. Given such literature gap, we will briefly present our understanding of restorative justice through Bueno's model, and the way in which this vision of justice could penetrate the field of transitional justice.

5.3. *Toward a Model of Restorative Justice*

Fig. 1 pretends to illustrate our vision of restorative justice (see Fig. 1).

According to this model, a model of justice would be restorative if the following criteria are present:

1. Restorative justice, is based on a *restorative philosophy* consisting of, on the one hand, the principle of non-violence and the principle of interconnectedness, and on the other hand, of underlying values such as respect, humility, solidarity and love. In this sense, the restorative justice model and the restorative philosophy share both the same values;
2. The restorative justice model is based on a "*restorative rule of law*" system that includes all harms and is not only limited to the crimes that have been established by law. Therefore, according to restorative justice, focus is made "on the harms of wrongdoing more than the rules that have been broken".[114]

---

112) Laura Stovel, *When the Enemy comes Home: Restoring Justice after Mass Atrocity*, Restorative Justice Conference, Vancouver, June 1-4, 2003 <www.sfu.ca/cfrj/fulltext/stovel.pdf>, 29 March 2012.

113) On the one hand, despite the TRC's deep restorative elements, such as the space provided to victims to be heard and acknowledged, the possibility of providing a broader explanation about the past and a form of accountability based on truth and not retribution, trust building would have required "white South Africans to take responsibility and atone for their support for apartheid – it would require full restorative justice" *Ibid.* On the other hand, *Gacaca courts* provide a concrete example of a mixture of restorative and retributive elements: "confessions *and* accusations, plea bargains *and* trials, forgiveness *and* punishment, community service *and* incarceration" Shaw and Waldorf, *supra* note 106.

114) Mark Umbreit and Marilyn Peterson (eds.), *Restorative Justice Dialogue: An Essential Guide for Research and Practice* (Springer Publishing Company, New York, 2010).

Primary Goal: To Restore the Harm and Reintegrate the Offender

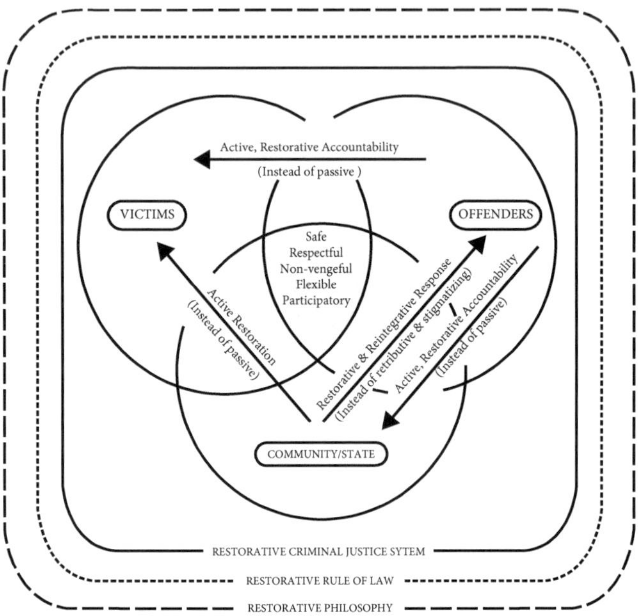

Secondary Inter-related Goals: Trust and Reconciliation

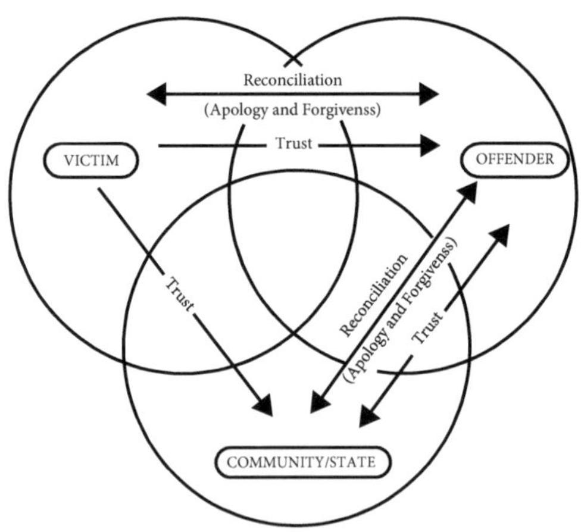

Fig. 1. Restorative justice in times of normality.

3. The *primary* goal of restorative justice is the restoration of the harm of victims, offenders and communities. Other goals, such as forgiveness, apology, trust, and reconciliation, are ideal and essential goals of restorative justice, but remain *secondary*;
4. Restorative accountability: In restorative justice the community/state should intent to restore the harm of the victim and the harm of the offender. The latter, in exchange, should intent to actively participate in the restoration of the victim's harm, the community's harm and his/her harm. Coercive measures, such as restorative imprisonment should take place only if necessary and without the intention of punishment infliction;[115]
5. The process of restorative justice should be *flexible* enough to meet the needs of victims, offenders and communities. It should therefore "provide opportunities for *dialogue*, direct or indirect, between victims and offenders as appropriate";[116]
6. The State should be present throughout the restorative justice process to guarantee security, the respect of human rights and the right execution of decisions taken either by a judge or mediator or collectively by the interested parties;
7. The whole process should be governed with respect and without any form of revengeful attitudes.

After having presented our understanding of the theory of restorative justice with regards to ordinary crimes we will now explain how this vision of justice can penetrate the field of serious violations of human rights. We should clarify though, that the concept of restorative justice is understood in exactly the same way as it has been explained, meaning an approach of justice that intents to restore the harm. The difference resides, though, in the context in which we pretend to analyse the application of restorative justice: a context of transitional justice involving massive crimes. The restorative approach would therefore need to adapt itself to the characteristics that involve mass victimization, meaning a collective dimension due to the elevated number of victims and offenders and the international dimension of the international community, which is obviously concerned by the gravity of the crimes. Accordingly, the model of restorative justice in transitional justice contexts, or as we have called it, "restorative transitional justice", would look as follows (see Fig. 2).

Accordingly, the question of *"restorative transitional justice"* could be defined as *"the variety of processes and mechanisms established to restore, to the extent*

115) Walgrave, *supra* note 80.
116) Umbreit and Peterson, *supra* note 114.

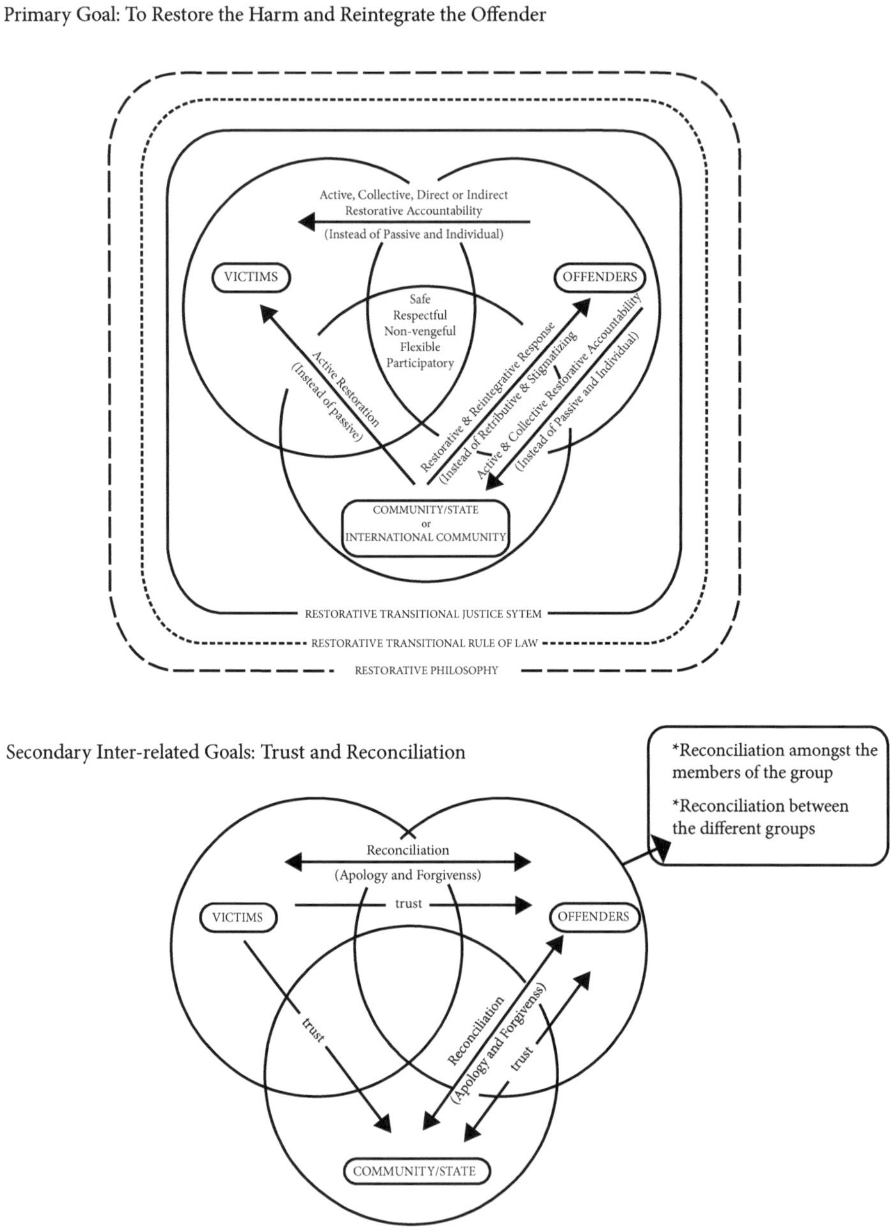

Fig. 2. Restorative justice in times of transition.

possible, the individual and social harm caused by mass abuses".[117] International, national and/or local-level transitional justice mechanisms may only gain the restorative adjective if they embrace the above mentioned restorative elements. In other words, neither truth commissions nor traditional justice mechanisms are inherently restorative; a real restorative transitional justice mechanism would be the one that intents, as much as possible, to restore the massive harm that has been caused by an offense, and consequently, find solutions to the already described weaknesses of the conventional legal system.

Approaching transitional justice from a restorative perspective would imply a "change of lenses" through which to look at the phenomenon of mass victimization. Such perspective would consequently alter the meaning of the key issues of transitional justice and the way in which they should be dealt with. In fact, in contrast to the legalistic approach whose goal is very much based on retribution, the key issues of transitional justice, when approached from a restorative point of view, cannot be dissociated from the goal of restoring the harm.

Accordingly, on the one hand, restorative truth, as the TRC report notes, would consist of "a truth that would contribute to the reparation of the damage inflicted in the past and to the prevention of the recurrence of serious abuses in the future".[118] Truth would therefore be a means to restoration and acknowledgement instead of punishment and stigmatization; knowing and unrevealing the truth would only serve to achieve constructive goals such as restoring the harm of the victim through the offender's acknowledgement of the facts and constructive restorative actions, liberate the heavy emotional burden of both victims and perpetrators through a story telling process and constructing the sociological and criminological truth of the past. In addition, we argue that the absence of retribution would encourage a real and deep truth unveiling process. Further and importantly, since group offenses involve many perpetrators, dialogue and group truth-telling processes should take place to better construct a recording memory of the past.

Restorative accountability in transitional justice would avoid any form of intentional punishment infliction and connect accountability to restoration and reintegration through measures like truth, community service, symbolic actions, compensation, among others. Like with restorative truth, restorative transitional justice should provide the opportunity for offenders to collectively restore the direct and/or indirect victims' and social harm. We subscribe therefore to Arsovska, Valinas and Vanspauwen's argument according to which transitional justice should require "a broad understanding of accountability which goes beyond mere individual responsibility. 'Accounting' for a violent past will include not only a

---

117) Bueno, *supra* note 86.

118) Truth and Reconciliation Commission of South Africa, *Report*, 5 vol., Vol. 1. (Juta Publishers, Cape Town, 1998).

recognition of what happened and the responsibilities associated to it, but also a commitment to make up for those wrongs and to prevent them in the future".[119]

As to the issue of reconciliation, we argue that the justice system of transitional justice societies must intent, to the extent possible, to respect the larger goal of national peace and reconciliation; a goal that goes beyond the justice system and touches every citizen of the ragged society; a necessary goal that, in our opinion, will be better met and respected through restorative justice, to the expenses of the conventional legalistic vision of justice. As previously mentioned, there has always been a conflict between peace and justice. However, as rightly said by UN Secretary-General Ban Ki-moon "the debate on how to 'reconcile' peace and justice or how to 'sequence' them has lasted more than a decade. Today, we have achieved a conceptual breakthrough: the debate is no longer between peace and justice but between peace and what kind of justice".[120] In contrast to the retributive dimension of the conventional justice system that threatens the goal of peace and reconciliation, "restorative justice offers a means of resolving this peace vs. justice dilemma";[121] restorative justice proposes a vision of justice that respects this indispensable goal and softens the road to achieve it. In Aukerman's words, "both retributive and restorative justices envision reconciliation as a product of full accountability for wrongdoing. But while retributive accountability involves proportionate punishment, restorative accountability demands an acknowledgement by offenders of their culpability and a willingness to make good. While retributive justice allow society to punish an offender as a means of achieving reconciliation, restorative justice requires society to include the offender in the process of reconciliation".[122] In our opinion, the justice system must bend over peace and reconciliation, which is a necessary and urgent state of a conflict-ridden society, and not the opposite.

6. Conclusions

Through this article we pretended to highlight some of the limitations of the dominant retributive approach when dealing with the issues of transitional justice in

---

119) Jana Arsovska et al., 'From micro to macro, from individual to state: restorative justice and multi-level diplomacy in divided societies', in Ivo Aertsen *et al.* (eds.), *Restoring Justice after large-scale violent conflicts: Kosovo, DR Congo and the Israeli-Palestinian Conflict* (Willan Publishing, Devon, 2008) pp. 444-460.

120) Valentina Torricelli, *The Contribution African States Can Make to the ICC Review Conference*, <www.africanarguments.org/2010/03/11/the-contribution-african-states-can-make-to-the-icc-review-conference/>, 29 February 2012.

121) Paul McCold, et al., *An Introduction to Restorative Peacebuilding. Briefing Paper 1. Restorative Peacebuilding Project. Working Party on Restorative Justice* (Alliance of NGOs on Crime Prevention and Criminal Justice, New York, 2007).

122) Aukerman, *supra* note 99.

Colombia, particularly in a complex context of ongoing conflict that involves consolidated illegal armed groups disposing of extraordinary financial means from the drug business. Given such inconveniences, we presented the restorative justice model as possible justice approach susceptible of bringing about solutions to the good administration of the issues of transitional justice.

Today, though, the uncertainty remains as to the attitude of the ICC towards national restorative transitional justice mechanisms. Could a country, experiencing an ongoing conflict, deal with the issues of transitional justice in a purely restorative way under the era of the ICC? Would it be forced to create retributive justice mechanisms to avoid an intervention of the latter? Only time and experience will illuminate the dialogue between the ICC and the restorative justice approaches.

Nevertheless, as we have previously explained, Colombia has done an effort in establishing state organised transitional justice mechanisms which intent to comply with the ICC's demands while trying to achieve peace. In fact, these mechanisms may be tainted by the retributive or the restorative justice approach or by a mixture of both. For example, whereas the judicial process of the JPL contain elements of both approaches, other mechanisms, like those established by Law 1106 contain to certain degree some restorative elements.

However, as previously explained, the discourse and the theory of transitional justice in Colombia has been mainly dominated by the retributive approach to justice, due in great part, to the presence and shadow of the ICC, which considers criminal justice as the only response to mass atrocity and the only way to avoid impunity in this scenario. We argue, though, that the excessive focus on this approach has dismissed other possible approaches to justice that may considerably enrich the field of transitional justice.

We consider, thus, that the ICC should be prudent enough with those countries that couldn't find a solution to their conflicts before the ratification of the Rome Statute. In the particular Colombian case, which is actually dealing with the issues of mass victimisation during a very complex conflict situation, the ICC should only exercise a guiding role intended to contribute to the consolidation of the Colombian national justice mechanisms, which may obviously integrate a restorative justice oriented approach.

Multilayered Justice in Northern Uganda: ICC Intervention and Local Procedures of Accountability

Steven C. Roach
Associate Professor, Department of Government and International Affairs
University of South Florida-Tampa, Tampa, FL, USA

Abstract
In an effort to redress the effects of the civil war in Northern Uganda, local, state and international officials have begun to study the feasibility of re-adapting the procedures of local justice, including *mato oput*, a local procedure practiced by the Acholi tribe. This article examines this evolving multilayered project of justice in Northern Uganda. It addresses two features of this model: (1) the central features of local justice, in particular *mato oput*, and (2) the complementary relationship between *mato oput*, the state, and the International Criminal Court's (ICC) victims' unit and the victims' trust fund. It argues that closer and more effective ties between the ICC and local procedures of justice can be developed. Not only does this relationship constitute an evolving framework for addressing the political realities of ICC intervention, but it also raises many important practical implications for reaching out to the local population.

Keywords
International Criminal Court (ICC); accountability; local justice; accommodation; sovereignty

The ongoing civil war in Northern Uganda has taken its toll on the local population. In an effort to redress the effects of the civil war in Northern Uganda, local, state and international leaders and officials have sought to revive the ancient procedure of *mato oput*, practiced by the Acholi people in Northern Uganda. *Mato oput*'s wider application, in this context, would address an important, emerging reality: that the ICC cannot investigate and prosecute many of the worst perpetrators, many of whom are children that the Lord's Resistance Army (LRA) forcibly conscripted.[1] Not only would it expand the scope for administering justice on the local level: it might also complement the ICC's activities by allowing more perpetrators to voluntarily confess their guilt.

But many legal scholars and ICC officials remain uncertain if the revival of *mato oput* will offer an effective alternative to the ICC and its high evidential standards

---

1) See Justice and Reconciliation Project, "Special Report: The Cooling of the Hearts," (2011).

(admissibility).[2] Some remain ambivalent towards the ICC's intervention in Northern Uganda, claiming that the ICC's indictments of the Lord's Resistance Army commanders have discouraged these indicted perpetrators from surrendering to state authorities.[3] Still others remain more optimistic towards the ICC's gradual accommodation of traditional justice mechanisms.[4] In their view, local procedures of justice can work effectively with the ICC and national courts to further accountability and peace in the region and to help resolve the disparities between local and international justice.

As we shall see, ICC officials have been actively addressing the needs of the Ugandan victims traumatized by the political violence, even though the ICC has yet to complete any trials that would provide compensation to victims. Such increasing activity, however, raises an important question: How will local procedures complement the ICC's own non-punitive measures and civil society mechanisms? And how should we understand the conflict between the ICC and *mato oput*? I argue that closer and more effective ties between the ICC and local procedures of justice can be developed. This is not to say that local procedures of justice can and will substitute for the ICC and vice versa. Nor that the ICC will prosecute below the top brass in this country, namely, Joseph Kony and his top commanders, two of whom are now dead. Rather, it is to say that the revival of the *mato oput* (ancient) procedure in 2000 represents a plausible and timely opportunity to advance an effective multilayered model of justice.

In the first section of the article, I shall address the central features of *mato oput* and the key challenges posed by its implementation, including the role of the national government. I then move on to address the ICC's role in punishing the very worst perpetrators and the prospects and limits of its victims' unit. Here

---

2) See *e.g.*, Louise Mallinder, "Can Amnesties and International Justice be Reconciled?", *The International Journal of Transitional Justice*, 1(1)(2007): 208-230; Tim Allen, *Trial Justice. The International Criminal Court and the Lord's Resistance Army* (London: Zed Books, 2006); Thomas Unger and Marieke Wierda, "Pursuing Justice in Ongoing Conflict: A Discussion of Current Practice," in Kai Ambos et al, supra note 15, , Judith Large and Marieke Wierda (eds.), *Building a Future on Peace and Justice: Studies on Transitional Justice, Peace and Development* (The Hague: Springer, 2009).

3) Adam Branch, "Uganda's Civil War and the Politics of ICC Intervention," *Ethics and International Affairs* 21(2)(2007).The ICC, it should be noted, does not accept any blanket amnesties and has refused to comply with the demands for dropping the indictments, even though the national government implemented an amnesty law national amnesty law in 2000 to allow perpetrators to confess their guilt in exchange for amnesty.

4) *See e.g.*, Steven C. Roach (ed.), *Governance, Order, and the International Criminal Court: Between Realpolitik and a Cosmopolitan Court.* (Oxford: Oxford University Press 2009); Steven C Roach, "The Turbulent Politics of the International Criminal Court," *Peace Review* 23(4) (2011):546-551; Renee Jeffrey, "Forgiveness, Amnesty, and Justice: The Case of the Lord's Resistance Army in Northern Uganda," *Cooperation and Conflict* 46(1): 78-95; Sarah H.M. Nouwen and Wouter G. Werner, "Doing Justice to the Political: The International Criminal Court in Uganda and Sudan," *European Journal of International Law* 21(4)(2010): 941-965.

I argue that ICC intervention has been negatively perceived, largely because of the assumed dichotomy between international/punitive and traditional/non-punitive justice. The problem with this assumption is that it overlooks the need of comparing and potentially reconciling the legal instruments of victims' justice at the ICC and the local level. Finally, in the third part, I address how outreach can move us beyond some of these legal problems and limits by raising awareness of the ICC's mechanisms and the stronger ties between local/communal groups and ICC officials.

1. Traditional Justice in Northern Uganda

Of the many traditional procedures of justice found in Northern Uganda, *mato oput* has attracted arguably the most attention among scholars. Practiced by the Acholi tribe consisting of fifty different clans, it is an intra-tribal procedure designed to resolve disputes and promote reconciliation among the different clans. Its revival in 2000 reflects the somewhat daunting challenge of revising its patriarchal structure to address the needs and rights of women. Nonetheless, as an intra-tribal procedure of justice, *mato oput* remains one of the most well-known forms of local justice practiced by the Acholi people in Northern Uganda. Others in Northern Uganda include *kayo cuk, tolu kakwa* and *moyo pliny*.[5] Of these other traditional mechanisms, only *moyo pliny* has been adapted to address the elements of war crimes covered by the Rome Statute, notably child conscription. Like *moyo pliny, mato oput* involves the sacrifice of livestock and healing through ritual. Its distinctive approach to healing involves the consumption of the bitter tasting *mato* root (*mato oput* literally refers to the "bitter root"). When mixed with a local brew, *kwete*, consisting of the blood of sacrificed lambs or goats, it becomes a viscous, bitter substance, which both the perpetrators and victims are required to drink at a tribal ceremony. This procedure allows the afflicted parties to consume the bitterness of the vengeance of their victims, symbolizing the act of moving beyond hatreds, distrust, and hostilities.[6]

Mato oput's primary goal, then, is to promote reconciliation through truth-telling and symbolic/ritual acts. Like the other traditional mechanisms mentioned above, it emphasizes the restoration of peace and tribal well-being and provides an alternative to punitive mechanisms such as national and international trials. As such, it is comprised of four modes: (1) the voluntary feature of the legal process, (2) establishment of truth mediation, (3) guilt acknowledgement and

---

[5] Lino Owor and Tim Murithi, "Transitional Justice and War Crimes in Northern Uganda," Justice and Reconciliation Project," JRP-IJR Policy Brief No. 1 (2011).

[6] Locals use the metaphor, "cooling of the hearts" to express the psychological redress for the perpetrators and victims.

(4) reparation and reconciliation via symbolic acts and spiritual appeasement.[7] These modes, however, differ in substance from the formal punitive mechanisms of international and national justice (trials).

Unlike formal criminal systems, which hold trials to punish and isolate the perpetrator's guilt, *mato oput* is an informal procedure of justice, relying on the goodwill and good faith of the community to foster an environment of mutual trust among the members of the tribal community. The voluntary nature of the process is intended to encourage confessions and/or truth telling and to diminish the perpetrator's fear of reprisal by warring members of groups.[8] Placing faith in the community's willingness to forgive is therefore an important customary element and/or value associated with *mato oput* and traditional justice. For not only does such faith initiate the process of administering justice; it also performs the important psychological function of "cooling the hearts" of those impacted by the violence. As such, voluntary truth-telling initiates the first step of the *mato oput* process, namely, to come to terms with one's guilt.

The clan leaders or elders oversee the second step of compensation: determining the amount of compensation or the number and/or size of goat and lambs to be sacrificed and split. Truth mediation in this respect refers to the intervention by the elders in the negotiations between the victims' families and perpetrators. Here the Ker Kwaro Acholi (KKA), the local institution of the Acholi, led by the paramount chief, serves as trusted mediator in conflicts, typically involving the killing of a family member (although disputes can also involve lesser offenses). As the leader of the Councils of Elders, the chief therefore serves three important, discernible functions for settling disputes and conflicts in the Acholi region: (1) to evaluate the admission of guilt and confessions (truth-telling), (2) to determine what amount of compensation is adequate to commence and perform the healing process (which I will discuss below in the context of war), (3) and to conduct and oversee the rituals or symbolic acts. The confession, in order to be considered genuine, must be done on a strictly voluntary basis; the task of the chief of the Ker Kwaro and the Council of Elders, for that matter, is to ensure that the confession has not been pressured or coerced. Because of the trust placed in his authority to judge the motives and guilt of perpetrators, the Ker Kwaro institution enjoys a high level of standing. The legitimate authority of the institution enables the chief to serve as the caretaker of local custom.

An important feature of the chief's legitimacy, then, is his extensive knowledge of local custom and law. The chief plays an active role in the ceremony-when

[7] Erin K. Baines, "The Haunting of Alice: Local Approaches to Justice and Reconciliation in Northern Uganda," *The International Journal of Transitional Justice*, Vol. 1(2007): 91-114; *See also* Ketyy Anyeko Erin Baines, Emon Komakech, Boniface Ojok, Lino Owor Ogora and Letha Victor, 'The Cooling of the Hearts': Community Truth-Telling in Northern Uganda, *Human Rights Review* 10 (2011).

[8] *See supra* note 1 at 10.

both sides are required to drink the bitter root. In fact, he is responsible for intervening in the ceremony, often improvising the acts and movements (of rooting out resentment and vengeance). These movements can, in some cases, take on an elaborate and unique structure. As one person explains of a ceremony he observed: "Both clans eat the exchanged food separately, and after (they finish) both start approaching the other holding sticks as if they want to fight and the Ker Kwaro chief calms them down as they hit the mediators' stick as a barrier preventing them from reaching the other side."[9] As such, the Ker Kwaro offers timely and creative intervention in the *mato oput* ceremony and is intended to spontaneously enhance the symbolic power of the rituals. Other traditional forms of local justice place less emphasis on intervention to achieve the desired effect of reconciliation. For instance, *gomo tong* (or "the bending of the spears"), another longstanding inter-tribal procedure in the Acholi region, signifies the symbolic power of mutually moving beyond hostilities. Here both sides place their bent spears beside the fire to express their shared commitment to peace. But *gomo tong*, which is rarely, if ever used, is not considered compatible with *mato oput*.

Mato oput also varies in its application from clan to clan. Some of the ceremonies, for instance, are conducted in an open forum in public display for all the affected tribes; others take place at private residences. As one report describes it:

> There are some strange mato oput styles in Palogar sub-county. They do the mato oput at the home of the victim, do not use Kwete or oput herb. All they do is prepare a kind of sorghum grain called Lawera. Its husk is removed, and the grain ground to flour, and it's that flour that the mediator with his finger scoops and puts in the mouth of every one at the ceremony of reconciliation, and the husk is sniffed by everyone.[10]

These variations of ritual acts stem in part from the diversity of the clans of the Acholi tribe in the northern region of Uganda (there are about four or five different tribes in Northern Uganda and about fifty in all of Uganda). The issue that such diversity raises for studying the adaptation of *mato oput* is whether the resources exist for expanding its application (to address the numerous casualties of the civil war). It is here where the role of the Ugandan government figures to make an important difference by providing the additional compensation needed to conduct the rituals on a mass scale. Thus, like *gacaca* (traditional) justice in Rwanda, *mato oput*'s revival as an alternative procedure stresses an important objective: that the national government must assume some responsibility for implementing a local approach to justice and reconciliation.[11] This also means that it should use

9) *Mato Oput* Project (2009). Available at http://www.ctafrica.org/default.asp?contentID=581, p. 15.

10) *Ibid.* p 4.

11) *Gacaca*, it should be noted, has also raised concern regarding state power, in particular the tacit practice of victors' justice in which the Rwandan government has held accountable only

its authority to ensure that a local procedure of justice is not unduly imposed on other groups espousing different beliefs. Some Evangelical Christian groups living in the area, for instance, do not accept *mato oput*, considering it in some cases, as a form of devil worship.[12]

The question that arises, then, is whether the adaptation of *mato oput* will unduly compromise the integrity of existing, context-specific *mato oput* ceremonies? Will its adaptation ensure that it does not unduly conflict with the implementation of other judicial mechanisms? Much of this will depend on the capacity of other judicial mechanisms to accommodate the social context of local justice and to confront concerns of the imposition of international justice. As the anthropologist Sverker Finnstrom points out, "the preference for traditional justice should reflect a greater understanding of the social contexts and acts, and not simply the concepts of forgiveness and reconciliation that Westerners and Christian groups like to invoke."[13] If this is true, then scholars and policymakers will not only need to further assess the role of the national government in mediating these differences, but they will also need to further understand the appropriate, complementary application of international restorative mechanisms.

1.1. *Challenges and Prospects of* Mato Oput: *National Trials and Local Custom*

Critics of *mato oput*'s revival claim that the mass application of *mato oput* will only undermine or compromise its traditional, localized application. As the proponents of this project of *mato oput* revival put it:

> For most, the adaptive ideas of assistance with compensation and promoting reconciliation through a mass mato oput ceremony lie beneath the threshold of change that is acceptable for pragmatic purposes of applying mato oput to conflict.[14]

The change needed in this sense is a willingness to confront the sheer brutality of the ongoing civil war that has engendered deep–seated grievances among the local population. The length and brutality of the war has led to the reluctance to forgive the LRA leaders. Indeed, nearly sixty-six per cent of the victims in Northern

---

the Hutu perpetrators of genocide, immunizing Tutsi military personnel from prosecution. See Timothy Longman, "An Assessment of Rwanda's Gacaca Court," *Peace Review* 21(2011): 304.

12) Note that many Christian groups remain open to and accepting of *mato oput*. *See supra* note 9 at 107.

13) Swerker Finnstrom, "Reconciliation Grown Bitter? War, Retribution, and Ritual Action in Northern Uganda," in Rosalind Shaw, Waldorf, Lars and Pierre Hazan (eds) *Localizing Transitional Justice: Interventions and Priorities After Mass Violence* (Palo Alto, CA: Stanford University Press, 2010), p. 137. On the issue of religious tension see Joanna Quinn, "The Thing Behind the Thing: Christian Responses to Traditional Practices of Acknowledgement in Uganda," *Review of Faith and International Affairs* 8(1)(2010): 3-12.

14) *See supra* note 10 at 28.

Uganda have indicated that they would prefer punishment or retribution for the worst perpetrators; only twenty-two percent preferred a traditional or non-punitive option.[15] Such support for retribution suggests that there may be a limit to how much the local people are willing to forgive (or to rely on *mato oput* to promote reconciliation). Local justice, as Martha Minow suggests in a broader context of transitional justice, is "a method of response that is institutional and inherently political."[16] Minow goes on to state that "such reconciliation would assist stability and democracy, but it also would require other measures: restoring dignity to victims would be part of this process, but so would dealing respectively with those who assisted or were complicit with the violence. Otherwise, new rifts and resentments are likely to emerge and grow."[17]

But recognizing victims' and defendants' rights requires not only the legal and political resources to compensate and offer social assistance to victims: it also entails legal mechanisms that prioritize the needs of the individual, including one's privacy. As we shall see, there is a limit to formal trials and formal mechanisms of victim redress; for rather than emphasizing communal values or healing, they tend to focus on the individual, or what we may call personal closure. But closure can be every bit as vague as reconciliation. It is not clear, for instance, how or when closure takes place, or why trials, for that matter - which provide evidence of guilt or innocence - allow victims to put the events behind them. Affected family members may experience closure, but remain vengeful. Formal mechanisms of restorative justice can actually isolate the individual from the rest of community by compensating only those affected by the perpetrator on trial. In this way, such mechanisms remain consistent with their punitive counterparts, such as trials and sentences, which seek to isolate the guilt of the community as a means of promoting communal healing. But the isolation of guilt, in this case, remains tenuously linked to such healing, and in fact, some might argue that it does little to eliminate the (source of the) grievances and hatred.

Mato oput, as we have seen, is predicated on a very different, albeit challenging premise: that respecting the dignity of individual victims is a collective, shared process that entails mutual forgiveness by the perpetrator, victim's family, and community. It requires these parties to participate equally in the healing process via tribal ceremonies. Personal closure, in this sense, needs to be distinguished from the communal (and inter-communal) reconciliation involving informal mediation by the chief of Ker Kwaro. As already indicated, without forgiveness,

---

15) Kai Ambos, Judith Large and Marieke Wierda (eds.), *Building a Future on Peace and Justice: Studies on Transitional Justice, Peace and Development* (The Hague: Springer, 2009) p. 268.

16) See Martha Minow, *Between Vengeance and Forgiveness* (Boston, MA: Beacon Press, 2007), p. 22. On this point, see also Ruti Teitel's normative analysis of the false dichotomy between universalism and particularism. Ruti Teitel, *Transitional Justice* (Oxford: Oxford University Press, 1999).

17) *Ibid.*, p. 23.

the voluntary admission of guilt means very little: *mato oput* can only proceed when such admission is followed by the affected family members and the victim's willingness to forgive. In effect, *mato oput* requires that forgiveness not be "commanded." As the Justice and Reconciliation Project notes:

> forgiveness comes before mato oput. Mato oput is a ceremony that marks an end to every kind of anger that exists among the affected people. For the sake of this war, I think you should forgive so that the abducted children come home.[18]

But getting the perpetrators of such unprecedented violence to voluntarily confess will not be an easy task. Again, many fighters remain fearful of reprisal by the LRA, should they voluntarily confess. Because the LRA forcibly conscripted and kidnapped children, many of the recruits were forcibly separated from their families and communities and hardened by the effects of war. Local supporters of *mato oput* point to this fact to demonstrate that communal or ceremonial justice may be the best way to reintegrate the community. In their view, the ICC's indictments and its intolerance of Uganda's 1999 amnesty law - which was designed to end the violence by allowing LRA fighters to confess in exchange for immunity- have exacerbated tensions by obstructing the national government's efforts to prosecute the LRA leaders (and by extension, discouraging young conscripted fighters to disarm and voluntarily confess).[19] Critics of the ICC's indictment, as we have seen, argue that the indictments have hindered the broad application of *mato oput*, by discouraging people from speaking out against amnesty, and by allowing the heightened threat of reprisal to prevail (by allowing Joseph Kony and his three commanders to remain at large). Perhaps even more important, it remains unclear if the returning fighters or perpetrators will have the resources to adequately compensate the victors.

Given these concerns, *mato oput* supporters will have to rely on the government for broad support/funding, even though the government may not be willing to accept responsibility for crimes that they believe have been committed by the LRA.[20] But for some, this remains a justifiable trade-off for ending the war and allowing the government the opportunity to assume a constructive role in

---

[18] *See supra* note 1, at 9.

[19] *Ibid.* pp. 10 and 12. Despite these concerns, some fighters have signalled their willingness to follow the path of *mato oput*. Two LRA fighters, for example, Sunday Otto and Richard Odong, surrendered to the government in exchange for (conditional) amnesty. And although the Ugandan government has yet to act on their requests for conditional amnesty, the two have confessed their guilt and requested to be tried under *mato oput* in order to begin rebuilding their lives. It should be stressed that *mato oput* offers the substantive hope that these fighters will confess and seek to reunite with their community, thereby redressing the deep-seated grievances that can perpetuate and erupt into new violence.

[20] Note that the Ugandan government has signalled some willingness to compensate, though it has not yet specified how it would compensate the victims under the peace accords.

mediating the conflict and future national healing. As David Lumedo, a scholar of *mato oput*, points out:

> There are two warring parties led by Yoweri Museveni and Kony. The two have killed in both ways. However the government is like a father and Kony is like a child of that father who has become rebellious. So anything that a child has committed is the responsibility of the father.[21]

Still, the government's responsibility remains a contentious issue, especially given its past record of violence. Many still perceive the government as corrupt and unable to utilize its scarce resources to strike an effective balance between punitive and non-punitive mechanisms. Under the Juba Peace Agreements (2006-2008), for instance, the Ugandan government established its International Crimes Division (ICD) of the High Court of Uganda in order to try the worst perpetrators for war crimes. In all, the agreements sought to deal with the relation between ICC proceedings, national criminal proceedings and traditional processes in a rather ambitious manner. The aim of establishing this national war crimes court was to provide an alternative punitive mechanism to the ICC, so that the national government could encourage the LRA commanders to surrender and/or to voluntarily put down their arms. But the Juba Peace Accords eventually broke down in 2008, primarily because of the LRA leaders' refusal to take part in the 2008 round of peace talks. The decision was based largely on the threat posed by the ICC's indictments of the LRA commanders and the ICC Chief Prosecutor's refusal to drop the indictments.

Nonetheless, if there is a silver lining to this cloud of uncertain accountability, it's that the failed talks produced the growing realization that a comprehensive, multilayered model of justice will be needed to address the deep-seated effects of the civil war. The recent report issued by the Justice and Reconciliation Project reflects the growing consensus surrounding this idea:

> ...the majority felt that the senior LRA commanders could not adequately be adjudicated by transitional justice processes, mainly because of their strategic role in creating and sustaining the conflict....traditional justice processes require a face-to-face interaction between perpetrators and victims and their communities, and this provision may not be sustainable in the case of senior LRA or government commanders whose victims would identify directly with their suffering. In supporting traditional justice, the government believes that a modular form of traditional justice application can offer redress to war crimes.[22]

But this declaration raises an important question: Can *mato oput* be adapted to systems and mechanisms that prosecute the elements of war crimes, such as

---

21) Ultimate Media Consult, Acholi Want More Prominent Role for Mato Oput," *UG Pulse*, 9 December 2008, p. 6.

22) *See supra* note 1, at 6.

gender crimes? The national government can of course remedy this uncertainty by holding trials for the more serious offenses. But trials can also be expensive. And it is not certain if national trials will meet the legitimacy standards (impartiality) of the ICC. Again, the national government's involvement in the civil war has made many weary of its integrity and legitimacy. Note that prior to these peace efforts and the government's attempts to sponsor *mato oput*, Yoweri Museveni, the President of Uganda, recently established the Commission of Inquiry of Human Rights Abuses to investigate the past abuses from 1962-1986. The scope of the commission applied to all atrocities committed during the prior regime. However, in restricting the purview of the investigation to only these years, Museveni also sought to prevent investigation of the actions of his own government.[23] Like other weak truth commissions, such as Guatemala, the Uganda truth commission mandate lacked strong legal powers, like the subpoena.[24] Joanna Quinn notes that "… the public at large, which had for so long been disenfranchised, seemed reluctant to talk about what happened and sensed that their participation in the work of the commissions could lead to renewed retribution."[25] If this is true, then a truth commission may prove much less desirable than *mato oput* in complementing the punitive and, as I have argued, non-punitive mechanisms of the ICC. At the very least, it suggests that the legitimacy of localized justice holds greater promise than state justice in initiating and driving the formation and sustainability of a multilayered project of justice.

Summing up: the principal challenge facing the broader adaptation of *mato oput* is the effective reconciliation of punitive and non-punitive justice. Legally and practically, this challenge raises the issue of how *mato oput* will properly complement the ICC and national mechanisms of punitive justice.[26] To be sure, there are considerable disparities between these mechanisms, which remain both politically and socially divisive. But as I have argued, it is also the attention paid to these disparities that has detracted from another important challenge: namely, that reconciling the ICC's measures of corrective justice with *mato oput*'s corrective procedures (that occur at the beginning of reconciliation) might very well reflect an evolving component of a multilayered justice approach.

23) *See supra* note 13, at 138 and 139; see also Joanna Quinn, "What of Reconciliation? Traditional Mechanisms of Acknowledgment in Uganda," in Joanna R. Quinn (ed), *Reconciliation(s): Transitional Justice in Postconflict Societies* (Montreal: McGill's University Press, 2009), pp. 185-187.

24) For an excellent discussion of the commission between the Guatemalan commission and the South African Truth and Reconciliation Commission, see Jonathan Tepperman, "Truth and Consequences," *Foreign Affairs* 81(2) (March/April 2002).

25) *See supra* note 23, at 185.

26) For a detailed discussion of this topic, see Kai Ambos, "The Legal Framework of Transitional Justice: A Systematic Study with Special focus on the Role of the ICC," in Ambos, et al., *supra* note 15.

2. Between Local and International Justice: The ICC's Victims' Trust Fund and Outreach

In the 2007 Office of the Prosecutor (OTP) report, the Chief Prosecutor stated the ICC's willingness to accommodate local, alternative forms of justice under its complementarity principle.[27] The report, however, did not specify any of the conditions or criteria for accommodation.[28] Rather, it stressed the distinction between positive and negative complementarity, in particular how positive complementarity involves the normative aspects of assistance, dialogue and restorative justice, while negative complementarity refers to retribution. The distinction has attracted considerable scholarly attention of the normative features of administering justice.[29] My aim in this section is not to assess the specific details to the complementarity principle, but to examine how these above features of positive complementarity provide the practical basis for explaining the ties between the ICC's restorative mechanisms and *mato oput*. In particular, I shall demonstrate how the victims and outreach units can be linked in a positive, complementary manner to *mato oput*'s informal way of administering justice.[30]

Nonetheless, what is promising of this contextual link is that the victims' unit mandate of the ICC goes well beyond its predecessors, the international criminal tribunals, especially in terms of incorporating several of the recommendations of the General Assembly Resolution (1985), such as the right to fair treatment, the right to restitution, and the right to medical, psychological and social assistance. But the mandate also raises the issue of how the ICC should proceed in raising awareness of this constructive link between the ICC's formal approach to victims' rights and compensation and the informal methods of *mato oput* mentioned earlier. This is one reason, as we shall see, why outreach becomes an important

---

27) The complementarity principle requires the ICC to defer *prima facie* to states, but to administer justice, if the territorial state proves unable and unwilling to investigate and prosecute in a genuine manner.

28) See Alexander Greenawalt, "Complementarity in Crisis", *Virginia Journal of International Law*, 50(1)(2009): 131-134. In the 2009 Office of the Prosecutor (OTP) report, for example, Moreno-Ocampo stated that the ICC's complementarity principle "does not exclude alternative forms of justice."

29) *See e.g.* Mohamed El Zeidy, *The Principle of Complementarity in International Criminal Law: Origins, Development, and Practice* (The Hague: Brill Publishers, 2008); Jan Kleffner, "The Impact of Complementarity on National Implementation of Substantive International Criminal Law," *Journal of International Criminal Justice*, 1(1)(2003); Carsten Stahn, "Complementarity: A Tale of Two Notions," *Criminal Law Forum* 19 (2008): 87-113.

30) See Markus T. Funk, *Victims Rights and Advocacy at the International Criminal Court* (Cambridge: Cambridge University Press, 2009). It is important, as already noted, that we not overstate the results of the developing link between these legal mechanisms. After all, the victims' program and outreach are nascent features of the ICC. As such, the practical link between the ICC restorative mechanism and traditional justice mechanism needs to be addressed on a case-by-case basis.

resource for reconciling these two differing modes of victims' justice; for it helps to facilitate the ties among NGOs, civil society groups, and local peoples by raising awareness of the ICC's legal process.

2.1. *Victims' Trust Fund*

Unlike the ICC's Victim's Unit, which is part of the Court itself, the victims' Trust Fund is a body with a separate legal personality. The fund has two mandates: (1) reparations in which the Court orders the perpetrators to pay for reparations; (2) and general assistance, which consists of voluntary contributions from donors to offer material support and physical rehabilitation for victims and families in the ICC situations.[31] Recently, the Netherlands donated 250,000 euros to the Trust Fund to help, as Dr Uri Rosenthal, the Netherlands Minister of Foreign Affairs, states, "to positively contribute to the lives and dignity of victims within the jurisdiction of the ICC."[32] Under the first mandate, the Court determines how much and to whom should be paid pursuant to Article 75 (1) of the Rome Statute, which states that "ICC authorities either upon request or on its own motion, in exceptional circumstances, shall determine the scope and extent of the damage, loss and injury to, or in respect of, victims, and will state the principles on which it is acting." The victims, it should be noted, cannot initiate the proceedings or recommend amounts to be paid.[33] Only the Court can initiate such proceedings, or in this case, determine how and when the victims will receive information and monetary compensation.

But the past record of international criminal tribunals suggests that the Rome Statute's provisions for compensation may be difficult to enforce. As William Schabas states of the practical difficulties:

> The concept of international compensation is seductive, but it is not without many practical obstacles. Experience of the ad hoc tribunals suggests that by and large most defendants succeed in claiming indigence. ...The irony is that these people are the very people who are widely believed to have looted the countries where they once ruled. It may simply be unrealistic to expect the new Court to be able to locate and seize substantial assets of its prisoners."[34]

---

31) *See, e.g.*, "Kisumu: Registry and the common Legal Representative for Victims Consults with Victims." ICC-CPI-20110921-PR724(2011).

32) International Criminal Court, "The Netherlands contributes 250,000 euros to the Trust Fund for Victims." ICC-TFV-20110824-PR713.

33) Article 79 of the Rome Statute provides several conditions for deciding amounts. These include: "The Court may order money and other property collected through fines or forfeitures to be transferred, by order of the Court, to the Trust Fund; the Trust Fund shall be managed according to criteria to be determined by the Assembly of States Parties."

34) William A. Schabas, *An Introduction to the International Criminal Court*. Third edition (Cambridge: Cambridge University Press), p. 338.

As Schabas suggests, enforcing the ICC's demands on reparations will require well-coordinated action among investigative units and states. But even if it fails to enforce reparations, the ICC and its supporters will continue to actively raise more funds under the TFV's mandate to compensate for any inadequate assets from the perpetrators. According to Elisabeth Rehn, a Trust Fund Board Member, donor contributions "will enable the TFV Board to complement reparations awarded in case a convicted perpetrator has insufficient resources to pay indirectly for reparations."[35] It might also allow the Court to complement reparations to non-retrievable assets of perpetrators. What this suggests is the following: that as more states join the Court - and the ICC receives more support from NGOs and other actors - the Fund will also become larger, helping to further offset the effects of non-retrievable assets.

Nonetheless, the determination of the amount of compensation will depend on the circumstances of each trial. This raises a curious implication: how *mato oput*'s communal basis of redress will reduce the need for or complement the compensation of victims under the ICC. Will, in other words, *mato oput* diminish the need for social and economic assistance and even monetary compensation if the ceremonies produce the desired effect of reintegration? Moreover, can some of the money awarded by the ICC also go towards the compensation needed to implement *mato oput*? Answers to these questions will depend on the decision-making power of the Elders and the willingness of ICC-compensated victims. Still, it is unlikely that any of the victims will use their monetary compensation received from the ICC to defray the costs of ceremonies, since the Ugandan government is already expected to defray most of the costs. Besides, it may be several years before the ICC can complete the trials to award the victims with monetary compensation.

On the other hand, if the ICC can eventually hold and complete the trials of the LRA commanders, then specialized social and psychological assistance/treatment and witness protection may help the victims to rebuild their lives or homes, thereby contributing to the healing process in the region and the nation. To recall, compensation under *mato oput* provides the chief of the Ker Kwaro with the resources (sacrificed animals) to conduct and mediate the ceremony; it does not address the material well-being of the person or individual. In this case, compensation enacts the symbolic process of healing. With the TFV, however, compensation will be based on lost income/wages and the emotional distress caused by the trauma (medical costs, for instance). This difference between individual versus societal need echoes the longstanding debate over the effectiveness of the South African Truth and Reconciliation's plan for monetary compensation: namely, whether reparations should be devoted to social communal reconstruction and/or development, or go directly to the individuals affected by the political violence.

---

35) *See supra* note 31.

In the context of Uganda, many fear that personal compensation will further divide the people; while others claim that corruption and bureaucratic concerns will interfere in societal rebuilding.[36] Whether or not personalized or collective assistance is the proper path, some have claimed that the efforts at bringing legal accountability to the Acholi region have focused too narrowly on corrective justice rather than more broadly on social justice or social and economic development.[37] While this may be true, the rule of law also remains an important precondition for promoting and maintaining social and economic development, and for helping to reduce the political tensions caused by ICC intervention, or the conflict between traditional and international judicial mechanisms. I am not arguing that ICC intervention should either be limited or provisionally restricted during civil wars, but rather that an effective multilayered justice system can help to reduce the political tensions associated with foreign legal intervention by reconciling the legal discontinuities of local and international justice models.[38]

One of these discontinuities, as we have seen, involves the private and public (communal) priority of the TFV and *mato oput*. Victims' (rights) privacy, because it is not addressed by *mato oput*, offers an important and specialized form of redress. This is especially true where the state government fails to uphold the privacy and/or protection of individual witnesses. For instance, the ICC's and civil society groups' recent consultation with the victims of the Kenyan situation suggests that most would prefer to have their identities concealed from public. In this case, nearly all the victims consulted, wished to have their identities concealed from the public.[39] Their reason for insisting on this was that the lingering tensions in the affected areas of violence still constituted a threat to their personal security. The TFV's involvement in Uganda is likely to turn on this issue of promoting the privacy of individual victims. But because Kony and his three commanders have yet to be apprehended and surrendered to The Hague, no one quite knows just when the victims in this case will be able to participate in the proceedings, or when they will be compensated.[40]

---

36) Cecily Rose, "Looking beyond Amnesty and Traditional Justice and Reconciliation Mechanisms in Northern Uganda: A Proposal for Truth-telling and Reparations," *Boston College Third World Law Journal* 28(2): 546 and 547.

37) *See supra* note 3, at 193.

38) *Cf* Branch, *supra* note 3, at 194.

39) "International Criminal Court, "Trust Fund for Victims Launches Programme in the Central African Republic." ICC-TFV-20110616-PR6852011.

40) It should be noted that the ICC though is unlikely to drop its indictments not only because it needs to uphold its mission of promoting the global rule of law, but also because the national war crimes court alternative would deprive many victims of their formal judicial rights. The Ugandan national court, in other words, would lack the resources and capacity to provide comparable (if any) assistance to victims. Local peoples would have to depend on *mato oput* for redress, even though supporters of *mato oput* have already signalled their acceptance of the ICC's special role of trying the very worst perpetrators.

Nevertheless, the ICC's integrated and separate mechanisms of corrective/ victims justice will address an important limit of *mato oput*: the redress of the most severely traumatized victims. In addition to the distinct body of the TFV, the Office of Public Counsel for Victims (OPCV) represents a promising mechanism of its victims' unit. The OPCV, it should be stressed, remains the first global office of its kind in international criminal law. As Article 16(1)(b)(c) provides, it is designed "to assist victims in obtaining legal advice and organizing their legal representation, providing their legal representation with adequate support assistance and information, and to ensure the effective participation of victims in proceedings before the Court." Such advanced legal representation will require effective participation in the legal process and help to raise the awareness of the participatory victims' legal options for redress. As such, additional security measures, such as witness protection (as mentioned above), will not be inconsequential to *mato oput*, since they will help to redress the fear of reprisal by LRA commanders.[41]

Such mechanisms would also address another practical limit of *mato oput*, namely, gender crimes. Although the *mato oput* project states that *mato oput* can be re-adapted to address this crime, it remains unclear if *mato oput* can effectively stipulate the conditions for such specialized redress. Given the mass scale of rape, the ICC's progressive list of specified elements of sexual crimes would certainly address this open-ended concern. However, critics of this novel list of sexual crimes argue that its specificity or "naming of harms" can lead to omissions that allow some crime or harm to go unrecognized.[42] Some have even pointed out, as we saw earlier, that the threat of such harm detracts from the impact of severe poverty or structural violence; that the political and legal controversy surrounding the compatibility of punitive and non-punitive justice also involves accommodating and promoting the social context of local justice and exposing the gap between a formal system and an informal one at the local level.[43] However, as I have argued, this political question has less to do with the politics of ICC intervention than with the lack of attention paid to how the ICC's restorative measures should be properly reconciled with *mato oput*. We still need, in other words, to explain why the rule of law, via a multilayered system for justice, constitutes an important precondition of further social integration and development.

---

41) Article 17(2) i-v) of the Rome Statute stipulates "Adequate protective and security measures and formulating long- and short term plans for their protection; assisting them in obtaining medical, psychological and other appropriate assistance; making available to the Court and the parties training in issues of trauma, sexual violence, security, and confidentiality; and recommending, in consultation with the Office of the Prosecutor, the elaboration of a code of conduct, emphasizing the vital nature of security and confidentiality."

42) *See supra* note 2.

43) See Elizabeth Stanley, "Transitional Justice: From the Local to the International", in Patrick Hayden (ed), *The Ashgate Research Companion to Ethics and International Relations* (Aldershot: Ashgate, 2009), pp. 275-292.

In sum, the ICC's formal approach to victims' participation appears to address two important limits to *mato oput*: (1) the very worst perpetrators cannot be forgiven, and (2) the existent lack of any specialized assistance for the victims regarding compensation. Victims of the violence not only need special protection, but also the legal resources to receive adequate legal representation. As such, much of the ICC's efficacy in this respect would be contingent on its collaboration with NGOs and non-state actors. This is why we also need to consider the ICC's outreach unit, and how, as a mechanism of raising awareness, it might help to further mediate local and international justice and reduce the uncertainty surrounding the consequences of the ICC's punitive and non-punitive role.

2.2. *Outreach*

Outreach refers to a mechanism of transitional justice designed to raise local awareness of the activities of an organization. Both the ICTY and ICTR implemented outreach programs in the former areas of Yugoslavia and Rwanda respectively.[44] The success of these programs encouraged ICC officials to develop a more sweeping program, one that would reach out to local civilian populations. At the Fifth Session of Assembly States Parties (2005), ICC officials agreed to adopt a strategic plan for reaching out to the local population. The plan was ambitious in design. For not only did it seek to promote the rule of law and greater accountability, but it also sought to further peace and reconciliation. As Patrick Vinck and Phuong Pham put it: "outreach was designed to demonstrate that judicial arbitrariness is no longer an acceptable mechanism."[45] As such, the outreach unit constitutes a network of ICC officials, lawyers (legal practitioners), activists, media personnel, civil society groups, and local communal groups. Its procedural aims are: (1) to offer accurate and comprehensive information to affected (general) communities regarding its role, (2) to provide further participation of the local communities in the activities of the Court, (3) and to offer access to and understand prosecutorial proceedings among affected communities.

The ICC has sought to reach out to the civilian populations in a number of ways, including showing coverage of trials and hearings, holding workshops, setting up radio talk shows and informational meetings, and conducting surveys of the ICC's activities. Not only have these particular measures helped to counter

---

44) It should be noted that outreach efforts were implemented at these tribunals, but were never well-developed. Some studies suggest that this contributed to more harm and injustice in the affected regions. For an excellent discussion of these events, see Victor Peskin, *International Justice in Rwanda and the Balkans: Virtual Trials and the Struggle for State Cooperation* (Cambridge: Cambridge University Press, 2008).

45) Patrick Vinck and Phuong N. Pham, "Outreach Evaluation: The International Criminal Court in the Central African Republic," *The International Journal of Transitional Justice* 4 (3) (2010), p. 442.

misinformation by state officials: they have also helped to shape the people's opinions and attitudes toward the ICC, as we shall see. Despite these benefits, critics argue that outreach "comes at the expense of domestic efforts to achieve justice."[46] Still others insist that outreach needs to further "educate the stigma of rape" in the Eastern Congo.[47] However, in the context of Uganda, the outreach unit has begun a more concerted campaign to educate the domestic population on gender, having launched an internet-based Short Message Services (SMS) system to address the topic of gender crimes and the Court's activities. ICC authorities have also established a strong network of gender-based NGOs/CBOs (community-based organizations) and has "held several consultative and bi-lateral meetings with over 89 NGOs" which have reached out to schools and universities.[48] Moreover, the number of people participating in these meetings was estimated at 21,180, considerably more than in the Democratic Republic of Congo (DRC).

Recently, ICC outreach representatives joined two hundred women to celebrate Women's Day in Uganda, providing information to grassroots women participating in the event.[49] *Mato oput* supporters, as we have seen, have continued to stress the issue of gender violence, or the need to incorporate it into the truth telling and elder mediation processes. One way it could do this is to have the tribal Elders consult with ICC officials, NGOs, and communal groups in order to determine how best to express or specify the war crime elements of the perpetrators' (voluntary) guilt. This of course would be a voluntary measure on the part of both the ICC and *mato oput* officials.[50] But the ICC's outreach unit could enhance this area of *mato oput* adaptation by expanding its discussions and workshops to help construct a threshold understanding of the justiciability of these elements.

It is important to stress, then, that such creative, mutual assistance will depend on the continued growth and acceptance of the ICC outreach unit itself. Recent studies suggest that there is a growing base of support for outreach and its role in producing the needed communicative links between global and local officials. In a recent survey conducted by Patrick Vinck and Phuong Pham, awareness about the ICC in Uganda increased from 25 percent to 60 percent in 2007.[51] What this suggests is that outreach's resources can be used to enhance the local population's

---

46) Elaine Baylis, "Reassessing the Role of International Criminal Law: Rebuilding National Court through Transitional Networks," *Boston College Review* 50(1)(2009), p. 52.

47) S. Bartels, D. Scott, D. Leaning, R. L. Mukwege, R. Lipton, and M. Van Rooyen, "Surviving Sexual Violence in Eastern Democratic Congo, *International Journal of Women's Studies*, 11(4) (2010), p. 4.

48) International Criminal Court, *Outreach Report, 2009*. Available at www.icc.org. p. 3.

49) *See* "ICC Outreach Unit joins women in war affected communities in celebrations marking International Women's Day in Uganda. ICC-CPI-20100309-PR504(2011).

50) *See supra* note 1.

51) *See supra* note 43, at 423.

understanding of the legal complications and restrictions of ICC intervention vis-à-vis *mato oput*. But the above survey also indicates a positive correlation between support for the ICC and these figures, suggesting that the ICC's use of the media helped to positively shape the opinion and attitudes of the people. In 2010, outreach initiated dialogue with the local population by establishing radio talk shows that would clarify among other things, the ICC's provision against trying anyone under the age of 18 at the time that the alleged crimes were committed.[52]

Take, for instance, the outreach unit's activities in the DRC. Here the outreach unit has helped to implement new media in Kinshasa (regarding its activities) and set up various seminars and workshops organized in and around Goma. It has advertised its activities on NGO websites, including its announcement and explanation of the arrest of Thomas Lubanga, the first perpetrator to stand trial in The Hague (who has been convicted and sentenced). Moreover, the NGO, RCN-Justice and Democracy has developed training programs on post conflict, which focus on the plight of internally displaced peoples. This and other outreach programs have produced interesting results. In 2007, Vinck and Pham conducted a survey, which found that 27 per cent of the people surveyed in the capital of Kinshasa were aware of the ICC, or at least had some knowledge of it. Compared to the above-mentioned survey conducted in Uganda - which showed that the level of awareness had increased nearly 32 per cent in Uganda (from 28 per cent to 60 percent) - these percentages indicate a relatively small increase from the 2005 levels.[53]

But do these developments reflect the positive perceptions of the ICC (or support) in Northern Uganda and other situations? And how can further information help to mitigate the unruly politics of ICC intervention which remains one of the primary concerns of many for constructing an effective multilayered form of justice? Answers to these questions still remain unclear because of the difficulties of gaining access to particular regions. However, recent research of the Central African Republic (CAR) indicates that ICC outreach has had some positive and transformative impact. Vinck and Pham, for instance, conducted various surveys, which showed that much of the awareness of the ICC in the CAR came primarily from radio and television, and less from its workshops and discussion sessions. Yet the effect has varied along class or socioeconomic group lines, with high levels of awareness coming from well-educated citizens. Their general population survey indicated that 95 per cent of the population found the ICC to be important.[54] In a follow-up questionnaire, nearly 27 per cent of the people believed that the ICC

---

52) See "ICC Outreach Unit Facilitates Children Dialogue in Uganda." ICC-CPI2010.

53) The discrepancy appears to reflect the varying levels of violence in the two countries, as well as the difficulties of reaching more people in the Congo.

54) *See supra* note 43, at 439.

would bring justice. However, on the issue of neutrality, only 10 percent found the ICC not to be neutral. But of the minority holding this opinion of the lack of neutrality, 34 percent attributed the lack of neutrality to the ICC's assisting the national government.

In sum, the outreach unit continues to build broad coalitions and networks of actors that have raised awareness of the ICC's operations and objectives. In the 2009 Outreach Report, for instance, ICC officials recommended, among other things, strengthening the capacity of NGOs and the media, ensuring that the local journalists attending The Hague proceedings offer accurate information of the trial, and conducting more surveys by third parties.[55] Given these recommendations, some continue to insist that outreach needs to be expanded: that it remains primarily focused on the capital cities rather than the country-side.[56] What this suggests is that the state's willingness to help develop a multilayered system of justice will be just as important as the ICC's efforts to enhance understanding of its complex, albeit constructive operations in Northern Uganda.

Conclusion

The ICC's intervention in Northern Uganda has raised concern about the role of international justice. Much of this underscores the ICC's interference in the talks between the Ugandan government and LRA rebel leaders. Such interference has called increasing attention to not only the political tensions between the ICC and national government, but also the ICC and local supporters of *mato oput*. As we have seen, local supporters of *mato oput* insist that international and national forums of punitive justice cannot adequately address the pervasive effects of the thirty-five year civil war, or offer the needed resources to promote forgiveness and prevent vengeance from erupting into violence. But these supporters also realize that *mato oput*, in its current form, must be adapted to or at the very least, reassessed in terms of the legal standards of the international criminal court, including its progressive list of war crimes (gender). This in turn has focused much, if not all the attention on the challenge of reconciling the disparities between punitive and non-punitive mechanisms of international and local justice and integrating the diverse mix of accountability mechanisms.

Accordingly, discussion of adapting *mato oput* to meet the standards of international justice have focused on these disparities between the ICC's punitive mechanisms of justice and *mato oput*'s non-punitive mechanism of reconciliation.

55) See *supra* note 5, at 8.

56) Marlies Glasius, "What Is Global Justice and Who Decides? Civil Society and Victim Responses to the International Criminal Court's First Investigations," *Human Rights Quarterly* 31(2)(2009), p. 519.

Unfortunately this has tended to downplay the important, emerging relationship between the ICC's restorative mechanisms and *mato oput*. The TFV, as we saw, provides various specialized formal measures and/or remedies that can complement *mato oput*'s informal mechanisms of ritual justice/reconciliation. These measures include witness protection and social and economic assistance to the victims who have been severely traumatized by the violence perpetrated by the LRA commanders. Together they raise an important implication for developing an effective multilayered model of justice: namely, that *mato oput* cannot possibly address all cases of human rights abuse, especially the most traumatized victims who would require special protection to cooperate with authorities.

In short, it is important to stress that the *mato oput* project is a complex undertaking and that part of this is due to the difficulty of reconciling punitive and non-punitive mechanisms. However, as I have argued, this difficulty should not detract from the aim of demonstrating how formal and informal mechanisms of restorative justice can mutually complement one another, and how this might diminish the tensions associated with the disparity between the punitive and non-punitive mechanisms. Indeed, it suggests that adapting *mato oput* will in part turn on the limits and potential of these formal resources of restorative justice and that the ICC's outreach unit will play an important role in helping to develop an effective multilayered justice model in Northern Uganda.

Financing the International Criminal Court

Jonathan O'Donohue[1]
Legal Adviser, International Secretariat, Amnesty International, London, UK

Abstract
In its first ten years, the International Criminal Court (ICC) cost approximately EUR 750 million. For this investment, it has conducted investigations in seven situations and commenced proceedings against 29 persons. However, it has only completed one trial and has yet to achieve significant impact in, arguably its most important function, promoting complementarity. With another eight situations under preliminary examination, its workload and budget requests are expected to increase. Some states are questioning its value for money and looking to restrict its expenditure. This paper examines the realities and challenges of financing the ICC. Firstly, it identifies emerging negative attitudes towards the cost of international criminal justice. Secondly, it describes ICC budgetary practice between 2002 and 2012. Thirdly, it considers the principle factors that should drive the ICC's workload and therefore its budget. Finally, it examines proposals to cut costs and their potential impact on the ICC's work.

Keywords
International Criminal Court (ICC); budget; funding

1. Emerging Negative Attitudes towards Funding International Criminal Justice

When the Rome Statute of the International Criminal Court (Rome Statute) was adopted on 17 July 1998, the modern system of international justice was relatively new.[2] The International Criminal Tribunals for the former Yugoslavia (ICTY) and Rwanda (ICTR) were just hitting their stride and their budgets had started to increase rapidly. One of the attractions for states supporting the establishment of a new and permanent ICC would have been that it could respond to impunity in situations where genocide, crimes against humanity and war crimes have been committed promptly and efficiently without the need to establish *ad hoc* mechanisms, including expensive infrastructure and core administration.

By July 2002, when the Rome Statute entered into force and the ICC was established, the mounting costs of the ICTY and ICTR were the subject of frustration

[1] The author has led the Coalition for the International Criminal Court's Budget and Finance Team since 2001.
[2] Rome Statute (1998), 2187 U.N.T.S. 90.

and criticism by states and even some senior United Nations (UN) officials.[3] However, in addition to confidence that the ICC would be a more efficient model for the future, there were two countervailing developments. Firstly, work was underway to develop strategies to improve the efficiency of the ICTY and ICTR and to complete their work. Secondly, an alternative cheaper model to the ICTY and ICTR had been developed. Internationalized criminal courts would sit in the countries where the crimes were committed and would be comprised of national and international staff, at potentially much less expense.[4] There was also the expectation that some internationalized courts would conduct fewer cases than the ICTY and ICTR. For example, the Special Court for Sierra Leone (SCSL) was mandated to investigate "those who bear the greatest responsibility" for crimes against humanity and war crimes committed in the country and was predicted to complete its work within three years at a total of USD 56.2 million, less than half of the original budget prepared by the UN Secretary-General.[5] Unlike the ICTY and ICTR which were funded by the UN's budget, the SCSL would be funded by voluntary contributions, despite concerns raised by the Secretary-General that

---

[3] *See* Dominic Raab, 'Evaluating the ICTY and its Completion Strategy', 3 *Journal of International Criminal Justice* (2005), p. 88: "[i]t was increasingly questioned in the UN General Assembly's Fifth Committee, whether the ICTY (and ICTR) were providing value for money". *See also* Ralph Zacklin, 'The failings of Ad Hoc International Tribunals', 2 *Journal of International Criminal Justice* (2004).

[4] Special Panels for Serious Crimes in East Timor made up of both international and national judges and staff had been established in the Dili District Court in 2000 by the United Nations Transitional Administration in East Timor to prosecute serious criminal offences committed around the 1999 independence referendum. A proposal in 1999 to establish a Kosovo War and Ethnic Crimes Court failed to materialize partly due to financial concerns. Instead, an International Judges and Prosecutors Programme had been established in 2000 as part of the United Nations Mission in Kosovo (*see* Thordis Ingadottir, 'The Financing of Internationalized Criminal Courts and Tribunals', in Cesare P.R. Romano, Jann Kleffner, Andre Nollkaemper, (eds.), *Internationalized Criminal Courts and Tribunals: Sierra Leone, East Timor, Kosovo and Cambodia* (Oxford University Press, Oxford, 2004) p. 271). In July 2002, the Special Court for Sierra Leone had started work. Negotiations were also being conducted between the United Nations and the government of Cambodia that would lead to an Agreement in June 2003 to establish the Extraordinary Chambers in the Court's of Cambodia. Furthermore, in June 2002, the ICTY had recommended that a division composed on national and international judges be created in the State Court of Bosnia and Herzegovina "with specific responsibility for the conduct of cases involving serious violations of international humanitarian law" (*see* ICTY, *Report on the judicial status of the International Criminal Tribunal for the former Yugoslavia and the prospects for referring certain cases to national courts* (S/2002/678)).

[5] *Ibid.*,

> The original budget proposal for the Special Court for Sierra Leone, which was prepared again by the UN Secretary-General with ICTY and ICTR in mind, was $114.6 million (US$30.2 for the first year, and US$84.4 for the following two).When it became clear that voluntary contributions would not even come close to this figure, the budget was scaled down to half of that, or US$56.2 million for the first three years of operation.

"[a] special court based on voluntary contributions would neither be viable nor sustainable".[6] The International Judges and Prosecutors Programme in Kosovo and the Special Panels for Serious Crimes in East Timor would be funded primarily from their respective UN mission budgets.[7]

Ten years later, attitudes to the cost of international justice have changed significantly in response to the actual experiences of the ICTY, ICTR, internationalized criminal courts and (as explained in part 2) the ICC. Although the ICTY and ICTR committed to their completion strategies, neither has met the timeline set out in Security Council Resolution 1503 to "complete all work in 2010".[8] The ICTY now estimates it will complete appeals by 2016.[9] The ICTR reports it can do the same by the end of 2014.[10] The budgets of both Tribunals started to decrease in 2010-2011. However, at the same time, a new Residual Mechanism has been created to continue the longer-term functions of both Tribunals after they close.[11] The first budget request for the Residual Mechanism was USD 50 million.[12]

Moreover, some internationalized criminal courts have in practice taken much longer to conduct their work and are costing much more than expected. The three-year timeline for the SCSL proved to be a gross under-estimate. Ten years later in 2012, it has completed its fourth and final trial at a total cost so far of approximately USD 256 million (more than four times the original estimate). If, as estimated, the appeal is completed approximately six months following the sentencing judgment, the initial judicial workload could be completed before the end of 2012.[13]

A similar prediction that the Extraordinary Chambers in the Courts of Cambodia (ECCC), established in 2006, would complete its work within three years at a cost of USD 56 million funded by voluntary contributions has proved equally unrealistic. At the end of 2011, it had cost over USD 150 million with only one case

[6] *Report of the Secretary-General on the Establishment of a Special Court for Sierra Leone* (S/2000/915), para. 70. *See also* Ingadottir, *ibid.*, pp. 277-281.

[7] Ingadottir, ibid., pp. 276 and 283.

[8] UN Security Council, *Resolution 1503 (2003)* (S/RES/1503 (2003)), para. 7.

[9] ICTY website, 'Completion Strategy', <http://www.icty.org/sid/10016>, 23 August 2012.

[10] ICTR, *Report on the completion strategy of the International Criminal Tribunal for Rwanda* (as of 11 May 2012), (S/2012/349), para. 100.

[11] These include protection of victims and witnesses, supervision of enforcement of sentences of convicted persons, providing assistance to national jurisdictions seeking to investigate and prosecute crimes plus a number of *ad hoc* judicial functions. *See* ICTY website, 'The Mechanism for International Criminal Tribunals', <http://www.icty.org/sid/10874>, 23 August 2012.

[12] Report of the UN Secretary-General, *Budget for the International Residual Mechanism for Criminal Tribunals for the biennium 2012-2013* (A/66/537).

[13] An Agreement to establish a Residual Special Court for Sierra Leone has been reached to continue residual functions after the Special Court completes its last case. However, the budget has yet to be agreed. It will also be funded by voluntary contributions. *See* Geraldine Coughlan, 'Much remains to be done in Sierra Leone', *Radio Netherlands Worldwide*, <www.rnw.nl/international-justice/article/much-remains-be-done-sierra-leone>, 23 August 2012.

completed, a second in progress and major question marks over whether a third or fourth case will proceed. Comparing the costs per case of the SCSL and the ECCC to the ICTY and ICTR, the savings are not that significant.[14]

Furthermore, a lack of voluntary contributions for the SCSL and the ECCC led to delays, serious financial problems and performance issues. The late Professor Antonio Cassesse, the first President of the ICTY, in his independent expert report on the SCSL found:

> The lack of stable funding has plagued the Court. In particular, it has made it very difficult to develop a long term plan. It has also affected recruitment, since most staff are recruited on a "just in time" basis and many potential staff are not interested in joining a court with an insecure future.[15]

The UN General Assembly has been forced to step in to rescue the SCSL from collapse by funding shortfalls in voluntary contributions from its budget for special political missions.[16] In light of these and other problems experienced by the SCSL and the ECCC, the latest trend appears to be favouring an internationalized criminal court model that is more embedded in the national justice system and legacy-focussed based on the perceived success and efficiency of the War Crimes Chamber of the Court of Bosnia and Herzegovina which forms part of the State Court.[17] Established in March 2005, the War Crimes Chamber, which is co-funded by the government of Bosnia and Herzegovina and donor states, has made more progress in conducting investigations and prosecutions with significantly less funds.[18]

---

14) *See* Marieke Wierda and Anthony Triolo, 'Resources', in Luc Reydams, Jan Woutersp and Cedric Ryngaert (eds.), *International Prosecutors* (Oxford University Press, Oxford, 2012) p. 125.

15) *See Report on the Special Court for Sierra Leone, submitted by Independent Expert Antonio Cassese*, 12 December 2006, para. 43, <http://www.sc-sl.org/LinkClick.aspx?fileticket=VTDHyrHasLc=&t%5babid=176>, 23 August 2012. *See also* Patrick Winn, 'Khmer Rouge tribunal nearly broke, risks collapse' *Alaska Dispatch*, 22 August 2012, <http://www.alaskadispatch.com/article/khmer-rouge-tribunal-nearly-broke-risks-collapse>, 28 August 2012.

16) *See* Report of the UN Secretary-General, *Request for a subvention to the Special Court for Sierra Leone* (A/66/563).

17) UN Secretary-General, *The Report of the assessment mission on the establishment of an international judicial commission of inquiry for Burundi* (S/2005/158), paras. 57-60 recommended this model over the SCSL taking into account factors including efficiency and cost-effectiveness.

18) Bogdan Ivanišević, *The War Crimes Chamber in Bosnia and Herzegovina: From Hybrid to Domestic Court* (2008), International Center for Transitional Justice, p. 24:

> The trials at the BWCC are far less costly than those of international tribunals. Between 2002 and 2007 the ICTY cost the international community 124 million euros per year. The average cost of the BWCC and the Special Department in the Prosecutor's Office for 2005 to 2009 has been 13 million euros to date. From 1994 to 2005 the average cost of each first instance ICTY judgment by accused was 15 million euros; at the International Criminal Tribunal for Rwanda (ICTR) it was 26.2 million. At the State Court the average cost was around 955,000 euros in 2006, around 680,000 euros in 2007, and the estimated cost for 2008 is a little less than 400,000 euros.

To date, it has completed more than 60 cases.[19] However, despite the progress in its workload, international judges and prosecutors were unable to hand over fully to the national authorities as planned in 2009.[20] As part of the national justice system, the Chamber has also faced strong domestic political opposition. Verbal attacks by some senior politicians, attempts to reject the jurisdiction of the State Court by the authorities of Republika Srpka and denials that war crimes had been committed have been common. In 2009, the state Parliament rejected the extension of the mandates of international judges and prosecutors and the High Representative of Bosnia and Herzegovina used his special powers to over-rule the decision.[21] The use of similar national justice system models in Kosovo and East Timor also resulted in serious challenges, including lack of resources, which undermined the efforts to address impunity.[22]

Irrespective of the important work being conducted by international and internationalized criminal courts in delivering justice to victims, perceptions have developed over the last ten to 15 years that international criminal justice is expensive, inefficient in terms of the number of cases that can be prosecuted for large sums of money and the costs and timelines are very difficult to predict, more often than not escalating far beyond initial estimates. This has tested the commitment of the international community to international criminal justice and its approach to the fight against impunity. Some states have delayed or refused to pay their assessed contributions, most notably resulting in a recruitment freeze being imposed on the ICTY and ICTR between May 2004 and 1 January 2005.[23] The vast

---

See also Rupert Skilbeck, 'Funding Justice: The Price of War Crimes Trials', <www.wcl.american.edu/hrbrief/15/3skilbeck.pdf>, 23 August 2012.

19) State Court of Bosnia and Herzegovina's website <http://www.sudbih.gov.ba/?jezik=e>, 11 September 2012.

20) *See* Human Rights Watch, *Justice for Atrocity Crimes: Lessons of International Support for Trials before the State Court of Bosnia and Herzegovina*, March 2012, p. 3.

21) *See* Amnesty International, *Annual Report 2009*, pp. 81-82. *See also* Amnesty International, *Whose Justice? The women of Bosnia and Herzegovina are still waiting* (EUR 63/006/2009), pp. 18-28.

22) In 2008, Amnesty International stated that the International Judges and Prosecutors Programme in Kosovo "has largely failed for a variety of reasons, including flaws in its conception and execution, limited resources and the low priority that international justice has been given in comparison to other UNMIK goals". *See Kosovo (Serbia): The challenge to fix a failed UN justice system* (EUR 70/001/2008). The Special Panels for Serious Crimes in East Timor suffered from a serious lack of funding and cooperation and were suspended in 2005 with more than 500 cases outstanding. *See* David Cohen, 'Seeking justice on the cheap: Is the East Timor Tribunal Really a Model for the Future?', 80 *Asia Pacific Issues* (August 2002). *See also* David Cohen, 'Indifference and accountability, the United Nations and the Politics of International Justice in East Timor', 9 *East West Centre Special Reports* (June 2006).

23) ICTY, The *Twelfth annual report of the International Tribunal for the Prosecution of Persons Responsible for Serious Violations of International Humanitarian Law Committed in the Territory of the Former Yugoslavia since 1991* (A/60/267–S/2005/532), para. 2:

majority of states have also decided not to make voluntary contributions to the SCSL and the ECCC. Some measures taken to contain costs have threatened the independence of the institutions.[24]

This situation raises significant challenges for the ICC. There is a risk that the ICC will be viewed as simply a permanent and, therefore, much more expensive version of the ICTY or the ICTR. However, the ICC has a radically different nature and purpose to act only when states fail to investigate and prosecute genuinely genocide, crimes against humanity and war crimes and, even more importantly, to act as a catalyst for states to fulfil their responsibilities by promoting complementarity. Although it is not expected that the ICC will ever be cheap, this unique mandate offers the Court the opportunity to distinguish itself from its predecessors by championing national justice for potentially many more victims and stepping in to investigate and prosecute crimes only when necessary.

2. Funding the International Criminal Court (2002 to 2012)

2.1. *The Budget Process*

Before the ICC started work on 1 July 2002, states parties to the Rome Statute put in place the main budgetary framework whereby the Assembly would consider and decide on the ICC's budget request, in accordance with Article 112 (2) (d). The Financial Regulations and Rules adopted by the Assembly at its first session provided that the Registrar would each year request budget proposals from the Office of the Prosecutor and other heads of organizational units and "elaborate a consolidated draft programme budget" for the ICC.[25] The Rules were carefully worded to ensure the independence of the Prosecutor in the process and not to give the Registrar control over the substance of the Prosecutor's request. To ensure proper oversight of the budget, the Assembly established a Committee on Budget and Finance (Committee) which is made up of 12 "experts of recognized standing in finance matters."[26] The members, who are independent, consider the ICC's budget proposal and make recommendations to the Assembly.[27] The Assembly considers

---

> the Tribunal's own work was greatly affected by the imposition of a hiring freeze by the international community whose interest in the Tribunal's important work was overshadowed by events elsewhere. During the period of the freeze, the Tribunal lost over 10 per cent of its staff, which also led to a decline in staff morale.

See also Ingadottir, supra note 4, pp. 276-277.

24) *See* Wierda and Triolo, *supra* note 14, pp. 157-160.

25) Assembly of States Parties, *Financial Regulations and Rules*, Rule 103.2.

26) Assembly of States Parties, *Establishment of the Committee on Budget and Finance* (ICC-ASP/1/Res.4), Annex, para. 2.

27) Although the independence of the Committee is not expressly stated in the resolution establishing the Committee, the Assembly affirmed the independence of its members at its

the recommendations and makes a final decision on the budget at its annual session.[28] The total approved budget is then apportioned between states parties "in accordance with an agreed scale of assessment, based on the scale adopted by the United Nations for its regular budget".[29] This allocates a percentage of the budget to each state party taking into account its gross national income and other criteria.[30]

An Office of Internal Audit was established at the ICC to ensure internal financial control over financial transactions and administrative systems.[31] In addition, an External Auditor was appointed by the Assembly to audit the ICC annually. It was expressly tasked with making "observations with respect to the efficiency of the financial procedures, the accounting system, the internal financial controls and, in general the administration and management of the Court."[32]

2.2. *Budget Practice in the First Decade*

The first ICC's budget proposals presented a new flexible and scalable institution that would maximise efficiency and economy. The ICC committed itself to developing performance based budgets as opposed to budgets driven by organizational structure.[33] It stated that the ICC would focus on prosecuting "the most important perpetrators" and establishing a "well functioning complementarity regime."[34] This would limit judicial activities and hence the budget of the ICC.[35] Despite its strong commitment to complementarity, in practice the ICC focussed both its activities and budget requests primarily on its own investigations and prosecutions. Little was allocated to take measures promoting national justice.[36] A draft

---

second session. *See* Assembly of States Parties, *Strengthening the International Criminal Court and the Assembly of States Parties* (ICC/ASP/2/Res.7), para. 12.

28) Financial Regulations and Rules, Regulation 3.5.

29) Rome Statute, Article 117.

30) *See* UN Committee on Contributions web page <http://www.un.org/en/ga/contributions/budget.shtml>, 10 August 2012. The current minimum percentage is 0.001 per cent and the maximum is 22 per cent.

31) Financial Regulations and Rules, Rule 110.1.

32) Financial Regulations and Rules, Regulation 12.3.

33) ICC, *Draft programme budget for 2004 prepared by the Registrar* (ICC-ASP/2/2), para. 8.

34) *Ibid.*, paras. 15 and 18.

35) *Ibid.*, paras. 15-17.

36) Although the proposed budget for 2005 established a Jurisdiction, Complementarity and Cooperation Division (JCCD) in the Office of the Prosecutor which was tasked with dealing with the "complementarity regime", the Division was designed to focus primarily on analysing situations to determine whether the ICC had jurisdiction and to promote cooperation rather than pressing states to fulfil their responsibilities (*see* ICC, *Draft Programme Budget for 2005 prepared by the Registrar* (ICC-ASP/3/2), paras. 44-47 and 216-232). The only mention of the latter mandate was a weak commitment that the Jurisdiction and International Cooperation Section of JCCD "implements OTP policy with respect to complementarity, both by building tools to assess genuine national proceedings and by working within the limits of available resources to encourage genuine national proceedings where possible" (para. 228).

Policy Paper on Preliminary Examinations issued by the Office of the Prosecutor in 2010 affirmed that the ICC "will seek to encourage where feasible genuine national investigations and prosecutions by State(s) concerned and to cooperate with and provide assistance to such State(s)".[37] However, it indicated that such efforts would be taken only in relation to "those who appear to bear the greatest responsibility for the most serious cases", i.e. only cases which the ICC would prosecute.[38]

The Committee reviewed the annual budgets proposed by the ICC and made recommendations to the Assembly – almost exclusively for cuts. Some of the initial recommendations were criticized for micro-managing the work of the ICC by questioning the strategic decisions of the senior officials of the ICC.[39] Other recommendations risked undermining the independence of the Prosecutor. For example, the Committee recommended that the resources for a third investigation team requested to start in November 2004 should not be approved and deferred until 2005.[40]

Initially, the ICC was generally accepting of the Committee's recommendations. It opposed some of the recommendations during the Assembly, but mostly it was willing to accept cuts on the condition that it would be allowed flexibility in deciding on how to absorb them.[41] The Assembly's Working Group on the Programme Budget which was coordinated by different chairs each year took different approaches to considering the Committee's recommendations. Some chairs and states clearly viewed the process as a formality to rubber-stamp the Committee's recommendations and sought to limit consideration of the recommendations. Others considered that the Assembly was obliged, at a minimum, to review the recommendations (particularly those that were controversial) and their potential consequences for the ICC's work.[42] In addition, almost unprecedented in any other international institution, non-governmental organizations (NGOs) actively followed each budget process. The Coalition for the International Criminal Court's

---

37) ICC Office of the Prosecutor, *Draft Policy Paper on Preliminary Examinations*, 4 October 2010, para. 94.

38) *Ibid.*, para. 17.

39) *See for example* Coalition for the ICC's Budget and Finance Team, *Submission to the Third Meeting of the Assembly of States Parties*, 26 august 2004, paras. 31-35, <http://www.iccnow.org/documents/CICCBudgetTeam_CommentsCBFreport26Aug04.pdf>, 15 August 2012.

40) Committee on Budget and Finance, *Report of the Committee on Budget and Finance* (ICC-ASP/2/7), para. 37.

41) For example, in her statement to the seventh session of the Assembly, the Registrar stated: "[s]o long as the Court retains sufficient flexibility to adjust its allocation of resources where necessary, the Court believes that it will be able to meet its needs within the limits of the Committee's recommendations". *Statement by Silvana Arbia, Registrar of the ICC*, 17 November 2008.

42) *See* Amnesty International, *International Criminal Court: Recommendations for developing an effective budget process* (IOR 40/008/2007), p. 12 <http://www.amnesty.org/en/library/info/IOR40/008/2007>, 14 September 2012.

Budget and Finance Team analysed the ICC's budget proposal each year and made submissions to the Committee.[43] It then reviewed the Committee's recommendations and lobbied the Assembly on whether or not to adopt them.

2.2.1. *Over-Budgeting and Under-Spending*

The ICC faced significant challenges in developing its budget requests because, in order to submit a proposal for approval to the Committee and the Assembly, it had to start the preparation process in January of the year before the budget started. In essence, the ICC had to predict how many investigations would be launched, whether suspects would be arrested, whether trials would begin and what stage they would reach. This was an almost impossible task for the new institution and resulted in overly ambitious and inaccurate assumptions. For example, in the 2005 budget request, the Office of the Prosecutor stated that it planned to conduct one full trial and begin a second even though no one had actually been arrested and surrendered to the ICC.[44] The first trial did not start until 2006 and took six years to complete.

At its first session, the Committee recognized that costs estimated for 2004 "in many cases were unlikely to be realistic, since likely expenditure needs were unforeseeable".[45] It expressed concern about the possibility of over-budgeting and under-spending if the ICC's assumptions were not achieved.[46] However, it was generally sympathetic to the ICC's situation and did not recommend major reductions because it concluded that "the programme budget was reasonable in the circumstances and because it wished to ensure that the ICC had sufficient resources to cover a range of realistic eventualities in 2004".[47] The ICC went on to under-spend by approximately 20 per cent between 2004 and 2006 (see Table 1).

Even though resources unspent by the ICC were used to pay other state party costs, the practice indicated a lack of budgetary control.[48] Measures were

---

43) The Coalition has established a number of thematic teams composed of its interested members. The Teams follow developments at the ICC and the Assembly and engage in relevant research and advocacy. While the work of the Budget and Finance Team reflects the positions of those Coalition members most active on particular issues and its submissions are prepared in consultation with other Coalition teams, its advocacy cannot be construed to represent the views of all organizations/members of the Coalition. At its second session, the Assembly adopted a Resolution entitled *Recognition of the coordinating and facilitating role of the NGO Coalition for the International Criminal Court* (ICC-ASP/2/Res.8).

44) *Draft programme budget for 2005*, *supra* note 36, para. 159.

45) *Report of the Committee on Budget and Finance*, *supra* note 40, para. 13.

46) *Ibid.*, paras. 13-14.

47) *Ibid.*, para. 13.

48) Financial Regulation 4.7 provides that:

> As of 1 January following the year in which the audit of the accounts of the financial period is completed, the amount so apportioned to a State Party shall be surrendered to such State Party if its contribution for that financial period has been paid in full and shall be applied to liquidate, in whole or in part, first, any advance due to the Working Capital Fund; secondly, any

Table 1

Budgetary period	ICC's budget request	Budget recommended by Committee	Budget approved by the Assembly	Percentage of approved budget actually spent by ICC
1/09/2002 to 31/12/2003	€30,893,500	N/A	€30,893,500	69.5
2004	€55,089,100	€52,319,755	€53,071,486	81.4
2005	€69,564,000	€64,956,000	€66,784,200	83.4
2006	€82,454,400	€79,767,300	€80,417,200	79.7
2007	€93,458,300	€88,563,200	€88,871,800	90.5
2008	€97,570,100	€90,173,600	€90,382,100	93.3
2009	€102,626,000	€101,229,900	€96,229,900	92.5
2010	€102,980,100	€102,681,600	€103,623,300	95.2
2011	€107,022,700	€103,919,600	€103,607,900	103.7
2012	€122,265,300	€112,019,210	€108,800,000	

therefore taken to improve the ICC's ability to accurately estimate its budgetary requirements. In 2005, upon the Committee's recommendation, the Assembly moved its main annual sessions from September to November/December to allow the ICC to develop its assumptions as closely as possible to the start of the budgetary year.[49] While this provided some assistance to the ICC, in practice assumptions still had to be developed in March/April of the preceding year. It was still too early to make accurate predictions about possible expenditure. Most significantly, at its third session in 2004, the Assembly established a EUR10 million contingency fund for:

> a) Costs associated with an unforeseen situation following a decision by the Prosecutor to open an investigation; or
> b) Unavoidable expenses for developments in existing situations that could not be foreseen or could not be accurately estimated at the time of the adoption of the budget; or
> c) Costs associated with an unforeseen meeting of the Assembly of States Parties.[50]

The Contingency Fund was expected to be the solution to over-budgeting and under-spending. It gave the ICC the ability to request in its budget proposal resources to cover expenses that were clearly foreseeable and, at the same time,

arrears of assessed contributions; and thirdly, assessed contributions for the calendar year following the year in which the audit is completed.

49) Committee on Budget and Finance, *Report of the Committee on Budget and Finance on the work of its second session* (ICC-ASP/3/22), para. 30.

50) Assembly of States Parties, *Programme budget for 2005, Contingency Fund, Working Capital Fund for 2005, scale of assessments for the apportionment of expenses of the International Criminal Court and financing of appropriates for the year 2005* (ICC-ASP/3/Res.4), Section B.

gave it the flexibility to access significant additional funds quickly, if it needed them during the budgetary year. However, instead of improving budgetary accuracy in the next years, the situation continued to deteriorate. Again in 2006, the ICC requested resources for two trials even though, at the time it was presented, no one had been arrested. Rather than recommending that assumptions be corrected and the budget adjusted, the Committee concluded they were reasonable.[51] The ICC corrected its approach in 2007 and scaled back its assumptions to only provide for the trial of Thomas Lubanga Dyilo who had been surrendered to the ICC in March 2006. But, even then, by September 2007, it was clear that the ICC was again poised to under-spend significantly for the year. The Committee expressed its concern that the causes of under-spending went further than setting the assumptions:

> The Committee concluded that the budget continued to contain a substantial level of capacity that had not been utilized. This could undermine budget discipline within the Court and diminished the ability of the Committee and the Assembly to assess budgetary needs.[52]

The Committee noted that part of the problem lay in the fact that each year, the ICC was using the approved budget of the previous year as the baseline for its annual request and not the predicted expenditure in the current year which, with the under-spending, was at the time significantly less.[53] Previously it had also noted that the ICC's budget request "related to only perceived growth from the previous year rather than justifying the overall budget."[54]

2.2.2. *Arbitrary Cuts and 'Zero-Growth'*

To reduce the consistent pattern of under-spending, the Assembly began requiring the ICC to absorb requests for new activities and additional costs within its existing resources. In 2007 for example, the Assembly adopted the Committee's recommendation not to approve the ICC's request for an additional EUR 1.49 million for staff salary inflationary increases even though, under the UN system applied by the ICC, the Court had to pay the costs.[55] The ICC was initially open to the practice of absorbing costs as long as it retained the flexibility to re-distribute funds internally. In some years, the ICC itself volunteered to absorb new costs. Its 2011 budget request even went as far as proposing to absorb all

---

51) Committee on Budget and Finance, *Report of the Committee on Budget and Finance on the work of its fifth session* (ICC-ASP/4/27), para. 23.
52) Committee on Budget and Finance, *Report of the Committee on Budget and Finance on the work of its ninth session* (ICC-ASP/6/12), para. 30.
53) *Ibid.*, para. 38.
54) Committee on Budget and Finance, *Report of the Committee on Budget and Finance on the work of its seventh session* (ICC-ASP/5/23), para. 48.
55) *Ibid.*, para. 51.

the costs of the new investigation in Kenya, apart from resources for witness protection.[56]

At its seventh session, shortly after the emergence of the global financial crisis in 2008, the Assembly took the unprecedented step of cutting the ICC's budget beyond the overall amount recommended by the Committee. Although the Assembly approved the budget incorporating the Committee's recommendations, it reduced states parties' appropriations by a further EUR 5 million, justifying the decision on the fact that "the Court has, since its inception, spent less than the full amount of its annual appropriations".[57] Many states were uncomfortable with the approach and insisted on language in the Assembly's report and budget resolution stressing that the decision was based on a "one-time, exceptional basis" and emphasized "that this method of budgetary consideration, in particular making exceptions to the Financial Regulations and Rules, should not be pursued in the future".[58]

However, within two years, a group of the highest paying states made up of France, Germany, Italy, Japan and the United Kingdom had adopted a common position of 'zero-growth'. In practice, they called for the ICC's budget not to increase beyond the budget allocated for the previous year, even if its activities increase or other costs rise and regardless of the Committee's recommendations. The approach has been opposed by many states parties that face similar economic problems and by NGOs who have argued that it "is simply not realistic nor, if it is imposed, will it lead to efficiency."[59] NGOs have instead urged the Assembly to focus on addressing transparency problems and finding savings, where possible, through efficiency efforts.[60]

For the 2011 and 2012 budgets, the divergent positions of states parties resulted in compromises imposing cuts beyond those recommended by the Committee. For 2011, the Assembly reached a compromise to allocate the amount of the 2010 budget plus the rate of inflation for the Netherlands (1.3 per cent) representing a nominal decrease of EUR 300,000 below the total recommended by the Committee. However, the issue came to a head the following year at the tenth session of the Assembly, when the ICC requested a much higher increase of almost EUR 20 million for 2012 (a total of EUR 122 million) to conduct two new investigations in

---

56) ICC, *Proposed Programme Budget for 2011 prepared by the Registrar* (ICC-ASP/9/10), para. 11.

57) Assembly of States Parties, *Programme budget for 2009, the Working Capital Fund for 2009, scale of assessments for the apportionment of expenses of the International Criminal Court, financing appropriations for the year 2009 and the Contingency Fund* (ICC-ASP/7/Res.4), Section D.

58) *Ibid.*

59) Coalition for the International Criminal Court Budget and Finance Team, *Comments and recommendations to the tenth session of the Assembly of States Parties*, 29 November 2011, <http://www.iccnow.org/documents/CICC_Budget_and_Finance_Team_Paper_ASP10.pdf>, 24 August 2012.

60) *Ibid.*

response to the UN Security Council's referral of the situation in Libya and the Pre-Trial Chambers approval of the Prosecutors request on Cote d'Ivoire.[61] There was also a request to increase legal aid for the defence and victims to meet a projected increase in judicial activities for the year and increases in staff costs. The Committee reviewed the request and made recommendations that would reduce the 2012 budget to EUR 112 million.[62] This was unacceptable to 'zero-growth' supporters, who, despite the obvious increase in the ICC's activities, maintained their position going into the tenth session. It prompted the President of the ICC in his opening statement to the session to state:

> While I understand the concerns of the States Parties who have argued for a zero nominal growth budget, I have to say plainly that imposing such a budget in 2012 would be profoundly damaging to the Court's ability to deliver fair and expeditious justice.[63]

After lengthy negotiations, which dominated much of the session, the Assembly reached a compromise to allocate EUR 108 million to the ICC for 2012.[64] It also decided only to replenish the Contingency Fund to EUR 7 million, following the ICC's use of the fund in 2011.[65] In a verbal statement to the Assembly, the Registrar expressed her concern that the cuts would make it nearly impossible for the ICC to engage in activities that had previously been mandated by the Assembly.[66]

2.3. *Efficiency Efforts and Other Measures to Improve the Budget Process*

Despite the budgetary discourse, efforts have intensified to find efficiencies in the ICC's work as a way to keep costs to a minimum and to establish more confidence

---

61) The figures cited include the total amount of the proposed budget for 2012 (ICC, *Proposed Programme Budget for 2012 prepared by the Registrar* (ICC-ASP/10/10)) issued by the Registrar on 21 July 2011, plus a supplementary budget request submitted in advance of the Assembly's session on 6 December 2011 (Assembly of States Parties, *Official Records of the Assembly of States Parties to the Rome Statute of the International Criminal Court, Tenth session, New York, 12 – 21 December 2011* (ICC-ASP/10/20), Part II, External audit, programme budget for 2012 and related documents, Section E and Annex), less EUR 0.8 million resolving from revised estimates for the Libya situation (Section F).

62) This includes the Committee's original recommendations in the *Report of the Committee on Budget and Finance on the work of its seventeenth session* (ICC-ASP/10/15), plus it's subsequent recommendations on the supplementary budget presented by the ICC in advance of the tenth session. *See Official Records of the Assembly of States Parties to the Rome Statute of the International Criminal Court, Tenth session, ibid.*

63) President of the International Criminal Court Judge Sang-Hyun Song, *Remarks to the Assembly of States Parties 10th session,*12 December 2011, <http://www.icc-cpi.int/iccdocs/asp_docs/ASP10/Statements/ASP10-ST-Pres-Song-Remarks-ENG.pdf>, 24 August 2012.

64) Assembly of States Parties, *Programme budget for 2012, the Working Capital Fund for 2012, scale of assessments for the apportionment of expenses of the International Criminal Court, financing appropriations for 2012 and the Contingency Fund* (ICC-ASP/10/Res.4).

65) *Ibid.*

66) Wierda and Triolo, *supra* note 14, p. 140.

in the ICC's financial practice. Since 2009, the ICC has been working with the Committee to improve its internal efficiency and the Committee has recognised that the ICC "had made considerable progress in its efforts to find and quantify possible efficiency savings".[67] In its latest report, for example, the ICC states that it established efficiency gains that it quantified to EUR 2.9 million in 2011.[68] Furthermore, the ICC initiated in 2012 a process to take stock of the lessons learned in its ten years of operation and to reflect upon measures that could be envisaged in order to expedite the judicial proceedings and enhance their efficiency, including amendments to the legal framework.

In December 2011, the Assembly tasked its Study Group on Governance "to engage with the Court and the Committee, with a view to enhancing the transparency and predictability of the budgetary process".[69] To date this has focussed primarily on further improving the assumption setting process, given the increasing complexity of predicting and budgeting for progress in cases where judicial decisions are pending that will determine whether a case will continue or its timelines.[70] As part of its 2013 budget request, the ICC has also, at the request of the Committee, set out predicted increases in key areas of its work for 2014-2016, including staff costs, capital investment replacements and premises costs, "to ensure that there were no surprises when a clearly identifiable expense comes due".[71]

2.4. *Implications for the Next Years*

At the time of writing, the ICC has just issued its 2013 budget request for EUR 118.75 million representing an increase of EUR 9.95 million from 2012.[72] EUR 6 million is for interim premises costs as the host state's agreement to pay the costs of the lease and maintenance is expected to expire at the end of 2012.[73] Other increases arise from two Kenya trials which are scheduled to commence in April 2013 and staff cost increases.[74] The rise is indicative of other increases that will likely arise in future years, in particular as suspects are arrested and surrendered to the ICC and new investigations are opened. Increases in staff salaries, allowances and

---

67) *Report of the Committee on Budget and Finance on the work of its seventeenth session, supra* note 62, para. 48.

68) ICC, *Seventh Status Report on the Court's progress regarding efficiency measures* (ICC-ASP/11/9).

69) *Programme budget for 2012, the Working Capital Fund for 2012, scale of assessments for the apportionment of expenses of the International Criminal Court, financing appropriations for 2012 and the Contingency Fund: supra* note 64, Section H, para. 1.

70) ICC, *Proposed Programme Budget for 2013 of the International Criminal Court* (ICC-ASP/11/10), paras. 15-17.

71) *Ibid., para.* 30.

72) *Ibid.*

73) *Ibid.*, para. 36.

74) *Ibid.*, para. 29.

benefits are expected to rise significantly in the next years.[75] These are currently unavoidable as the Assembly has been advised that, if the ICC were to depart from the UN Common Cost System, it could give rise to legal challenges.[76] Securing sufficient resources to meet these increases in the current political context will no doubt prove very difficult. As explained below, much will depend on the approaches taken in the next budget processes by the ICC, the Committee and the Assembly.

2.4.1. *The Approach of the ICC*

The ICC ultimately controls how much resources it will request and how it presents its proposals. If the ICC presents transparent and strongly justified budget requests that promote efficiency, scalability and implement a coherent strategic plan to address impunity, they will likely resonate more with states parties and have more chance of success. To achieve this, the ICC will need to counter-act the damaging effects of absorbing costs in recent years. Although this practice has increased the implementation of the annual budget, the process of moving resources within the ICC to meet these additional needs has resulted in confusion about how resources are actually allocated and spent. This has undermined confidence in the process. For example, in 2009, the Committee pointed out that even though the overall implementation rate of the annual budget had increased to 93.3 per cent of the funds allocated for 2008 "the implementation of the Court's budget did not always correspond to the realization of the underlying assumptions. It noted for example, that overspending had occurred in a number of areas".[77] The ICC will also need to request the resources it needs to conduct its work effectively. NGOs have criticized the ICC for responding to budgetary pressure by under-funding certain aspects of its work, in particular on victims' issues, outreach and defence.[78] A recent effort to amend the legal aid system has proved particularly controversial with NGOs stating "[t]he focus of the review has been piecemeal, driven by budgetary pressure to reduce legal aid rather than a genuine review of the existing system".[79]

---

75) Following the UN Common System, staff costs increased by EUR 2.96 million in 2012 and EUR 3.88 million in 2013. The ICC predicts similar increases for 2014-2016. *See Proposed Programme Budget for 2013 of the International Criminal Court*, Table 7.

76) *Official Records of the Assembly of States Parties to the Rome Statute of the International Criminal Court, Tenth session, supra* note 61, Part II, External audit, programme budget for 2012 and related documents, Section H.

77) Committee on Budget and Finance, *Report of the Committee on Budget and Finance on the work of its twelfth session* (ICC-ASP/8/5), para. 17.

78) *See for example* Coalition for the ICC's Budget and Finance Team, *Comments on the Proposed Programme Budget for 2012 of the International Criminal Court and other matters*, 17 August 2011, <http://www.iccnow.org/documents/Commentary_on_2012_Budget_17_August_2011.pdf>, 24 August 2012.

79) Coalition for the International Criminal Court's Legal Representation Team, *Submission and recommendations on the 'Proposal for a review of the legal aid system of the Court in accordance*

In addition to developing fully justified budgets, the ICC can also play a constructive role in the Assembly's review of the budget request and the Committee's recommendations. In its 2012 budget resolution, the Assembly requested the ICC:

> to prepare, if it proposes any increase of the budget for 2013, a paper which details the Court's options where reductions would be made in order to bring the level of the approved budget for 2013 in line with the level of the approved budget for 2012, as well as how those reductions would impact on the Court's activities.[80]

When faced with a similar request the year before, the ICC refused pointing out that "in order to be able to submit a budget option with no growth or a minimum one, States Parties should first prioritize among the Court's different mandates and identify those that should be reduced or eliminated".[81] Although the ICC has some basis to argue that it is unreasonable for the Assembly to expect the Court to identify where cuts should be made to achieve 'zero-growth', a detailed analysis of the implications of a 'zero-growth' budget presents an opportunity to force the Assembly to consider the consequences more clearly in its decision making.

2.4.2. *The Approach of the Committee*

Despite the Assembly's recent decisions to go beyond the Committee's recommendations in reducing the ICC's budget, the Committee remains a key participant in the process capable of providing informed and independent assessment of the ICC's needs. Its independent review is central to the integrity of the whole budget process. However, last year, the Committee commented that "the Court is reaching the point when the expectations on the type and level of activities and on the level of resources may be diverging" and went on to set out a number of potentially damaging measures that would reduce costs (some of which are considered in part 4 below).[82] This included an urgent review of legal aid for both the defence and victims, considering alternative ways of conducting reparation and outreach and considering alternative mechanisms both for financing and for delivering certain services, including through voluntary contributions.[83] These are strong indications that, contrary to its independent mandate, the Committee may be willing to adopt the 'zero-growth' approach in its work, even though it is

with resolution ICC-ASP/10/Res.4 of 21 December 2011', 9 March 2012, http://www.iccnow.org/documents/CICC_Paper_on_Legal_Aid_9-03-12.pdf, 14 September 2012.

80) *Programme budget for 2012, the Working Capital Fund for 2012, scale of assessments for the apportionment of expenses of the International Criminal Court, financing appropriations for 2012 and the Contingency Fund, supra* note 64.

81) *Official Records of the Assembly of States Parties to the Rome Statute of the International Criminal Court, Tenth session, supra* note 61, Part II, paras. 41-42.

82) *Report of the Committee on Budget and Finance on the work of its seventeenth session, supra* note 62, para. 14.

83) *Ibid.*, paras. 15-26.

strongly disputed and only supported by a small number of governments. Such a move would make it extremely difficult for the ICC to obtain increases in resources.

2.4.3. *The Approach of States Parties*

While it is expected that some states will continue to call for 'zero-growth', it remains to be seen how states that have been supportive of increasing the budget to meet additional costs and workload will respond to these calls in the longer-term. To date, states parties have been able to justify some of the cuts imposed on the ICC based on its regular under-spending. However, as the Committee recently noted "absorption of new activity within existing resources, even with re-engineering, can only go so far".[84] The significant cuts imposed for 2012, make it less likely that under-spending will arise to the same extent in the next years. Indeed, in 2011, the ICC over-spent for the first time. In the 2013 budget proposal, the Office of the Prosecutor states that it has reached its "absorptive capacity" and "further reductions would either result in an investigation being terminated, or further slow down all investigations to levels that would potentially increase costs in other related areas".[85] Furthermore, the recent practice of requiring the ICC to absorb increases in staff costs, if continued, would create the situation of staff costs consuming the resources allocated for its activities. The Assembly will face these and other difficult decisions in the next years that will test their commitment to respecting the Rome Statute and to pursuing the fight against impunity.

3. The Principal Budget Driver

An underlying question in the current discourse is: what should drive the ICC's workload and consequently its budget? There is currently no consensus on this issue. Those advocating 'zero-growth' promote a resource-driven ICC. Those opposed have yet to clearly articulate an alternative approach. A number of options are explored below, including a capacity-driven ICC, a demand-driven ICC and an impunity-driven ICC.

3.1. *A Resource-Driven ICC*

This approach means that the Assembly decides the budget for the ICC by setting a financial envelope based on what states are willing to pay and the ICC must

---

84) *Report of the Committee on Budget and Finance on the work of its seventeenth session, supra* note 62, para. 18.

85) *Proposed Programme Budget for 2013 of the International Criminal Court, supra* note 70, para. 114.

adapt its workload to meet the resources provided. It provides certainty for states parties and arguably forces the ICC to maximise its use of the resources provided to be as efficient as possible. However, as explained below, the approach is inconsistent with the Rome Statute and it risks underfunding the ICC at times when its workload is high, threatening the effectiveness of its work. There is a particular risk of this at present when the ICC's investigations and preliminary examinations are high but the caseload is relatively low and could increase at any time. In worst cases, resources restrictions imposed by this approach could deter the ICC Prosecutor from responding to situations where crimes are being committed or render her office unable to proceed effectively with investigations or other activities.

3.2. *A Capacity-Driven ICC*

There are a number of limitations set out in the Rome Statute and other practical factors that define the ICC's capacity. In particular, the Rome Statute provides initially for 18 judges and the permanent premises will contain three courtrooms that will determine the maximum number of cases that can proceed at any given time, without additional judges or courtroom facilities.[86]

In principle, the idea of defining the ICC's maximum capacity in terms of caseload and increasing the budget to that point has appeal. The approach promotes the ICC running at full capacity and, therefore, achieving maximum efficiency. However, the capacity limitations contained in the Rome Statute only relate to certain aspects of the ICC's structure, and they were not intended to be absolute. For example, Article 112(2)(e) foresees the Assembly altering the number of judges presumably to meet an increase or decrease in workload.

As with the resource-driven approach, the capacity-driven approach establishes a cut-off line beyond which the ICC will be unable to respond to impunity. The current allocation of 18 judges is relatively small considering that only six are assigned to the Trial Division. If those judges work on only one case at a time, that will limit its trial capacity to two concurrent cases. Already, the ICC has established four Trial Chambers, but that includes outgoing judges completing their

[86] The ICTY has struggled to conduct 10 simultaneous trials with three courtrooms, 18 permanent judges and additional *ad litem* judges. *See* ICTY, *Assessment and report of Judge Patrick Robinson, President of the International Tribunal for the Former Yugoslavia, provided to the Security Council pursuant to paragraph 6 of Security Council resolution 1534 (2004)* (S/2010/270), para. 5:

> The high number of cases running simultaneously has placed pressure on the Tribunal's resources. The Tribunal's courtroom capacity and staffing levels are insufficient to adequately support 10 ongoing trials, and the number of trials has also impacted on the speed of translations, which are relied upon in all cases, but particularly those involving self-represented accused.

trials. It would only take a few more arrests for the ICC to be either looking at assigning judges to multiple cases or asking the Assembly to increase the number of judges and other resources to expand its capacity.

3.3. *A Demand-Driven ICC*

This approach promotes flexibility for the ICC to be reactive and for its work and budget to follow the demands placed on the Court. However, who creates the demand? And, how does that impact on the independence of the Prosecutor? With two Security Council referrals, four state referrals and one accepted Article 12(3) declaration by a non-state party in the first ten years,[87] there are clearly external demands from states and the international community for the ICC's work. But even in these situations, the independent Prosecutor makes a final decision on whether to proceed. In addition, even where there are not demonstrable demands, the Prosecutor can, subject to authorization by the Pre-Trial Chamber, initiate preliminary examinations and investigations *proprio motu*. In some situations, there may be strong opposition to the ICC's action.

3.4. *An Impunity-Driven ICC*

A similar but more objective approach that is most consistent with the object and purpose of the Rome Statute, including its mandate to promote complementarity, is the impunity-driven approach. The ICC was created to play a key role in ending impunity. It is therefore only logical that the level of the commission of these crimes in situations under its jurisdiction and the degree of the effectiveness of national authorities responding to them should be major objective factors in determining the ICC's workload. An impunity-driven approach provides the ICC with the maximum flexibility to respond to impunity under its jurisdiction, whenever and wherever it exists.

Despite its obvious compatibility with the Rome Statute, this approach is unlikely to be appealing to some states since the commission of crimes and the national responses to them are largely outside the control of the Assembly. When the commission of crimes and the number of situations are high, the ICC will require resources to conduct preliminary examinations. When national

---

87) A declaration pursuant to Article 12 (3) was also submitted by the Palestinian National Authority on 22 January 2009. On 3 April 2012, the Office of the Prosecutor issued a decision stating it "has assessed that it is for the relevant bodies at the United Nations or the Assembly of States Parties to make the legal determination whether Palestine qualifies as a State for the purpose of acceding to the Rome Statute and thereby enabling the exercise of jurisdiction by the Court under article 12(1)".

authorities are genuinely unable or unwilling to investigate and prosecute, the ICC will require resources to investigate and prosecute the crimes.

3.5. *The Extent of the Assembly's Powers to "Consider and Decide" the ICC's Budget*

Article 112(2)(d) of the Rome Statute establishes that the Assembly shall "consider and decide the budget of the Court". It is clear that this role extends beyond a mere procedural responsibility. No-one would suggest that the Assembly is bound to approve and fund each ICC budget request in full. Indeed, it is commonly agreed that the Assembly has a responsibility, including through the Committee, to provide budgetary oversight ensuring the effectiveness and efficiency of the ICC. Therefore, there are clearly some limitations that the Assembly can impose to ensure that the ICC is able to carry out its mission most effectively at the lowest reasonable cost.

However, that is not to say that the Assembly has an unfettered power to set the budget at any level it chooses, regardless of the impact on the ICC, as contended by states supporting the resource-driven approach. In accordance with the principle of *pacta sunt servanda*, set out in Article 26 of the Vienna Convention on the Law of Treaties, states parties to the Rome Statute are bound by the treaty and it must be performed by them in good faith. This must also apply in the budget-setting process. Budgetary decisions that preclude the ICC from performing the mandate set out in the Rome Statute would be inconsistent with states parties' obligations.

Article 112 of the Rome Statute establishes the Assembly as a management oversight, not a management, body. Article 112(2)(b), for example, expressly limits management oversight by the Assembly of the Presidency, the Prosecutor and the Registrar "regarding the administration of the Court". A plain reading excludes oversight of the substance of the ICC's prosecutorial or judicial functions. The drafting history shows that the term "administration" was specifically selected to avoid a broader interpretation that could interfere with judicial independence.[88] Indeed, the independence of the judges and the Prosecutor set out in Articles 40 and 42(1) of the Rome Statute respectively are central principles which states parties are committed to respecting, including through the budgetary process. Nowhere in the Rome Statute does it provide that any of the decisions or powers of the Prosecutor or the judges depends on resources available or the Assembly's willingness to approve resources. Budgetary decisions which infringe on such independence are therefore inconsistent with the Rome Statute. As identified

[88] *See* S. Rama Rao, 'Article 112: Assembly of States Parties', in Otto Triffterer and Kai Ambos, (eds.), *Commentary on the Rome Statute of the International Criminal Court: Observers' Notes, Article by Article* (C.H. Beck, Munich/Hart, Portland/Nomos, Baden Baden, 2008) pp. 1690-1691.

above, there is a specific risk of such interference if either the resource-driven or the capacity-driven approach is applied. Similarly, unless it is accepted that the Prosecutor ultimately creates the demand, the demand-driven approach also threatens the independence of the Prosecutor by linking resources to perform its activities with external demand.

States parties must also consider the spirit and purpose of the Rome Statute system in setting the budget. This is clearly set out in the Preamble, in which states parties;

> [affirm] that the most serious crimes of concern to the international community as a whole must not go unpunished and that their effective prosecution must be ensured by taking measures at the national level and by enhancing international cooperation… [determine] to put an end to impunity for the perpetrators of these crimes and thus to contribute to the prevention of such crimes… [and recall] that it is the duty of every State to exercise its criminal jurisdiction over those responsible for international crimes[.]

To have an impact in the fight against impunity, the ICC must be more than a boutique court that only has the resources and capacity to respond to a limited number of situations. It must be able to respond to impunity wherever it exists both by encouraging states to fulfil their complementarity obligations to investigate and prosecute genuinely crimes and stepping in to investigate and prosecute crimes when states fail to fulfil their responsibilities, even at times when crimes are being committed in a large number of situations. If the budgetary approach renders it incapable of doing so, the ICC will become irrelevant and accused of bias for responding to some situations and not others. The impunity-driven approach is the only approach that fully respects the spirit and purpose of the Rome Statute.

4. Cost-Cutting Proposals

Independently of the overall approach to the budget, a number of initiatives have been proposed to reduce the costs of the ICC. Some of these initiatives, if implemented, would seriously undermine the effectiveness of the ICC's work.

4.1. *Voluntary Funding of 'Non-Core' Functions*

At its 17th session in September 2011, the Committee recommended that the Assembly consider alternative financing mechanisms for the ICC noting "[t]here may well be other areas of the current Court activity that could benefit from a mixed financing system of assessed and voluntary contributions, such as outreach and public information".[89] However, it did not examine whether, in the light of

[89] *Report of the Committee on Budget and Finance on the work of its seventeenth session, supra* note 62, para. 25.

experience of other international criminal courts and bodies, voluntary contributions could really be an effective alternative.

Voluntary funding of services for international justice mechanisms is not new. For example, the ICTY's outreach programme has been funded exclusively by voluntary contributions. Some aspects of the ICC's work have also been funded by voluntary contributions. Its internship program has been funded by the European Union, although it is expected to end in 2012.[90] A decision was also taken by the Assembly at its ninth session to fund family visits for indigent detainees through a voluntary fund.[91] The Assembly established the fund and rejected funding family visits from the main ICC budget despite a decision by the ICC Presidency that "a positive obligation to fund family visits must be implied in order to give effect to a right which would otherwise be ineffective in the particular circumstances of the detainee".[92]

Given the serious problems experienced by the SCSL and ECCC in obtaining voluntary contributions to conduct their work, voluntary funding is not appropriate for all aspects of the ICC's work. Some states have increasingly referred in the budget discourse to funding 'core judicial activities', implying that many functions considered non-judicial should fall outside the ICC's budget and be funded voluntarily.[93] NGOs have challenged this approach stating:

> The proposals ignore the reality that the implementation of the ICC's mandate depends on a range of interrelated functions. The ICC's investigations, prosecutions and trials cannot be conducted effectively unless they are supported through field engagement and presence, witness protection, legal aid, and outreach and victim participation activities to ensure victims can access their rights under the Rome Statute. Lessons learned, including from the ad hoc tribunals, demonstrate that investment in these areas is essential to the meaningful delivery of fair and credible justice. All such activities are "core" to the ICC's mandate and should be budgeted through the annual budget.[94]

---

90) Alternative funding mechanisms are being considered, such as establishing a Junior Professional Officer Programme funded by sponsoring governments. *See Report of the Committee on Budget and Finance on the work of its eighteenth session*, (ICC-ASP/11/5), para. 54.

91) Assembly of States Parties, *Programme budget for 2011, the Working Capital Fund for 2011, scale of assessments for the apportionment of expenses of the International Criminal Court, financing appropriations for 2011 and the Contingency Fund* (ICC-ASP/9/Res.4), Section X.

92) ICC Presidency, *Decision on "Mr Mathieu Ngudjolo's Complaint Under Regulation 221(1) of the Regulations of the Registry Against the Registrar's Decision of 18 November 2008"*, para. 37.

93) *See for example* UK, *Statement to the Tenth Session of the Assembly of States Parties*: "The British Government is, of course, committed to ensuring that the Court has the funding it requires to maintain its core judicial activities and to handle the workload that it is required to take on"; Italy, *Statement to the Tenth Session of the Assembly of States Parties* "Italy is of the view that the Court must be afforded all those financial means that are necessary for the performance of its core judicial activity".

94) Coalition for the ICC, *Letter to states parties on the 2012 budget*, 6 July 2012, <http://www.iccnow.org/documents/CICC_Letter_on_the_2012_ICC_Budget_-_6_July_2011.pdf>, 24 August 2012.

The Committee's attention to the possibility of mixed assessed and voluntary funding of outreach and public information has attracted particular attention.[95] Although the practice of voluntarily funding the ICTY and ICTR's outreach programmes provides some precedent, the ICTY has repeatedly cited outreach as a 'core function'.[96] It also requested that the programme be funded from the main ICTY budget in 2002-2003. However, that was rejected.[97] Furthermore, ICC outreach is now widely recognized as an essential function, including by the Court, which will in most cases investigate and prosecute crimes thousands of miles away from victims and affected communities.[98] Indeed, both the Assembly and the 2010 Review Conference have acknowledged the importance of this work in achieving the ICC's mandate. In 2004, the Assembly stated in its annual resolution on Strengthening the International Criminal Court and the Assembly of States Parties that it:

> [r]ecognizes the importance for the Court to engage communities in situations under investigation in a process of constructive interaction with the Court, designed to promote understanding and support of its mandate, to manage expectations and to enable those communities to follow and understand the international criminal justice process and, to that end, encourages the Court to intensify such outreach activities.[99]

In the same way that victim protection was originally funded by voluntary contributions at the ICTY and later incorporated into its core budget, there is clearly good reason for other essential elements of the contemporary international criminal justice system, as it develops, to be funded through assessed contributions. Proposals to do the opposite and to revert to voluntary funding for essential ICC tasks already incorporated in its budgets fly in the face of years of experience and risk inadequate funding of 'core' work.

---

95) *See* Coalition for the ICC, *Letter to states parties on ICC Communications for International Justice Day*, 20 July 2012, <http://www.iccnow.org/documents/CICC_Letter_on_ICC_Communication_and_outreach-20.07.12.pdf>, 24 August 2012.

96) *See for example* ICTY, *Tenth annual report of the International Criminal Tribunal for the Prosecution of Persons Responsible for Serious Violations of International Humanitarian Law Committed in the Territory of the Former Yugoslavia since 1991*(A/58/297–S/2003/829), 10 August 2003, para. 287.

97) ICTY, *Eighth annual report of the International Tribunal for the Prosecution of Persons Responsible for Serious Violations of International Humanitarian Law Committed in the Territory of the Former Yugoslavia since 1991* (A/56/352–S/2001/865), 17 September 2001, para. 232.

98) *Proposed Programme Budget for 2013 of the International Criminal Court*, *supra* note 70, para. 194:

> "in the case of outreach activities and victim participation, through these core functions the Court delivers justice in a meaningful way to the actual communities affected by the crimes under the Court's jurisdiction by ensuring that they have a stake in the Court's judicial process and effectively managing their expectations."

99) ICC-ASP/4/Res.4, para. 22. *See also* Review Conference, *The impact of the Rome Statute system on victims and affected communities* (RC/Res.2), para. 3.

Voluntary contributions raise a number of challenges specific to the ICC. As demonstrated by the loss of funding for the internship programme after 10 years, the permanent ICC will find it difficult to find long-term funding for specific functions. Most major donors, including governments, fund project-based work not the continuing activities of permanent institutions. Adapting long-term funding needs into projects – such as funding specific tasks in some situations - will inevitably result in uneven funding based on donors priorities. The fund for family visits of detained persons is a prime example. It has only received two voluntary contributions since it was established in 2010, both from Germany which strongly opposed funding the visits through the core budget and offered its initial contribution as part of the compromise to establish the voluntary fund.

Recognizing the different degrees to which other international and internationalized criminal courts have been funded through voluntary contributions,[100] it should be acknowledged that the higher the level of the ICC's dependency on voluntary contributions will result in a higher exposure to the risk of under-funding, in particular, but not exclusively, at times of global financial problems.

4.2. *Increasing Judicial Budgetary Responsibility*

In 2008, at the same time as the Committee and states were disputing the Presidency's decision setting out an obligation to fund family visits for indigent detainees, the Committee stated:

> In several instances the Committee was advised of judicial decisions which had both short- and long-term impacts on the budget, and of pending appeals that would overturn decisions or policies of the Registrar. In order to improve transparency, the Committee recommended that the Registrar should provide a statement of financial implications to Chambers on matters under consideration, preferably prior to decisions being taken. The Committee also recommended that the Presidency should advise Chambers of the need to take appropriate account of costs in their deliberations.[101]

Although many states were supportive of the idea of providing information to the judges of the financial implications in advance of their decisions, many were concerned about sending a message which could be interpreted as interfering with the independence of the judges. Ultimately, the Assembly endorsed the recommendation for the Registry to provide financial information to the Chambers

---

100) Whereas, the SCSL and the ECCC were funded almost entirely by voluntary contributions, voluntary funding for the ICTY makes up less than one per cent of its total budget. ICTY website, *Support and Donations*, <http://www.icty.org/sections/AbouttheICTY/SupportandDonations>, 24 August 2012.

101) Committee on Budget and Finance, *Report of the Committee on Budget and Finance on the work of its eleventh session* (ICC-ASP/7/15), para. 54.

whilst highlighting the independence of the judiciary, but it did not go as far as taking measures to call on Chambers to consider costs in their deliberations.[102] Nevertheless, the Committee repeated its recommendations in its May 2012 report and requested the ICC to provide a report, to be considered in the context of the 2013 budget request, "on all judicial decisions taken in 2010, 2011 and from January - August 2012 having a significant impact on the budget".[103] The Committee clearly recognizes judicial decisions as a significant cost driver over which the Assembly currently have little control, especially at the current time when the judges are playing a key role in defining how the ICC works in practice through their jurisprudence and case management. Judicial decisions clearly can have a significant budgetary impact. But where does budgetary oversight stop and external pressure that interferes with the independence of the judges begin?

The Assembly already appears to have made this judgement in its previous decision on the Committee's recommendations. The continued prompting for the Assembly to go further than communicating financial information to judges by taking measures to direct the judges to consider costs during their deliberations, especially as budgetary tensions increase, could be interpreted as pressuring judges not to make decisions that are perceived as costly or to choose cheaper and less effective options when they exist. Such pressure would be inconsistent with Article 40 (1) of the Rome Statute and Principle 2 of the Basic Principles on the Independence of the Judiciary, which states:

> [t]he judiciary shall decide matters before them impartially, on the basis of facts and in accordance with the law, without any restrictions, improper influences, inducements, pressures, threats or interferences, direct or indirect, from any quarter or for any reason.[104]

The appropriateness of the Committee's recommendation is further called into question by the fact that the ICC's Mission Statement already commits the ICC to conduct "expeditious proceedings" and "achieving desired results with minimal resources".[105] The Statement was developed based on the "one court principle" and highlights "[e]ven where independent, the Court's staff and elected officials form part of the same institution and share a common mission".[106]

---

102) *Official Records of the Assembly of States Parties to the Rome Statute of the International Criminal Court, Seventh session, The Hague, 14 – 22 November 2008* (ICC-ASP/7/20), Part II: External Audit, internal audit, programme budget for 2009 and related documents, para. 13.

103) *Report of the Committee on Budget and Finance on the work of its eighteenth session, supra* note 90, para. 50.

104) *Basic Principles on the Independence of the Judiciary* endorsed by General Assembly resolutions 40/32 of 29 November 1985 and 40/146 of 13 December 1985.

105) ICC, *Strategic Plan of the International Criminal Court* (ICC-ASP/5/6), Part III.

106) *Ibid.*, para. 15.

4.3. *UN Funding of Security Council Referrals*

The UN Security Council has referred two situations to date to the ICC Prosecutor – Darfur and Libya. However, part of the compromise which led to the adoption of both resolutions included the following stipulation:

> [The Security Council] *Recognizes* that none of the expenses incurred in connection with the referral, including expenses related to investigations or prosecutions in connection with that referral, shall be borne by the United Nations and that such costs shall be borne by the parties to the Rome Statute and those States that wish to contribute voluntarily.[107]

The text is not consistent with the intent of the drafters of the Rome Statute (which included the five permanent members of the Security Council) as reflected in Article 115(b) of the Rome Statute. It provides that the expenses of the ICC shall be provided by "funds provided by the United Nations, subject to the approval of the General Assembly, in particular in relation to the expenses incurred due to referrals by the Security Council". The text also raises constitutional issues for the UN as Article 17 of the UN Charter provides the General Assembly, not the UN Security Council, with exclusive authority over budgetary matters.[108] The Relationship Agreement between the International Criminal Court and the United Nations expressly tasks the General Assembly with entering into such arrangements.[109]

Although the Assembly appeared to accept that that it should bear the costs of the Darfur situation, by the time it came to consider the costs of the Libya situation during the difficult 2012 budget discussions, the mood among states was less accommodating. At its tenth session, the Assembly invited the ICC to "include this matter in its institutional dialogue with the United Nations and report thereon to the eleventh session of the Assembly."[110] An effort was also taken by states to address the issue through the annual General Assembly resolution on the ICC. However, that only achieved an invitation for all states to consider voluntarily contributing to the ICC's expenses.[111] This places states parties and the ICC in a difficult situation. On the one hand, supporters of the ICC see Security Council referrals, in the absence of universal ratification, as positive measures which both

---

107) UN Security Council, *Resolution 1593 (2005)* (S/RES/1593 (2005)), para. 7; UN Security Council, Resolution 1970 (2011) (S/RES/1970 (2011)), para. 8.

108) *See* Robert Cryer, 'Sudan, Resolution 1593, and International Criminal Justice', 19 *Leiden Journal of International Law* (2006), pp. 206-208.

109) *Negotiated Relationship Agreement between the International Criminal Court and the United Nations* (ICC-ASP/3/Res.1), Article 13 (1).

110) *Programme budget for 2012, the Working Capital Fund for 2012, scale of assessments for the apportionment of expenses of the International Criminal Court, financing appropriations for 2012 and the Contingency Fund, supra* note 64, Section G.

111) General Assembly, *Report of the International Criminal Court* (A/RES/66/262), OP 12.

enable the ICC to respond to situations anywhere in the world and which build the global credibility and acceptance of the institution. On the other hand, they are concerned that the UN Security Council can take action that expands the expectations on the ICC to deliver justice without accepting any financial responsibility for the work and costs that referrals generate.

In pursuing UN funding of Security Council referrals, the Assembly will need to consider whether, if they are successful, it would generate opposition among Security Council members towards future referrals. Not all obstacles relate to an unwillingness to pay. In particular, the 2000-1 Foreign Relations Authorization Act prohibits the US from funding the ICC and could preclude the US from supporting referrals.[112] Furthermore, what influence would the General Assembly have over the budget setting for investigations and cases resulting from Security Council referrals? At present, the Assembly is struggling to secure the commitment of the ICC's strongest supporters to fund its work. The involvement of non-states parties that are not committed to the ICC or its efforts to end impunity could be counterproductive and even potentially interfere in its work. Another possible solution could be for the Assembly to set a target of voluntary contributions which must be reached before the ICC proceeds with an investigation in response to a Security Council referral. However, this could significantly delay the ICC's response to the crimes. There is no basis for such mechanisms in the Rome Statute and limitations imposed by the Assembly would risk interfering with the independence of the Prosecutor to decide whether to proceed in response to a referral.

5. Conclusions

The ICC has come into existence at a time when questions are being raised about the long-term feasibility of funding international criminal justice at the international level. The ICC has the opportunity to distinguish itself from other international and internationalized criminal courts by demonstrating its efficiency, control over its operations and finances and its value by achieving impact. However, ten years into its work, all three aspects of its work are being questioned and damaging cost-cutting efforts are being considered that would undermine its work.

Although many external factors have contributed to this situation, the onus must be on the ICC itself to build a stronger budgetary support base of state parties by continuing to pursue maximum efficiency and asserting financial control and direction. This does not require radical re-thinking. The ICC's original vision of a flexible and scalable institution that maximises efficiency and economy

---

112) American Non-Governmental Organizations Coalition for the International Criminal Court website, 'Anti-ICC Legislation', http://www.amicc.org/usicc/legislation, 24 August 2012.

reflects sound principles for the Court to build upon. In particular, by delivering fully justified budgets for the whole ICC and by developing convincing estimates of how its budget will need to increase and decrease to meet its fluctuating workload, without costs spiralling out of control, the ICC can counter-act the damaging effects of years of cost absorption. Some progress has been made in this regard in the 2013 budget proposal.

Most importantly, the ICC needs to demonstrate its value. Criticism that the ICC has only delivered one trial for EURO 750 million is not entirely fair. Much of the lack of progress results from states failing to arrest and surrender suspects. However, the proceedings the ICC are able to conduct must be expeditious, ensuring that the rights of the accused and victims set out in the Rome Statute are respected, and the ICC must be seen to conduct all its functions efficiently and effectively. The current lessons learned process being conducted by the ICC is, therefore, particularly important.

Complementarity is the big prize of the Rome Statute system and is, in many respects, an important part of the solution to the current budgetary problems. If the ICC can develop more effective and transparent strategies, particularly at the preliminary examination phase, to press states to fulfil their responsibilities, the measures could provide the biggest long-term cost savings for the ICC's budget and ensure justice for victims on a scale not achievable through the ICC's limited cases. Until these strategies are put in place and sufficiently resourced, the ICC will continue to be measured against its predecessors on the number of trials completed and commenced.

The ICC cannot succeed without the goodwill and support of the Assembly and the independent functioning of its Committee. If the Assembly continues to impose damaging cost-cutting measures in the next years, the ICC will run into serious problems and the hope of ending impunity that inspired massive support from governments and civil society around the world will fade. The Rome Statute system was designed to respond to impunity wherever it exists. Its workload and its budget must be impunity-driven. The future of international criminal justice depends on it.

Enunciating Genocide: Crime, Rights and the Impact of Judicial Intervention

Mark Findlay
Professor of Law, Law School, Singapore Management University
Professor of Criminal Justice, Law School, University of Sydney, Australia

Abstract
As a consequence of recent decisions from the ICJ and the ICTR, it is clear that genocide can be pursued through the international courts both in terms of criminal liability and also rights/responsibility legal paradigms. This article suggests that this duality in possible contexts and processes of judicial determination, while being procedurally problematic, is in keeping with the human rights direction of international criminal justice. In addition, by opening the legal consideration of genocide to questions of individual liability as well as state-sponsored rights abuse, judges are now able to consider the more realistic complexity of genocide atrocity and thereby to address the diverse legitimate interests of victims. Particularly, by enabling and expanding juridical activation as the medium for legally enunciating the Genocide Convention, the determination of genocide and its consequences may benefit from enhanced certainty when reflected against the constitutional legality of the courts.

Keywords
genocide; human rights judicial determination; international criminal justice; accountability

1. Introduction

The interplay between state-to-state suits for genocide, and the criminal prosecution of genocide are important developments in both international criminal justice, and international humanitarian law. The fact that the International Court of Justice has ruled that genocide may be alleged as a delict against a state by another state before this court opens up a consideration of the role judges can play in enunciating the spirit and the process of the Genocide Convention. With the Rome Statute claiming for the International Criminal Court (ICC) jurisdiction to try individuals charged with genocide, and the *ad hoc* tribunals deliberating on such charges, complemented by domestic criminal prosecutions of the crime, then the nature and scope of judicial engagement with genocide is both particularised. In addition, the rights and liability approaches now available in bringing genocide to judicial determination offer a more holistic consideration of the atrocity, its perpetration, and its consequences through considerations of individual criminal liability, and collective state responsibility for the abuse of rights which genocide declares.

Now, insofar as international judicial determinations are concerned, legal reaction to genocide can be pursued through international criminal law (vested in domestic courts, the *ad hoc* UN tribunals, and the ICC) or through human rights law (before global rights courts such as the ICJ). This article will attempt to understand the consequences of these parallel developments both for the execution of the Genocide Convention and for the development of a richer judicial engagement with this horror. Some of the aspects of, and the differences between, both approaches require analysis against the aims of criminal justice and their possible attainment.[1] The article concludes that an important alliance between international criminal law and international rights law is developing for the enunciation of genocide, which is leading to an enhanced role for judicial determination in the global response of the global community. The interesting purpose for the article is to discuss the duality in possible routes to and contexts of judicial determination, against the aspirations particularly for legitimate victim interests which either style of justice (criminal or rights-based) may offer.[2] The empirical dimension of this analysis might eventually be to test whether the wider goals of international criminal justice (with their origins in criminal liability, rights protection, and security and peace-making) are better met through the addition of a human rights judicial paradigm. Do human rights considerations 'add value' to the emerging reach of international criminal justice over genocide via recognition of the need to look at states' responsibility for rights protection along with individual liability for crimes of genocide? What are some of the problems/limits faced in this duality?

2. International Criminal Justice – Rights Responsibility and Criminal Liability in Tandem?

Some commentators argue that the *justice core* of international criminal justice is now best explained in terms of "the imminent rise of human rights sanctioned by international criminal tribunals as the emerging paradigm of international relations and law".[3]

---

1) Mark J. Findlay and Ralph J. Henham, *Transforming International Criminal Justice: Retributive and Restorative Justice in the Trial Process* (Willan, Cullompton, 2005).

2) Mark J. Findlay, 'Locating Victim Communities within Global Justice and Governance', in Adam Crawford, (ed.), *International and Comparative Criminal Justice and Global Governance* (Cambridge University Press, Cambridge, 2011a) 109–139.

3) Frédéric Mégret, 'The Politics of International Criminal Justice', 13(5) *European Journal of International Law* (2002) 1261–1284, p. 1266.

Directly following the experiences of World War II, there was a new and fresh commitment to formalising basic human rights principles at an international level. The Genocide Convention[4] and the Universal Declaration on Human Rights[5] were both adopted in 1948 by the United Nations General Assembly in a climate of renewed humanitarianism and peace-keeping. The update and expansion of the Geneva Conventions in 1949[6] show how international laws had a significant influence on the development of international humanitarian law. The Geneva Conventions, especially through the rights protections of prisoners and those directly affected by military conflict, have had a rich influence over the development of a wider, non-military human rights framework internationally.

Further, the creation of post World War II crimes tribunals represents the earliest attempts to direct the remit of international humanitarian law towards individual rather than state interests, by incorporating rights violation within criminalisation and picking up their consequences in criminal sanctioning. Behaviours that offend the human rights of individuals were criminalised, and as mentioned before, for the first time individuals were prosecuted for international crimes. In this sense, the international criminal tribunals, in particular the ICC, can be seen as the institutional culmination of the belief that *because individuals live under the international legal system that must necessarily have rights and obligations flowing from it,* this generates a clear connection between international criminal justice and human rights.

The emerging body of criminal procedure now adopted in international criminal courts also displays the influence of human rights, not just through the conventional due process protections favouring accused persons, but also by recognising legitimate victim engagement.[7] However, as with international human rights legislation or institutions, there are complex challenges to enforcing international criminal justice rights in many situations of conflict and resistance, genocide not being the least of these. Even so, the recognition that international criminal justice rights and procedures should complement judicial human rights

---

4) UN General Assembly, *Universal Declaration of Human Rights*, 10 December 1948, Resolution 217 A (III).

5) UN General Assembly, *Convention on the Prevention and Punishment of the Crime of Genocide*, 9 December 1948, Resolution 260 (II) ("the Genocide Convention").

6) International Committee of the Red Cross (ICRC), *Geneva Convention for the Amelioration of the Condition of the Wounded and Sick in Armed Forces in the Field* (*First Geneva Convention*), 12 August 1949, 75 UNTS 31; ICRC, *Geneva Convention for the Amelioration of the Condition of Wounded, Sick and Shipwrecked Members of Armed Forces at Sea* (*Second Geneva Convention*), 12 August 1949, 75 UNTS 85; ICRC, *Geneva Convention Relative to the Treatment of Prisoners of War* (*Third Geneva Convention*), 12 August 1949, 75 UNTS 135; ICRC, *Geneva Convention Relative to the Protection of Civilian Persons in Time of War* (*Fourth Geneva Convention*, 12 August 1949, 75 UNTS 287.

7) Diane M. Amann, 'Harmonic Convergence? Constitutional Criminal Procedure in an International Context', 75(3) *Indiana Law Journal* (2000) 809–873.

protection has meant that the global governance influence of rights and justice can more centrally guide the global community's response to humanitarian challenges such as genocide.[8] The analysis to follow will unpack both approaches while at the same time arguing that their parallel and intersecting development through judicial determination offers:

- Greater certainty and actionability for the genocide convention, and more broadly,
- A measure of whether the wider aims for international criminal justice (such as the protection of victims from genocide) are advanced through judicial determinations directed against criminal liability and human rights responsibility, individual or state-centred.

3. The Reach of Criminal Liability

Zahar and Sluiter[9] refer to the codification of genocide as a crime under the Genocide Convention of 1948 in terms of a "rare gift to international criminal law where the nascent UN tribunals generally have to struggle to give shape to ill-defined crimes".[10] The key elements of genocide's codification were added, unchanged, to the statutes of the ICC, the International Criminal Tribunal for the Former Yugoslavia (ICTY), the International Criminal Tribunal for Rwanda (ICTR), and the Special Panels for East Timor.[11] As one of only four crimes over which the ICC has jurisdiction, genocide is centrally located within the limited offence framework of international criminal laws.

Many nation-states which have ratified the Genocide Convention now implement the offence within their domestic legislation. It is through the national courts as yet that genocide has been most actively criminalised.

In 1996, as a consequence of its majority decision in the *Case Concerning Application of the Convention on the Prevention and Punishment of the Crime of Genocide* (*Bosnia and Herzegovina* v. *Yugoslavia*),[12] the International Court of

---

8) Mark J. Findlay, *Governing through Globalised Crime: Futures for International Criminal Justice* (Willan, Cullompton, 2008).

9) Alexander Zahar and Goran Sluiter, *International Criminal Law: A Critical Introduction* (Oxford University Press, Oxford, 2008).

10) *Ibid.*, p. 156.

11) UN Security Council, *Statute of the International Criminal Tribunal for the former Yugoslavia*, 25 May 1993, Resolution 827, Article 4; UN Security Council, *Statute of the International Criminal Tribunal for Rwanda*, 8 November 1994, Resolution 955, Article 2; UN General Assembly, *Rome Statute of the International Criminal Court*, 17 July 1998, A/CONF. 183/9, Article 6.

12) *Case Concerning Application of the Convention on the Prevention and Punishment of the Crime of Genocide* (*Bosnia and Herzegovina* v. *Yugoslavia*), Preliminary Objections, Judgment, I.C.J. Reports 1996, p. 595.

Justice (ICJ) found that it had jurisdiction to deal with the case on the basis of Article IX of the Convention, dismissing the additional and remaining non-genocide related bases of jurisdiction invoked by Bosnia-Herzegovina. This decision cleared the way for actions to be brought state against state concerning allegations of genocide as serious violations of international humanitarian law. In its much criticised decision in 2007 on the *Case Concerning Application of the Convention on the Prevention and Punishment of the Crime of Genocide* (*Bosnia and Herzegovina v. Serbia and Montenegro*)[13] (hereafter referred to as the ICJ Genocide Judgment), the ICJ held - although not unanimously - that Serbia was neither directly responsible for the Srebrenica genocide (earlier determined as such by the ICTY and with which the ICJ agreed), nor that Serbia was complicit in it. However, the court did rule that Serbia had breached the Genocide Convention by failing to prevent the Srebrenica genocide, for not cooperating with the ICTY in punishing the perpetrators of the genocide, in particular in respect of General Ratko Mladić, and for violating its obligation to comply with the provisional measures ordered by the Court. In this respect, the UN's principal human rights tribunal accorded with the UN's criminal tribunal on the Balkans conflict in confirming genocide as appropriate for judicial determination both in terms of criminal and international human rights jurisdictions.

After recognising the development of a dual judicial capacity to deliberate on genocide charges, this brief article analyses how understanding and responding to genocide as a crime and genocide as a violation of human rights now:

- Can be enhanced by a dualist juridical activation at the international level in order to enjoy the force of law in both criminal and human rights paradigms; and
- how by taking the global consideration of genocide beyond the enunciation of commissions and conventions, and locating it centrally within a judicial remit, the determination of genocide and its consequences now have a far greater potential for certainty and actionability through:
    - reflection against the constitutional legality of the courts,
    - distillation within the elaboration of judicial narrative, and
    - elaboration through the accretion of argued and judicially deliberated jurisprudence in criminal and human rights jurisdictions.

Regarding this combined judicial consideration of genocide through the lenses of human rights and criminal liability, Judge Peter Touma of the ICJ observed:

13) *Case Concerning Application of the Convention on the Prevention and Punishment of the Crime of Genocide* (*Bosnia and Herzegovina* v. *Serbia and Montenegro*), Judgment of 26 February 2007, I.C.J. Reports 2007, p. 43.

> Hopefully, the activities of these two judicial institutions of the United Nations [The International Court of Justice and the International Tribunal for the former Yugoslavia]... contribute in their respective fields to their common objective – the achievement of international justice – however imperfect it may be perceived.[14]

Yet, in seeking to have the crime of genocide and the human rights violations it represents adjudicated through international courts, is too much being asked of judges to perform this crossover? Particularly with respect to the International Court of Justice, is it appropriate to require that court to determine the responsibility of states by employing a similar methodology which interrogates the minds and actions of senior state figures, in appreciating the way a criminal court would approach liability? Does this collapsing of rights and crime determinations risk that judicial decision-making may lose some of its definition and rigour? I argue it does not. The reason for this confidence is that as a consequence of the manner in which the international criminal tribunals and courts have received their mandates, international criminal justice has a clear human rights dimension and this is an important distinguishing characteristic of the development of international trial justice compared with national systems. For instance, referring to Article 5 of the Rome Statute, genocide (defined in Art 6), crimes against humanity (defined in Art 7), war crimes (defined in Art 8), and crimes of aggression (defined in Art 8) are deemed crimes which fall within the jurisdiction of the ICC. Against these crimes, the Rome Statute invokes aims directed towards peace and security which are as much about rights protection as punishment and retribution.

The State Parties to the Rome Statute (through its Preamble) recognise that crimes against humanity *threaten the peace, security and well-being of the world*, and in doing so within the wording of the Rome Statute, the ICC is declared to be committed to ameliorating such ends. For the ICC, the maintenance of international peace and security asks more than what the retributive justice model can supply – that is the punishment of the guilty – it looks at the impact of the crime far more comprehensively, and engages with the consequences for victims as well as the responsibility of perpetrators. Adjudicating liability becomes a vehicle for responding to what has personally impacted the victim, and the court's determination of the crime needs to be mindful of the conditions for peace and security that must reflect these considerations.[15]

Peace and security in the context of the ICC includes the prevention of conflict-related risks to the lives of potential victims. Where crimes that threaten international peace and security are committed (that fall within the jurisdiction

14) Dermot Groome, 'Adjudicating Genocide: Is the International Court of Justice Capable of Judging State Criminal Responsibility?', 31(4) *Fordham International Law Journal* (2007) 911–989, p. 911.
15) Findlay, *supra* note 2.

of the ICC), a referral should be made to empower the ICC to facilitate international accountability by restoring peace and security for the victims of such conflicts. Peace and security, as concerns for the ICC process, look beyond the perpetrators of global crime, focusing the Court's attention principally on the victims of such crime. The objective of ensuring peace and security seeks to prevent harm to potential victims both now and in future, and hopes to repair and restore the damage done to those who are already victims of global crimes within the Court's jurisdiction. Peace sees the broken community moving beyond the tensions that brought about the particular conflict, and providing protection for present risk, and security looks past the frictions that might ensue from the current conflict towards a peaceful future for victims and their communities.

If we take the wider aims of the ICC as expressing legitimate aims for international criminal justice, and that these aims reflect rights protection as well as punishment and retribution, then in addressing the crime of genocide, it is only natural that the two justice paradigms should be operational for a more comprehensive realisation of global justice. This being so, we can seek within international criminal justice judicial determinations the duality of rights and retribution, while at the same time seeing that duality as available through the consideration of the global rights judiciary as well as the judges in the international criminal courts and tribunals.

4. Adjudicating Responsibility and Liability

For the purposes of this article I will consider the judicial role in ruling on genocide internationally as now taking two forms –

- the determination of individual criminal responsibility through the international criminal courts and tribunals; and
- determining the human rights responsibilities of State Parties in conflict by the ICJ.

This distinction is not meant to minimise the capacity of judges within all levels of international criminal justice to consider both dimensions of genocide (rights and crime). Rather it is intended to add to that capacity by providing an additional jurisdictional avenue for opening up the process of judicial determination, and directing it to individuals and to states.

As suggested above, while the methodologies employed in judicial interpretations for both decision processes may invite similar considerations, the outcomes are distinctly different and the enforcement consequences represent separate motivations. Liability is directed to the criminal actions of the individual. I have in other writing criticised the artificiality of such determinations when global crimes are so often perpetuated in collective enterprises or demonstrate the intentions and aggregations of many minds.[16] To address this to some extent beyond the individual, responsibility is accorded by the ICJ to State Parties, and while it is the behaviours and thinking of state officials which is taken to evidence state responsibility, the judicial determination concerns the role of states as rights violators.

The possibility of approaching genocide from both directions of individual and collective action offers a more realistic and satisfying consideration of such encompassing atrocity. In addition, looking at liability and responsibility broadens the extent to which individuals and states can be drawn into law's regulatory net.[17]

Also, in an earlier work I argue that the legitimate interests of victims cannot be satisfied by either only liability or responsibility determinations.[18] Criminal liability and ensuing punishment generate retributive understandings and may comfort victims and future victims through promises to end impunity, and the suggested safety that general deterrence may project. To evoke all the restorative aspirations such as restitution, reparation, and recognition which victims are seeking in addition to criminal punishment, there is a need for the wider interrogation of victimisation that may not be offered by the selective discourse of adversarial testimony and questioning.[19] Consideration of human rights violations, particularly by states, offers a richer opportunity than would trial narrative focused on liability, to appreciate the complexity of global victimisation. In addition, the anticipated outcomes of a responsibility rather than liability determination are more likely to address restorative and conflict resolution necessities, particularly if offending states accept their duties (or are shamed into accepting them) following on from responsibility allocation for mass rights violations.

Another conflation of the liability/responsibility duality to consider when looking at the practical benefit of the two potential judicial determination approaches in tandem, is through the processes of proof. The definitional element that most distinguishes genocide from other international crimes is its *mental state* requirement that the perpetrator have the "intent to destroy in whole or in part a national, ethnical, racial or religious group, as such"[20] commonly referred to as the *special intent* of genocide. Although the term *genocide* is popularly used to describe many serious crimes committed on a discriminatory basis, its legal definition limits its prohibition to specified acts committed with the intent to destroy a particular protected group. This requirement, that a specified actor has a specific intent, means

16) Mark J. Findlay, 'Collective Responsibility for Global Crime – Limitations of the Liability Paradigm', in Ralph J. Henham and Mark J. Findlay, (eds.), *Exploring the Boundaries of International Criminal Justice* (Ashgate, Aldershot, 2011b) 47–74.

17) *Ibid.*

18) Findlay, *supra* note 2.

19) For a discussion of the limited testimonial fabric of the international criminal trial, *see* Mark J. Findlay and Sylvia Ngare, 'Sham of the Moral Court: Testimony Sold as the Spoils of War', *Global Journal of Comparative Law* (forthcoming).

20) The Genocide Convention, Article 2.

that genocide cannot exist in the abstract, absent a clear demonstration that its perpetrators possess the *intentional mental state* of genocide.

The judicial determination of intent is important both for the proof of genocide as a crime and as a rights violation. That said, the process of judicial determination in either situation evidences the different purposes for which judges in rights or criminal tribunals employ fundamental considerations of fact on which to base decisions on liability or responsibility.

5. Genocidal Intent – Relationship with Liability and Responsibility

While the criminal conduct of genocide may seem to mirror that which also satisfies crimes against humanity, and such was the conventional determination as far back as the Nuremburg tribunal hearings,[21] the need for proof of intention is the distinguishing evidentiary element for proving genocide crimes, and a reason why criminal prosecution may be more difficult than the determination of responsibility for rights violation. Another complicating feature in a reliance on prosecuting liability as a satisfactory legal mechanism for addressing genocide is the uniquely collective nature of the atrocity.

> Generally speaking, genocide...is intended...to signify a coordinated plan of different actions aiming at the destruction of essential foundations of the life of national groups, with the aim of annihilating the groups themselves. The objectives of such a plan would be disintegration of the political and social institutions, of culture, language, national feelings, religion, and the economic existence of national groups, and the destruction of the personal security, liberty, health, dignity, and even lives of the individuals belonging to such groups.[22]

The collective dimension of genocide is an evidentiary factor in the more factually amenable determination of responsibility for rights violation, where a senior state official takes action to manifest a largely shared genocidal intent and directs the criminal conduct which is perpetrated through many hands. The exploitation of misplaced nationalism or misunderstood necessities for defence may not be enough to satisfy the special intention required of individual genocidal liability, while it provides more than enough evidence of responsibility for mass rights violation.

The corporate state entity possesses no capacity to formulate intent itself – its intent is revealed only through the demonstrable intentions of state actors with the *de jure* or *de facto* authority to engage the state's participation in the

---

21) Antonio Cassese, 'Genocide', in Antonio Cassesse *et al.*, (eds.), *The Rome Statute of the International Criminal Court: A Commentary* (Oxford University Press, Oxford, 2002), p. 335.

22) Raphael Lemkin, *Axis Rule in Occupied Europe: Laws of Occupation, Analysis of Government, Proposals for Redress* (Carnegie Endowment for International Peace, Washington, D.C., 1944), p. 79.

criminal conduct. The ICJ, in holding that states could be responsible for genocide, developed a two-part test for determining whether the genocidal acts could be attributed to states in question, and thus determined where the court would look for genocidal intent. The first of these tests determines "whether acts of genocide…were perpetrated by 'persons or entities' having the status of organs of the Federal Republic of Yugoslavia…under its internal law".[23] Using this test, the court examined the internal law of the respondent to determine if any person or entity engaged in genocidal acts had a legal relationship to the Federal Republic of Yugoslavia. In the absence of a direct legal relationship, the Court examined whether acts of genocide were perpetrated by persons or entities under the 'effective control' of the state as that term was defined in the *Nicaragua* v. *United States* case.[24]

Having established this proof pathway for attributing state responsibility through the minds of senior officials, the ICJ had to encounter similar proof questions which exercised the ICTY judges' minds when deliberating genocide prosecutions such as in the *Milošević* case. Such a matter of proof, at least in the realm of evidentiary rules, suggests a decision-making situation where the judicial tasks of determining either responsibility or liability intersect, even though the material brought to bear in order that these proof requirements are satisfied may take distinctly different forms (individual or constructive intent). In addition to the foundations of proof differing, for the lawyers and their arguments in either fora, the burden and standard of proof may take on different requirements. Such divergence is further confirmation that criminal liability determination and rights violation responsibilising are distinct but equally significant judicial determinations of genocide. The processes for making such determinations also reveal flexibility in constructing the perpetration of genocide from the individual mind of a single perpetrator to the imputed collective motivations of states.

Different deliberative pathways of judicial determination can be a product of distinguishable purposes for judicial decision-making. On the other hand, an overemphasis on the differences between liability and responsibility determinations can unnecessarily distract analysis away from the central concerns for judicial determination, rights or crime-based. Returning to a consideration of the aims of international criminal justice, despite in its formal incarnation the focus on criminal liability within the international criminal trial, there is little doubt that the intention of even retributive justice for global crime cannot be separated from concern for the rights of victims. It is through the rights focus of international criminal justice that much of its influence over global governance rests.[25]

---

23) ICJ Genocide Judgment, *supra* note 13, p. 386.

24) *Case Concerning the Military and Paramilitary Activities in and against Nicaragua* (*Nicaragua* v. *United States of America*), Judgment of 27 June 1986, I.C.J. Reports 1986.

25) Findlay, *supra* note 8.

6. Criminal Justice and Rights Consciousness - Rights and Governance

It is arguable that the foundations of international criminal justice in their current form can be traced back as a natural consequence of the development of international humanitarian law. In this respect, international criminal justice institutions and processes may be seen as the result of:

- the logical development from victor's justice and the war crimes tribunals following World War II;
- a reaction to international atrocities;
- evidence of a growing potency of international organisations and NGOs in making rights a global governance issue; and
- the new place of humanitarian rights in international relations.

The human rights focus of international criminal justice is essential for its global governance potential.[26] From domestic to global governance, international humanitarian law recognises the need to make nations-states responsible for mass rights violations such as genocide as a measure of their civilised governance record. Global governance particularly through an institutional UN model can be seen as essentially informed by a human rights consciousness. The institutions created by this governance mechanism (such as rights courts and criminal tribunals) should reflect such a consciousness. Because the influence of international criminal justice institutions on global governance is disproportionately significant,[27] the courts and tribunals of international criminal justice have a magnified rights-protection responsibility.

To be confident that it is appropriate more than expedient to move judicial decision-making over genocide from questions of individual criminal liability to considerations of rights violation by states, and in so doing produce a more convincing global justice account, it is useful to overview how a rights consciousness has directed the development of the most recent phase of international criminal justice. With this understanding, it is possible to consider judges in global human rights courts and criminal tribunals advancing with a common mission of global justice as it applies to genocide, and thereby directly influencing the peace and security mission of global governance.

It is not only for international criminal justice institutions to respect human rights in their procedures, but much more, through their wider conflict resolution and victim interest aims, to see the rights of victims and their communities, and potential victim communities, at the forefront of the international criminal

---

26) Payam Akhavan, 'Beyond Impunity: Can International Criminal Justice Prevent Future Atrocities?', 95(1) *American Journal of International Law* (2001) 7–31.

27) Findlay, *supra* note 8.

justice mission. However, critics of a tribunal-based approach to international criminal justice suggest that the true peace-keeping potential of international criminal justice and global governance is achieved more through the collective recognition of human rights (offered through international human rights conventions and their monitoring) than through the prosecution of violations against these.[28] If this position has merit then the claim by the ICJ for jurisdiction over the rights violations of state genocide is a welcome complement to the rights and governance potential of international criminal justice. The ICJ in its declaratory role provides a measure of civilised governance through its capacity to declare states responsible, while not requiring findings of liability or determinations of punishment, so criticised by those who wish to see a more transitional role for international criminal justice.

In the wider sense of international relations, rights recognition and protection come as a package with the delivery of humanitarian aid, or with the establishment of trade relations or with of new states configurations.[29] This rights agenda around political economy, even at a normative level, confirms at a normative level at least a human rights epoch in the current state of global governance. It would be wrong, however, to conceive of this development as uniform, universal and non-problematic. It would also be an overstatement to assume that human rights recognition and protection are the only motivation behind international criminal justice, despite its wider peace-making aims.

7. Motivations of International Criminal Justice

As mentioned earlier in this article, arguably, the prevailing motivation for the international jurisdiction of criminal justice as expressed in instruments such as the Rome Statute is a humanitarian rights response to the violation of individual rights posed by genocide, war crimes, crimes against humanity and crimes of aggression. Along with the end to impunity, which the ICC claims will be a consequence of the selective prosecution and punishment of these crimes, the Preamble to the Statute indicates that the focus of the Court's justice aims is primarily ensuring peace and security for victims and potential victims.

International criminal justice provides justice for victims in that it offers access to justice, inclusivity within the justice process, and integration within justice

28) Mark Drumbl, 'International Criminal Law: Taking Stock of a Busy Decade', 10(1) *Melbourne Journal of International Law* (2009) 38–45.

29) Barbara Crossette, 'Hurting the World's Poor in Morality's Name', 21(4) *World Policy Journal* (2004) 57–62; Morgan J. H. Warners, *Abortion in U.S. Foreign Relations: The Mexico City Policy 1984–2001* (Utrecht University Press, Utrecht, 2009); Richard Fanthorpe, 'Humanitarian Aid in Post-war Sierra Leone: The Politics of Moral Economy', in Sarah Collinson, (ed.), *Power, Livelihoods and Conflict: Case Studies in Political Economy Analysis for Humanitarian Action. HPG Report 13* (Overseas Development Institute, London, 2003) 53–66.

communities.[30] Yet, there is limited selective evidence of a genuine victim constituency developing for international criminal justice, one where humanitarian obligations can translate into the satisfaction of legitimate interests.[31] Translating justice for victims into identifiable trial outcomes is problematic, even in the language preferred by the ICC (perpetrator accountability, creating a historical record, deterring future crime, restoring peace). Even if there is some merit in concluding any of these outcomes from the selective prosecution and punishment of token offenders before the ICC, the rights protection impact of such outcomes is far from certain.

7.1. *Making Perpetrators Accountable*

International criminal justice intends to establish accountability for individual perpetrators and thereby to end the impunity of those who would otherwise evade justice for massive global crimes. Recently, the then Chief Prosecutor of the International Criminal Court directed this humanitarian aim against the late Libyan dictator Colonel Gaddafi in an early stage of the recent uprising against the Gaddafi regime.[32] The prosecutor's intention was to suggest that the actions of individual heads of state and the military figures who served the regime would not be outside the concerns of international criminal justice at any stage of their development, and even prior to formal indictments.[33] While the allegations against Gaddafi did not focus on genocide, the Prosecutor's rhetoric referred to crimes against countless victims of the regime, and the need to protect the rights of citizens against such individual and collective terror.

Controversial as its manifestation in that case might be, the aim of making perpetrators accountable (also prominent in the prosecutorial discourse also directed against Charles Taylor),[34] however, relies on externalities beyond the control of the court (such as violent military incursion or individual amnesty) in order to entice potential offenders to participate in the justice process where they would otherwise be immune from through political or commercial protection and

---

30) Gioia Greco, 'Victims' Rights Overview under the ICC Legal Framework: A Jurisprudential Analysis', 7(2/3) *International Criminal Law Review* (2007) 531–547.

31) Mark J. Findlay, 'Activating Victim Constituency in International Criminal Justice', 3(2) *International Journal of Transitional Justice* (2009) 183-206.

32) *Pre-Trial Chamber Issues Three Warrants of Arrest for Muammar Gaddafi, Saif Al-Islam Gaddafi and Abdualla Al-Senussi*, 27 June 2011, International Criminal Court, Press Release, <www.icc-cpi.int/NR/exeres/D07229DE-4E3D-45BC-8CB1-F5DAF8370218.htm>, 17 September 2012.

33) Tony Cadman, *The international criminal court's many flaws can't simply be glossed over*, 28 June 2012, The Guardian, <www.guardian.co.uk/commentisfree/2012/jun/28/international-criminal-courts-flaws-overlooked>, 17 September 2012.

34) Colin Waugh, 'Don't Be a Dictator in the Wrong Continent at the Wrong Time,' 20 June 2012, *New African Magazine*, <www.newafricanmagazine.com/features/politics/dont-be-a-dictator-in-the-wrong-continent-at-the-wrong-time>, 17 September 2012.

segregation. Amnesty is liberally applied in less formal justice processes such as Truth and Reconciliation Commissions (TRCs) to induce cooperation, and even the international criminal courts and tribunals offer such protections to key witnesses and informants despite the potential criticism of compromising objective justice in so doing.

The formal international criminal justice style of selective intervention (selective prosecution in particular, which is a critical feature of international criminal trials) raises questions as to how impartiality in the delivery of justice is possible for international criminal trials. This reservation concerning the political partiality of international criminal justice gains added weight, given the sectarian determination of offenders and victims in situations where crisis is contested across geo-political favouritism in international relations. Thus, for example, it was suggested in relation to the first case before the International Criminal Court that the government in the Democratic Republic of Congo (DRC) offered up the accused from an opposition militia in order protect themselves and their operatives from prosecution. The Ituri area of the DRC conflict that was targeted for investigation by the ICC in its first trial, was the most distant from the political centre and much riven with opposition influence and authority. In this area, evidence was also less clear as to whether the President and his supporters had any connection to the atrocities alleged to have been committed, whereas there was some evidence of his involvement in supporting militia groups associated with serious crimes in other areas and regions. Thus, with the ICC focusing on crimes in Ituri, its activities could be politically acceptable to the central authorities by "displaying the least capacity to destabilise the current government".[35] Further, the individuals selected for prosecution - Lubanga, Katanga and Ngudjolo – "represent the ICC's attempts to maintain good working relations with the Congolese government in order to facilitate ICC investigations during ongoing conflict and to maintain the support of the Court's principal donors in the context of the Congolese elections and their direct aftermath".[36]

Selective application and activation are not criticisms reserved for international criminal justice alone. International human rights law is equally vulnerable to being selectively directed on political rather than merit-based grounds. Add to the feature of partiality the restriction on engaging human rights law with non-state actors, and the rights paradigm may not cure the problem of selective benefit, whether one seeks judicial determination in a criminal liability or a rights protection route.

---

[35] Phil Clark, 'Law, Politics and Pragmatism: The ICC and Case Selection in Uganda and the Democratic Republic of Congo', in Nicholas Waddell and Phil Clark, (eds.), *Courting Conflict? Justice, Peace and the ICC in Africa* (Royal African Society, London, 2008), p. 40.

[36] *Ibid.*, pp. 41–42.

7.2. *Historical Record*

The development of the historical record through international criminal justice is considered, particularly by victims, as an important humanitarian consequence of global justice intervention. For genocide, the treatment of any such record as atrocious against the standards of civilised society is critical for victims to claim the restitution and healing they deserve from genocide deniers and sceptics. In addition, records outside the courtroom such as commemorative monuments have been shown to facilitate victim and community participation and healing.[37] Again, however, questions can be raised as to whose truth is being recorded in situations where stories are deeply contested and alternate versions of history are up for grabs.[38] For example, the decision of the ICTR in the *Akayesu* case represented the first time that an accused was convicted of genocide for crimes which explicitly included sexual violence, evidenced as rape in war.[39] Despite what is now known of the systematic use of sexualised violence in the Rwandan conflict, charges of sexual violence were not initially included in the indictments, because of the as yet undetermined status of rape in war as evidence of any of the crimes within the tribunal's jurisdiction.[40] The Prosecutor at the time felt that prosecution would not succeed on these grounds because of a belief that women victims would not wish to testify. However, Judge Pillay, who presided in the *Akayesu* case, investigated sexual assault evidence with two female witnesses called to testify to other crimes. The Judges expressed extreme dismay that witnesses were not asked about this earlier, and the Prosecutor subsequently amended the indictments to include further charges of sexual violence.[41] Following on from this, the rape victims were accorded by the judges unique freedom to describe the facts of their violation without relying, as would normally be the case, on the questioning of the lawyers from both sides. Does this case and the manner in which evidence of gross sexual violation evolved, more disturbingly does recognition that adversarial examination of oral testimony in a court-room scenario, where the rules of evidence limit telling the whole story and indictments ignore large components of that story, mean that the trial so conceived will never be the appropriate arena for historical record in the fullest sense?

---

37) Frédéric Mégret, 'Of Shrines, Memorials and Museums: Using the International Criminal Court's Victim Reparation and Assistance Regime to Promote Transitional Justice', 16(1) *Buffalo Human Rights Law Review* (2010) 1–56.

38) Findlay, *supra* note 31.

39) *Prosecutor* v. *Jean-Paul Akayesu*, Case No. ICTR-96-4-T, Judgement, ICTR Trial Chamber, 2 September 1998 ("*Akayesu* case").

40) Chérie Booth, 'Prospects and issues for the International Criminal Court: Lessons from Yugoslavia and Rwanda', in Philippe Sands, (ed.), *From Nuremberg to the Hague: The Future of International Criminal Justice* (Cambridge University Press, Cambridge, 2003), 166–173.

41) Cate Steains, 'Gender Issues', in Roy S. Lee, (ed.), *The International Criminal Court: The Making of the Rome Statute: Issues, Negotiations, Results* (Kluwer Law International, The Hague, 1999).

It could be said from the limits of the adversarial trial frame that an intimate and dynamic recognition of rights violation is a hostage to legal form. Even so, witnesses receive a range of protections through this form and these also are not to be minimised when rights are evaluated. One of the reasons we have argued so strongly for trial transformation in international criminal justice is to spread the due process net wider than what is available for vulnerable victim witnesses who testify to atrocity where and when they remain exposed to their perpetrators.[42]

7.3. *Deterrence*

The rights dimension of international criminal justice is directed towards what can be referred to as general deterrence against the perpetration of atrocities elsewhere, through the punishment of offenders and thereby the denial of impunity for them and those in the future. This protective consequence of justice relies on the assumption that potential offenders will be discouraged from activities which would otherwise constitute global crimes by the prosecution of those who have committed such offences in other places. In a more contextual measure of deterrence, prosecution is said to discredit destabilising political forces within the nation, and even when those prosecuted retain popular support, to limit the long term power of these groups through exclusion from the international sphere.[43]

The causal problem associated with deterrence is the assumption, firstly, that these potential offenders will anticipate the likelihood of apprehension, and once apprehended, next they will expect that stages of justice will be swift and certain. That is of course even if these potential offenders hear of the prosecution, know of its details, and are not privy to the intensely political variables that weigh on selective prosecution. In addition, they might just be powerful enough, or have powerful enough friends, to ignore an ICC warrant. None of these assumptions necessarily hold in the mind of such offenders any more than they seem to for offenders of lesser crimes in domestic criminal justice systems where apprehension is much more likely and prosecution much less selective. Nevertheless, even if direct deterrence is not necessarily effective, some argue that the broader impact of international criminal tribunals is to have ..."mainstreamed" accountability in international relations and thus instilled long-term inhibitions against international crimes in the global community.[44]

Would a rights-protection route add value to the deterrence conundrum? The decisions of the ICJ are essentially expressive. Beyond identifying normative standards that should prevail following judicial determination, it might be hoped that

---

42) Mark J. Findlay and Ralph J. Henham, *Beyond Punishment: Achieving International Criminal Justice* (Palgrave Macmillan, Basingstoke, UK, 2010).

43) Akhavan, *supra* note 26.

44) *Ibid.*, p. 27.

an ICJ judgement would have some force in dissuading a repetition of the behaviour that was the substance of the rejected argument. But this is no more empirically certain than the ICC's aspiration for an end to impunity through an ICC judgement.

What might be ascertained in the desire for deterrent impact is that widening the shaming context from criminality to rights invasion may shore up a wider community approbation against the behaviour. After all, deterrence is as much dependent on the reaction of the community in which the perpetrator has presence and status, as it is a pressure on individual conscience.

7.4. *Restoration of Peace*

Is it fair to suggest that peace will be a logical outcome when military intervention precedes say the involvement of the International Criminal Court or the tribunals in trying to establish individual accountability for military conflict which in part challenged peace in the first place? In terms of its conflict resolution function, international criminal justice is selective to the extent that only certain conflicts are deemed to merit such intervention, and intervention moves from the victors to the vanquished. The Israeli/Palestinian conflict, for instance, is very unlikely to receive global justice intervention as part of any Middle East peace package, not because the premium of peace is not critical in this context but because the cost involves in judicial intervention for the institutions of rights and justice would challenge their hegemonic legitimacy.[45]

International criminal justice mechanisms are said to facilitate the restoration of peace and state reconstruction, as well as essential community reconstruction post-conflict. The ICC trust fund is material evidence of this commitment, limited as it may be. However, the reality is that international criminal justice in its formal incarnation is only directed towards protecting geo-politically significant transitional states, and against states where such intervention is considered by the UN Security Council (UNSC) members to be politically viable. In many areas of global conflict where the states concerned have powerful friends, these situations avoid the initiation and consequences of international criminal prosecutions.

The same criticism cannot so consistently be turned on the selective adjudication of the ICJ. Whether it is because this court does not impose determinations of liability, or that it is restricted to declaratory judgements, that in exercising its rights protection mandate the court has a more even-handed recent history in confronting hegemonic political domination. In addition, it is possible that opening up genocide to rights-based determinations against State Parties may

---

45) *United Nations Fact Finding Mission on the Gaza Conflict*, UN Human Rights Council, <www2.ohchr.org/english/bodies/hrcouncil/specialsession/9/FactFindingMission.htm>, 17 September 2012.

diminish the critical political pre-trial determinations of why rather than who to prosecute.

Perhaps it is in their distance from political expedience that gives the judiciary at large a capacity to make accountable through their deliberations the perpetrators of the world's worst crimes (states or individuals). Once the pressure on prosecutorial discretion is passed, the context of judicial determination will be more likely to receive the case on its merits. Judicial deliberation is a sharp mechanism for making politicised legal initiation accountable to more balanced adjudication. For the purpose of this analysis, a further level of accountability open to judges who determine crime and rights abuse is their facility to hold the justice process at all its levels accountable for the satisfaction of legitimate victim interests.[46]

8. More than Rights – Accountability through Judicial Intervention

Recently, Caroline Fournet, while detailing the widest social and political avenues for accountability in responding to genocide, and noting the limitations of legality in this regard, chose not to go past the importance of legal accountability measures:[47]

> Notwithstanding the evolution on the international scene, legal accountability – prosecutorial forms of accountability – remains at the core of the concept: lack of legal accountability means impunity, which inevitably ensures the recurrence of the atrocities. As Zolo rightly observes,
>
> > It can hardly be denied that widespread impunity is a fact and there is an important link – though not decisive or exclusive – between the political-judicial restoration of social equilibrium and the start of a process of peace-making.
>
> However, international criminal justice has not yet proven to be capable of remedying widespread impunity, except to a minor degree and with normative ambiguities.

Her inference of a possible judicial-political interface in the accountability mix is also recognition that judicial power is critical in calling to book the incipient politicality of international criminal justice, and international rights protection.

As we have done in our earlier case for transforming the international criminal trial into a more restorative and responsive justice mechanism,[48] Fournet argues that by augmenting the judicial presence in international justice delivery, there is more likely to be greater victim satisfaction through the enhanced accountability that judicial determination affords. Such augmentation can, in the present

---

46) Findlay, *supra* note 31.

47) Caroline Fournet, 'Mass Atrocity: Theories and Concepts of Accountability – On the Schizophrenia of Accountability', in Ralph J. Henham and Mark J. Findlay, (eds.), *Exploring the Boundaries of International Criminal Justice* (Ashgate, Aldershot, 2011) 97–114, p. 97.

48) Findlay and Henham, *supra* note 1.

analysis, involve a dual application of responsibility and liability determinations in global rights courts and criminal tribunals. Even where non-judicial alternative accountability frames can claim a better capacity in creating historical record, judicial determination has a sharper capacity to legitimate confidence in the accountability project:

> By its dramaturgy, justice has the power, in the course of the debates, to intensely arise consciousness of what has happened, of the horror of the crime itself (Robert Badinter).
>
> As previously mentioned, truth commissions have the immense benefit of offering a flexible option particularly "suited to achieving [accountability, reconciliation and the transition from an authoritarian past] in countries where limited resources, the absence of a strong and impartial legal system, and other circumstances make a judicial approach infeasible".[49] Furthermore, as Havel observes, "truth commissions (as they are now evolving) have the markedly superior characteristic, rarely apparent in criminal trials, of systematic consideration of the victims of the investigated oppression".[50] Still, notwithstanding the advantages offered by TRCs, accountability, short of prosecution, is bound to fail in achieving its universal goals of prevention and of guarantee of non-repetition.[51]

Accountability through judicial deliberation is not a new concept. In fact, one of the arguments in favour of a trial model for international criminal justice is that judges can ensure that justice is seen to be done. Following on from questioning:

- the rights focus of aims for international criminal justice
- the practical attainability of peace and security aims
- the widening potential for peace and security through crime and rights judicial determinations; and
- the better satisfaction of legitimate victim interests through liability and responsibility adjudication frames,

there is arguably a prescient responsibility for judicial determination of rights in action, so that the aims of international criminal justice which claim to advance rights are more than aspirations.

9. Conclusion

It is an important alliance between international criminal law and international human rights law that is leading to an enhanced role for judicial determination in

---

49) Jason S. Abrams and Priscilla Hayner, 'Documenting, Acknowledging and Publicizing the Truth', in M. Cherif Bassiouni, (ed.), *Introduction to international Criminal Law* (Transnational Publishers, Ardsley, New York, 2002) 283–293, p. 291.

50) Brian F. Havel, 'Public Law and the Construction of Collective Memory', in M. Cherif Bassiouni (ed.), *Introduction to international Criminal Law* (Transnational Publishers, Ardsley, New York, 2002), p. 389.

51) Fournet, *supra* note 47, pp. 40–41.

the global response to genocide. An interesting and also important byproduct of this is how the judicial manifestation of rights responsibility and criminal liability in international legality may be fortified through this alliance, thereby increasing the potential of law and legal institutions to respond to global atrocity. As Groome observes:[52]

> In the *ICJ Genocide Judgment* - its first judgement enforcing the 1948 Genocide Convention - the ICJ has thus created, in effect, a relationship of dependency upon the work of other international criminal courts. Given the likelihood that future allegations of genocide will be brought not only before the ICJ, but the ICC, the relationship between the ICJ and the ICTY as defined by the *ICJ Genocide Judgment* will also, no doubt, come to define the relationship between the ICJ and the ICC.
>
> We may expect a State Party to initiate a claim of genocide in the ICJ shortly after any such alleged conduct takes place and long before any final determination of individual criminal responsibility in an international criminal tribunal. The ICJ - dependent upon the work of other tribunals - will necessarily have to wait upon their final judgments.

Even so, it would be foolish to pin the hopes of genocide victims on judges and trials (determining responsibility or liability) as an adequate global recourse to the horrors of genocide, and the call to accountability which it demands. Despite my assertion that a binary approach in responding to genocide (rights and crime) is better managed in the hands of an accountable judiciary, and stimulating a burgeoning jurisprudence which builds history and legal certainty around atrocity, and reflects the wider legitimate victim interests, I would be selling this assertion too hard were it not measured against the limits of international legal institutionalism. Particularly in the context of the atrocity trial, Mark Drumbl rightly sounds caution in the face of overstatement:[53]

> The atrocity trial pins blame on the ugliest and most reprehensible individuals. In reality, however, atrocity is the product of many factors. Individual action is one of these. But disappeared from the truth-telling process is the involvement (or nonfeasance) of state actors and international organisations. Also disappeared is the catalytic role of benefiting bystanders, transnational capital and colonial histories. The truths told by international criminal law are convenient. They are manageable. By blaming the few for the murder of the many, these truths comfort. They do not embarrass too much or too many. But the origin of atrocity is much more discomfiting and discomforting. If we move into a mindset where the current truths of international criminal law become totalising and exclusionary of all others, then we achieve some justice but we actually settle for a very crimped understanding of justice. One of the reasons why international criminal law may have limited transformative potential — despite the lofty rhetoric — is because it only scratches the surface of what justice actually entails following mass atrocity.

I have suggested, in this brief review, that opening up parallel pathways for judicially determining genocide, from the perspectives of criminal liability and

52) Groome, *supra* note 14, p. 916.
53) Drumbl, *supra* note 28, p. 44.

rights-protection responsibility, builds on a present trend in international criminal justice to recognise punishment and protection. The peace and security aims of international criminal justice are compatible with, and may be supported by, this binary development of judicial determinations regarding genocide. However, the global justice aims do not offer simple pathways for their attainment, and the consequential aspirations that they protect legitimate victims' rights are far from certain. Judicial deliberation, therefore, needs to adopt an accountability dimension to test whether determinations of responsibility or liability for genocide will advance legitimate victim interests if enunciated through a criminal liability or rights responsibility frame. In so doing, judicial deliberation should bring closer together the enunciation of genocide as a global crime and an affront to human rights.

Public Support for the International Criminal Court

James Meernik
Professor of Political Science, University of North Texas, Denton, TX, USA

Abstract
The legitimacy of the International Criminal Court and especially public acceptance of its actions will be crucial to its success in apprehending suspects, conducting fair trials and garnering the support it needs in the international community. I contend that individual opinions about the ICC will be anchored in the degree to which the Court is seen as upholding or undermining the dominant narrative within one's salient, identifying groups regarding who committed international crimes and why. I utilize data from a World Public Opinion survey of seven nations in the Middle East, Central Asia and Africa to investigate public support for the ICC's case against President Al Bashir of The Sudan. I argue that support is contingent upon individual membership in salient groups as defined by religion, region and ethnicity. Those who might be expected to view the ICC's actions as in conflict with the dominant narrative of these groups regarding who was responsible for the crimes under investigation and the perceived bias of the ICC and the West against their group were less likely to support the ICC.

Keywords
International Criminal Court (ICC); *Al Bashir* case

1. Introduction

The International Criminal Court is, at the time of writing, actively investigating or prosecuting alleged violations of international law regarding war crimes, crimes against humanity, and genocide in eight situations. These situations involve the countries of Uganda, the Democratic Republic of the Congo, Central African Republic, Ivory Coast, Libya, Kenya, Mali and The Sudan. While no one case is more intrinsically significant than the others, the ICC's efforts to apprehend and try those alleged to be responsible for the suspected genocide in the Sudanese Darfur region have brought tremendous attention to the Court and especially its indictment of Sudanese president Omar Al-Bashir. Indeed, the ICC's efforts to bring the suspected perpetrators to justice, the strongly critical reaction by many African governments and the defiance of the Sudanese leadership have made this a critical test case for the ICC. The credibility of the promise inherent in the creation of the ICC to end impunity for those who have committed violations of international law is at stake. So too is the credibility of the United Nations Security Council that referred the case to the ICC.

There is an increasing sense among many supporters and critics of international justice that politics is playing a prominent role in the work of the ICC. All the situations listed above involve African states, which has led to charges of bias and neo-patrimonialism. Many critics charge that the ICC has not pursued justice within these cases in an even-handed fashion. They contend that by thus far not charging, for example, government leaders in Uganda and government allies in the DRC, the ICC has ignored the wrongdoings of the powerful and the crimes of its benefactors.[1] Furthermore, because of the authority of the United Nations Security Council to refer situations to the ICC, the Court must engage in selective prosecution that suits the interests of the major powers (e.g., The Sudan, Libya cases), as well as selective "non-prosecution" of states whose Security Council supporters block referrals (e.g., Syria). The accumulated weight of these charges of bias and politicization, regardless of their merits, may begin to undermine the legitimacy and prospects for international justice.

The legitimacy of the International Criminal Court will be crucial to its success in apprehending suspects, conducting fair trials and garnering the support it needs in the international community. In particular, public support of the ICC will be especially critical. Scholars have only recently begun investigating public views on international justice and the various international tribunals, but they have shown that there is a great deal of misinformation and misunderstanding among the affected publics that can lead to scepticism, distrust and ultimately perceptions of interference and illegitimacy.[2] The viability of international justice will depend upon the work of the tribunals, and the ICC in particular, to communicate their mission and their methods to these publics to avoid charges of bias.[3] As de Guzman[4] writes, "Indeed, the globalization of communications increasingly means that an institution's legitimacy depends on the opinions of ordinary citizens around the world". If public perceptions of international courts are tainted by accusations of victor's justice, western domination or disregard for local interests and values, the power of international justice to prosecute wrongdoers and end impunity will be damaged. Indeed, the affected states and their people may well

---

[1] *See* News Release, HRW, ICC: Investigate All Sides in Uganda (4 Feb. 2004), *at* http://www.hrw.org/en/news/2004/02/04/icc-investigate-all-sides-uganda.
See also Tim Allen, *Trial Justice: The International Criminal Court and The Lord's Resistance* (Zed Books, 2006), Army, 98.

[2] Janine Clark, 'The Limits of Retributive Justice: Findings of an Empirical Study in Bosnia and Hercegovina' 7 *Journal of International Criminal Justice* (2009) 463-487; Eric Stover and Harvey M. Weinstein, *My Neighbor, My Enemy* (Cambridge: Cambridge UP, 2004).

[3] Mark. Drumbl, *Atrocity, Punishment, and International Law* (New York: Cambridge Univ. Press, 2007); Tim Kelsall, *Culture under Cross-Examination: International Justice and the Special Court for Sierra Leone*. (Cambridge: UK Cambridge University Press, 2009).

[4] Margaret de Guzman, 'Choosing to Prosecute: Expressive Selection at the International Criminal Court', 33 *Michigan Journal of International Law* (2012) 265-.

resort to other methods of achieving their political ends, such as other transitional justice strategies, or even violence.

The purpose of this chapter is to assess what factors lead individuals to support the work of the International Criminal Court. I focus on public support in several African, Middle East and Central Asian countries for the prosecution of Sudanese President Omar Al-Bashir. First, I review the historical background of the Darfur ituation in The Sudan and the ICC's efforts to hold leaders accountable. Second, I develop a theory of individuals' views on President Al-Bashir's prosecution that focuses primarily upon the importance of identification with the accused, knowledge of the situation (in this case, Darfur) and education. I test the hypotheses on data from a World Public Opinion survey of seven African, Middle East and Central Asian states. Last, I conclude with suggestions regarding how future research can contribute to the development of a more comprehensive model and what sort of data would be required to better evaluate public support for international justice.

2. Background

The Darfur region is in the west of The Sudan and is largely populated by a non-Arab and non-Muslim population. While this part of what is now The Sudan has experienced political turmoil and conflict prior to the recent spike in violence, the region's current troubles began in earnest in 2003 when the Sudan Liberation Movement and the Justice and Equality groups took up arms against the Arab and Muslim-dominated government in Khartoum. They accused the Sudanese government of favouritism toward the Arab population and a neglect of Darfuri problems and concerns. The Sudanese government responded through the use of military force to put down the rebellion. While the Sudanese military and police were part of this operation, it was the government-affiliated militias, known as the Janjaweed which have been accused of some of the worst of the atrocities in killing civilians and driving them from their homes. The Janjaweed militias consist largely of the Arabized populations of the area, for which the Sudanese government has disclaimed any responsibility. As the Sudanese military proved incapable of successfully battling the insurgency, the Janjaweed militias assumed a greater role in the fighting, which then sharply escalated. Estimates of the number of those killed in the fighting range from the thousands to hundreds of thousands, while the number of refugees who have fled the fighting, especially into neighbouring Chad may be as high as one million. Since 2003 there have been numerous international and regional efforts to stop the violence and reach a peace agreement, as well as the deployment of African Union forces to police attempts at cease-fires.

Accusations of genocide were levelled against the Sudanese government by many governments and NGO's that kept international attention focused on the conflict. Then in March of 2005 the United Nations Security Council referred the situation in Darfur to the International Criminal Court. The Security Council referral, under Article 13 of the Rome Treaty, was based upon its Chapter VII powers in the UN Charter to look after international peace and security. Prominent opponents of the ICC—the United States and China—abstained on the resolution vote. While The Sudan is not a party to the Rome Treaty (it signed, but did not ratify the treaty), the Security Council resolution requires that all parties to the conflict in Darfur cooperate with the ICC. Shortly thereafter, the ICC Office of the Prosecutor (OTP), led by Luis Moreno Ocampo, began its investigation and gathered evidence on the Darfur situation from the government of The Sudan, the African Union, the United Nations and other groups and organizations.[5]

In April of 2007 the ICC issued arrest warrants for the former Minister of the Interior, Ahmed Haroun, and for Janjaweed militia leader, Ali Kushayb, in keeping with its focus on those senior leaders most responsible for violations of international law. Haroun and Kushayb were both charged with multiple counts of war crimes and crimes against humanity for human rights atrocities in Darfur. The government of The Sudan denied that the ICC had any right to intervene in its affairs and refused to cooperate. In July of 2008 the Prosecutor filed an application for an arrest warrant for Sudanese President Omar Al-Bashir charging him with multiple counts of war crimes, crimes against humanity, and most notably, genocide. Subsequently in March of 2009 the ICC Pre-Trial Chamber I issued its first warrant of arrest for President Bashir, but without the genocide charges. The OTP appealed the Pre-Trial Chamber's decision to exclude the genocide charges and it was subsequently determined by the Appeals Chamber that the Pre-Trial Chamber had applied an erroneous standard of evidence regarding the genocide charges. The OTP's application for the addition of the genocide charges was sent back to the Pre-Trial Chamber. Subsequently in July of 2010 a second arrest warrant was issued with the genocide charges added. Thus, President Al Bashir became the first sitting head of state to be charged with violations of international law by the ICC.

Reaction in The Sudan against the ICC's initial arrest warrant was swift. The Sudanese government expelled many international aid organizations in retaliation for the arrest warrant. The government condemned the ICC's efforts. An aide to President Bashir was quoted by the BBC as asserting that, "This decision is exactly what we have been expecting from the court, which was created to target Sudan and to be part of the new mechanism of neo-colonialism".[6] President Bashir contemptuously stated that the ICC could "eat" its arrest warrant. Thousands

---

5) See the ICC documentation on the situation in The Sudan at http://www.icc-cpi.int/menus/icc/press%20and%20media/press%20releases/2005/the%20prosecutor%20of%20the%20icc%20opens%20investigation%20in%20darfur?lan=en-GB .

6) "Warrant Issued for Sudan's Leader", 4 March 2009. As found at http://news.bbc.co.uk/2/hi/7923102.stm.

turned out into the streets of Khartoum to protest the indictment. Many African and Arab governments came out in opposition to the arrest warrant and argued that it could make reaching a peace settlement in Darfur all the more difficult. There were also many supporters of the ICC indictment, including many western governments and NGOs who spoke out in favour of the indictment.

Since the initial indictment in March of 2009 President Al Bashir has remained in power in The Sudan and has even flown to other African and Arab states, whose governments have refused to arrest Bashir despite the UN Security Council resolution that called on all states to cooperate with the ICC. The African Union went so far as to issue the following declaration at its July, 2009 meeting in Libya:

> DECIDES that in view of the fact that the request by the African Union has never been acted upon [requesting that the UN Security Council ask the ICC to defer its investigation of the situation in The Sudan], the AU Member States shall not cooperate pursuant to the provisions of Article 98 of the Rome Statute of the ICC relating to immunities, for the arrest and surrender of President Omar El Bashir of The Sudan.[7]

Since that time President Bashir has flown throughout the continent in continued defiance of the ICC arrest warrant as African and Middle East states persist in refusing to honour the warrant or the Security Council's resolution mandating cooperation with the ICC.

The investigation into the Darfur situation and most especially the indictment of Al Bashir as a sitting head of state involved in an ongoing conflict have generated tremendous visibility for the ICC. Much of it, especially in the context of the ICC's focus on situations in Africa, has been rather negative. While indictments of popular or powerful leaders can almost always be expected to generate interest and opposition, the impact of this indictment has been particularly important as the ICC seeks to establish its credibility, impartiality and value to the international community. As these criteria for success are realized through unbiased case selection, successful apprehension of suspects and fair trials of suspected war criminals, the ICC becomes further embedded in the fabric of international politics and security affairs. To the extent the ICC is unable to demonstrate its credibility, impartiality and value to its many diverse audiences around the world because of (mis)perceptions particularly regarding its selection criteria for investigations, perceptions of its legitimacy may be jeopardized.

It is crucial to understand how perceptions and support for the ICC are determined. We can expect that many of the decisions to investigate and indict will prove unpopular as people and their leaders will question why a particular country or specific individual is being targeted when there are so many other atrocities

---

[7] Decision on the Meeting of African State Parties to the Rome Statute of the International Criminal Court (ICC) Doc. Assembly/AU/13(XIII), as found at http://au.int/en/sites/default/files/ASSEMBLY_EN_1_3_JULY_2009_AUC_THIRTEENTH_ORDINARY_SESSION_DECISIONS_DECLARATIONS_%20MESSAGE_CONGRATULATIONS_MOTION_0.pdf.

occurring around the world. Whether one sees merit in such arguments or not, especially in light of the impossibility of investigating all potential violations of international law throughout the globe, is irrelevant. The ICC's legitimacy and ultimately its success will depend on a foundation of support, or at least acceptance of its actions as necessary for peace and security. As Ramji-Nogales writes, achieving "legitimacy is of paramount importance to transitional justice mechanisms".[8] Therefore, it is crucial to understand what factors lead individuals to support ICC investigations and indictments. In particular, it is important to understand such support, or the lack thereof, in these difficult and controversial cases where the lofty aims of international justice collide with the complexity and passions of local politics. Public support for the ICC in its indictment against President Al Bashir is thus a critical test case, especially in those nations and among those people who are likely to be the toughest critics of the ICC—the populations of states nearby and similar to The Sudan. I conduct just such an analysis with data from a World Public Opinion survey that contains information on individual opinions in several African, Middle Eastern and Central Asian nations. First, however, I outline a series of expectations regarding expected support for or opposition to the ICC's indictment of President Bashir.

3. Theoretical Framework: Understanding Public Opinion and International Courts

3.1. *Research on Public Opinion and International Tribunals*

The current state of knowledge regarding public support for international criminal tribunals is embryonic. Much of the research points to the importance of institutional factors, such as the process by which tribunals are created, their location, and other institutional characteristics.[9] A variety of polls on public attitudes toward the various tribunals finds a great deal of mixed opinion, especially regarding the International Criminal Tribunal for the Former Yugoslavia and the people of the former Yugoslavia, which have garnered the most study. A 2005 report by the United Nations Development Programme Early Warning System found that 23.3% of those surveyed in Bosnia believed that the ICTY had "done a good job and justified its existence", while 36.8% believed that the ICTY had not performed well, but was still necessary.[10] Positive evaluations

---

8) Jaya Ramji-Nogales,' Designing Bespoke Transitional Justice: A Pluralist Process Approach,' 32(1) *Michigan Journal of International Law* (2010) 12–13.

9) William W. Burke-White, '*Regionalization of International Criminal Law Enforcement: A Preliminary Exploration,*' Texas International Law Journal. 729 (2003) 736–37.

10) UN Development Program Early Warning System Special Report (2005) 'Justice and Truth in Bosnia and Herzegovina: Public Perceptions' http://www.undp.ba/, accessed 7 December 2009, 12.

of the Tribunal vary considerably across ethnic groups. Kosovar Albanians typically register the highest levels of support for the ICTY, followed by Bosnian Muslims, Croatians and Serbians.[11] Essentially, public support is strongly and inversely related to the number of those from one's ethnic group in detention at the Tribunal. Clark finds that Croatian and Serbian interviewees, "...unanimously claimed that the Tribunal was biased against their own ethnic group".[12] Even more troubling, she finds that an "overwhelming majority" of Bosniaks were angry and disappointed by ICTY sentences.[13] As Mirko Klarin argues, however, "public opinion in the former Yugoslavia is influenced very little by what the prosecution and the judges are actually doing in The Hague". Rather, he argues that local elites and the media shape the discourse on the Tribunal, in large part because until recently the people of the region were ruled by the very same individuals who have been investigated and often indicted by the Tribunal.[14]

Unfortunately, locating good data on public opinion regarding the performance of other tribunals, such as Rwandan or Sierra Leonean international courts (The International Criminal Tribunal for Rwanda and the Special Court for Sierra Leone), is problematic. While some researchers have conducted small-scale surveys or have done more extensive work in particular regions of these countries, generalizing from these findings requires caution. Nonetheless, as Ford[15] shows, the populations in these nations generally are not hesitant to offer an opinion about international justice, but do not always understand how the tribunals operate and what their responsibilities are. There is limited evidence to suggest in the case of Sierra Leone that support for the SCSL varies somewhat depending on the respondent's degree of identification with those whom the SCSL is prosecuting. Opinions on the SCSL tend to be filtered through individuals' ethnic and political ties with the accused, measured as one's region. Individuals from areas where the Sierra Leonean factions drew their support and whose leaders are on trial tend to

---

11) Donna E. Arzt, 'Views on the Ground: The Local Perception of International Criminal Tribunals in the Former Yugoslavia and Sierra Leone', 603 *The Annals of the American Academy of Political and Social Science* (2006) 226-239; UN Development Program Early Warning System Special Report (2005), 'Justice and Truth in Bosnia and Herzegovina: Public Perceptions' <http://www.undp.ba/> accessed 7 December 2009, 12; A-S. J. Hatay, 'Peacebuilding and Reconciliation in Bosnia and Herzegovina, Kosovo and Macedonia 1995-2004' <http://www.pcr.uu.se/publications/other_pub/Reconciliationreport_jacobsson_050615.pdf>, accessed 8 December 2009.

12) Clark, *supra* note 1, p. 471.

13) Mirko Klarin, 'The Impact of the ICTY Trials on Public Opinion in the Former Yugoslavia,' 7 *Journal of International Criminal Justice* (2009) 89-96, at p. 92.

14) Klarin *supra* note 10, 90.

15) Stuart Ford, 'A Social Psychology Model of the Perceived Legitimacy of International Criminal Courts:

Implications for the Success of Transitional Justice Mechanisms,' *Vanderbilt Journal of Transnational Law* 45 (2012) 405-476.

be less supportive of the SCSL.[16] As Ford points out, "In short, the survey evidence from Sierra Leone is consistent with the social psychology model, which predicts that whom the court indicts can have a large negative effect on how the court is perceived by affected groups that identify with one of the "sides" in the conflict."[17]

In an innovative piece of research Ford demonstrates that research regarding the importance of institutional features on public support and legitimacy is not supported in studies of public attitudes. Indeed, since institutional features such as location, mandate and staff composition are largely fixed, they cannot account for variations in opinion across individuals in a country. Rather, since support tends to depend on individual factors such ethnicity, national identification and religion, we must look elsewhere for a coherent theory of public opinion regarding international justice. He finds such a theory in a social psychology model of individual attitudes. Ford writes:

> Both theory and numerous attitude surveys indicate that where there is a high degree of identification between groups within the affected population and the "sides" in the conflict that led to the involvement of a court, the affected population's perception of the court will be determined largely by whom the court prosecutes. When the court's indictments and prosecutions conflict with a group's dominant internal narrative about responsibility for the conflict, members of the group are likely to perceive the court as biased and unjust, which allows the group to discount the indictments and preserve its internal narrative.[18]

Ford utilizes a social psychology perspective that frames individual opinions regarding the legitimacy of international courts and support for international criminal justice institutions as predicated on the extent to which the institutions target individuals for prosecution in a manner that conflicts with individuals' ethnic/religious/national group's internal narrative regarding the origins of violence, and their responsibility for violations of international law. Through motivated reasoning and confirmation bias in which individuals tend to reach pre-existing conclusions, discount information that conflicts with their conclusions and seek out information that supports their conclusions, individuals form biased opinions about international justice. When evidence regarding the performance of such courts conflicts with their group narrative regarding the origins and responsibility for conflict, it is strongly discounted. This scepticism and distrust regarding evidence at variance with the group narrative allows individuals to avoid the uncomfortable cognitive dissonance that arises from the prosecution of their countrymen.

---

16) Edward Sawyer and Tim Kelsall,'Truth vs. Justice? Popular Views on the Truth and Reconciliation Commission and the Special Court for Sierra Leone,' 7 *Online J. Peace & Conflict Resol.* (2007) 36, 59.

17) Ford, *supra* note 15 at 447.

18) *Ibid.*

An individual may have attachments to a variety of groups that are fundamentally important in defining his or her identity. These groups, in turn, provide the individual with a context within which his existence may be interpreted; a narrative regarding the history of the group and especially its triumphs and tragedies; and a community that provides a social support system that tends to the welfare of the individual and to the sustenance of the group's narratives. These group identities may be formed on the basis of nationality, ethnicity, religion, and other such intrinsically meaningful human units of organization. The strength of individuals' emotional and intellectual reliance on these groups to understand and make sense of the world creates a powerful tie that can serve many purposes for group leaders. In particular, those who claim to speak for such groups can use these strongly felt attachments to rally support against rival groups and those who might do harm to the group or its dominant narratives. Therefore, we should expect that membership in these groups will exercise a substantial effect on an individual's willingness to support institutions that would challenge their dominant narratives and thus be perceived as threatening to the survival of the group.

Ford's social psychology model provides a useful framework for understanding individual views on international tribunals generally, and about the ICC in the *Al Bashir* case. Furthermore, Ford's work comports well with what several scholars have been finding with regard to the ICTY—opinions are premised principally upon ethnic identify. To the extent that the ICTY's (in this case) actions regarding whom to prosecute and how severely to punish the guilty have comported with individuals' ethnic group's internal narrative regarding the origin of the wars and responsibility for the crimes committed, approval of the ICTY has been more likely (e.g., Bosnian Muslims). However, as the ICTY's decisions to prosecute and punishment have conflicted with such narratives, as they tend to focus on the wrongdoings of individuals' ethnic group more than others and tell an origin of war story that diverges from the dominant ethnic narrative, support for the ICTY has declined (e.g., Serbs, and especially Bosnian Serbs). Therefore, identification with the individuals under indictment or on trial at international tribunals tends to be the dominant determinant of support for such tribunals. Support is conditional, circumstantial and dynamic.

3.2. *A Group Identification Model of Individual Support for the ICC*

I begin by making two key assumptions. First, as Ford and others cited above have amply noted, information and understanding regarding international tribunals is fairly low among people living in the nations that are the object of these courts. A lack of information and understanding, however, will generally not act as a hindrance to the development of opinions. Individuals will express views on the performance of international criminal justice institutions and their general sense of whether such institutions are "good" or "bad" things. As a consequence therefore, I contend that individual opinions will be anchored in the degree to which the court, in this case the ICC, is seen as upholding or undermining what is the dominant narrative regarding the conflict within one's salient, identifying groups.

To test the model outlined below I utilize data from a World Public Opinion survey of seven nations in the Middle East, Central Asia and Africa. After excluding cases with missing data, I find that of 5161 survey respondents who were asked the following question, "ICC has charged Pres of Sudan, Omar Bashir w/war crimes & crimes against humanity for his role in displacing & killing civilians. Do you approve of the ICC taking this action?", 3028 individuals (58.7%) expressed support, while 2133 individuals (41.3%) expressed opposition. This is the question that measures the dependent variable—support for the ICC in the case against President Bashir. Below I outline those factors that should be relevant in determining how the ICC's actions are perceived through the lens of individuals' key group identifying characteristics.

3.2.1. *Region*

In the case of the International Criminal Court and the prosecution of Sudanese President Omar Al-Bashir, there are three, critical identification factors that might be expected to play a role in individual opinions: regional identification, ethnic identification and religious identification. As many critics have noted, the International Criminal Court has largely focused on African conflicts for investigation and prosecution (although this will soon change), which has led to charges of bias and Western legal imperialism.[19] The resulting negative press that the ICC has confronted may well have colored individual support for its prosecution of President Bashir. If individuals from Sub-Saharan African states generally accept the narrative that the ICC is politically biased against African states and has unfairly singled out that continent's conflicts for investigation and prosecution, then we should expect that there would be a tendency to not support the ICC. Painting individual opinions regarding the ICC with such broad brush strokes is not the most nuanced approach to understanding such attitudes. Obviously, opinion across Africa and within Sub-Saharan African states is likely to vary among other group identity characteristics and other factors as well. For our purposes, however, it is possible to begin making such distinctions at a more general level to determine their predictive accuracy and whether further refinement of such measures is necessary to accurately portray which group identity characteristics are most meaningful in these evaluations. Therefore, I suggest the following hypothesis:

---

[19] See Oette Lutz, 'Peace and Justice or Neither". 8 *Journal of International Criminal Justice* (2010) 345-364 for a review.

Hypothesis 1: Individuals from Sub-Saharan African states will be more likely to oppose ICC prosecution of Sudanese President Omar Al Bashir.[20]

3.2.2. *Religion*

Second, the group identification model suggests that another critical factor that determines the strength of an individual's attachment to a group and its narrative is religion. We saw in the case of the ICTY that religion, although closely tied to nationality and politics, was a potent factor in determining one's opinion about that Tribunal. In the case of The Sudan, one finds two, key situational characteristics that could be expected to invoke the power of religion and a religion-inspired narrative of the events in Darfur that would be especially relevant for those of the Muslim faith. First, the conflict in Darfur, although it is complex and involves cross-cutting alliances among various religious/ethnic groups, is often portrayed in the popular media as a struggle between the Christian and animist Darfuris against the Muslim, Arab majority. The ICC's indictment against the Muslim leaders of The Sudan might well be expected to generate hostility among other Muslims both because of who is and is not being singled out for prosecution. Second, one cannot overlook that the West, led by the US, has intervened with international coalitions (often working with the same European states who are the strongest supporters of the ICC) into two Muslim majority states this century. Such actions have further fuelled charges that the West (and often by extension, the international community) is anti-Muslim and is seeking to impose its values and politics on those who belong to the religion. Such charges fit comfortably into a similar narrative regarding the perceived bias of the ICC (even though the US is not a party to the Rome Treaty, it essentially acquiesced to the UN Security Council referral of the Darfur situation to the ICC) and form part of a larger narrative regarding a culturally and politically imperialistic West. Therefore, we might expect that those who identify themselves as Muslim, regardless of nationality, will be more likely to oppose the prosecution of President Al Bashir. An Al Bashir prosecution invokes the power of these narratives that question the very purposes of international justice, and most especially its selection of targets for prosecution.

Hypothesis 2: Individuals who identify as Muslims will be more likely to oppose ICC prosecution of Sudanese President Omar Al Bashir.[21]

3.2.3. *Ethnicity*

Another potent group identity characteristic is ethnicity. One of the fault lines that has run through international politics, especially since World War II, the creation of Israel and more recently with the various military interventions by

---

20) The Sub-Saharan African states included in this analysis are: Kenya and Nigeria.

21) Religion is measured using responses to the question, "What is your religion?". Several choices are provided, including, Christian, Muslim and Jewish.

the West and UN in the Middle East involves the division between the West and the Arab world. To be sure, these political differences and the internal narratives that all sides employ to make sense of these clashes are informed by religion, politics, economics and other factors. But like religion, such narratives among the identity groups are made all the more potent in cases like the Darfur situation. The division between Darfur and the rest of The Sudan involves religion and ethnicity as the Darfuris are largely non–Arab. Thus, charges of ICC or Western bias against Arabs because of the prosecution regarding the actions of Arab leaders are likely to resonate deeply, especially as such actions fit comfortably within the larger narrative of the anti-Arab West. Thus, we should expect that support for the ICC's indictment against President Al Bashir will be particularly weak among those individuals from Arabic states.

Hypothesis 3: Individuals from largely Arab states and territories will be more likely to oppose ICC prosecution of Sudanese President Omar Al Bashir.[22]

3.2.4. *ICC Knowledge and Education*

As Ford shows in his extensive review of public opinion and international courts, knowledge about the workings of all tribunals is usually in pretty short supply among all affected countries. Nonetheless, this does not prevent individuals from offering opinions on the basis of more intuitive understandings and perceptions, as well as more emotional bases of opinion formation. Therefore, we should not expect either an individual's extent of knowledge about the ICC and the Darfur situation or her level of education would correlate with support for the ICC. However, in other research, knowledge of the Geneva Conventions was shown to be strongly related to support for punishment of those suspected of having committed war crimes.[23] In this case we have data on the respondents' awareness of the situation in Darfur. Such a measure of knowledge may actually possess some intrinsic value even if it does not tell us anything about the respondents' knowledge of the ICC. Knowledge of the Darfur situation implies some awareness about the extensive violence there, and perhaps the charges of genocide that have been a preeminent feature of the conflict. This may lead to support for prosecution. Therefore, I still expect that greater awareness of the ICC and greater levels of education will tend to be positively related to support for the ICC's prosecution of President Bashir.

Hypothesis 4: The greater the level of an individual's awareness of the Darfur situation, the more likely (s)he will support ICC prosecution of Sudanese President Omar Al Bashir.[24]

---

22) The Arab states and territories included in this analysis are: Egypt, Iraq and Palestine.

23) James Meernik and Kimi King, *A Model of Individual Choices Regarding Justice Options After Conflict.* Unpublished manuscript.

24) We use the following question to measure individual awareness of the Darfur situation, "How much have you heard about violence in the Darfur region of Sudan, which has led to over

Hypothesis 5: Individuals with more years of education will be more likely to support ICC prosecution of Sudanese President Omar Al Bashir.[25]

3.2.5 *Attitudes toward the International Community*

It is also important to factor in individual attitudes toward the larger, proper response to the Darfur situation more generally, regardless of what actions the ICC may or may not take. If individuals believe the situation is severe enough and the implications for human rights substantial, we might expect them to be more inclined to some form of external intervention to address the situation. Individuals who believe that such humanitarian intervention is needed should be more predisposed to support the ICC prosecution of President Bashir. To determine individual views on external intervention, I utilize the following question:, "Should UN bring in shipments of aid, protected by military if necessary, even against will of govt or would this be a violation of sovereignty? Those who support external intervention such as this and are not troubled by concerns over infringements on another country's sovereignty should be more accepting of the ICC prosecution of Al Bashir as this issue is also portrayed by critics as a violation of The Sudan's sovereignty. Additionally, support for the United Nations may also correlate with acceptance of the other major international institution involved in the Darfur situation—the International Criminal Court. We should find that those individuals who support intervention as a means of protection should also be more likely to support intervention to prosecute.

Hypothesis 6: Individuals who support UN intervention should be more likely to support ICC prosecution of Sudanese President Omar Al Bashir.

3.2.6 *Control Variables*

I include three variables to control for the influence of socio-economic and demographic characteristics. First I include a measure of the size of the community in which the individual lives. In general we might expect that those living in urban or more populated areas would be exposed to a greater diversity of opinion and knowledge about Darfur and the ICC. Thus, a positive relationship may exist here. I also include an ordinal measure of age and a measure of gender to determine if support for the ICC's investigation against President Bashir is influenced by these factors.

---

a million civilians being driven from their homes & 100K + civilians being killed?". The possible responses were "a lot"; "some"; "a little"; "nothing at all" in ranked order.

25) We use the following measure of education: 1 = "illiterate"; 2 = "Primary, basic, elementary school or less"; 3 = "Some of High/Preparatory/Secondary School or equiv"; 4 = "Completed High/Secondary School. Includes HS diploma or equiv"; 5 = "Some of college/intermediate or associates degree"; 6 = "Completed University/Bachelors degree"; 7 = "Post Graduate Degree".

4. Analysis

To model the determinants of individual opinion formation regarding the ICC investigation and indictment against Sudanese President Omar al-Bashir I employ a probit model with robust standard errors, clustered according to the country of the respondent. The nations in the sample are: Egypt, Iraq, Kenya, Nigeria, Pakistan, Palestine Territory, and Turkey. This clustering will help prevent problems associated with heteroskedastic standard errors, which might have biased the results. First, after leaving out observations with missing data on both the dependent and independent variables, I note that of all the respondents in the analysis, 59.2% support the ICC's case against Al Bashir. The model predicting support performs quite well. Of the 4830 cases in the analysis, the model correctly predicts 76.7% of those who support the ICC, and correctly predicts 75.3% of those who do not favour ICC prosecution. The overall predictive accuracy of the model is 76.3%. This represents an improvement of 42% over predicting the modal category in every instance (the modal, or most frequently occurring response is support for the ICC—59.2% of the respondents in the model). Therefore, there is good reason to believe that the type of model outlined in this chapter—one premised on group identity characteristics as suggested by Ford—makes a great deal of sense (see Table 1).

Most importantly, I find that the group identity characteristics are generally salient and in the predicted direction. Those who identify as Muslims in the survey were unlikely to support the ICC. The coefficient for this variable is negative and

Table 1. Predicting Individual Support for the ICC Case against Sudanese President Al Bashir.

Variable	Coefficient	Standard Error	Z Statistic	P Value	Marginal Impact
Muslim	-0.518	0.121	-4.280	0.000	-0.189
African State	0.231	0.098	2.350	0.019	0.087
Arab State	-0.524	0.134	-3.900	0.000	-0.201
Darfur Knowledge	-0.076	0.098	-0.780	0.436	-0.029
Education	-0.054	0.034	-1.610	0.108	-0.021
UN Should help in Darfur	1.309	0.167	7.820	0.000	0.486
Community Size	0.141	0.070	2.020	0.043	0.054
Age	0.013	0.025	0.510	0.613	0.005
Gender	-0.010	0.122	-0.080	0.936	-0.004
Constant	-0.042	0.224	-0.190	0.852	

N = 4830 Percent Correctly Predicted = 76.3%

statistically significant. To gauge the impact of Muslim identification on support for the ICC I use the marginal effects coefficients, which tell us the expected increase in probability of observing support for the ICC, when holding all other variables at their mean or modal value. In this case, the marginal effect of Muslim identification on ICC support is -.189. This means that those individuals who identified as Muslim were approximately 19% less likely to support the International Criminal Court in its case against the president of The Sudan. But while Muslim support for the ICC's case against Bashir is found to be negative in the multivariate model, when we examine a simple breakdown of support we see that in fact Muslims are split evenly between those who support and do not support the ICC. Of those identifying as Muslims in the sample, 49.7% support the ICC, while amongst all other individuals, 80.7% support the ICC. Thus, in comparison to the rest of the respondents, Muslims are less likely to support the ICC but this does not tell the whole story. The reason we find a negative coefficient is that in comparison to these other groups, Muslims are less likely to support the ICC.

We also see that individuals from Arab states and territories—Egypt, Iraq and Palestine—are less likely to support the ICC. This coefficient is also negative and statistically significant. The marginal effect of -.20 tells us that individuals in these nations are approximately 20% less likely to support ICC prosecution of President Al Bashir, all other things being equal. When we examine the simple breakdown of the data to gauge support for the ICC from these Arab states and territories we find that 40.5% of individuals from these areas support the ICC in comparison to 69.8% among all the other respondents. Here we do see a strong link between group identity and support for the ICC.

However, those who are from African states were actually more likely to support prosecution. The coefficient for this variable is positive and statistically significant. The marginal impact of .23 tells us that respondents from Africa states—Kenya and Nigeria—were 23% more likely to support the ICC. In general, 77.4% of Kenyans and Nigerians support the ICC. Thus, in contrast to those we identify by religion or ethnicity, we do not find that a "regional" identification leads to a lack of support. Indeed, the evidence would suggest that in comparison to individuals from Egypt, Iraq, Palestine and Pakistan, individuals from African states are significantly more supportive of the ICC case against Al Bashir. Thus, the effect of one's identification with a salient group, such as one's co-nationals, or in this case, co-regionals is more complex. While many Kenyans and Nigerians may well believe that the ICC is biased against Africa (indeed, Kenyans have been brought before the ICC in The Hague in one case), they may identify more with the victims in the Darfur conflict who are generally labelled as African rather than Arab. Thus, the more important identification may be with the Africans who are being attacked by the Arabs. If the more powerful and dominant narrative among respondents in these states is the injustice done against these Africans by Arabs rather than the larger "injustice" of the ICC's focus on Africa, then their support of

ICC prosecution makes a great deal more sense. Ultimately, this finding illustrates the need for caution and more nuanced theoretical explanations of support for international criminal justice that recognize how individuals may be influenced by cross-cutting group identifications and the importance of their identification with one of these particular groups over other competing groups and conflict narratives (see Fig. 1).

We can see these trends in support across all the countries in the sample in Fig. 1. The reader will see that support for the ICC is quite strong in both African nations with Kenya the most supportive (80.3%) and Nigeria just somewhat less at 74.5%. Of the Arab states and territories, the ICC enjoys the most support in Egypt (47.5%), closely followed by Iraq (43.4%), with support lagging far behind in the Palestinian territories (26.4). Support for the ICC in Pakistan stands at 51.2%, while among respondents from Turkey the ICC enjoys 68.8% support. Thus, in all but the Arab states and territories, the ICC case against President Al Bashir enjoys support. Its support in Iraq and Egypt, while not rising to a majority still stands at somewhat respectable levels in the 40 percent range. It is only in the Palestinian territories, perhaps because of their long-standing frustration with international institutions and the major powers to resolve their concerns, that we find a substantial and negative view of the ICC.

The variable that exercises the most substantial effect on the likelihood of ICC support concerns whether the individual was in favour of United Nations intervention in Darfur more generally. The coefficient for this variable is positive and statistically significant. Such individuals are 48% more likely to support the ICC, holding all other variables constant at their mean value. Clearly, support for interventionist policies seems to overlap. When individuals are in favour of the UN

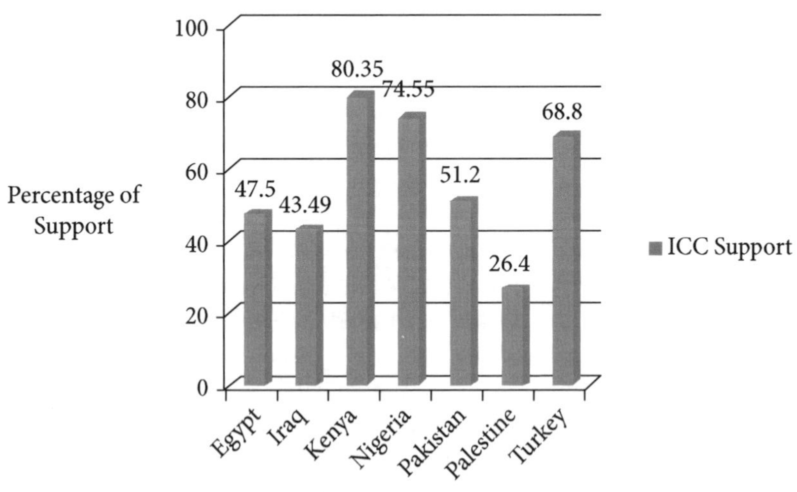

Fig. 1. Support for ICC to prosecute Sudanese President Bashir.

taking action to respond to humanitarian disasters, at a very general level they are implying that the responsibility to protect takes precedence over sovereignty concerns. Individuals who privilege interventionist rationales and objectives for one type of involvement seem to be quite likely to do so in cases of other types of interventions. This suggests that in the future one critical component of models of individual attitudes and international justice will be respondents' underlying predisposition to privilege humanitarian intervention over sovereignty. This consideration and the preference for sovereignty over intervention was the critical determination in the Bush administration's withdrawal of the US signature from the Rome Treaty, as well as the logic behind the refusal of the Chinese, Russian and other governments to sign on to the treaty. The extent to which individuals privilege the importance of humanitarian needs over more abstract principles of sovereignty and even group identity will be critical in determining support for a variety of interventions, especially judicial involvement.

As previous research suggested,[26] but in contrast to my hypothesis, we find that knowledge and education appear to exercise little influence on individuals' support for the ICC. The coefficients for both the variable measuring the individual's level of knowledge of the Darfur situation, and the variable measuring the individual's level of educational attainment were statistically insignificant. To determine if correlation between the two variables might be depressing their statistical significance, I reran the analysis to assess the impact of each variable without the presence of the other. Both remained statistically insignificant. As scholars have suggested, what matters most seems to be one's identification with salient religious, ethnic and national groupings. In fact, some research suggests that even when individuals acquire more relevant knowledge their opinions of international justice grow more, not less, negative.

We do find that there is a positive relationship between community size and support for the ICC. Individuals who live in larger communities are more apt to express support for the ICC and its case against President Al Bashir. This may well indicate something of an urban/rural split in respondent attitudes. If we engage in a bit of generalization to consider rural respondents as more conservative than their urban counterparts, this finding may suggest evidence of a political effect. We would expect that, ceteris paribus, individuals with a broadly conservative mindset would be more distrustful of foreign institutions and foreign intervention. Subsequent studies should also control for the influence of this notion of rural versus urban opinions, albeit with a more nationally-sensitive measure of such ideologies. Finally, I find that neither the control variable for age nor the

---

[26] Diane F. Orentlicher, Open Society Justice Initiative, Shrinking the Space for Denial: The Impact of the ICTY in Serbia 86 (2008), *available at* http://www.humansecuritygateway.com/documents/OSJI_Shrinking_the_Space.pdf.

control variable for gender, as determined by their coefficients, appears to exercise any meaningful influence on support for the ICC.

5. Conclusion

The findings of this chapter strongly support the notion that individuals view international justice through a slightly biased lens. Support for the International Criminal Court's case against President Al Bashir of The Sudan was contingent upon individuals' religion and ethnicity (as measured by the dominant ethnic group of their state). Those who might be expected to view the ICC's actions as in conflict with the dominant narrative of these groups regarding who was responsible for the crimes under investigation, the perceived bias of the ICC and the West against their group, and the violation of the sovereignty norm were less likely to support the ICC. Individuals who identified as Muslims and individuals from Arab states were most likely to oppose the ICC case against Al Bashir. Individuals from Sub-Saharan African states, however, were actually more likely to support the ICC. Support for UN humanitarian intervention, however, was the strongest predictor of support for the ICC. The results demonstrate both that Ford's social psychology model of individual attitudes on international justice can be employed in large N studies and that it is possible to develop a theoretically informed model of individual attitudes.

This research demonstrates how winning the support of publics and thereby deriving legitimacy from positive impressions will be difficult for the International Criminal Court. The Court should not expect that those who share the ethnicity, nationalism or religion (and most likely some combination of all three) of those whom it indicts and who subscribe to the narrative proffered by these indicted individuals to justify and contextualize their behaviour will be its supporters. Just as the ICTY has had to accept that it may never win over the hearts and minds of a majority of Serbs, so too should the ICC expect that this disconnect between its prosecution strategy and the perceptions of the larger population from which its targets are drawn will continue. To be sure this will not happen in every case as there will be some people who are more than ready to be rid of local warlords and even leaders and would be strongly in favour of any actions that would advance that end. But this divergence of views premised on group identification is as fundamental to judicial politics as it is to human nature. As Clark writes, "Thus, in certain circumstances, short-term negative perceived legitimacy may simply be the price that must be paid for international criminal courts to be successful".[27]

---

27) Clark, *supra* note 7 at p. 72.

The findings here are suggestive of several fruitful and fascinating lines of inquiry. First, since the Al Bashir indictment concerns just one ICC case, future research should broaden the survey data base by including popular opinion in more of the countries that have become involved in ICC cases, such as Kenya, Ivory Coast, Libya, and hopefully as the ICC progresses beyond African conflicts, to people in states in other regions. There are several organizations involved in international polling that are developing a wide body of expertise that can be utilized by scholars with sufficient support to fund such work. Second, survey questions need to be expanded to probe respondents' attitudes on the fairness and effectiveness of the work of international tribunals, as well as underlying attitudes and values that may be predictive of support for the ICC more generally. As the ICC begins to issue more verdicts it will be especially useful to evaluate public opinion on its judgments and especially its punishments. Third, it will be critical to ascertain not just whether respondents believe the ICC or an international criminal tribunal is the most appropriate venue for settling such disputes, but whether individuals believe other forms of transitional justice, especially local efforts, would be more meaningful and effective. Such questions also pertain to what individuals believe are the fundamental purposes of transitional justice. Is it retribution? Truth telling? Deterrence? As transitional justice becomes more established as a field of inquiry, but without a great deal of evidence regarding support for such efforts and their impact, opinion surveys will play a critical role in the development of theory and practice.

Afterward

The volume presented here is a joint effort by scholars from across the globe to critically assess the state of the modern international criminal justice system from its inception in the middle of the nineteenth century to today. The topics covered here presented the progress of and challenges to the international criminal justice systems: from the ideal of ending impunity to the everyday obstacles facing the courts. Our goal is to begin a discourse that recognizes the pitfalls of the international criminal justice system as remarkably similar to those of national systems. Through a systematic evaluation of the existing courts and their effects in the real world on states, victims, and offenders, and their impact on the development of the law related to their jurisdictions, both on the international and national level, the authors hope that lessons can be drawn for a more promising future delivery of criminal justice by international and domestic judicial bodies. After all, it is only through addressing the problems and weaknesses that a more efficient and equitable system can emerge.

We also hope that we have shown the importance of bridging practitioner and juristic concerns with criminological insights that can aid in understanding not only motivational factors, but impediments to the broader goals of the modern international criminal justice system. As a work in progress, scholars of law, criminologists and practitioners should continue to examine the challenges brought to light in this volume. Future research should focus on the impact of the international criminal justice system at national levels, the role of the victims and the impact of the criminal justice processes on them as individuals and collective victimized groups, the boundaries of international criminal law's effect, the legitimacy of the institutions, the everyday operating procedures of the courts, and the overarching impact, if any, of a deterrent effect.

International tribunals will remain a dominant force in world politics. As such, these courts, and especially the International Criminal Court, will become more institutionalized in their operations and in their unique role among national and transnational actors involved in the management of political conflict and violence. We should find that as a result of their development as institutions and the acceptance of their role in international affairs, these tribunals will become more predictable in their actions and in their impacts, thereby facilitating scholarly and practitioner inquiry. It is incumbent upon the scholarly and practitioner communities to systematically evaluate the inputs and outputs of the tribunals to help everyone better understand what international courts can and cannot deliver for the world. Only through such research can we truly appreciate the realities of international criminal justice.

Dawn L. Rothe, James D. Meernik
Editors

Dawn L. Rothe *is an Associate Professor of Criminology at Old Dominion University, Director of the International State Crime Research Consortium and Director of the PhD Graduate Program. She has extensively published on issues related to the international criminal justice systems, state criminality, and crimes of globalization with five books and over six dozen peer reviewed articles and book chapters.*

James D. Meernik *is a Professor of Political Science at the University of North Texas. His scholarship concerns international criminal law, human rights and international conflict.*

Þórdís Ingadóttir *is an Associate Professor at Reykjavik University, co-director/director in the Project on International Courts and Tribunals and the Project on the Impact of International Courts and Tribunals on Domestic Criminal Procedures in Mass Atrocity Cases.*

Subject Index